Toy Wars

Toy Wars

THE EPIC STRUGGLE BETWEEN G.I. JOE, BARBIE, AND THE COMPANIES THAT MAKE THEM

G. WAYNE MILLER

TIMES BOOKS

RANDOM HOUSE

All rights reserved under International and
Pan-American Copyright Conventions.
Published in the United States by Times Books,
a division of Random House, Inc., New York, and in Canada by
Random House of Canada Limited, Toronto.

Portions of this work were originally published in the
Providence Journal-Bulletin in different form.

Neither Hasbro nor Mattel, which own the rights to G.I. Joe
and Barbie respectively, have endorsed this book.

Library of Congress Cataloging-in-Publication Data
Miller, G. Wayne.
Toy wars: the epic struggle between G.I. Joe, Barbie, and the companies that
make them / G. Wayne Miller.
p.   cm.
Includes bibliographical references and index.
ISBN 0-8129-2984-5 (alk. paper)
1. Hasbro, Inc. 2. Toy industry—United States. 3. Hassenfeld, Alan Geoffrey. 4. Businessmen—
United States—Biography.
HD9993.T694H376 1998
338.7´68872´0973—dc21 97-18248
CIP

Random House website address: www.randomhouse.com
Printed in the United States of America on acid-free paper
98765432

Book Design by Oksana Kushnir

To G. Calvin Miller,
my American beauty

．

May you forever keep a story in your heart,
old Fusser.

CONTENTS

Author's Note   xi

Lucky Pennies   3

BOOK ONE ▪ 9

1. The Last Hassenfeld   11
2. Plastics   19
3. Real American Heroes   33
4. Rose of Tibet   50
5. A Wedding and a Funeral   79
6. Bean Counting   85
7. Star Wars   96

BOOK TWO ▪ 113

8. X-Men   115
9. Made in Japan   138
10. The King Lays an Egg   162
11. Black Tuesday   180
12. Sharks   205

13. Extremes   220
14. Kid Number One   234

BOOK THREE ▪ 239

15. Gotham City   241
16. Lillymere   260
17. Brand Names   270
18. Mortal Combat   285
    Epilogue   302
    Notes   307
    Bibliography   319
    Acknowledgments   325
    Index   329

AUTHOR'S NOTE

One winter evening some while ago, I happened to have dinner with Alan Hassenfeld, chairman and chief executive officer of Hasbro, a corporation with eleven thousand employees and nearly $3 billion in annual revenues. We were in Hasbro's private dining room, the Greenhouse Cafe. Except for an occasional appearance by the chef, whose cuisine was the finest, we were alone.

After dessert, we lingered over a bottle of wine. Alan was in fine spirits. He was reminiscing about his childhood, how he'd always suspected he'd been, in his words, an afterthought. He laughed. "I used to kid my parents and my brother and my sister about how I really was supposed to be the firstborn but my plane was delayed seven years!" he said. He went on to talk about being sent to sleep-away camp when he was four and boarding school when he was fourteen, of spending many Saturdays fishing alone while his mother and father were at the country club. I was surprised by Alan's candor, although, I would learn, it was characteristic of him.

Sitting across the table from him, I thought of other discoveries I'd made on the long journey that became this book. I'd found Alan to be warm, intelligent, temperamental, and sometimes endearingly goofy. He was colorfully unconventional, even paradoxical. He had no children of his own, but he was the head of the largest toy company in the world. He was Jewish, and his family had been prominent in Zionist causes for three generations, but his stepchildren were Arabs. He was a smoker, but his favorite philanthropy was a hospital. He was forty-six, but he still talked to his mother at least once every day.

I thought also of Alan's only brother, Stephen, chairman and CEO of Hasbro until he died, of AIDS, in 1989. Stephen was a business genius who'd built a schlocky little toy company into a Fortune 500 firm; Alan was the English major who'd come aboard because it was his ticket to the Orient, which enchanted him—but not because Hasbro manufactured there. While Stephen was making his mark on Wall Street, Alan was writing short stories and dating beautiful women. Although successful in his corner of Hasbro, he'd never expected, never wanted, to run the whole business. When tragedy forced his hand, he knew the long shadow of his brother would be upon him. Just how long, he could not have imagined.

This book is about Alan and the shadow. It's about Alan's struggle to succeed in an enterprise that even a brilliant brother found perilous.

This is also the story of an American family.

Although publicly traded since 1968, the company founded in the 1920s by Polish immigrant Henry Hassenfeld, grandfather of Alan and Stephen, had always taken paternalistic pride in its employees. Even during the 1980s, when Hasbro was one of the fastest-growing corporations in America, Alan and Stephen still walked the factory floor, still knew most of their workers' names. As revenues surpassed $2 billion under Alan, the spirit of the good old days was increasingly jeopardized. Alan did not walk the factory floor. In Rhode Island, where it all began, he no longer even had much of a factory.

▪

When I first approached Alan about writing this book, more than five years ago, I wanted only to witness the birth of a toy, one that was mass-produced.

Hasbro's hundreds of products included Monopoly, Batman, Star Wars, G.I. Joe, Mr. Potato Head, Nerf, Play-Doh, Raggedy Ann, Candy Land, Scrabble, Barney, Sesame Street, and many more. Of these, G.I. Joe most intrigued me. The quintessential American boy's toy, Joe, like Barbie, had transcended "plaything." It had become an icon, and its popularity over three decades suggested that in its story truths would be revealed. I intended to chronicle all aspects of the creation of a G.I. Joe action figure: earliest idea, research, design, engineering, marketing, manufacture, and sales. Such an account of G.I. Joe indeed is to be found within this book.

But I wasn't long inside the world of toys before other avenues beckoned. Some brought me to Hollywood, where studio executives have helped merge television series, feature movies, restaurant and amusement park tie-ins, software, publications, and merchandise into a seamless commercial web. Some led to the Paramus, New Jersey, headquarters of Toys "R" Us, the world's largest retailer of toys. The most important took me to Wall Street, ultimate seat of power in the children's industries.

Here, at the busy intersection of art, industry, and commerce, I would learn something about children and the adults who influence them, for toys are universal.

▪

I set off with certain preconceptions, many traceable to my childhood. How vividly I remembered the night before Christmas, when excitement kept me awake until nearly midnight. The next morning, when the presents seemed piled higher than the tree! Fresher were memories of my own children on Christmas Day—their uncontained joy at discovering what Santa had brought. Watching a child play, even the casual observer must conclude that nothing delights and amuses like a toy.

Toys, of course, do more. They are props in rehearsing behavior, and building blocks for fantasy, in turn the foundation for creativity and self-expression. "Toys are to a kid what a hammer is to a carpenter—they enhance his ability to build things," said child psychologist Lewis P. Lipsitt, founder of Brown University's Child Study Center. "They teach about the way the universe is. They either symbolize or directly represent things in the adult world." Some are emblematic of innocence, childhood's most precious and fleeting gift. And unlike TV, whose influence on child development is also substantial, toys go everywhere, even to bed, and often through life. Poke around in the attic of many a grown-up and you'll find their treasured toys.

▪

The world I ventured through is rarely seen by outsiders and almost never by writers. It was, in many respects, a place unlike what I'd expected. Most strikingly, it was largely devoid of children; when glimpsed, they nearly always were the subjects of focus groups or characters in TV commercials, print ads, and catalogs. It was a world that could be zany, but not uniformly fun; some of the most painful moments I have witnessed in two decades of journalism occurred inside a toy company. And far from being exempt from the capitalist dynamics that govern the production of, say, toasters or cars, the toy industry, if anything, is more susceptible to them. A so-called fashion business, it is always at the mercy of fad; change is constant, sudden, and rarely predictable, like children themselves. These are the factors that have driven the largest toy companies, in concert with entertainment firms, to seek the stability promised by brands such as G.I. Joe and Barbie. They are the same factors that create enormous pressures to perform or be gone, from chief executive officer to junior marketer.

On my journey, I witnessed many discussions about what kids might want and many fewer about what they need or what might enrich them. Perhaps it was naive of me to have expected anything different, given that the large toy and entertainment firms are publicly traded and stockholders by and large demand nothing beyond a good return. Sizzle sells, whether on TV, the silver screen, or in the form of injection-molded plastic.

During our many interviews, Hasbro executive Al Verrecchia often reminded me of who Hasbro's (and America's) stockholders are: not wealthy individuals exclusively, but big institutional investors, firms such as Fidelity that manage pools of little people's money with a single mandate. "The assets that are in the California teachers' retirement program, the Rhode Island retirement program—that's where the ownership of corporate America is," Verrecchia said. "Those institutions are brutal; you see it in the newspaper every day. They want profitability." The consumer is complicit. As the history of the auto industry has demonstrated beyond all question, quality, price, and self-serving desire are supreme.

■

When I set off in early 1992, I envisioned a journey of two years. Two years passed, and I was immersed in a restructuring in which nearly a thousand workers were shuffled and more than a hundred fired, an agonizing process tainted with intrigue and caprice. Three years passed, and DreamWorks SKG, Steven Spielberg's new studio, had extended a hand to Hasbro. Four years, and Mattel was intent on taking over its arch-rival, a corporate clash that is the climax of this narrative. As I write this, competition between the two continues, with no end in sight.

I have little doubt that historians one day will describe the period I chronicle as one of epochal change in children's culture. Interactive software and the Internet emerged as powerful forces in young lives. Although some voices continued to speak out, advocates for quality children's TV for the most part abandoned the battle; children's fare suffered accordingly. Managers with MBAs supplanted old-fashioned toy people in the executive suites. In ever closer concert with manufacturers, the major retailers increased their market shares and began to limit the variety of toys they sold. Hasbro and Mattel developed insatiable appetites for their smaller brethren. The adoption of brands as a fundamental philosophy directed innovation toward preexisting lines and away from outside invention; the maturing of global marketing spread American toys, and the values associated with them, worldwide. This process was abetted by hundreds of millions of dollars in advertising every year by the two industry leaders alone and was magnified by the vast promotional campaigns of their studio, restaurant, and merchandising partners.

Increasingly, a small group of executives determined how the children of the world would play. This is regrettable. This is in the best interests of capital, not kids.

■

If Alan Hassenfeld were to name his most important ambition, I imagine it would be making Hasbro socially responsible. It may be his toughest struggle, for while he is a humanitarian at heart, Alan must answer to two masters. One buys his products. The other buys his stock.

Unlike his struggle with the shadow, this one is not over.

G. Wayne Miller
Pascoag, Rhode Island
September 20, 1997

Toy Wars

LUCKY PENNIES

Alan G. Hassenfeld had no appetite for breakfast when he awoke the morning of February 14, 1996, after a long night of little sleep. Only cigarettes and coffee interested him. He dressed in a blue suit and favorite pair of loafers, pinned a purple button to his lapel, kissed his wife good-bye, and walked alone in bitter cold from the Waldorf-Astoria to the Pierre, a hotel thirteen blocks away. Through his socks, his feet were in contact with the seven lucky pennies he'd found recently on the streets of New York. They gave him some small measure of comfort for the ordeal ahead.

Hassenfeld recognized many of the hundred or so people in the Pierre's Grand Ballroom, a cavernous chamber outfitted with velvet drapes, mirrors, and crystal chandeliers below a gold-trimmed ceiling. They were mutual fund managers, institutional investors, and analysts employed by the host of the Eleventh Annual Toy and Video Game Conference, William Blair & Company, a Chicago investment firm.

Some considered Hassenfeld a capable, even exemplary, captain of industry. Others believed he was chairman and chief executive officer of Hasbro Inc., America's 423rd-largest public corporation, only because a Hassenfeld had headed the firm since its founding early in the century. They couldn't understand why a man of his stature wore rubber bands as bracelets and a scarf indoors in winter—but rarely a necktie or jacket, or even a shirt with a collar. They didn't share his humor, which could be uncommonly silly for a man of almost fifty. And they remained incensed that Hassenfeld and his board three weeks ago had rejected a merger offer from longtime rival Mattel that would have brought shareholders more than $53 for stock that had been languishing near $30 a share. What was wrong with him? He, his sister, and his mother, a strong-minded woman who'd been a member of the board for thirteen years, had stood to gain almost $600 million themselves! Not only had he rejected the offer—in doing so, he had opened Hasbro to a withering attack that, in the darkest moments, seemed certain to destroy it.

The lights dimmed and Hassenfeld took the podium. With his wire-rim glasses and full head of untamable brown hair, he looked as if he could just as easily be lecturing on Faulkner or Twain, two of his favorite authors.

"Good morning," he began, his voice slightly tremulous, but only to someone listening for it. "Today we are here to review our 1995 performance and share with you Hasbro's outlook for 1996 and beyond. For that reason, I will not be talking about the now ended Mattel proposal."

Looking to the last row, Hassenfeld saw Mattel's two leaders. Chairman and CEO John W. Amerman was a slender man of average height whose white hair, baritone voice, and expensive tailoring projected an image of someone considerably larger; at sixty-four, his passions were golf, German shepherds, and Thoroughbred horses. Sitting to his left was Jill E. Barad, forty-four, who had risen to chief operating officer and president largely on her success with Barbie, a doll that promised glamorous fantasy to little girls and handsome bonuses to executives. Worldwide sales of Barbie the previous year had reached $1.4 billion, an extraordinary feat no other toy of any kind had ever accomplished. Amerman and Barad were unusually attentive, for today was the first time this year Hassenfeld had faced the industry's powers. Mattel insiders pictured themselves as sharks, and the agony they'd caused Hasbro over the last month—the battering punishment that had pushed Hassenfeld and his inner circle to exhaustion, if not the verge of breakdown—had more than confirmed that reputation. Even if Alan didn't discuss Mattel's spurned offer, Amerman and Barad might learn more clues about the damage they'd inflicted. No telling when they might be tempted to strike again.

Even before launching its stunning takeover attempt, with a fax to

Hassenfeld the morning of January 16, precisely two hours after he'd returned from winter vacation, Mattel had become the new darling of the toy industry. Its flagship brands—Barbie, Fisher-Price, Hot Wheels, and Disney—were all vigorous, helping the company to end 1995 with its seventh consecutive year of record sales and earnings. No toy company had ever made $358 million, but one had come close. Only two years ago, at this same conference, Hassenfeld had reported the largest revenues and earnings in Hasbro's history. Without gloating, which was not his style, he'd reminded Wall Street that a thousand shares of Hasbro stock purchased for less than $15,000 in 1982 would have been worth almost $1 million twelve years later. He'd joked about his mother's approval of such arithmetic and shown a slide of his greatest philanthropic achievement: a newly opened children's hospital in his hometown, that bore his company's name.

Two years earlier Mattel had been in second place, a position that vexed its corporate soul.

▪

Unlike his older brother, Stephen, a masterful orator who'd preceded him as chairman and CEO, Alan did not relish public speaking, even to friendly audiences. Financial presentations were his nemesis.

Ordinarily he relied on humor to get under way, but his advisers had persuaded him this was no time for frivolity. Nor had it been considered wise to begin with one of Hasbro's brilliant television commercials, as he customarily did to lighten the atmosphere at what otherwise was a half day or more of undiluted dreariness. And he would not close with his usual remarks about Hasbro's commitment to social responsibility, which was at the core of his corporate and personal beliefs. Wall Street had wearied of Hassenfeld's causes. Especially in light of the Mattel offer, Wall Street was interested only in earnings and the price of stock—and how the chairman intended to multiply both. Wearing a purple button with the letters "ESV," for enhance shareholder value, would not suffice. Hassenfeld had to get directly into the numbers—the area of the business where, he was first to admit, he was least expert.

He began with the fourth quarter of 1995, the first billion-dollar quarter in Hasbro history, and moved on to the full-year results. Hasbro's revenues had risen modestly, and earnings, while down, were nothing to be ashamed of: $155 million, or $1.76 a share. Many a private businessman would have uncorked champagne over such numbers, but Wall Street judged Hasbro (like Mattel) by the merciless measure of growth. It was an expectation established by Stephen, and one price to be paid for continuing membership in the Fortune 500.

"While our 1995 full-year results were essentially flat," Alan said, "we have momentum coming into the new year." The games and international divisions, he reported, had had impressive years. Batman and Star Wars toys remained hot, and retail sales on many other lines were encouragingly strong. Mr. Potato Head, Hasbro's first hit more than forty years ago, was the surprise star of *Toy Story,* the Christmas season's box office smash. All had contributed to Hasbro's continuing strong balance sheet.

And it was there, in the middle of cash flow and debt, that Hassenfeld's heart started to race and the Grand Ballroom began to go black.

Almost seven years into his chairmanship, Hassenfeld still sometimes felt like an impostor. It was a feeling of wicked wonder, like that experienced by the Tom Hanks character in the movie *Big:* a boy who one day wakes up an adult in the eyes of the world—an adult who just so happens to be a major toy company executive responsible for, and in love with, the design and development of toys. Unpleasurable moments at financial forums were the price to be paid for being "Kid Number One," as Hassenfeld sometimes called himself, but this was different from any discomfort he'd experienced before.

Lucky pennies and all, Hassenfeld was about to faint.

He reached for a glass of water, praying it would sustain him.

▪

He did not faint; his twelve-second pause seemed eternal to him but went unremarked upon by almost everyone else. He drank his water, found his confidence, and continued with his presentation, rich with references to global brand building, the key to Mattel's success and, he now believed, his own company's future. Financials dispensed with, he rolled a dozen of Hasbro's finest new commercials, outlined some of the steps he would take to improve his company's performance, and hinted at even greater changes to come. Hassenfeld closed with a kind of prediction he'd never made: a specific dollar amount for increased profit in the year ahead, offered as a token of his newfound resolve to enrich his stockholders. General applause and a private handshake from Amerman followed. The ugly questions his advisers had prepared him for—"Alan, if you can't enhance shareholder value, will you step down?" "Alan, how bad is the blood between you and John Amerman?"—failed to materialize.

"It's done, baby! Behind you!" said Wayne S. Charness, Hasbro's vice president of corporate communications, as their chauffeur-driven Lincoln Town Car traveled south on Fifth Avenue toward Hasbro's showroom, crowded with buyers this third day of the American International Toy Fair, the worldwide industry's largest show. Hassenfeld was in front, legs tucked into his chest, breathing in a Parliament cigarette, oblivious of anything but the remembrance of his presentation. Charness adjusted the seat to give his boss more room.

"With the adrenaline pumping the way it was at the beginning, I was almost overready," Hassenfeld said. "I think that's why I went blind for a minute."

"It was beautiful," Charness said.

"You wouldn't say anything different."

"I tell you when you stink." Charness assured him that no one in the audience knew what had happened in those twelve dark seconds.

"I was really, really scared," Hassenfeld said.

"It's over," Charness said, but his reference was only to that morning. For new pressures awaited Hassenfeld as he neared the Hasbro showroom, on West Twenty-third Street. His board would meet the next day, and directors were ornery. They'd been put on the defensive for rejecting Mattel's offer—"Fifty-three dollars a share," they kept hearing, "are you crazy?"—and if Mattel had truly given up, as some doubted, other sharks could be circling. No one was pleased with the previous year's dismal performance in Hasbro's domestic toys division, headed by Hassenfeld's oldest business friend, Alfred J. Verrecchia, a man whose prodigious financial and administrative skills had helped propel Hasbro to the top. Relations with Toys "R" Us, Hasbro's biggest customer, were badly strained since Hassenfeld had inadvertently disclosed information during the Mattel affair that had led *The Wall Street Journal* to report that the giant chain was the subject of a federal investigation.

And it was all well and good to promise great things for 1996, but quite another to deliver. Having failed on earlier promises of improved performance, Hassenfeld had a credibility problem. The stress was not unlike seven years ago, when cruel fate had handed him the chairmanship of what was then the largest toy company the world had ever seen.

Still, as his Town Car turned onto West Twenty-third, Hassenfeld was starting to relax. Toy Fair had always been his time—a week of hosting celebrities, showing off the latest toys, dining with family and friends, and otherwise being Kid Number One. Hassenfeld genuinely enjoyed people. He enjoyed pleasing them, feeding them, telling them stories, making them laugh.

The first smile of the day crossed his face when he was asked what he'd dreamed the night before. In 1994 he'd seen, of course, Jill Barad posed with pillows and three dozen Barbie dolls on a red satin sheet when *People* magazine named her one of that year's "50 Most Beautiful People." And he'd seen her on the cover of this week's *Brandweek,* a marketing magazine, with the headline G.I. JOE'S WORST NIGHTMARE. Joe, Hasbro's most famous toy and one of Hassenfeld's sentimental favorites, had ended 1995 below $15 million in sales, a pitiful performance, especially in contrast with Mattel's signature product.

"It was weird," Hassenfeld said, deadpan, about his dream. "Barbie was raping G.I. Joe." It was uncharacteristically crude of Hassenfeld, and as he stepped into the cold, he hastened to add: "Just kidding!" Then he ran across the street and disappeared into the fabulous showroom—a palace, really—that his late brother had built.

BOOK ONE

1

■

THE LAST HASSENFELD

I

he hearse bearing the body of Stephen Hassenfeld left New York the afternoon of June 26, 1989, and reached Mitch Sugarman's Mt. Sinai Memorial Chapel in Providence, Rhode Island, by nightfall. After being washed in accordance with ancient Hebrew custom, Stephen was dressed in a burial shroud, a simple garment that is white, to symbolize death's democracy, and pocketless, a reminder that nothing material from this world survives to the next. At the family's request, a business suit was placed over the shroud. Stephen was laid out in Sugarman's finest mahogany casket and wheeled into the chapel, where a memorial candle with a Star of David burned.

The coffin was closed. Dark haired and handsome in life, an impeccable dresser with exquisite taste in everything, Stephen in death was devastated by AIDS, which had finally claimed him after almost a month in a coma in Manhattan's Columbia Presbyterian Hospital.

Stephen's callers the next day were only those closest to him. His mother, Sylvia, was in from New York, along with his sister, Ellie Block; during Stephen's hospitalization, the details of which they'd kept fiercely private, they'd maintained a bedside vigil. Stephen's life partner and longtime business associate, Robert Beckwith, came, as did Leslie Gutterman, Rhode Island's foremost rabbi.

As midnight neared and his mother and sister wearied, Alan insisted they leave, to get what rest they could. Jewish tradition requires that the deceased be attended until burial, and Sugarman ordinarily hired elderly holy men. But Alan did not want Stephen with strangers. He'd insisted on watching, on reciting the Book of Psalms, by himself. Sometime in the predawn hours he put down his book, opened the casket, and tucked into a pocket of Stephen's suit the notes and pictures his nieces and nephew wanted their uncle to have. Alan had a note of his own, and he placed that in the pocket, too. Then he removed one of his rubber bands and placed it on Stephen's wrist.

Through his tears, Alan spoke of his love for his only brother and best friend, seven years his senior. His thoughts wandered to their childhoods on Providence's East Side—the fancy Porsche Stevie had driven, his reputation as a debater at the prestigious Moses Brown School, how Stevie always came to the rescue when Alan's shenanigans landed him in trouble with Mom. He pondered the tragedy of Stephen's disease, which Stephen had confirmed only to Beckwith. Only when Stephen was on his deathbed did his family confront the truth behind the maladies that had slowly consumed him until, at his last public appearance, Hasbro's annual meeting in his beloved New York showroom, not two months before, this man who'd once regularly worked eighteen-hour days was exhausted by a routine thirty-minute presentation. Forty-seven years old, Stephen had died without finding the way to unburden himself.

▪

He was called the father of the modern toy company, but that hardly did Stephen D. Hassenfeld justice. In 1980, when Stephen became Hasbro's chairman and chief executive officer, toy companies were but a quirky footnote on Wall Street. Investors were wary of businesses built on the whims of kids, for good reason: one hit, and men became millionaires overnight; one bomb, and bankruptcy beckoned. Hasbro had been no exception, having made tremendous profits in the mid-sixties with the introduction of G.I. Joe and then sputtering into the seventies as Joe's popularity waned. Hasbro lost more than $1 million in 1978; two years later it made a modest $5 million, its stock traded at but $6 a share, and revenues were only $104 million. Mattel, the worldwide industry leader, was eight times as big and vastly more profitable.

Under Stephen's leadership, Hasbro in the next five years surpassed $1.2 billion in sales, clobbering Mattel, whose investments outside of traditional toys had left it deeply in debt. *Forbes* magazine rated Hasbro first in a thousand-corporation survey of increased value during that tumultuous period, well ahead of other highfliers such as Wal-Mart and Berkshire Hathaway. Given Hasbro's roots in textile remnants, it was, quite literally, a rags-to-riches story.

Alan had been a force in all this, but a less potent one than Stephen. President and chief operating officer, he was responsible primarily for international, the side of the business he'd joined after graduating from the University of Pennsylvania, where he'd majored in English and creative writing. Stephen involved Alan in major decisions, and both took pains to describe their relationship as teamwork, an accurate description; until Alan married in spring of 1989, they'd even shared a house in Rhode Island, home of corporate headquarters, and apartments in Palm Beach and New York. But there was never a doubt who was in control, never a suspicion the younger brother coveted the older's job, for truthfully he did not.

"It's the old Chinese philosophy," Alan would say. "Two tigers can't live on the same hill."

▪

Until cardiac arrest sent him into irreversible coma, Stephen had believed he would recover. A wonder drug would be found, a miraculous new therapy perfected, something. He'd never discussed succession at Hasbro with Alan or anyone else. Stephen had confidence in his brother's potential, but he'd never wanted to believe he would be tested this way.

"Should I? . . ."

Alan was talking aloud again. In the scented shadows of the funeral home, he imagined Stephen would respond.

How tempting it was simply to walk away!

A millionaire many times over, Alan could return to writing, an earlier passion he still carried within. He could devote himself to philanthropy, a new and growing interest, or pursue his distant dream of being a diplomat or holding political office. Alan had never shared his brother's single-minded focus. Life for him was a great feast, meant to be sampled in its many delicious varieties.

What would Stevie or their late father, Merrill, Stephen's predecessor at Hasbro, have wanted him to do? For that matter, what would their grandfather, Hasbro's founder, have thought? It was difficult to imagine that any of the Hassenfelds, even softhearted Merrill, would have approved of the final brother simply walking away. But Alan had someone else to consider: his wife, Vivien, a granddaughter of Prussian nobility who'd schooled in England and built a successful Hong Kong design firm. She'd married Alan barely two months before expecting to continue her cosmopolitan lifestyle, not be anchored in Rhode Island, a post-industrial backwater that had no charm she could discern, except, perhaps, for Newport. Alan knew Vivien would support any decision he made, but her happiness was a concern he could not blithely ignore.

Alan didn't question where Mom stood. He never had, not through his youth or later at Hasbro, when, regardless of where they were in the world, she telephoned her sons at least daily. Sylvia was a noted philanthropist, prominent in domestic and international Jewish causes, but no small share of her stature rested on the foundation of Hasbro. It mattered not that, unlike her firstborn, Alan had come reluctantly to the firm. Alan was the only one she had now in a position of corporate power, for her daughter, Ellie, herself a philanthropist, was of a generation whose women were kept from the executive suite.

And if he did seek the chairmanship of Hasbro—he supposed it was his for the asking, although he could not be certain until the board met—how would he fill this void Stephen had left? Alan's strengths were product, merchandising, manufacturing, and overseas. He knew little about balance sheets and investor relations—Wall Street, the treacherous soil on which the legend of Stephen had grown. The prospect of following him there was terrifying.

As dawn came, Alan thought he could hear Stephen giving him advice. Alan accepted it.

"He would have killed me," Alan said, "if I had basically thought of anything different."

▪

From the funeral parlor Stephen was taken to his home in Bristol, on the east shore of picturesque Narragansett Bay. Stephen was no sailor, but during the America's Cup campaign of 1983, which was staged from Newport, he'd chartered three large sailing vessels for the exclusive summer-long use of business associates, family, and friends. Alan kept on his desk a photograph of him with his brother on one of those long-ago cruises.

Alan placed white roses on the casket, and he and the small gathering of family and friends bade Stephen farewell. The hearse returned to Providence, to Temple Emanu-El, where bronze tablets and a stained-glass window inscribed with the names of Hassenfelds attested to the family's prominence for most of the century. Stephen's senior executives awaited the deceased in the warmth of the summer day. Of the inner-most circle, only Robert Beckwith was not standing with them, was not a pallbearer; the Hassenfelds had not asked him. But as he ascended the temple steps, he was hugged by all five of Stephen's senior people, each of whom Stephen had made a wealthy man.

Stephen A. Schwartz, chief marketing executive during the years of fastest growth, had been instrumental in returning G.I. Joe from retire-ment in 1982—the single most critical factor in building Hasbro's huge cash reserve, which Stephen had applied to acquisitions, which in turn had brought growth. Schwartz had a tremendous ego, but it was not un-deserved. He was smart and stubbornly ambitious, a fast-talking native New Yorker endowed with great product sense. Two more of the indus-try's most profitable lines of the 1980s, Transformers and My Little Pony, had been introduced by Hasbro on his watch.

Lawrence H. Bernstein stood next to Schwartz, his close friend. Bern-stein was the best salesman Hasbro had ever had—an exceptionally en-tertaining man whose jokes and mannerisms were reminiscent of Sid Caesar, a comic he'd idolized growing up in 1950s Brooklyn. Bernstein could make the unique claim of having coaxed Stephen, after too much wine, into reenacting a Marx Brothers routine at a company gathering. "The Three Musketeers" was what Bernstein had called himself, Schwartz, and research director George A. Dunsay, no longer with Has-bro. Standing there, consumed by grief at the loss of a man he loved, Bernstein could not possibly have imagined what fate would soon befall the surviving two Musketeers.

Barry J. Alperin, executive vice president and the only officer besides Alan to serve on the board at that time, was the lone intellectual on the temple steps. An aficionado of ballet, opera, and theater, as Stephen had

been, Alperin had grown up in Providence, where his family's philanthropy brought him into contact with the Hassenfelds. Alperin was an attorney, a bespectacled man steeped in the arcana of acquisition law.
Before his death, Stephen had given Alperin a new responsibility in marketing and product development, including development of a secret
video game whose code name was NEMO. Like Bernstein, Alperin
could never have guessed what his future at Hasbro held.

With Alperin was George R. Ditomassi Jr., Stephen's games vice president, entrusted with Candy Land, Chutes and Ladders, and other timeless jewels. Ditomassi had come to Hasbro with Stephen's acquisition of
Milton Bradley, America's premier maker of games and puzzles. Dito, as
he was known, had style that rivaled Stephen's. He was that rare man who
could wear gold without seeming tacky or pretentious.

And then there was Al Verrecchia, who knew more about the business
than anyone but Stephen himself.

Of all the chairman's men, Verrecchia most looked the part of senior
executive. Six feet three, broad shouldered, fit, and uncommonly handsome, Verrecchia favored suits and wing-tip shoes, always freshly shined.
Employees sometimes joked that his hair must obey different laws of
physics, for a strand was never out of place. Having spent twenty-five
years with Hasbro and recently promoted to president of manufacturing,
Verrecchia had no equal with numbers. Many an underling had experienced a chill when he perched his reading glasses on the tip of his nose,
took up his mechanical pencil, ruler, and calculator, and started into their
business plans. Verrecchia knew the underside of Hasbro: the late 1960s
and early 1970s, when Merrill, as president, had been forced to put up
his personal property as collateral on high-interest loans needed to cover
the payroll. It was Verrecchia who'd negotiated those loans, Verrecchia
who'd begged resin suppliers for extended terms to keep the molding
machines running, Verrecchia who'd analyzed when individual pay-
checks were cashed so that he could dole out the precious dollars to cover
them.

Despite their grief, Stephen's senior managers had not lost sight of succession. Few doubted the board would grant Alan the chairmanship if he
sought it, but they had no clues about how, when, or even if he would
restructure the top after taking charge. Alan's U.S. office was next to his
brother's at world headquarters, and he was everywhere at Toy Fair, but
there was an ethereal quality to him. With his international duties, he was

always traveling, and when he was home, he was as likely to regale them with tales of expeditions through early post-Mao China as with marketing strategies for toys. Alan's closest confidants at the company were his mother and brother, and his wife to most was a stranger. No one knew his vision for Hasbro, because he'd never had to spell one out.

■

In his eulogy, Rabbi Gutterman spoke to more than company executives, for Stephen Hassenfeld would not only be remembered for stock options and dividends. Factory workers whose names and birthdays he'd never forgotten were present, together with politicians, religious and community leaders, and beneficiaries of corporate and family philanthropy. "If every person Stephen Hassenfeld touched with happiness brought a flower to his grave," Gutterman said, "he would sleep tonight beneath a wilderness of roses."

Led by a state police escort, Stephen's funeral procession was more than three miles long. Those familiar with such matters said it was the largest motorcade in Rhode Island history, surpassing even presidential visits.

II

SEVEN DAYS AFTER ALAN had thrown the last spadeful of earth onto his brother's grave, next to Merrill's in Lincoln Park Cemetery, the directors of Hasbro Inc. gathered in a conference room on the mezzanine floor of the company's New York showroom. Alan spoke a few words to the board, and he, his mother, and Alperin left.

Directors were aware that Stephen's hospitalization and rumors about its true cause had troubled Wall Street before the chairman's death. Their concern was compounded by Hasbro's uncharacteristically flat performance in 1987 and 1988. Had Stephen lost his touch—or was Hasbro simply catching its breath after its extraordinary run? Whatever the case, Alan, this man with the rubber bands, gave Wall Street the jitters. Would he and Sylvia—they effectively controlled almost a third of Hasbro's stock—decide to sell? Speculation that the Walt Disney Co., entertainment giant MCA, video-game maker Nintendo, and Mattel were interested in acquiring the firm had led to a run on Hasbro stock. If Hasbro remained independent, more probable after adoption of a so-called poison pill a week after Stephen was hospitalized, would Alan be up to the job? *The Wall Street Journal* was among the doubters. It recently had described him as his brother's "shadow."

Behind closed doors, director E. John Rosenwald Jr. had the floor. Newly named vice chairman of the Bear Stearns Companies, one of New York's foremost investment bankers, Rosenwald had been a close friend of Stephen's and was the most powerful member of the Hasbro board, except for Alan. Shortly after the funeral, Alan had visited him in his Fifth Avenue penthouse. Sitting on the terrace as the sun set over Central Park, the youngest Hassenfeld had poured his heart out. "I'd be a little bit different from my brother," he'd told Rosenwald, "but I know the business and I want my shot."

Rosenwald related their discussion to the directors, some of whom had spoken privately with him of their inclination to sell Hasbro and, having turned a tidy profit, be done with it. He talked of the depth of Hasbro's management team and praised Alan's intelligence, experience, and desire. "He deserves his shot," Rosenwald said. "His name is on the door, too. He has spent his whole life here and he's ready to roll and he has a plan and I think you should support him."

The vote was unanimous. Alan returned with Sylvia and Alperin and was congratulated. He had not heard, of course, Rosenwald's caveat about the last brother—sole surviving grandson of the founder, a Polish immigrant who'd arrived in America, virtually penniless, at the age of thirteen.

"If it doesn't work out," Rosenwald had said, "we can always sell the company."

2

■

PLASTICS

I

*E*astern European Jews already lived in fear when word of the events of Palm Sunday in 1903 reached them. Armed with clubs and shouting, "Kill the Jews!" a drunken mob had swarmed the streets of Kishinev, Russia, desecrating synagogues, destroying shops and homes, and murdering some four dozen with terrible cruelty. Nails were driven through the heads of victims, and eyes were gouged out. Infants were ripped from their mothers and thrown from upper stories onto the street. Women were raped, mutilated, and left to die while the police and militia stood by, intervening only occasionally—only to stop the Jews who tried to defend themselves.

If Osias Hassenfeld needed further incentive to send his family to America, new home for hundreds of thousands of Eastern European Jews who'd fled already, Kishinev provided it. The Hassenfelds lived in Ulanow, a minor trading center at the confluence of two rivers in Galicia (now Poland) that was but a day's travel from this latest pogrom. Most of Ulanow's nearly 3,500 residents were Jews; most, like Hassenfeld, were deeply religious and desperately poor. Shtetl life was hardscrabble, particularly for a man with a wife and five children. Lacking the means to bring his entire family to America, Osias sent two sons first. In the spring of 1903 he gave Hillel, sixteen, and Henry, thirteen, what little money he could spare, the names of relief societies that could help them to an Atlantic port, and the address of an uncle already in New York, and bade them farewell.

They arrived by steamer and settled on Manhattan's Lower East Side, which was teeming with foreigners like themselves. Educated in an Orthodox religious school, the Hassenfeld brothers spoke no English. They had no trade, only memories of the shtetl, where peddling—an occupation requiring salesmanship, patience, and, for those most successful, ambition and imagination—was available to all. Henry peddled electrical supplies, Hillel gas mantles, before both moved on to textile remnants. Their new business brought them in contact with Rhode Island, where mighty mills had ushered in a golden age. Rhode Island had another appeal for two natives of Galicia: a tradition of tolerance that dated to its founder, seventeenth-century religious libertarian Roger Williams. Jews had found the state as early as the 1670s and opened one of the continent's first synagogues a century later in Newport. By the 1900s nearly two thousand Jewish families lived in Providence, the capital. Their community flourished, with many moving rapidly into the middle and upper classes.

Henry Hassenfeld left New York in 1915, after marrying a Rhode Islander he'd met on a trip to Providence. Marion Frank's father, a peddler himself once, had prospered in scrap textiles, and he helped his new son-in-law start a Rhode Island business of his own. Hillel joined Henry, and by 1920 Hassenfeld Bros. Inc. of North Main Street, Providence, boasted two telephones and a quarter-page ad in the city directory. Not content with selling rags, the brothers sought an entrée into manufacturing. Stuck with an overrun of book-binding cloth he couldn't move, Henry seized on an idea. Why not use the fabric for pencil boxes? A suitable design was arrived at, and Henry and Hillel took samples to F. W. Woolworth and S. S. Kresge. Both chains placed orders, enabling the Hassenfeld brothers to build their first factory, in 1922. Among their first employees were their sister, Esther, a clerk, and brother Herman, a foreman, who'd finally made it to America with their parents and the fourth Hassenfeld son. Penniless leaving Galicia, Henry and Hillel could now afford to bring their family to the new land. They were just in time. In their occupation of Ulanow, Russians had embarked on a pogrom.

▪

Expansion was the story of the 1920s and 1930s. Empty pencil boxes were a lost opportunity, so the Hassenfeld brothers filled theirs with rulers, compasses, notebooks, erasers, and pencils purchased from outside suppliers. Buying from outside was a lost opportunity as well, so Henry and Hillel began manufacturing pencils. Having outgrown its first factory, Hassenfeld Bros. moved into a 65,000-square-foot facility in 1929; eleven years later the company moved again, to nearby Central Falls, into a plant seven times as big. Sales by 1940 surpassed $500,000, and more than 250 workers were employed during the peak season. The Hassenfelds were deeply involved in resettling hundreds of Eastern European and German Jews facing an evil unimaginably worse than pogroms; Henry, who outlived Hillel, would later build a pencil plant in the young and economically struggling republic of Israel. "Making money, being successful—that's not enough," he explained. "You have to believe in something. You have to have something to live and work for."

Hillel had no children, but Henry and Marion had four. Their two sons were barely adults when they joined the firm: Harold as a supervisor, Merrill as a salesman. Harold gravitated toward pencils, and eventually toward Tennessee, where in 1946 the Hassenfelds bought Empire Pencil Co., a manufacturer. Merrill's legacy would be in toys. He joined Hassenfeld Bros. upon graduation from the University of Pennsylvania, and it was during his apprenticeship, on the eve of World War II, that the Hassenfelds happened on yet another way to sell their boxes: with crayons, modeling clay, and paints, a marketing twist that might fill the slack periods in the school supplies market. A creative man, Merrill saw no reason to stop there. Why not fill their boxes with play stethoscopes and pill bottles, as several toy companies already did? A line of junior doctor and nurse kits was born. When war darkened coastal cities, Merrill put whistles, armbands, flashlights, and warden's caps into his boxes, and junior air raid warden kits went to market. Henry rewarded his son with the presidency in 1943. Merrill confirmed that wisdom with junior cosmetics kits, inspired by the play of his young daughter, Ellie, who was always into Sylvia's vanity. ("Keeps Mother's expensive cosmetics safe," one ad assured.) Cosmetic kits led to jewelry, sewing, embroidery, mailman, and school kits, toys that reflected a generation's philosophies of rearing its young.

▪

One day in 1951, a man carrying a box paid a visit to Merrill. George Lerner was a toy inventor from Brooklyn. His box contained plastic noses, ears, eyes, eyeglasses, mustaches, hats, a pipe, and hair. You stuck these into vegetables and fruits to create amusing characters, Lerner explained. Any fruit would do, although potatoes seemed best. Mr. Potato Head had been packaged briefly as a premium for a cereal company, but when that ended, Lerner had been unable to interest anyone else. What a waste of food! the toy honchos told him. And what about when Junior loses the darn thing behind the couch? The whole house would stink! Lerner moved down his list to Hassenfeld Bros., a bit player in toys.

Merrill was interested—Lerner's little novelty *was* amusing, for reasons difficult to articulate. He recognized the peril, but what was the worst that could happen? Mr. Potato Head would bomb, then disappear quietly. Toys did that all the time. And Hassenfeld Bros. could afford a loser. Stationery and pencils remained moneymakers, and the Hassenfelds' slowly expanding toy line was profitable, sufficiently so that they were inching into the high-risk business of licensed promotional items, with Donald Duck doctor kits, Mickey Mouse pencils, and Roy Rogers pistol pencil cases. Mr. Potato Head might even be a good candidate for television advertising, a new medium no toy company, big or small, had yet tried. Given his sorry history of rejection, how much could Lerner want for his odd little creation anyway?

Lerner settled for a $500 advance against a 5 percent royalty. The following year, backed by newspaper ads and a TV commercial in a handful of local markets, Mr. Potato Head debuted. The 1952 catalog for Hasbro, as Hassenfeld Bros. was now calling itself, had renderings of the toy as an orange, apple, cucumber, banana, pepper, pear, and potato. "The most novel toy in years," the copy proclaimed. "The ideal item for gift, party favor, or the young invalid." And only a dollar.

Whatever Potato Head's secret—whether its sheer silliness or something more profoundly comic in the marriage of humanity to food—the toy struck a chord, with adults as well as children. Mr. Potato Head wound up on TV with Jackie Gleason and in newspaper stories nationwide. West Coast distributors paid exorbitant air freight to keep shelves stocked, and the Hassenfelds hired additional workers to meet demand. Merrill had been optimistic, but he'd never dreamed of moving a million units the first year. He knew what to do with his good fortune. The next year Mrs. Potato Head debuted with a son, Spud, and daughter, Yam. Hasbro was still primarily a pencil and school supplies firm, but Merrill had tasted a success that would draw him ever more deeply into toys.

I I

LARRY REINER, A YOUNG games designer of minor distinction, was attending a meeting at Ideal Toy Co., his employer, when his thoughts began to stray. It was shortly before Toy Fair 1963, and Ideal, an industry leader, had brought together its creative talents to explore ways to expand its popular Tammy doll line. Someone suggested knocking off a competitor that marketed uncle dolls, aunt dolls, and other doll relatives in a line called Little Chaps. Someone else suggested making Tammy's father a fireman and her uncle a cop. Reiner was drifting off.

Why not a soldier doll? he wondered. He did not have in mind another small, immovable plastic or metal soldier, steady sellers for decades. He envisioned a roughly ten-inch, flexible figure that could hold toy weapons, strike realistic poses, and fit into tanks and other toy combat vehicles. After the meeting, Reiner disclosed his concept to his boss. His boss told him he was crazy. "Boys will never play with dolls," he declared. Reiner was free to take his idea elsewhere, but good luck. No company could be so colossally stupid.

Licensing agent Stan Weston, whom Reiner met that February at Toy Fair, didn't think the idea was so crazy. Weston was an up-and-coming presence in the still embryonic business of toy licensing, having sold the rights to such properties as MGM's popular Dr. Kildare and Universal's Frankenstein and Mummy. Weston outlined Reiner's concept to Don Levine, Merrill Hassenfeld's marketing/research director. Working with Weston, Levine had developed monster games and Dr. Kildare doctor kits for Hasbro and was under orders from Merrill to broaden Hasbro's anemic boy's line. He was considering the toy rights to *The Lieutenant,* a TV military drama Weston was representing, but Reiner's concept intrigued him more. Trade skepticism would be a formidable obstacle, but the play potential was enormous and Levine's gut told him boys and their dads would buy in, provided the pitch was right. He left New York with a promise to get back to Weston.

Merrill was with Sylvia on another of their philanthropic missions to Israel when Levine assigned his tiny research and development staff the job of refining the concept. The earliest prototypes were crude: store-bought poseable wooden artists' mannequins, about a foot tall, dressed in hand-sewn army, navy, marine, and air force uniforms. The figures were equipped with weapons and accessories cobbled together from retail items and materials the designers had on hand. The toy still did not have a name.

Merrill returned from Israel knowing nothing of Reiner's concept. Levine showed him the latest models and drawings of faces and heads, which he proposed be sculpted and manufactured in extraordinarily meticulous detail. Levine suggested molding the arms, legs, and bodies in Rhode Island and assembling and packaging the toys there as well. He recommended molding and hand painting the heads—because of the detail, a labor-intensive process—in Japan, where labor was still considerably cheaper than in America. Hasbro had never made anything overseas, nor had it ever sold a doll of any kind, for boy or girl. Both considerations troubled Merrill.

But he was enamored of the merchandising potential: the fact that the figures would be sold with a wide selection of uniform sets, equipment packs, and, eventually, vehicles. Levine called his marketing plan the "razor/razor blade" principle: Sell a razor, and you'd sold ongoing demand for blades. His inspiration was Mattel, which had proved the concept with America's best-selling doll. Hardly any little girl got a Barbie without at least one of her accessories or outfits, each sold separately.

And like Levine, Merrill instinctively believed boys could be persuaded to play with dolls, given the right approach—an approach that began with the solemn vow never to use the word "doll," not even internally.

"This is exciting," Merrill said, "but I'm concerned." He could already hear the buyers.

"Merrill, I have such a feeling about this," Levine said. "I think this can be it."

▪

Merrill desperately needed a hit in the spring of 1963. Alone atop the toy division since the death of his father (and mother) in 1960, he was a seasoned toy man now—a cigar-smoking raconteur who drove a hard bargain but was blessed with warm charm. Hasbro's revenues had grown steadily throughout the fifties and sixties, but the success of Mr. Potato Head and several later toys had been accompanied by a harsh lesson of the fashion business: What goes up comes down. Tempted by the greater revenue potential of higher-priced items, Merrill had gone beyond traditional toys to mechanization. Only one item in the 1961 line had a motor, but five toys the next year did, including an automatic bowling alley, a cotton-candy maker, and an electric car. All were more expensive and difficult to manufacture than toys that emerged fully formed from a molding machine. All failed at market, contributing to the division's unprecedented loss of $2.7 million on sales of only $15 million. Down in Tennessee, brother Harold, chairman of the board, was grumbling.

Merrill was banking on Flubber, a puttylike compound based on the magic material in *Son of Flubber,* sequel to *The Absent Minded Professor,* a blockbuster movie. "From Disney to Hasbro to you—the new kid craze," the catalog copy proclaimed. "Flubber is a new parent-approved material that is non-toxic and will not stain. . . . Flubber acts amazing. It bounces so high. It floats like a boat. It flows and moves." The material was cheap to produce, but based on the popularity of the film, Merrill figured, correctly, that he could move large volumes at high margin. Hasbro's compound was backed by TV commercials, Sunday comics, and a comic book, heady stuff in an era before multimillion-dollar campaigns involving restaurants, retailers, and saturation advertising keyed to movie openings and videotape releases.

Flubber seemed to be answering Merrill's prayers—millions of units had sold since its introduction in September 1962—when the federal Food and Drug Administration began investigating reports that the compound, a mix of synthetic rubber and mineral oil, gave some children sore throats and caused others to break out in full-body rashes.

"Ridiculous," Merrill said in a statement on March 15, 1963. "Tests have been conducted by the laboratories of several leading medical schools and universities as well as by one of the outstanding private research laboratories in the country—and the results of every single test have indicated that the product is absolutely safe." Some of the subjects, Merrill failed to mention, were inmates at Alcatraz—a questionable, if controlled, protocol for a product designed for kids.

A week later a Kansas housewife filed a $104,000 lawsuit, an intimidating sum at the time, claiming Flubber had caused rashes so severe on her and her three-year-old son that both had required hospital treatment. After 1,600 reports of such reactions to Flubber and similar products from other firms, Hasbro in May recalled its compound and stopped all production. Allegedly unable to dispose of it at sea (Flubber floated) or burn it at the city dump (it produced noxious black smoke while failing to combust completely, the story goes), Merrill buried his inventory—several tons' worth—behind a new warehouse and paved it over for a parking lot. Company legend three decades later still held that on the hottest summer days, Flubber oozed through cracks in the pavement—a primordial reminder of the vagaries of the toy business. Profitable only two years before, Merrill's toy division lost nearly $5 million, conceivably a lethal amount, in 1963.

■

Certainly the time seemed right for the unabashed patriotism of G.I. Joe, the name Levine gave his line of dolls after watching a World War II movie. The cold war was testing a nation's belief in invincibility, but in 1963 the belief still held; a combat hero was in the White House, and the largest class of veterans in American history was raising the largest generation of children, the baby boom. Toys derived from characters in westerns, where the good guys always won, were big sellers from the 1950s into the 1960s, and many companies' lines reflected the era's fascination with the marvels of modern technology. With considerable pride, Merrill brought forth such toys as Art Linkletter's Magic Moon Rocks, Space Doctor Survival Kits ("as imaginative and exciting as the space age in which we live"), and the Think-A-Tron, a toy computer. Toys enriched children and delighted their parents, or so it was assumed. Merrill put a drawing of a mother, father, daughter, and son on the cover of his 1962 catalog with the wholesome slogan "A Hasbro Toy Is a Family Joy."

"Let's test it," Merrill instructed Levine.

No toy company did much in the way of market research then—Merrill's test consisted of bringing in a handful of buyers for a cigar, a dinner, and a private peek at G.I. Joe. They liked what they saw, provided Merrill launched the line with uncompromisingly masculine fanfare. "Do it," Merrill told Levine. What with Flubber and last year's losses, Hasbro would have to borrow some $15 million to ramp up production.

After putting him off for months, Merrill finally met with Stan Weston on the eve of Toy Fair 1964, when G.I. Joe was to be unveiled. Merrill offered him a 1 percent royalty on all future sales. One percent, take it or leave it. Weston was incredulous—5 percent was the standard of the time—but given that Hasbro had put so much already into development, he would settle for 3 percent. Merrill counteroffered with a flat $75,000, to be paid over five years, for perpetual rights to Joe. Weston asked for $100,000, to be split with Reiner. Merrill shook hands on the deal. Reiner was not pleased, but what could he do? Twenty-nine years old, he did not have the savvy that came later in a successful career as an inventor of toys, including Hasbro's Talking Barney. "If I had it all to do over, I'd get a royalty," Reiner would lament. "I get it from a lot of people that I was a schmuck!"

Buyers visiting the Hasbro showroom were not allowed to see the toys until after viewing a promotional film Hasbro's advertising agency had prepared. "Since the beginning of time," the voice-over said as the camera panned a boy who bore a resemblance to Timmy from TV's *Lassie,* "children have always played soldier—with wooden swords, broomstick rifles, with cast-lead soldiers, with plastic miniatures . . . but none of these gave a boy the feeling he was playing real soldier."

G.I. Joe, America's Movable Fighting Man, did. Every weapon, the film explained, was modeled after the regulation item; every uniform, canteen, and tent a miniature of the real thing. Nearly a foot tall (Barbie's height, a fact left unsaid), G.I. Joe had an astounding twenty-one movable parts, which enabled him to carry a flamethrower, toss a grenade, or storm a beach. The sound track was stirring military music, and actual combat footage was shown, but the strongest patriotic sentiments involved Joe's face: "Not just an artist's fancy," the voice-over claimed, "this *is* the face of G.I. Joe, carefully designed from composite photographs of twenty Medal of Honor winners." In truth, the model was a Hasbro artist's colleague, a good-looking but otherwise ordinary guy.

Buyers gave Joe mixed reviews. Orders were written, but not in the volume Merrill needed to cover his investment. His answer was to spend more, and advertisements were prepared for TV and print. The toy was in only a small number of stores when, that summer, Hasbro began running a commercial a day on a New York television station. Within a week G.I. Joe had sold out in New York, a market retailers watched closely. Advertising on the NBC network spread the craze coast to coast. Joe sold $5.3 million in 1964, returning Hasbro's toy division from its nearly $5 million loss to a profit of $895,000. Merrill expanded the line for 1965

and put another $2 million in advertising behind the toy. He was re-
warded with sales of $23 million and a divisional profit of nearly $6 million, a record—and a number the likes of which neither the corporation
nor the division would see again for many years, something that would
obsess Merrill's new assistant, his oldest son, Steve.

I I I

UNLIKE ALAN, WHO NEVER was too wild about Daddy's factory, Stephen
Hassenfeld was enthralled from the age of four or five. Weekends, vacations, summers—whenever opportunity beckoned, Stephen wanted to
be in Central Falls. Everything interested him: the injection molders, the
sewing machines, the assembly lines, and the executive suite, such as it
was in that towering redbrick building with the creaky old elevators and
grease-stained floors where Mr. Potato Head sprang to life. Years later,
when Stephen was CEO, factory workers would marvel at the memory
of the young lad sticking his nose everywhere, asking polite questions,
and making cheerful small talk as if he were one of them and not the
boss's son.

Stephen attended Providence's Moses Brown School, a private academy founded by Quakers in 1784. Flirting with the idea of becoming a
diplomat, he majored in political science at Johns Hopkins University,
where he joined a fraternity and was the only student among his peers to
have a credit card. Stephen struck his classmates as unusually mature—a
young man of quiet confidence who enjoyed a moment of fun but
seemed to know exactly where he was heading, which, despite his major,
was not the State Department. Early in his senior year, in the fall of 1962,
Stephen left Hopkins, never to return. "I could not see spending another
eight months reading English literature and political science when business had a greater appeal to me," he told an interviewer a few years later.
Stephen wanted to work for Merrill, but Merrill insisted he try something else first to confirm Hasbro was where his heart was. Stephen took
a job at a Providence advertising firm. In 1964 Merrill relented. He hired
Stephen, twenty-two, as his assistant.

The young man moved deliberately and fast, as if all those childhood
visits had been not merely to watch, but to devise a future plan. Hasbro's
sales and production departments had been swamped by G.I. Joe's

overnight success, and Stephen went right to work on the problem, introducing tighter controls and an information system that helped restore order. Within two years he had restructured Hasbro's national sales force, replaced outside manufacturers' representatives with Hasbro personnel, and improved the company's distribution network. Marketing held the greatest appeal, and he dove into packaging, advertising, and promotion with infectious enthusiasm. "At first meeting, you cannot avoid coming under Steve's spell," observed a writer for *Toy & Hobby World* in 1966, when Merrill had promoted his son to vice president of marketing. "We observed him for two solid days conduct a marketing seminar in Cranston, Rhode Island. Never once was he not in total control of the situation, and as fast as complex questions were thrown at him, he responded with the answers." Insiders appreciated his touch, too. "This is a young man who was born with a silver spoon in his mouth and has never felt it," an executive told the magazine.

Merrill named Stephen executive vice president in 1968, the year Hasbro went public, and president in 1974, when toy sales were $65 million (Merrill became vice chairman of the board). The presidency was the fulfillment of a boyhood dream, but it came at a time when Hasbro was struggling to survive. Merrill had essentially run the business as every old-fashioned promotional toy man did, according to the philosophy that great product drives great sales, and other details resolve themselves. Cash flow, inventory, receivables, working capital, bank credit—the other details—had suffered, putting Hasbro on precarious financial ground. The situation was so dire in early 1974 that Merrill and Harold had been forced to put up their personal property as collateral for loans at exorbitant rates, all they could get to carry the company through the post-holiday period, when sales ebbed but manufacturing for next Christmas was already tooling up.

Whether Merrill had contributed to the situation or not was immaterial to Stephen: he resented the hold the banks had and vowed to break it. He saw the solution in discipline and in Al Verrecchia, promoted to treasurer in 1974 and now Hasbro's highest financial officer. Stephen had worked eighteen-hour days, often seven days a week, since starting at Hasbro. He applied this energy to his new preoccupation, the numbers, drawing on Verrecchia's knowledge from a decade in the trenches. With the exception of one disastrous year when Hasbro bet heavily on several new products and lost, the company's balance sheet improved steadily during the last half of the seventies. With better forecasting and controls on production and distribution, inventory as a percentage of sales declined; with less money tied up in unsold goods, Hasbro built its cash reserves. And with a better cash position, Stephen could begin weaning the company off short-term debt, which in 1973 had reached $16 million, an alarming 21 percent of toy sales. He could also afford to invest more heavily in advertising and research and development.

Stephen did not tackle the balance sheet in isolation. The toy company of tomorrow—his, at least—must have balance and diversity and be first or second in sales in all major categories. Stephen set about building a preschool line, an outdoor line, and fashion doll and promotional doll businesses. He endeavored, for years in vain, to establish Hasbro as a force in games. He examined Hasbro's staples through the cold lens of profitability, weeding out items that didn't perform. Those that made money—Mr. Potato Head, Lite-Brite, doctor and nurse kits—got new looks and new advertising. Stephen insisted on approving every detail: every color choice, every package, every catalog page, every merchandising plan, every ad.

By the mid-seventies he was convinced Hasbro could be a player on Wall Street, even though Hasbro's stock had never been on any broker's list of smart buys. In his presidential letter in Hasbro's 1976 annual report, Stephen spelled out his financial objectives: revenue increases of 15 percent a year with earnings gains of 11 to 13 percent. "Is it to swim upstream to believe that a moderate-sized company like ours can build strong investor credibility and confidence?" he wrote. "We believe not."

▪

Merrill was working in his office, next to Stephen's, when he suffered a heart attack one day in March 1979. He died a short while later at Providence's Miriam Hospital. He was sixty-one.

A man with a weakness for fatty foods, Merrill had struggled for years with his weight and high blood pressure. His death was nonetheless a stunning blow. Stephen effectively had been running Hasbro's toy division for years, but the wisdom Merrill had gained over four decades in the business still served his precocious son well. As vice chairman, Merrill was the one who took the heat from brother Harold when things went wrong up in Rhode Island. And wrong they'd gone, with such ill-fated ventures as *Romper Room* nursery schools and day-care centers (closed after three straight years of losses) and *Galloping Gourmet* housewares (whose demise was hastened when termites ate warehoused wooden salad bowls). "He allowed us to get into things over our heads, allowed us to make mistakes, and when we made them, never came down hard on us," Stephen told a reporter interviewing him and Alan after their father's death. "We always sat and talked through those things."

The Hassenfelds had much to discuss among themselves after Merrill was gone. Although the balance sheet was not mortally wounded, 1978 had been a disaster, the first loss year since Hasbro had gone public: the villain, once again, was toys. Stephen had kept G.I. Joe on the market despite five straight years of declining sales, and his last effort to save the line, an abomination called Super Joe, had been a catastrophe at retail. Charlie's Angels, Stephen's latest challenge to Barbie, was in its second (and final) year and had lost all momentum. Total toy losses were $5.2 million, more than any year in company history. Meanwhile, pencils had turned in a tidy $2 million profit, best ever. With Merrill gone, the long-simmering dispute between Tennessee and Rhode Island boiled over.

If Stephen (still only thirty-seven) was such a boy wonder, how come he was taking Hasbro into the tank? Could such a man be counted on for the capital investments Empire Pencil needed to maintain its steady, if unspectacular, growth? Chairman Harold's answer was no.

On September 28, 1980, the firm founded by two immigrant brothers was cleft in two. Harold stayed in Tennessee. Stephen became chairman of the toy half, which kept the Hasbro name.

▪

A dark omen to his uncle, Super Joe had pushed Stephen to a rare sophistication in marketing. Henceforth, strategy would drive development; by themselves, love or sentiment would not be enough for a toy. Stephen rededicated himself to pruning or killing existing lines—"categories important to us in the past which have lived on largely because of the emotion of what they had meant to us," he wrote in his 1980 report. The most difficult casualty had been G.I. Joe, which Stephen killed altogether. This was sacrilege, but Stephen had a higher calling now.

The new Hasbro made $5 million in 1980, the most since the height of Joe's popularity in 1964. The firm ended the year with a record $16 million in cash and one of its most favorable inventory levels ever. All short-term debt had been liquidated, and long-term debt was dropping rapidly. Alan, with the company since 1970, had negotiated the largest licensing deal in Hasbro history: $2 million for foreign rights to G.I. Joe (who would be known overseas as Action Man), an unprecedented cash windfall that could not have come at a more opportune moment. The rest of Stephen's team was in place: Al Verrecchia and the Three Musketeers (Larry Bernstein, Steve Schwartz, and George Dunsay).

Still, as the company entered the Reagan era, no one was picking it for greatness; greatness was a word associated with number one Mattel, eight times larger than Hasbro and closing in on $1 billion a year in sales. If anything, what Stephen had accomplished in Rhode Island had been lost in the hoopla over a breathtaking new category of toy that was taking the nation's young by storm. Everyone knew video games were the wave of the future. Where, then, was Hasbro? Stephen had come to Toy Fair with nothing but more of his cute molded plastic, an appallingly deficient vision for which Hasbro was widely ridiculed as "Has-been."

No one, not even Stephen, could have predicted how this seeming misfortune would turn out to be such luck, so often the silent partner in fabulous business success.

3

REAL AMERICAN HEROES

I

Stephen Hassenfeld was not expecting to change his mind when the lights went down in Hasbro's presentation theater that day in 1981. There was a good chance he'd pitch a fit. For months the Three Musketeers had been clamoring for permission to bring G.I. Joe back. It was the hardest sell Bernstein, Schwartz, and Dunsay had ever had.

Explosive the first year, Joe sales had hit a phenomenal $23 million in 1965, dipped as opposition to the Vietnam War heightened, then inched back up as the war wound down and Stephen moved deliberately away from the line's hard-edged militarism. G.I. Joe Adventure Teams, launched in 1969, bore little resemblance to America's Movable Fighting Man, Merrill's flame-throwing, M-60-toting toy warrior. Adventure Team members had beards, wore dog tags that suspiciously resembled peace symbols, carried few weapons, and embarked not on combat missions but on quests, such as Mission to Spy Island. His tag line even changed, to America's Movable Adventure Man. Joe's biggest year was 1973, with $26 million in sales.

Adventure Teams had succeeded as a short-term gimmick, but something vital had been lost in Joe's pacifist makeover, and as sales declined again, Stephen struggled for a replacement. Martial arts swept through the popular culture, and Joe, in 1974, adopted Kung-Fu Grip. *The Six Million Dollar Man* was a TV hit, and Joe became bionic. Comic book superheroes made one of their periodic returns to popularity, and the tired old fighter became the Human Bullet and the disastrous Super Joe. The fall from 1973 was rapid: sales of G.I. Joe declined 75 percent in only three years. The end came in 1978, when Kenner's Star Wars figures redefined the market, reaching almost $100 million in sales, unprecedented for action figures, the genre Joe had begun. With Joe's sales at their lowest ever, Stephen sounded taps.

Stephen accepted blame for the toy's demise. If there was consolation, it was that Joe had reinforced like nothing else his belief that diversity, not reliance on a single mercurial line, was what might persuade Wall Street to take an inconsequential toy company seriously. But Joe was more than a painful marketing lesson to Stephen. Joe had been Hasbro's crown jewel, its Barbie; the argument could be made that without it, Hasbro would have come out of Flubber a nice little Tennessee pencil maker. Merrill had lived just long enough to see his fabled soldier breathe his last, and while he knew the fluky ways of toys as well as anyone, it had been a bitter disappointment. In the early 1980s the emotions surrounding Joe still ran deep with the Hassenfelds. Resurrection was not a matter to be taken lightly.

The Three Musketeers understood that, but believed an appeal to Stephen's head, not his heart, would give them a chance. They saw no reason why Star Wars' success could not be coopted in a reborn Joe. Seemingly the time was right: Jimmy Carter had been returned to the peanut farm, and Ronald Reagan, invoking the specter of the Evil Empire, had vowed to restore America's military might. Plastic had become expensive, so the new Joe would have to shrink to the size of Star Wars figures: just under four inches tall. But what was lost in stature, creative minds could recompense with heroic fantasy.

The first hint Stephen had that something was afoot was in 1980, when he was shown a crude concept, code-named Blastoff. Loosely grounded in World War II, Blastoff was little more than recycled early Joe. Stephen wasn't interested. Blastoff had no highly developed villains, no epic conflicts, no continuing adventures like those George Lucas offered. Stephen craved carefully scripted fantasies—which, like those underpinning the most enduring TV series, could be manipulated into years of line extensions and sales.

The Three Musketeers had heeded the lesson of Blastoff. Rather than return to the past, with its political baggage and old-fashioned truisms, Joe would be a fighting force for today, armed with the weapons of tomorrow, as imagined inside Hasbro. Patriotism would return, but not with marines storming Iwo Jima; like the Green Berets, the reborn Joe would be part of an elite antiterrorist team, ready at a moment's notice for operations anywhere in the world. Stephen said he'd consider it. It was early 1981.

The Three Musketeers were on a West Coast invention-scouting trip when Stephen phoned with his decision.

"Years ago, I told the Wall Street community the reason we're stopping G.I. Joe is because we became dependent on this one line and that's what hurt us in the past," he said. "And I can't think of a reason why we would be successful now." How could Joe compete with Star Wars, which continued to torch the market? Hasbro had no movie.

"You can't do this," Schwartz told his boss on his return the next day. "You can't on one hand hammer us that we are not growing the business—and then when we show you what we think is the way, not let us do it." He threatened to resign, and when he'd cooled, he said: "Give us one more meeting to show you the marketing." Stephen set a deadline of two weeks.

▪

Joe Bacal was center stage in the presentation theater when the lights went down. Bacal and Tom Griffin, Stephen's friends, headed Hasbro's New York advertising firm.

Bacal began by recapping the incredible success of *Star Wars* and its sequel, *The Empire Strikes Back.* A third title, *Return of the Jedi,* was due in 1983, giving Joe, which Schwartz wanted to launch in 1982, a one-year window of opportunity. "We don't have a movie," Bacal continued, "but we do have the book." He handed Stephen a mock cover of a comic book, which Marvel Comics had produced for the presentation. The pencil art was exciting, the colors bold; the title, *G.I. JOE: A Real American Hero,* was called out in distinctive type. Patriotic music blared as Bacal whirled through storyboards of the lavish, all-animated commercials they would develop. Technically the commercials would be for the comic: drawings of characters, weapons, and vehicles would be shown, but not representations of the actual toys. Therein lay the key. Driving back to New York from a meeting with the Three Musketeers, Bacal and Griffin had hit upon an ingenious idea.

As the Reagan years wore on, children's TV would be substantially deregulated, paving the way for the freewheeling era of *Mighty Morphin Power Rangers*. But broad deregulation was something marketers only yearned for in the early eighties. Networks and stations still adhered to a voluntary set of guidelines (established by the National Association of Broadcasters) limiting toy commercials. Specifically discouraged was extensive animation, which might mislead minds too young to distinguish reliably between fantasy and reality. "Fantasy is such a healthy part of play," Bacal would later say, "and they weren't permitting it except under the most rigid circumstances, like having to say 'You can imagine' before you could say anything." But there was no rule against commercials for comics; no one had ever seen the need. "You're kidding," Marvel's chairman said when Schwartz offered him $3 million to advertise the new title. Schwartz wasn't kidding. He trusted kids to make the connection between comics and toys.

"We're going to reach more people than Star Wars reached with the movie," Bacal explained to Stephen. "We're going to be able to put the fantasy of G.I. Joe into the kid culture."

A charming man in social circumstances, Stephen was a bear at presentations. He challenged, suggested, dictated, praised lavishly when it was warranted. He rated commercials on a scale of one to ten, rejecting any lower than eight. He practiced a limited democracy, soliciting commentary from everyone in the room before setting the course and demanding strict adherence to it. He was strangely mute on this day. Bacal finished his presentation, and the lights went up.

Stephen was standing, tears in his eyes, at the back of the room. "I wish my father had been alive to see this," he finally said. "I'm going to tell my father."

He left the room, bound for Lincoln Park Cemetery.

■

Fifty-one million dollars' worth of Real American Heroes were sold in 1982, and the toy was the overwhelming new boys' sensation that Christmas. Hasbro's marketing was carefully crafted to fit public sentiment, a renewed militarism nonetheless tainted by lingering memories of Vietnam; like Reagan, Joe was walking a line. "We want kids to understand that G.I. Joe is not a warmonger," Schwartz told a reporter. "We feel that we have a commitment to the kids of America and to their parents to properly represent the role of the military today, which is as a peacekeeping force, not an aggressor."

Joe's was indeed a benign patriotism. Parents, many of whom had marched against the war, accepted this, or at least did not let principle interfere with their sons' desires. New Joe's sales tripled in two years, producing a cash flow that allowed Hasbro to underwrite a television series that quickly became entrenched at the top of the syndicated market.

As the line neared $185 million in sales (in 1986), a third more than Kenner's Star Wars toys at their apex, Hasbro mined its fantasy deeply. As a multipurpose team, Joe could go anywhere, pilot any vehicle, and fire any weapon, two favorites being the twin-barreled Heavy Artillery Laser and the Dreadnok Thunder Machine. Stephen sanctioned violence but strictly forbade depiction of its consequences. "They told me, 'You can have all the firepower you want, but please: no one gets killed or injured. No nuclear bombs, no bullets, only laser beams,' " an artist for the TV series told *The Wall Street Journal*. "It was funny. Even the sharpshooters had to shoot at an object like a boulder that would fall on the enemy's head and knock him unconscious." In toy form, Joe's plastic weapons did not shoot, although spring-fired technology had long existed. Grandson of a man who'd narrowly escaped a bloody pogrom, Stephen would not cross that line.

Hasbro was not content with conventional tactics of line extension, for this was not the 1960s, when Toy Fair sizzle, a promotion or two, and a couple of ads were enough to drive sales. Joe's TV program was freshened continually. The G.I. Joe Fan Club reopened. A nationwide "Real American Hero" search generated huge publicity, and under the guise of teaching heroism, a program offering free posters and coloring kits took Joe into a hallowed place: grammar school classrooms. A magazine was sold, along with the comic. Outlicensing sent Joe into homes and onto playgrounds with breakfast cereals, lunch boxes, trading cards, T-shirts, sneakers, sleeping bags, videocassettes, arcade and video games, snorkels, masks, and swim fins. Outlicensing was particularly lucrative, for not only did it further seed the toy into children's culture—it generated millions in royalties, nearly all of which could be applied directly to the bottom line.

Joe alone might well have set the stage for Stephen's greatest triumph, but Hasbro seemed to have happened into a wondrous gestalt, as Bacal would call it. My Little Pony, a line of toy horses with manes girls would happily comb for hours, debuted in 1983 with $21 million in sales, a volume that tripled the next year. Transformers, an Americanized version of a popular Japanese toy, topped $100 million in its first year, 1984. Both became successful TV series and movies. Hasbro's earnings in 1983 were $15 million on revenues of $225 million, both company records, but more important for what was ahead, cash reserves swelled to previously unimaginable levels. Wall Street was listening to the intense young toy maker from Rhode Island now, and the toy maker was rewarding his senior executives with fabulous stock options and raises.

"You want to talk about heady days," Bernstein would recall much later, when his fortunes had turned. "That was a time when people were calling a broker at least hourly."

II

STEPHEN HASSENFELD RETURNED FROM Toy Fair 1984 in rare spirits. The new G.I. Joe and My Little Pony lines had been enthusiastically received, and the launch of Transformers had the retail trade abuzz. Hasbro Preschool had scored with Gloworm dolls, Smurf activity sets, and Big Bird toys. The acquisition of Knickerbocker Toy Co. had established Hasbro in the plush business; another takeover in 1983, of Glenco, gave Stephen a solid presence in the infant care market. Although he did not hold the master licenses, Stephen had negotiated limited rights to use Snoopy, Garfield, Cabbage Patch Kids, Strawberry Shortcake, and Disney characters in such niche products as coloring sets and an old Hasbro standby, the Sno-Cone machine.

In April, in a report targeted to Wall Street, Stephen expertly analyzed changing demographics and how he was positioning Hasbro to exploit them. "The rising number of two-income families means more discretionary spending on children," he said. "The number of toy buyers is also on the rise. Growing numbers of two-home and single-parent families mean the children often have two sets of toys. Longer life spans mean more grandparents—and grandparents generally treat grandchildren very well." In case there was an investor who hadn't heard his sermon by now, Stephen repeated a fundamental tenet: "Steady growth comes from balance."

But Hasbro was yet to achieve the degree of diversity, or success, the chairman wanted. Millions of dollars had been spent over many years trying to develop a fashion doll to break Barbie's maddening dominance, to no avail. More frustrating had been Hasbro's efforts to get into games. Since the 1960s barely a year had passed without the company introducing some new title that Stephen had hoped would crack this high-margin market, immensely profitable for those few firms that had found the key. Word Nerd, Quick Jump It's a Skunk!, Baboon Ball, I Want to Bite Your Finger (the Dracula Game)—all had been embarrassing failures. Only Hungry Hungry Hippos, which Hasbro introduced in 1978, had staying power. Whatever the magic formula, Stephen couldn't discover it on his own. He knew he would have to buy it.

Stephen had long had his eye on the Milton Bradley Company, just over an hour away in the old Yankee bastion of Springfield, Massachusetts. No marketer could look without gnawing envy at Milton Bradley. The company sold Chutes and Ladders, Candy Land, and Go to the Head of the Class, timeless diversions that were as much a part of millions of childhoods as sandboxes and swings. Yahtzee, Strategy, Battleship, and Life brought families together for hours of predictably safe fun. Bradley sold a full selection of chess, checkers, and dominoes sets. And was there a home anywhere without the company's jigsaw puzzles, finest in the land? By penurious management of its classics and savvy introduction of the best new games, Bradley had gone without a loss for thirty-five consecutive years (until 1983). It owned Playskool, whose cachet in preschool was rivaled only by Fisher-Price, and its overseas sales and marketing organizations dwarfed Hasbro's. For all the right business reasons, Bradley made sense. But there was more to it than that. In 1984 Stephen was behind the wheel of a sports car, zippy on the corners and unbeatable from the light. Milton Bradley was a Bentley, rich with pedigree and aristocratic mystique. The company's roots predated the presidency of Abraham Lincoln, and its first game had been sold nearly a half century before Henry Hassenfeld left the shtetl. Peruse Bradley's archives, and you got a sense of America's rise to greatness. Peruse Hasbro's, and you found plastic noses stuck onto potatoes.

Considering Bradley's size (revenues of $421 million in 1980, more than four times Hasbro's that year), Stephen had no hope of getting Bradley—until Vectrex, its new video-game system. Developed amid great optimism, Vectrex had become an open wound, sending Bradley in a single year from net income of $19 million to a loss almost as big. London-based Hanson PLC watched with heightened interest. An industrial conglomerate with extensive holdings in the United States, Hanson had grown by aggressive takeovers—of companies with products as diverse as hot dogs and bricks. Early in 1984 Hanson bought nearly 5 percent of Bradley's stock, apparently with the intention of making a run at the company. Panicked at the prospect of more than a century of proud independence evaporating overnight, Bradley bought back the stock—for $30.50 a share, considerably more than the open-market price. The buyback, $11 million in total, not only further damaged Bradley's deteriorating balance sheet: it touched off a tempest of speculation that put the company into play.

George Ditomassi, Bradley's executive vice president of marketing and a member of the board, was in chairman James J. Shea Jr.'s office the day Stephen Hassenfeld called.

"If you need a white knight," Stephen said, "I'd love to act on your behalf."

"Thanks a lot, Stephen," said Shea, who still believed he could save the day, "I'll let you know if I do."

Shea hung up. "Can you believe that?" he said, incredulous. "Hassenfeld wants to be the white knight!"

■

Twenty-three-year-old Milton Bradley was a struggling lithographer looking for new uses for his underutilized press when, in the summer of 1860, inspired by an old English game, he invented The Checkered Game of Life. The game mirrored his belief in the conflicting forces of ambition, expertise, and chance—which, in the end, might deliver a young man like himself to Happy Old Age or Ruin. That September Bradley traveled from Springfield with his game. "I have come to New York with some samples of a new and most amazing game, sir," Bradley said on his first call, a stationery store. "A highly moral game, may I say, that encourages children to lead exemplary lives and entertains both old and young with the spirit of its friendly competition." Descendant of a

Puritan who'd left London for Massachusetts in 1635, Bradley was a churchgoing Methodist.

Bradley sold forty thousand copies of Life that first winter, an impressive performance driven, in part, by an anxious nation's desire for amusing distraction on the eve of civil war. Bradley abandoned his other business, lithographs of a clean-shaven presidential candidate, a business that had suddenly soured when Abraham Lincoln grew a beard after his election. Life was followed by Games for the Soldiers, and Patriot Heroes, which capitalized on Union war sentiment; and Sunday School Cards, a set of colorfully illustrated biblical quotations. Before the war was over, Bradley was selling My Grandfather's Games, based on the traditional children's games of Fox and Geese and Three Hen Morris, and his first toys and puzzles. Croquet sets, Bradley's first foray into sports, were patented in 1866.

With the spread of public education in the latter part of the nineteenth century, Bradley began making school products: multiplication sticks, rulers, and stencils. He was not simply opportunistic; like most other manufacturers of children's products, he believed he was duty-bound to advance the well-being of children. Whether through puzzles, games, or toys, entertainment should be wholesome; if it could be educational as well, all the better. In the Rousseauian view of the time—a view that continued to prevail well into the twentieth century (an echo can be heard in Stephen Hassenfeld's prohibition against showing killing)—children were innocents, and it was an adult's moral obligation to protect and nurture as they made the journey to civilized status in the grown-up world. A few toys and games mirrored the racial prejudices common to the period, but Bradley and his peers would have been dumbfounded at the idea that adults would someday invest millions of dollars to manufacture and advertise products designed specifically to frighten or disgust children or empower them to vicariously maim and kill with the bloody results realistically displayed six inches from their eyes. The mind of a child was a sacred trust.

The Bradley line in the early 1900s reflected the founder's approval of technology, erudition, and commerce. The company sold Ring Off, A Wireless Telephone Game; the Auto Game; and the Air King Game, featuring a zephyr ("A safe way of navigating the air. No broken bones."). Thoughts from Longfellow, Books and Authors, and Bible Objects ("We are not advocates of Sunday games, therefore we do not recommend the playing of this as a *game* on the Sabbath") were popular. In the Toy Town series, youngsters could play bank, post office, library, conductor, school, policeman, and train. War was considered a noble endeavor for an emerging world power, and the Bradley catalog was filled with such military titles as Bombardment, Sharpshooters, and Battleship, especially as tensions in Europe grew as 1914 drew near. Toy soldiers were staples year after year, but the figures did nothing more than stand. Boys were to be shielded from the graphic horrors of war while preparing to someday heed patriotic duty.

Although Milton Bradley Company had moved heavily into products licensed from Hollywood and TV by the 1980s, the founder's commitment to wholesomeness and learning had not been lost. Go to the Head of the Class, Game of the States, Memory—these were nothing more than modern versions of eighty-year-old classics. Even the ill-fated Vectrex was supposed to come with "a variety of educational cartridges."

▪

James J. Shea Jr. knew he was taking a risk when, in the summer of 1982, he decided to plunge his venerable firm into video games. He'd been burned in nonvideo electronic games and toys (two straight years of losses) and video-game makers by the dozen had created fierce competition. "Your management has been reluctant to enter the video-game market because we believe that the market will shortly be oversaturated," Shea noted in his annual report for the year.

But the lure of the microchip was irresistible. By the time Shea succumbed, U.S. video hardware sales were $950 million annually, more than three times that of just two years earlier, and software sales, growing at the rate of 500 percent a year, had passed the $1 billion mark. Afraid the future would be lost without romancing this sophisticated newcomer, traditional toy firms, notably Mattel and Coleco, had jumped into the fray with such heavy hitters as Commodore, Atari, and Texas Instruments. Only Hasbro, ridiculed as "Has-been" for its old-fashioned attitudes, showed no evidence of temptation.

"It was felt that Vectrex did not compete directly with the existing game consoles in the marketplace and would offer a new dimension in game play," Shea noted in buying the California company that had developed the system. "An astounding breakthrough," trumpeted the Bradley catalog.

Vectrex was launched in the first quarter of 1983, the precise moment that Christmas softness in video-game sales accelerated into an industry-wide collapse (hardware sales fell 20 percent in 1983 and were only $165 million, less than a fifth of their peak, the following year). No retailers wanted ColecoVision or Mattel's Intellivision, never mind this newfangled entry from a company without a lick of experience in the category. Shea could not get the broad distribution he needed to make his numbers work, a dire situation that only worsened when buyers began canceling orders. It was a classic case of supply and demand: too many products, too few consumers. By the end of the year Shea was offering Vectrex at below manufacturing cost. And still it was stuck to the shelves, in those few stores that carried it.

Although company lore held that near mystical prescience on the part of Stephen Hassenfeld had kept Hasbro out of video games, the truth was he'd been tantalized like everyone else. But Stephen didn't trust his own people to develop a system from scratch, and none of the concepts shown by outside inventors had bowled him over. "They all began to look the same, and we backed off," he told *The New York Times* after serendipity had saved him. "Did I understand how much momentum this would give us? No." The momentum was best appreciated by examining the balance sheet, which in spring 1984 was heavily fortified by the success of old-fashioned plastic.

•

"We have an opportunity," John Rosenwald said to Stephen in April, when press accounts of the Hanson buyback and the resulting upward spiral in the price of Milton Bradley stock confirmed the depth of its troubles. The idea of a white knight was no longer quite as unpalatable to Shea, stunned by how rapidly the company he and members of his family had directed for more than forty years was slipping out of his control.

Rosenwald belonged to the new guard, whose members Stephen was hiring to replace the family cronies and small-time businessmen Merrill and Harold had put on the board. Stephen had snared Alex Grass, chairman and president of Rite Aid Corporation, the drugstore giant, and was soon to bring on Carl Spielvogel, chairman of a Madison Avenue advertising firm. If Stephen was going to travel in high circles, his closest companions would be first-class.

Rosenwald was the real catch. Senior partner (and future vice chairman) of the Bear Stearns Companies, an investment banking house that was in the thick of the merger and acquisition fever that gripped corporate America as Reaganism rolled on, Rosenwald, to Stephen, was what Wall Street was all about: graduate of Deerfield Academy, Dartmouth College, and Amos Tuck School of Business Administration; three residences, including one in Palm Beach, Florida; memberships in six exclusive clubs; trustee of Dartmouth and New York University Medical Center. More important for Stephen's plans, Rosenwald was like a competing financial firm's popular motto: When he talked, investors listened, and so did Stephen Hassenfeld. Of all Hasbro's directors, only Sylvia Hassenfeld, whom Stephen brought onto the board after his father's death, enjoyed greater respect from the chairman.

After talking to Rosenwald, Stephen took a commercial flight to New York with Verrecchia, his finance chief. Rarely had he been as excited, or as apprehensive. At $337 million in sales, Milton Bradley, albeit suffering, was nearly twice as large as Hasbro.

Verrecchia and Stephen met Rosenwald at the Waldorf-Astoria. For the next several hours, until late into the night, they planned their approach to Shea. To the best of their knowledge, Milton Bradley had only one other suitor—although in a volatile affair such as this, that could change rapidly, they knew. If there was any certainty, it was that no traditional toy company but Hasbro was in a position to make a credible offer. Coleco had been singed by ColecoVision and was yet to see the riches of the Cabbage Patch Kids, newly introduced. Intellivision had left Mattel with a staggering $394 million loss at the end of 1983. Things at Mattel were so bad that an investment banker recently had quietly approached Stephen to see if he'd be interested in being its white knight.

Stephen wasn't, not for Mattel.

▪

The suitor was Ronald O. Perelman, an investor with no background in toys, games, or puzzles.

Perelman seemed centrally cast for a leading role in the takeover wars of the eighties. Son of the owner of an inconsequential metal-fabricating firm, he'd earned an MBA from the Wharton School and married into money. His first deal was in 1978, when he borrowed nearly $2 million to buy a stake in a jewelry distributor; two years later he bought candy maker MacAndrews & Forbes, the more Anglican-sounding name under which he from then on operated. Next was the purchase of Technicolor, the film-processing firm; Perelman sliced it into pieces, selling most to reduce debt. By 1984, with backing from Drexel Burnham Lambert Inc.'s Michael Milken ("the Billionaire Junk Bond King"), the head of MacAndrews & Forbes was on the hunt again. Shrewd, socially conscious, and on his way to great wealth, Perelman counted private aircraft, property in the Hamptons, and friends such as Warner Bros. president Terry Semel among the important things in life. He'd divorced and would soon marry a beautiful gossip columnist turned TV reporter. Someday he hoped to be like Semel—a big-time player in TV and film. Perelman already had Technicolor. With its ties to Hollywood, Milton Bradley was not an illogical step.

Perelman's offer was $49 a share, while Stephen Hassenfeld's was $50, or about $360 million in cash and securities; with either, Shea's fiduciary responsibilities would be fulfilled. It wasn't difficult to imagine whom the founder would have chosen had he tumbled into such humiliating circumstances: the father of a newly revived classic toy or a guy who wasn't particular whether his money came from jewelry, junk bonds, or a wife. "Now I don't know the Hassenfelds, but I do know that we're looking at the third generation of brothers," Ditomassi said at a meeting of the Bradley board. "They're toy people. I hope that twenty years from now I'm still working for Milton Bradley in one form or another, and I think I have a better shot with the Hassenfelds and Hasbro than I do with Ron Perelman." The board began full-fledged negotiations with Hasbro.

Advised by Rosenwald's firm, which would reap almost $2 million in fees, Verrecchia put together the short-term financing, from banks that not so long ago had turned up their noses at Merrill Hassenfeld's kitschy little enterprise but were now only too glad to be pumping his son's hand. Working around the clock, the lawyers, accountants, and bankers ironed out the technical aspects of the deal while Shea and Stephen and their teams decided the new board, salaries, use of company cars, disposition of Bradley's Learjet, and titles: Stephen, president and CEO; Shea, chairman. Captured more than saved by his white knight, Shea could not bear to utter the word "acquire," but Hassenfeld did not believe "merger"

did the transaction justice. So, when it was announced in a carefully prepared press release on May 4, the words were used interchangeably. Privately there was less diplomacy. "Let me tell you something," Verrecchia
said. "You pay three hundred and sixty million, you didn't merge, baby. I
bought you."

There remained unfinished business: long-term financing. A Hasbro
board member who worked in the Rhode Island office of Drexel Burnham suggested Stephen and Verrecchia talk to Milken, and later that
spring they flew to Beverly Hills, where Milken had moved his headquarters. Milken entertained Hasbro's executives and introduced them to
T. Boone Pickens and other fabled corporate raiders—"guys that you
were reading about," Verrecchia recalled. "I was in awe." After two
decades of obscurity, the boys from Pawtucket were playing with the
high rollers. Milken appreciated Hassenfeld's style and was impressed
with Hasbro's cash flow and balance sheet, so unlike the stereotypical toy
company's. "I think you can do some subordinated debt," Milken said.
"Let me work for a few days, put together a proposal for you guys, and
we'll come back and talk about it again."

III

MANY GREETED THE ANNOUNCEMENT of the Bradley deal with derision:
at $360 million, double book value, Hassenfeld had been snookered. "An
early Christmas gift for Milton Bradley shareholders," one analyst sniffed
in *The Wall Street Journal*. To which Stephen responded: "You pay a vintage price for a vintage wine."

By year's end even the scoffers understood the magnitude of Stephen's
coup. Milken had delivered favorable financing and Shea had resigned,
leaving Stephen where he needed to be: alone at the very top. Hasbro
stock was trading as high as the low sixties. With full-year revenues of
$750 million and earnings (now that Vectrex was gone) of $52 million,
more than triple the year before, Hasbro in eight months had accomplished the seemingly impossible: it had displaced crippled Mattel as the
world's largest toy company. Barely a day passed without another acco-
lade. *Business Week* published a glowing piece. One Providence magazine
named Stephen and Alan (president now) "Businesspersons of the Year,"
and another put them on its cover, posed with Mr. Potato Head, as the

"Toy Tycoons." "I never thought I'd like the stock, but I do," an investment manager confessed to *The Wall Street Journal*.

Stephen handled the celebrity with poise. This had been a long time coming, and he was prepared, as only someone so unwaveringly confident for so many years could be. Asked repeatedly to explain his success, Stephen credited his father and grandfather. He talked, as old Milton Bradley himself might have, of how his company made not widgets, but the most intimate sort of goods that were vital to the development of a child. Hasbro had a holy relationship with its consumers, and responsibility did not stop with safe, high-quality toys. "It is to the young that we owe our existence and prosperity," Stephen said in announcing the Hasbro Children's Foundation, the most ambitious philanthropic enterprise three generations of Hassenfelds had ever undertaken. Like Merrill and Henry, Stephen believed reward carried obligation, although that did not mean he would simply hand out dollars to any cause. He would encourage innovative efforts in health care and special education and against child abuse and neglect, areas he believed had broad, urgent need.

But he drew the line at anything that might bring him into the political arena. It was safer and certainly tidier here, behind the sturdy walls of a private foundation that he completely controlled.

IV

THREE YEARS LATER Stephen's vintage wine had appreciated nicely in value. On the eve of Toy Fair 1987, he invited friends and associates to a cocktail party in Hasbro's new offices and showroom on New York's West Twenty-third Street, half a block from the Toy Building, where lesser entities leased single rooms or dingy suites. Waiters in black circulated with hors d'oeuvres and wine as Stephen, his eyes sparkling, escorted his guests through three floors of tasteful splendor, the likes of which the industry had never seen.

Robert Beckwith, Hasbro's corporate design director and Stephen's longtime companion, was among those there. An art history major in college, Beckwith, a young man with sophisticated tastes, had been hired to help the chairman recast Hasbro's image from little toy company to Fortune 500 corporation.

Deborah Sussman was there with her husband, Paul Prejza. Their firm, Sussman/Prejza & Company, had been the creative director behind the groundbreaking environmental graphics of the 1984 Los Angeles Olympics—the signs, colors, banners, flags, logos, and related visuals that gave that Olympics its memorable look. Impressed, Stephen had hired Sussman/Prejza for West Twenty-third's interiors, graphics, and signage. Nancy Rosen, Stephen's fine-arts adviser, was there. She'd searched galleries, museums, and private collections for the nearly fifty original pieces, in a broad range of media, that Stephen had selected. Barton Myers couldn't make it but had wanted to. An emerging name in architecture, Myers had found the way to transform a dilapidated old building into grandeur. Writers and editors for art, design, and architecture magazines were there.

West Twenty-third was a milestone for Hasbro, but it was not a revolution. Stephen had long believed his job was bigger than diversifying the portfolio and strengthening the balance sheet. For Wall Street to fully appreciate what he was about, he had to connect on an almost subliminal level. He had to create a distinctive corporate personality, one with no trace of the schlocky image investors carried in their minds of toy companies. For the better part of a decade, Stephen had worked toward that goal. In 1978 he had the company trademark redesigned, from a bland *H* made out of child's blocks to a more spirited depiction of two children at play, and ordered the new logo to appear on every ad, package, truck, building, letter, and envelope that bore the company name. He demanded perfection in Hasbro's old showroom, refusing to tolerate dirt on a rug or lint on a model's dress. He steadily refined the appearance of annual reports and catalogs, cleverly integrating prominent licensed characters into the design. He even worked on his own image, abandoning the informal, almost nerdy look of the early seventies for the crisp suit-and-tie persona of the early eighties. A consummate marketer, Stephen understood the many uses of advertising.

Hiring Beckwith in 1982 had brought Stephen new awareness. Fourteen years Stephen's junior, Beckwith nonetheless was sophisticated in ways Stephen was not, was educated and informed about architecture and the design world in ways the chairman was not. During the America's Cup summer in Newport, he was the one who suggested Stephen lease three yachts for the use of clients and friends; he then immersed himself in the details of producing a season-long event that people were still talking about years later. When Stephen decided he wanted a new headquarters in Rhode Island, Beckwith was asked to find the architect. When Stephen decided, shortly before the Bradley deal, he wanted a new showroom to replace Hasbro's cramped quarters on the thirty-first story of a nondescript skyscraper, Beckwith took charge. And when Hasbro bought Bradley, it was Beckwith who looked at the game-maker's showroom with its laminated shelves and frayed rugs and suggested Stephen close it and combine Bradley, Playskool, and Hasbro into one magnificent celebration of success.

Those who had not seen Stephen's palace—there truly was no better word—were awed that February night in 1987.

Stephen had spent almost $12 million and labored nearly two years inside an 1896 cast-iron building that most recently had been a discount department store. Myers had gutted the bottom of the building and begun anew. For corporate offices, he'd added a mezzanine level around the perimeter of the immense, high-ceilinged ground floor. The lobby and display areas took up all of the ground floor except the middle, which Myers cut out, opening up the basement for a cafeteria and congregating plaza and creating an enormous central atrium. Sussman/Prejza's color schemes lent dignity to the executive offices, where Stephen would receive investors, and bold excitement to the toy and game displays the more impressionable buyers would see. The art included a Roy Lichtenstein lithograph/silkscreen, a Jasper Johns print, an Andy Warhol screenprint, and a Richard Artschwager sculpture, *Exclamation Point,* a fair enough metaphor for Stephen's new world. Even Verrecchia, who counted pennies same as always, had to be impressed. This, indeed, was a statement.

And these were heady times. Stephen had but one worry, a deeply personal one. He was afraid that his sexual orientation, long the subject of rumor, would become publicized, causing the stock to drop, the investment community to turn its back on him, and the popular press to write lurid stories. What would he say to his brother, sister, and mother? As close as the Hassenfelds were, this was one intimacy he'd never shared. He believed his family would never understand.

4

ROSE OF TIBET

I

Sylvia Grace Kay met Merrill Hassenfeld while visiting a relative in Providence. She was nineteen, daughter of a prosperous Philadelphia hosiery manufacturer and descendant, on her mother's side, of wealthy Jews who'd come to America from Germany in the mid–nineteenth century. Sigmund Freud was a distant relative. She was a strikingly beautiful woman—refined, reserved, conversant with the lawyers and bankers in her father's circle. Merrill was a different sort, an easygoing, unpretentious young man who liked to finish a good meal with a cigar. Just out of college, he had an important position with the family business, and his future seemed assured. He asked Sylvia to marry him shortly after they met. "It was one of the instant chemistry things, I guess," she later explained. In 1940, about the time Hassenfeld Bros. was diversifying into junior doctor kits, Sylvia and Merrill were married.

Stephen David, their first child, was born on January 19, 1942; Ellen, their second, came nearly two years later. They lived in a middle-class neighborhood on Providence's East Side, near Temple Emanu-El and the house where Merrill had grown up. Dad was the softy of the family—a teddy bear, as his grown children would remember him, always happy to hug and kiss his kids and get down on the floor with them to play. Dad told marvelous stories and often came home with new toys in his briefcase. He golfed. He drove a Lincoln. He enjoyed his vacations. He indulged in hot dogs, doughnuts, Chinese takeout, and ice-cream sundaes, even after his doctors, concerned with his blood pressure and weight, advised him to forgo such foods and his wife endeavored to keep him on a diet. He took his boys to see the Red Sox and Brown University football games. And he took them to the factory, a place Stephen wanted to be from an early age.

Sylvia had stricter notions of how children should be raised. In her view, children did not leave the table until they'd finished everything on their plate. They did their homework immediately on return from school, spent regular time with Mother reading aloud, and followed current events on the evening news. Daughters took piano lessons and became Brownies; sons played organized sports and joined the Cub Scouts. Children passed the summer at sleep-away camp in the northern New England woods, studied at religious school, and were always well dressed. They did not associate with bad influences, nor did they have comic books or watch just anything on TV. They needed their fresh air and, for their leisure, were allowed Scrabble and Monopoly and the card game Fish. To help with all of this, Sylvia hired a laundress, a cook, and a live-in nanny.

Stephen took no issue with Mother's rules. A serious, introspective boy, he seemed to have inherited more of Sylvia's disciplined restraint than Merrill's nonchalance. Teachers at Moses Brown School judged him punctual, obedient, possessed of good posture, and neat. He had excellent penmanship but showed no evidence of a gift for music or art. His IQ tested at nearly genius level, but he was at best a mediocre student, graduating thirty-ninth in a class of forty-six. He was no athlete, but not for lack of effort. Early on at Moses Brown, Stephen participated in basketball, track, wrestling, swimming, tennis, and football, but by senior year had persisted only in tennis. "Once Steve realized that sports were not his forte," his yearbook noted, "he began to apply himself diligently to the intellectual side of extracurricular affairs."

Achievement was as important to Stephen as it was to Mother. It was not enough to be counselor at his old summer camp; he needed to be head counselor, and after applying himself, he was. If he could not excel inside the classroom, then he would outside. He was business manager two years for his school's literary magazine, and like his father, he had nat-ural presence before an audience, a talent that served him well in his three years on the Moses Brown debate club. Not satisfied with merely be-longing to Model United Nations, the nationwide student organization, he was general chairman of the Moses Brown chapter his senior year and had some notion, as he headed for Johns Hopkins University in 1959, that diplomacy might be his calling. It was an honorable profession, one that would please Sylvia.

▪

Alan Geoffrey Hassenfeld, born November 16, 1948, believed he was one child more than his parents intended. "Now that my mother and I talk about it," he would joke, "I was not necessarily thought about. My par-ents had a wonderful son and a wonderful daughter. And I came five years after my sister." Alan was a smiling baby with blond ringlets who grew into an outgoing little boy whose disposition was gentle, like his dad's. He was often into mischief. He did not like being confined in the back-yard, so he dug under the fence to freedom, only to be caught by Sylvia several blocks from home on her return from the beauty parlor. He did not like Mother's vegetables or liver, so he sat alone at the table many nights long after supper, finally being dismissed to bed with the certain knowledge that the offending portion would await him at breakfast. When he was five he was caught trying out a Hassenfeld Bros. junior doctor kit on a neighbor's daughter. Her mother paddled him and sent him home, to further punishment. When he was in third grade he stole a small gift for his grandparents from a store. He was spanked and grounded for two weeks.

He was nonetheless a carefree child, happy with his stamp collection, his trading cards, his Hardy Boys books, and his toys. They were typical for a boy of the fifties, albeit many came from Daddy's firm: Mr. Potato Head, marbles, six-shooters, toy soldiers manufactured from green plas-tic and tin. He was a devoted fan of Hopalong Cassidy and the many westerns that made it from Hollywood to children's TV. On Saturdays Alan would rise early, put on his cowboy outfit, and sit all morning at the tube. He liked the woods and was especially fond of fishing. A favorite spot was the nearby Seekonk River, mouth of the Blackstone, where, barely a mile upstream in Pawtucket, eventually the headquarters of Has-bro, the American Industrial Revolution had started in Samuel Slater's mill. Sometimes his parents brought him to their country club, which had a pond. While Merrill golfed and Sylvia socialized, Alan spent the day catching sunfish. "They didn't have to worry," he later recalled. "I'd be there at four o'clock in the afternoon, still fishing."

From an early age Stephen was fond of his younger brother, whose only demand, some attention, was a modest one. Stephen taught Alan to ride a bicycle and throw a football, and he did not exclude him from the company of his friends, as older brothers are wont to do. Except for Ellie, whose counsel Alan occasionally sought, Stephen was the only one in whom Alan could confide, a bond that was unbroken until the younger brother was middle-aged and had met the woman he would marry. Stephen was a comfort for Alan when their aunt and both paternal grandparents (Henry and Marion Hassenfeld) died in a ten-week period in 1960. He was sympathetic to Alan's asthma, which for many years required weekly trips to the doctor. And he invariably defended Alan when he'd crossed Mother.

Alan followed Stephen to Moses Brown, and it was then, as a freshman, that he read *Rose of Tibet*, a recently published novel. Alan's tastes had evolved from the Hardy Boys to Hemingway and Cervantes, authors who transported him to faraway places; but this book was unlike anything else he'd read. A man from London sets out to find his brother, lost on a trip to the Orient, and winds up inside a forbidden kingdom after a death-defying journey across the Himalayas. The Englishman falls hopelessly in love with a beautiful young Chinese woman, and together they plot escape from the kingdom's evil hold. *Rose of Tibet* was not great art, only great adventure, but Alan was enraptured. Here was a mysterious and exotic world, so different from his own. For some time he'd had a certain fascination with the Orient—he'd read about Marco Polo and Confucius—but now he ached to visit China, to live there, perhaps.

Going to sleep at night, he imagined himself in the arms of an Oriental temptress.

▪

By the time her second son was a teenager, Sylvia was making a name for herself. She was becoming, like her husband, a force in local, national, and international Jewish causes. She'd led a delegation to Auschwitz and been to Israel, and she was known for the dinners she hosted for visiting dignitaries and like-minded philanthropists from around the world. With

Hasbro's improving fortunes, the Hassenfelds had bought one of the last large undeveloped tracts on Providence's East Side, hired an architect and interior decorator, and put up a spacious split-level house surrounded by woods and complemented by a tennis backboard, in-ground pool, and cabana. Woodland Terrace wasn't for just anybody. Friends visiting Alan felt a distinct sense of grandeur, heightened by the presence of Sylvia, who didn't wear the kinds of clothes or jewelry other mothers did. Mrs. Hassenfeld shopped in New York. She always seemed attired for some special occasion.

One day when he was a freshman at Moses Brown, Alan was summoned by his parents into the den of their new home. They had something they needed to tell him. What with all of their travels lately, Sylvia said, and with Stevie and Ellie both away now at college, it would be better for everyone if he went to boarding school. Alan was stunned. How could they? He was just coming into his own at Moses Brown. He had a girlfriend—a nice Jewish girl, in fact—and all his friends were in Providence. Sylvia gave him no choice in the matter; his only choice was whether he would attend Exeter, Andover, Choate, Hotchkiss, or Deerfield. Alan chose Deerfield, and in the fall of 1963 he enrolled as a sophomore.

He was unhappy at first, but he came to like the school, two hours away by car in Massachusetts's Pioneer Valley. Alan was an ordinary student and an above ordinary athlete, a letterman in varsity tennis, a member of the fishing club, and on the business boards of the school newspaper and yearbook. He took up smoking. He began to write short stories and insightful vignettes about life's twists and turns. He spent the summer after junior year traveling Europe, the summer after graduation with a family in the small town of Mildura, Australia, as part of an Experiment in International Living program. While there, he fell in love with a sixteen-year-old girl who a short time later was in a car accident that left her in a coma. Keeping vigil in a hospital waiting room, Alan passed the hours twirling rubber bands; when his girlfriend died after two days, having never regained consciousness, he vowed to wear them in her memory for the rest of his life. "If you can't keep a promise to yourself," he would explain, "then you can't keep a promise to anyone."

Alan entered the University of Pennsylvania, his father's alma mater, in the fall of 1966. After taking a business course or two, a token gesture to

Mother, he declared his concentration to be English and creative writing. Let Dad and Stephen handle the toys.

"I didn't want to be considered the spoiled rich kid that automatically had his life planned," he later said. "I had to be independent."

Sylvia was not pleased, nor was she pleased with other aspects of her son's college experience. She did not approve of this new girl he was talking about marrying, for he was much too young for such a serious commitment. She did not see the good of his latest preoccupations, none of which involved a classroom. Alan had made the freshman squash team and was nationally ranked in his age group. He'd joined a fraternity. He pulled all-nighters and took his pals in his Pontiac Firebird on road trips to other colleges. Meanwhile his grades were gentleman C's. "Your dad and I have not worked so hard all of our lives to put a jock through school," Sylvia said on a visit to Philadelphia. "You better make up your mind about what you want to do." Alan wanted to be a novelist or an English professor, not exactly what Mother had in mind. He wanted to visit Asia, just not that part consumed by war. He enlisted in the Air National Guard, and after freshman year, in the summer of 1967, he left for basic training. He wasn't back at Pennsylvania more than three weeks when, in early 1968, he contracted hepatitis and mononucleosis and was forced to leave school.

As he recuperated at Woodland Terrace, Alan cast about for something to do. Stevie took him to Jamaica, but that was for only a few days. He did not want to be at the factory, for it had never cast a spell on him, and in any event, your daddy's firm was not the place to be in the countercultural year of 1968. When someone suggested he volunteer a few hours a week helping disadvantaged kids in a Providence grammar school, he was intrigued; during his summer in Australia, he'd worked with retarded children and found it gratifying. These Rhode Island kids were frighteningly poor. Sometimes he walked one or two of them home, to subsidized housing in a part of the city where crime was an everyday occurrence and the streets were filthy and had no trees. He'd never set foot in such a neighborhood, where the only white people were bureaucrats and social workers. I'm making a difference, he thought. I love this. It was a very sixties feeling for a rich kid, but it happened to be sincere, and it would not only last, but someday deepen.

He returned to school that fall. Sometime before the next summer, Stephen, by then Merrill's executive vice president, said he could use an extra hand in Asia, where vendors under contract to Hasbro made toys sold in America. Stephen knew of Alan's fascination with the Orient and doubted his brother could refuse, despite all this talk of big business being imperialistic.

Stephen was right. What fool would say no to a summer job in the Far East? Alan thought. His first assignment was to oversee operations in Shizuoka, Japan, a port city southwest of Yokohama, where a growing company named Bandai was manufacturing Amaze-A-Matics, a line of toy cars Hasbro would be introducing at Toy Fair 1970. Alan lived in a hotel and spent long days in a factory, but he socialized with Japanese in order to learn their language and culture. From Shizuoka he went south to Hong Kong, where another vendor manufactured heads for G.I. Joe and where Alan learned to run molding and flocking machines, which created the hair. Hong Kong was exactly what he'd imagined the Orient to be—exotic, sensual, a teeming garden of delights. Hasbro's overseas operations were still relatively small, and Alan knew then he could carve out a niche here, if he so chose, half a world from the long shadow of his brother and father. Like Hemingway in Paris, he could write. Certainly he'd not lack for material.

As he returned to college for his senior year, Alan decided he'd found his future.

I I

THE PERIOD FOLLOWING World War II saw the beginning of a fundamental transformation of the toy industry. America's baby boom, coupled with its postwar prosperity, created unprecedented domestic demand for toys. Wartime restrictions on the use of resin for nonmilitary purposes had ended, and rapid advances in plastics placed better, and less costly, raw materials at the disposal of manufacturers. Devastated by war but determined to rebuild its economy, Japan eagerly sought business from its former enemy. Several toy makers founded during and immediately after the U.S. occupation offered favorable rates, even when shipping was factored in, and by 1955 the leading American toy maker, Louis Marx's firm, was producing 5 percent of its $50 million line in Japan. By 1963, when Merrill Hassenfeld concluded that G.I. Joe heads could not be made profitably in Rhode Island, most leading American major toy makers had a presence in Japan. Having mastered mass production, the leading Japanese companies (Bandai, Takara, and Tomy) were becoming design and marketing forces in their own right.

Alan arrived on the scene shortly after Hasbro had moved production of Joe heads from Hong Kong to Japan, which was building a powerful export market in more lucrative commodities, automobiles and electronics among them. Such less economically advanced regions as Korea, Taiwan, and Hong Kong welcomed toys, which did not require great manufacturing sophistication, only a desire to learn, ready access to a port, and a plentiful pool of men and women willing to work under unpleasant and sometimes unhealthy or dangerous conditions for a few dollars a week. The payoff was not only in income to the workers, many of them peasants whose opportunities otherwise were severely limited. Perfecting the skills needed to run a toy factory to American standards brought the enterprise to the next step on the manufacturing ladder. Cheap labor had its rewards.

Alan had tracked Hasbro's Far East business during his senior year through copies of the telexes and cablegrams that went back and forth across the Pacific. He spent several weeks after graduation in Scandinavia and the Soviet Union, observing day-care centers for a study Stephen used in Hasbro's fledgling (and ill-fated) *Romper Room* nursery school business, and that fall announced his desire to join Hasbro full-time—provided three preconditions were met. "If ever at any time the moral values you have instilled in me growing up I'm asked to sacrifice, I'll leave the business," he told his father and brother. "Second, if ever I see the business bringing separation to our family, I'm walking away. And number three: I work *with* you, not *for* you." Merrill and Stephen had no trouble with any of that. Alan got an office in Rhode Island but would spend most of his time overseas.

Alan's primary responsibilities at first were negotiating vendor contracts and managing production and shipping with an eye to saving money and speeding output. But the niche he envisioned was broader than that. He saw firsthand the enormous creativity of Japanese toy companies and arranged for several of their products to be sold in America under the Hasbro name. He expanded Hasbro's global outlicensing network, particularly through Europe, and saw international royalties increase more than fivefold from 1971 to 1976. He arranged the sale of foreign rights to G.I. Joe in 1980, for $2 million in cash. His greatest strength was his charm. No ugly American, he was a bright young man who was interested in culture as well as business. Whether at a dinner or on the factory floor, he considered himself a guest, but he was not so foolish as to ignore the reality that being the boss's son opened doors. Alan allowed them to be opened, graciously. One led to Li Ka-shing, a Hong Kong businessman who'd fled China during the closing days of Mao's revolution. Penniless, he'd parlayed a small plastic flower-making business into a toy-manufacturing empire whose factories made heads, clothing, and accessories for G.I. Joe, among other products. Li became something of a mentor to Alan, and the two remained friends long after Li, having diversified into real estate and other enterprises, became one of the world's wealthiest men.

By 1972 Ping-Pong diplomacy had brought President Nixon to China. Three years later, the Vietnam War almost over, perceptive observers could discern signs that China's Guangdong province was reopening to the outside world. The portal was Hong Kong, that outpost of old British imperialism on its southern border. Increasing numbers of Hong Kong residents with family ties in Canton and neighboring regions were being allowed to visit, bringing with them Western views, fashions, and, soon enough, industry. The South Wind, as it was known, was carried largely on two trains. The first left Hong Kong early in the morning and stopped at Luohu, on the border, in time for lunch. Passengers crossed a covered bridge and were met by Chinese guards carrying AK-47s. As passports were checked and baggage inspected, passengers were given English editions of Mao's *Little Red Book* to pass the time. The second train set off for Guangzhou, arriving by early evening.

One morning in April 1975, Alan Hassenfeld boarded the train in Hong Kong for his maiden trip to China. He was one of a handful of Americans invited to the Canton Trade Fair, held in Guangzhou every spring and fall. He made it to the city without incident and was put up in a hotel with Australian, French, Italian, British, and American businessmen—like Hassenfeld, capitalist pioneers drawn by the promise of personal adventure and corporate profit. The roads were mostly unpaved, and cars were scarce. The electricity was spotty, and even in the hotel, one of Canton's finest, running water could not be guaranteed at night. Movement was restricted, and what little contact there was with everyday Chinese, barely emerged from the Cultural Revolution, drew expressions of curiosity and disbelief. Alan was in his element.

Before too many years passed, Li Ka-shing and other Hong Kong vendors with Hasbro accounts would be establishing factories in Guangdong and hundreds of millions of dollars' worth of toys would be made there every year for shipment to the American heartland. Business demands would keep Alan from his writing. But during the early period he wrote constantly—on planes, in hotel rooms, wherever opportunity presented itself. He kept his stories and essays but was reluctant to let anyone read them. Hounded by a writer one day when he was chairman and CEO, he rummaged around in his office and, sure enough, found some papers. He selected the top one, a sheet of stationery from the Hong Kong Hilton dated 1:30 A.M., November 5, 1976, and began to read aloud: " 'With trepidation, tonight weaves on. Here but not here, there but not there, in limbo and flux my mind wanders, anticipating what I am afraid to anticipate. Too quickly, yet too slowly, the night begins to dissipate. The shadows of light and dark flicker.' " Hassenfeld chuckled and said: "I must have been in one of my real moods!" He went on: " 'Before us lies the long, endless road once again, the lazy river no longer crimson as much as in years past. The walk across no man's territory and the covered bridge: the covered bridge of destiny. For some, freedom; for some, life; for others, death. For some it is the beginning of the long, endless road to enigma. With trepidation, my eyes turn to the covered bridge, the southern gateway to China. Times past—the look, the touch . . .' " He stopped again and said: "I was *very* philosophic that night!" After laughing, he continued reading: " 'Time passes so quickly—no longer is what was. Perhaps now is the only time, for now will never be again. So many reveries—but to make those dreams true. Guangzhou, the first step of the ladder, reached. But Shanghai and Beijing—Beijing and the doors of an unknown world on an endless road of enigma.' "

Perhaps it was the great physical distance that separated Alan from Rhode Island during that time. Perhaps it didn't occur to Stephen that a grown-up kid brother still needed recognition. Or maybe in Stephen's mind, assembly lines pale in comparison with a corporate vision. Whatever the reason, Alan in his early years at Hasbro sometimes felt his contributions were overlooked. He'd be back in Rhode Island for a few days, eager to go over his plans, and Stephen wouldn't find time for him until the very evening he was to fly back to Hong Kong.

"I needed, you know, the football pat on the rear end, and as loving a family as we were, I never got that encouragement from Dad or Steve,"

Alan said. "I learned that once you respect yourself, it no longer matters what others think."

III

STEPHEN HASSENFELD LIVED AT Woodland Terrace with his parents, as did Alan when he was not overseas, until near the end of 1978. Stephen was almost thirty-seven, and the fact that he still lived at home raised eyebrows but was not something anyone inside Hasbro talked about openly. For some time Alan had suggested the brothers move out (Ellie was married and lived in Illinois with her husband and three young children), and Stephen finally was persuaded. They took an apartment near Brown University, but then Stephen found a waterfront home in Bristol, south of Providence on Narragansett Bay. Alan was in Shanghai when he called with the news. This was an exceptionally pretty place at a reasonable price. In 1979 the brothers moved in.

As the eighties began, Stephen was engaged in almost nothing that could be described as leisure. After so long, everything at Hasbro was finally coming together; this was not the time to let up. Dinners were working sessions, vacations a few hours on the ski slopes between calls on customers and clients. Lovely as it was, Bristol was rarely more than a place to put head to pillow. Bristol was where the brothers reached decisions, talking into the wee hours of the night.

With his growing involvement in the financial community, Stephen was in New York more than ever. He was visiting an art gallery in 1981 when he met Robert Beckwith, twenty-four, who'd come to Manhattan after studying art history in college.

Son of a businessman and a woman who'd raised her children in a Victorian house she'd decorated with designer taste, Beckwith was a handsome, funny, perceptive young man with a natural sense of style. He found Hassenfeld charming. Stephen was a powerful and wealthy executive, but his smile was sincere and he delighted in making others laugh. When you were with Stephen, his full attention was only on you.

They had known each other several months when Hassenfeld persuaded Beckwith to accept a job at Hasbro as assistant to the chairman. For almost a year Beckwith accompanied Hassenfeld to financial, design, and marketing meetings, but those aspects of the business interested him less than they did his boss, and Hassenfeld agreed his talents would best be utilized directing the new corporate aesthetic. Beckwith had his work cut out for him. Stephen's Rhode Island office had Naugahyde furniture, fake wood paneling, and tube lighting, vestiges of Merrill's era; the New York showroom and corporate apartment, in a residential hotel, were similarly drab. Under Stephen's supervision, Beckwith brought architects, designers, and art advisers on board and began to construct the new image. West Twenty-third would be Hasbro's statement to the world— but Hassenfeld's statement to his own people, the worldwide headquarters, would be even more ambitious. Hassenfeld and Beckwith initially wanted to move to the suburbs from the old factory in Pawtucket where Merrill had moved headquarters. Hasbro bought land and commissioned architect Barton Myers to create a concept (a campus with five buildings radiating, like spokes on a gigantic wheel, from a glass-roofed hub), but Stephen, fearing he would lose employees in a suburban exodus, embarked instead on a renovation of existing headquarters that would wind up costing $52 million, double all of Hasbro's revenues the year he'd joined the company. Another $8 million would be spent on the European headquarters, near London.

Beckwith's influence went beyond business to the heart of the man. Hassenfeld had artistic sensibilities and a taste for finer things when they met, but a discerning eye saw possibilities for further refinement. Together, Stephen and Beckwith began to fashion an image of a man who commanded the attention of Wall Street and an international industry. They selected more flattering eyeglasses for the chairman, gave up Stephen's Rhode Island barber for a Madison Avenue salon, and replaced Hong Kong suits with European tailoring. They traded the old corporate apartment for one in Museum Tower, a chic new address next to the Museum of Modern Art that featured spectacular views of Manhattan, an $85,000 polished bronze front door, and Picasso and Matisse lithographs in the lobby—then brought in an art consultant to help choose the paintings and sculptures for the Hasbro suite. Stephen used Museum Tower for meetings, but also to host parties. Artists, designers, and admen Tom Griffin and Joe Bacal were among their guests.

Alone, Robert and Stephen shared quiet pursuits. They attended the theater and dined out, with the older man deepening his partner's appreciation of French and Italian food and fine French wines. Robert's passions were opera, dance, and art, and he drew Stephen, who already had such sensibilities, more deeply in; rare was the important opening or museum show in New York that passed without the two attending. Beckwith urged Stephen to broaden his social circle past family and business friends and reminded him of the value of periodically getting away, of savoring some of the fruits of two decades of the tireless labor that had brought the family firm into the Fortune 500. So they skied in Aspen, sailed the Caribbean, and, in summer, rented cottages in the Hamptons.

Years passed and Beckwith wanted them to have a place of their own, where there would be no need of the secrecy in which Stephen insisted on cloaking hotel registrations and rental agreements, no need for only Stephen to answer the phone when they were traveling together, no need for Stephen on some nights to have dinner with Beckwith and then, when they'd parted, a second dinner alone with Mother. For while Hasbro insiders and many in the toy, financial, and gay communities knew, Hassenfeld did not acknowledge their true relationship or his sexuality, not even to his family. Beckwith wanted him to be open. He tried to convince Stephen he was beyond touch—that Hasbro was so big that the personal lifestyle of its chairman would be but a footnote on Wall Street, not a scandal or a threat to the stock. "Your success should liberate you," Beckwith said, "not trap you further." Beckwith reminded Stephen of the great honor and wealth he'd brought to his family and friends. "You're forgetting how much people love and appreciate you," he said.

Stephen was away on business when Beckwith bought a house near the ocean. Stephen quietly approved. He had ideas for improvement, and an addition and remodeling were begun, and someday, he began to think, he would invite his family there for a weekend. And at some point during that weekend, he was increasingly of a mind to believe, they would all confront the truth.

∎

Hasbro had just wrapped up its eighth consecutive record year when, in January 1987, Stephen came down with a cold. The cold worsened, and soon he was bedridden. Stephen had always been healthy, and his stamina was legendary—four hours' sleep a night on average, with work weeks that regularly ran to seven days. Beckwith was concerned, but not yet alarmed.

Stephen recovered from this cold, but shortly before opening his showroom he was sidelined by another. Intuition told Beckwith something was wrong. Unbeknownst to anyone, he urged Stephen to be tested for AIDS. The result was positive. New York doctors began aggressive treatment that included AZT and other medications not yet approved for widespread use. Stephen brought no one into his secret but Beckwith, who was not infected (nor would be). The stigma of AIDS was cruel in 1987, with the general public still unconvinced that you could not get the disease from a handshake or a sneeze.

From diagnosis to deathbed, Stephen believed he would conquer the virus—or at least reach a lasting truce. His conviction was as strong as his 1970s belief that Hasbro could be the toast of Wall Street. He did not, however, make his disease a cause. It was Beckwith who followed the latest developments in the treatment of AIDS, scheduled the doctors' appointments, and monitored Stephen's adherence to the latest protocols; Stephen more or less just went along, as if investing his own energy would somehow give the disease the upper hand. Besides, he had a $1.3 billion corporation to run.

In July 1987 Stephen became sick with endocarditis, a potentially lethal heart infection, opportunistic in people with AIDS, that is characterized by fever, night sweats, fatigue, and abdominal pain. At Columbia Presbyterian Hospital, a catheter was threaded into his heart for the direct administration of antibiotics, and he was discharged, without staying a night, to the care of Beckwith and a home health care service. He regained his strength slowly, not leaving Museum Tower for several weeks but keeping his hand in the business via telephone and meetings with his brother and senior executives in his living room. They found him in pajamas and robe sometimes, but he was never depressed, never gave a sign that he was dealing with anything other than some momentary distraction. Outsiders knew none of this, of course, nor did they suspect something was amiss, at first. Summer is a time of low visibility in the toy industry, and except for announcement of first-half results, which Hasbro handled with a standard press release, the chairman had no need of contact with the public.

Stephen was well enough to return to the office in early October, but by then rumors had started to break free of Hasbro. They followed Stephen to Washington, where, on October 19, he spoke publicly for the first time since his endocarditis. The occasion was an annual conference of international investors. Hassenfeld was bright, although his assessment of his industry was gloomy, in part because a revitalized video-game market was eating into sales of traditional toys. "There's a malaise in the industry that we haven't seen in a number of years," he said, noting that even Hasbro, which had just reported a third quarter drop in profits, had not escaped. Asked about his health after his speech, Stephen related his experience with endocarditis. "He appeared healthy and high-spirited," a reporter wrote, "speaking to more than 100 international investors for at least 20 minutes, fielding questions afterward, then meeting for two newspaper interviews." Stephen praised the managers who'd taken on bigger roles while he was sick, singling out his brother and Al Verrecchia. He disclosed nothing about how he could have contracted endocarditis.

During the next fifteen months Stephen suffered from an ulcer on his left thigh that left him, for a while, with a limp. He had two episodes of Pneumocystis pneumonia; treated as an outpatient, and nursed by Beckwith, he recovered both times. By early 1989 his health was deteriorating again. Those in daily contact with him saw how easily he tired and knew he had difficulty digesting food. His suits fit loosely and he was uncharacteristically pale, developments increasingly difficult to hide. He rarely acknowledged that anything was happening, and when he did, it was with some vague allusion to the lingering effects of endocarditis and its treatment. "It's just an infection," he would say, or "a rash from the medication." None of his associates pressed Stephen, nor did his family, and the rare reporter who asked him to comment on speculation he had AIDS received polite but insistent denial. Beckwith urged Stephen to confide in Alan, at least, but Stephen would not. Nor did he want Beckwith to act as intermediary, a wish that Beckwith respected, but only reluctantly.

The time had come, Beckwith believed, for candor all around. He knew Stephen was dying.

▪

Stephen's last Toy Fair was only the third in his cherished showroom. He had much to preoccupy him other than his disease. G.I. Joe was marking its twenty-fifth anniversary, and alongside the corporate celebration was a protest beneath the chairman's window by an antiwar group that had elected the toy to its Hall of Shame. Donald Trump, who'd lent his name to a Milton Bradley game, came by West Twenty-third, as did Sgt. Slaughter, a professional wrestler. But these were secondary to Stephen's consuming interest. Hasbro seemed to have reached an earnings and revenues plateau, and the chairman was intent on getting past it. Not surprisingly, he had a plan.

Parts of it already were in place. Seeking sharper internal focus, Stephen in December had created three new divisions: Hasbro Toy, Playskool, and Manufacturing Services. He'd cut advertising and development costs for the first time in a decade, moves that had left Hasbro with an unprecedented $250 million in cash reserves in the first quarter of the new year. Stephen told analysts at Toy Fair 1989 that he intended to apply that hoard to acquisitions and other outside opportunities, not stock buybacks. He would not disclose what was in mind, but a secret dialogue already was under way with the creators of Cabbage Patch dolls for that license, held by Coleco—which, never fully recovered from ColecoVision, was in bankruptcy. Mattel's Amerman, chairman and CEO for only two years, was also bidding for the rights.

In developing his 1989 line, Stephen had been painfully aware of the emergence of Nintendo as a force in the U.S. toy market. Virtually single-handedly, Nintendo had brought the video-game industry back from the ruins of the early 1980s, largely on the wild success of Super Mario Bros. and its sequels, games as popular in the late 1980s and early 1990s as Mortal Kombat would be later. In just one year, 1987, Nintendo's net sales had risen 50 percent, to $1.5 billion, eclipsing Hasbro and sending all-too-familiar shock through traditional toy companies. Marketed to boys, Nintendo's games were a threat to Hasbro's action figures. Stephen's answer was an original, internally developed video-game system code-named NEMO, for Never Ever Mention Outside. Begun in 1986 under Barry Alperin's supervision, work was abandoned two years and $20 million later when developers could not meet a retail price of $199, Stephen's mandate. Until he came up with something else, Stephen took heart knowing that video games, big as they suddenly were again, did not interest girls. Girls wanted dolls. And Stephen, who'd coveted a piece of the fashion doll market for almost twenty years, was eager to try again.

It was not coincidence that the cover of Hasbro's 1989 catalog, Stephen's last, had a photograph of a single toy: Maxie. Successor to Charlie's Angels and the World of Love dolls, costly losers the chairman wished he could forget, Maxie had blond hair, blue eyes, a slender waist, ample bosom, and long legs. She wore a tiara, was dressed in a fur-trimmed pink tutu, and held a red rose. In other words, Maxie resembled

Barbie. Mattel was undaunted. Despite the millions Hassenfeld had invested, Barbie was trouncing this new pretender to the throne. This was Maxie's second year on the market, but despite the Toy Fair hype, the sales figures would soon suggest the doll wouldn't last much past December.

That was not the case with Sindy, a fashion doll that had been sold for years in Europe by an English company that recently had sold the rights to Hasbro. Sindy was performing strongly against Barbie in England, and the battle was only heating up. Amerman was incensed by what he'd been able to learn about Sindy for 1989. He considered it a carbon copy of Mattel's signature brand.

If it came to that, Amerman figured Mattel would have a good case in court, a place Barbie had been before.

I V

THE SPIRIT OF MATTEL issued forth from its co-founder, Ruth Handler, born Ruth Mosko, short for Moskowicz. "I am a fiercely independent woman, one who has always felt the need to prove myself, even as a child," she said in her autobiography. Last of ten children of Polish immigrants who spoke Yiddish, Ruth grew up in Denver and moved to Los Angeles after visiting California on vacation in 1937. She was nineteen, tantalized by Hollywood. She worked as a stenographer at Paramount Pictures and married her childhood sweetheart, Elliot Handler, a young artist who'd followed her west to pursue his studies. Elliot was shy, the very opposite of Ruth, but he had prodigious talent in industrial design. Ruth saw his sketches for the bookends, candelabra, and cigarette boxes with which they might brighten their one-room apartment and convinced him to buy the tools to build them, on a payment plan from Sears. Elliot set up shop in his half of a two-car garage, and when Ruth saw his first creations, she knew she could sell them. She was not thinking Sears. On her lunch break from Paramount one day, she went to a shop on Wilshire Boulevard with her husband's samples in a suitcase and insisted on seeing the owner. He placed a $500 order, and the Handlers were in the giftware business. Investors joined them, and their company diversified into jewelry, designed by Elliot. The handlers had two children, Barbara and Ken. By 1943, their firm had $2 million a year in sales.

Mattel was an offshoot, founded after a partner, Harold "Matt" Matson, left, encouraging the Handlers to join him in a new enterprise. Matson, whose nickname contributed the first four letters of the new company's name (Elliot provided the last two), was an accomplished craftsman. The war had restricted use of plastics, and the Handlers and their new associate decided to manufacture picture frames from wood. Matson produced samples from Elliot's designs, and Ruth found a factory and managed sales. Soon Elliot was designing dollhouse furniture, then toys. Learning that the heart of the toy business was in New York, at the Toy Building at 200 Fifth Avenue, site of Toy Fair, Ruth took a train there to arrange East Coast distribution for her husband's products. She arrived knowing no one and went home with a deal. In its first full year, 1945, Mattel made a 30 percent profit on sales of $100,000. Inspired by radio and television personality Arthur Godfrey, who played a ukulele on air, Elliot the next year brought forth the Uke-A-Doodle, a music toy; introduced at Toy Fair 1947, it became Mattel's first hit. Uke-A-Doodle was followed by a jack-in-the-box that played "Pop Goes the Weasel," the Bubble-O-Bill Bubble Hat, and, in 1955, the Burp Gun. Excitement over Burp Gun surpassed that for Merrill Hassenfeld's latest Mr. Potato Heads (the Spudettes, "Potatohead pets") at Toy Fair that year and helped the Handlers, who'd bought out Mattson, toward record revenues.

But Burp Gun was not the turn that pointed Mattel toward dominance. It was how the toy was marketed. By the middle of the 1950s Mattel was spending about $150,000 a year on television advertising, an impressive amount for that early in the TV era, but—like Hasbro, the first to use the medium to advertise a toy—was buying commercial time only in a few large cities, and only for the weeks before Christmas. (Other toy manufacturers had eschewed TV altogether, including Louis Marx, owner of the world's largest toy company. Marx's entire media budget in 1955 was $312.) The Handlers were intrigued when, in January 1955, an executive from their ad agency and a sales representative of the ABC television network asked if they would be interested in sponsoring Walt Disney's *The Mickey Mouse Club*, set to air that fall. ABC was guaranteeing 90 percent coverage of the nation's TV homes on the strength of the Disney name; for $500,000, Mattel could sponsor a weekly fifteen-minute segment in which three of its commercials could be shown. Sponsorship would have to be for a full year, and there was another catch: a contract could not be canceled. Aware that Mattel's net worth was not much more than $500,000, the Handlers asked their chief financial officer if they would be broke if the ads didn't bring in the millions in sales needed to justify such an outrageous expenditure. "Not broke," the numbers man said, "but badly bent." The Handlers signed, and commercials were prepared for their music toys and Burp Gun, a cap-firing toy whose somewhat complicated loading and firing could be demonstrated in an ad children readily understood.

The Mickey Mouse Club was an instant hit. Mattel shipped more than a million Burp Guns before Christmas, pushing corporate sales for the year to $6.2 million, an increase of 25 percent. "Remember the Burp Gun," proclaimed signs in the Mattel showroom at Toy Fair the next year. From then on buyers would be as concerned with the TV advertising as with a toy itself.

▪

The Handlers were in Lucerne, Switzerland, in 1956 when they happened on a doll in a store window. This was Lilli, a sort of playgirl based on a character in a German newspaper cartoon and sold mostly to adult men in tobacco shops and bars.

Almost a foot tall, Lilli had long blond hair, long slender legs, a narrow waist, and large, perfectly shaped (if nippleless) breasts—a softly pornographic idealization of Teutonic beauty. In her memoir, Ruth Handler describes finding Lilli dressed respectably enough in a ski outfit, but her appeal to German-speaking men, who kept her in their cars or used her as a sexual come-on to randy girlfriends, was her tight sweaters and short skirts, which could be removed.

Handler's interest in Lilli was tamer. She'd tried unsuccessfully for some while to persuade Elliot and his designers to produce a grown-up-looking glamorous doll. Her inspiration was watching her ten-year-old daughter play. Barbara and her playmates wanted only adult paper dolls, which they could attire in prom gowns, wedding dresses, or swimwear. "Pretending to be doing something else," Ruth recalled, "I'd listen, fascinated, to the girls as they played with these paper dolls hour after hour. And I discovered something very important: they were using these dolls to project their dreams of their own futures as adult women." The Handlers brought Lilli back to the States and the designers went to work.

Resculpted and bestowed with a fresher face, and manufactured in Japan, Barbie debuted at Toy Fair 1959. She wore a black-and-white bathing suit, shoes, and sunglasses and was offered at a suggested retail price of $3, additional outfits and accessories sold separately. Mattel had paid $12,000, an unheard-of sum in those days, for market research on Barbie. The results confirmed what Ruth Handler knew: girls loved the doll, and mothers hated her. "I know little girls want dolls with high heels, but I object to that sexy costume," one mother of three told the researchers. "I wouldn't walk around the house like that. I don't like the influence on my little girl. If only they would let children remain young a little longer." Another mother blushed when she saw Barbie. "It has too much of a figure," she said. For the first (but not last) time in the toy industry, breasts had become an issue.

Ruth bet on the girls. Mattel began production of twenty thousand dolls a week, a gamble that seemed a horrible mistake when buyers saw Barbie at Toy Fair 1959. "Little girls want baby dolls," one skeptic told Ruth, "they want to pretend to be mommies." As with the moms, the biggest hurdle was Barbie's anatomy, which, in human size, translated to measurements of 39-21-33, a physique another young entrepreneur of the period, Hugh Hefner, surely would have appreciated. "Ruth," the buyers said, "mothers will never buy their daughters a doll that has . . ." Virtually all male, they could not even bring themselves to pronounce the word "breasts" in the company of a woman. Not even Barbie's impressive television advertising created much enthusiam, although TV in the end would save Barbie.

Mattel's agency, Carson/Roberts, which also had the Max Factor cosmetics account, had spent months in scripting and production, hiring fashion stylists for the sets and learning through trial and error such tricks as freezing dolls before a shoot to keep the lights from melting them. Unhampered by strict regulations, Carson/Roberts animated Barbie, and the resulting commercials, tested extensively on children before airing, seemed to bring the doll to life. The ads aired beginning in March, and by summer the doll was selling out coast-to-coast. Handler increased production well beyond the original twenty thousand per week, and still three years would pass before the factories could catch up to demand. Mattel added hundreds of thousands of square feet of space in California and Barbie clubs sprang up across America. In the first two years of the doll, Mattel's revenues doubled, to over $25 million, and pretax earnings surpassed $2.5 million.

While not as glamorous as Barbie, or as pretty, Ruth appeared to be leading a life as fantastic as her doll. "Ruth works a full day, driving away in a pink Thunderbird at 8:15 A.M. every day with her husband, leaving a gorgeous $75,000 home in Beverly Wood," a *Los Angeles Times* writer observed in an article in September 1959. "That's something not every woman would do. But Ruth wouldn't have it any other way. 'If I had to stay home, I would be the most dreadful, mixed-up, unhappy woman in the world,' she cries."

Ruth's statement hinted of life inside Mattel. Elliot was the introverted genius, chairman only because business was a man's domain and Ruth calculated they'd get further with the titles that way; he was happiest when he was with kindred spirits in the R&D department he'd built. Ruth was the woman who'd left an infant son and a three-year-old daughter in California and taken a wartime train to New York to launch a business. She ran Mattel's marketing, finances, and administration. She was a perfectionist—a driven and demanding manager, much like a woman who one day would succeed her. Employees loved or hated her; there was no middle ground. "My mother wasn't very diplomatic always," Ken Handler told a writer profiling Ruth. "She could be very tough."

▪

By the end of 1971 Mattel was on its way toward realizing the Handlers' vision of a company that sold not just toys, but fun, in its many money-making varieties. "The World of the Young," as Elliot and Ruth called their grand ambition, echoed of Disney. By 1971 Mattel had acquired Ringling Bros.–Barnum & Bailey circus; Monogram Models; Metaframe, a manufacturer of pet supplies; Audio Magnetics, a maker of blank tapes; and Turco Manufacturing, which made playground equipment. The Handlers had formed a film partnership, Radnitz/Mattel Productions Inc. (its most notable title was 1972's Academy Award–nominated *Sounder*). The World of the Young was indeed global, with marketing, sales, and manufacturing centers throughout Asia, the Americas, and Europe. Mattel's pretax profits for the fiscal year ended January 30, 1971, were more than 10 percent of record sales of $345 million.

Or so the company claimed. In truth, Mattel was playing with the numbers, to hide a series of disasters compounded by a personal crisis. The first event was a fire in a Mexican factory in late 1969 that left Mattel unable to fill many of its Christmas orders, with a resultant loss of revenues. A product in which the Handlers had invested heavily—Sizzlers, a motorized version of its popular Hot Wheels cars—did not catch on at retail the next year, and the company was left with a huge unsold inventory. Optigan, an expensive piano-organ that Elliot was in love with, also failed. In its public financial reports, Mattel began to inflate its sales and income statements to meet Wall Street's expectations. The figures were lies, but they preserved the image of Mattel as a growth company and protected the stock, at first. Meanwhile cancer struck Ruth Handler, and she lost a breast in a mastectomy in June 1970. She returned to work five weeks later but claimed to have lost her mastery of, and all-consuming love for, the business. A dockworkers strike impeded shipments in 1971, and by March 1972, when year-end results were released, not even accounting tricks could disguise the truth. Blessed for so long, the Handlers seemed suddenly cursed. Elliot and Ruth reported a staggering pretax loss of $47 million on sales that had plummeted 25 percent.

"Fortunately, we feel most of our troubles are behind us," the Handlers said in their annual report.

They were not. Shareholders filed suit late that year, and the Securities and Exchange Commission began investigating the company early the next year when Mattel issued a press release saying it expected another loss for 1972—eighteen days after it had publicly predicted a profit. Ruth was forced out as president, although she continued as co-chairman with her husband until, in 1975, a special counsel working with the SEC confirmed Mattel had published false financial statements overstating its earnings. The Handlers lost their chairmanship and left the company, subsequently reimbursing Mattel for $112,000 in legal costs and contributing more than two million shares of their stock, about half of what they owned, toward a $34 million settlement of shareholder lawsuits.

And still Ruth's difficulties were not over. In February 1978 a federal grand jury indicted her and four others for mail fraud, conspiracy, and issuing false financial reports to the SEC, part of a scheme to increase the value of Mattel stock for the purpose of acquiring other companies and securing bank loans—in other words, to build the World of the Young. Ruth was accused of altering inventory, royalty, and tooling data. She maintained innocence, alleging that people who worked for her had cooked the books without her knowledge: "The marketing guys who had done most of the 'dirty work' were not indicted," she claimed. Nonetheless, in hopes of avoiding prison, Ruth pleaded no contest as the trial approached. She feared prosecutors would seek a long sentence because of her sex, despite the fact that the U.S. attorney was female. "Bring down a woman," Ruth said, "a famous woman, an uppity woman who had the nerve to climb to the top—just think of the reputations that could be made by bringing her down. I guess they knew I'd get much more press coverage for them, since no other woman had up to that time been the head of such a large corporation." In late 1978 a U.S. District Court judge sentenced her to forty-one years in prison and ordered her to pay a $57,000 fine but suspended both. The judge also sentenced her to community service of five hundred hours a year for five years. Hardly penniless, and only momentarily broken, Handler would go on to found a successful breast prosthesis company, Nearly Me, a curious if redeeming encore for the creator of Barbie.

▪

The World of the Young had been partly dismantled, the Handlers officially forgotten, when Intellivision began to collapse. Mattel had recovered from the dark days, reaching new profit and revenue highs in the early 1980s, but its ill-fated investment in video games nearly brought down the company. Financiers led by Michael Milken and two principals of E. M. Warburg, Pincus & Co., Inc., John L. Vogelstein and Lionel I. Pincus, saved it. Convinced of the long-term value of Mattel's core brands, they restructured the company's debt, invested millions of their own money, and found new lines of credit, freeing it to move forward— in traditional toys. Mattel sold what little was salvageable of Intellivision and the last vestiges of the World of the Young. Pincus and Vogelstein got seats on Mattel's board, as did another investor, Richard Riorden, who one day would be mayor of Los Angeles. Mattel had two good years, then stumbled again. Hoping to finally establish an enduring action-figure brand, Mattel invested heavily in a line of superheroes known as He-Man and Masters of the Universe. He-Man brought in $400 million in 1985, eclipsing Barbie (and G.I. Joe), then, in a decidedly nonheroic performance, sank to under $200 million the very next year.

Once again the company was swamped by unsold inventory. Mattel was heading toward another loss in 1986 when Vogelstein, chairman of the board's executive/finance committee, appointed a trio of men to run the company while a national search was conducted for a new chief executive officer and chairman to replace the retiring Arthur S. Spear. One of the men was John W. Amerman, head of the surging and highly profitable international division. Another was Thomas J. Kalinske, Mattel's president.

Finding no one better outside Mattel, Vogelstein decided on Amerman and, on February 19, 1987, named him chairman and CEO. Amerman's first priority was radical surgery, on an emergency basis. Within weeks he'd closed ten factories, eliminated five hundred jobs at headquarters, and accepted the resignation of Kalinske (who later became president of Sega of America). He instituted tighter control of inventory and receivables and cut tooling costs. And he declared his intention to make Mattel a growth company again in the United States and abroad. Mattel lost $113 million in 1987, penance for sins of the past, and returned to profitability in 1988, when Amerman's influence on the bottom line began to be felt.

V

AMERMAN WAS STILL WORKING for Warner-Lambert's American Chicle Division, maker of Chiclets gum, when Stephen Hassenfeld had begun to build his balanced portfolio in the 1960s.

Hassenfeld saw the success of Barbie and knew Hasbro had to compete in the fashion-doll market. His first efforts, Bobbie Gentry and Flying Nun dolls, on the market briefly in the late 1960s, fell short of the mark. His next try was the work of a more sophisticated marketer, albeit one with much still to learn. In 1971 the World of Love offered five dolls, each nine inches tall, each sold in hip clothing—or what passed for it in the view of a young man from Rhode Island whose signature item wore fatigues, not exactly the uniform of the Woodstock generation. As with Barbie, additional outfits and carrying cases were offered separately for the dolls, who were named Love, Peace, Flower, Adam, and Soul, an African American. Love, the lead doll, had long legs, blond hair, and a face vaguely similar to Barbie's. "Love is today's teenager," the catalog declared. "Love is what's happening."

Love was only memories after three years, but not Hassenfeld's conviction that Hasbro needed a fashion doll. He tried next with Leggy, "the super fashion model doll" whose most distinctive anatomical feature was announced in its name. Ten inches tall, Leggy came in blond and three other hair colors and was sold with bell-bottoms, halter top, gown, and stole. Leggy walked quietly into history in 1974. Hassenfeld stayed out of the market for two years, returning in 1977 with Charlie's Angels, based on the popular TV show. Hassenfeld was so excited about the line that he put a portrait of the show's three stars on the first page of his annual report. Far and away the most ambitious of Hassenfeld's challenges to Barbie to date, the dolls had a distinctly California look and came with more separately purchasable outfits than any Hasbro dolls ever—such attire as the Golden Goddess swimsuit set, the Night Caper gown, and the Black Magic metallic dress and jacket. Girls could buy the Hideaway House and Adventure Van and send their 8½-inch Angels snorkeling, skiing, or river rafting. But girls did not want water sports; girls wanted Barbie. The Angels disappeared in 1978, Hasbro's last loss year.

Larger issues preoccupied Hassenfeld into the eighties, but by mid-decade he was back with a fashion doll called Jem. Lead item in the 1986 line, Jem was not the bumbling response of an immature marketer who envied a competitor's success but did not know how to replicate it. Rather than aping Barbie, Hassenfeld had decided to go after the fashion doll market with a clear difference. Jem was sold with a carefully constructed fantasy that provided an alternative to Barbie without forsaking Barbie's glittery appeal. Mild-mannered music executive by day, Jem by night was the lead singer of a hot rock group, the Holograms, whose sworn enemies were a band known as the Misfits. Hassenfeld invested millions to bring to market nineteen dolls, more than three dozen outfits, and a wide selection of accessories and play sets. He arranged for television programming, made Jem the centerpiece of his new showroom at West Twenty-third's innaugural Toy Fair, and put the doll on the cover of his catalog for two consecutive years. And still success eluded him.

One reason was that, uncharacteristically, he'd still not drawn a lesson from his earlier failures. Every fashion doll Stephen had marketed in more than fifteen years had been a different size from Barbie, on the theory that girls buying his dolls would then have to buy his accessories and outfits, not Mattel's. In reality, girls tried to dress newcomers in Barbie outfits—and, when they didn't fit, lost interest. Like its predecessors, Jem was a different size from Barbie—an inch taller—and Barbie clothes hung off it. There were other strategic missteps. In creating the Misfits, Hasbro was using a good-versus-evil play pattern that worked flawlessly in action figures but had never done well with girls, raised in a culture where for the most part they still were expected to become wives and mothers, not warriors. Jem's added inch meant higher cost for not only dolls and accessories, but packaging and shipping as well; the result was a retail price that Mattel could easily undercut with Barbie. And unlike Barbie, who was versatile and at home in many segments, Jem existed in a single world, entertainment.

Still, Mattel took no chances. Whether through some loose-lipped employee or an unscrupulous buyer who'd broken the confidence of a Hasbro preview to curry favor in California, Mattel got word of Jem before it reached shelves. "Within five minutes of hearing what was happening competitively, we formed a defensive launch," recalled Judy Shackelford, executive vice president of marketing. "We had already been working on a music segment. We decided to turn Barbie into the lead singer." Pressured by Mattel, retailers didn't yield ground in their lucrative pink aisle, and Jem didn't get the shelf space Hasbro needed. Introduced simultaneously with Jem, Barbie and the Rockers was a big seller for Mattel. Buyers' initial enthusiasm for Jem evaporated as expectations of a $100 million line gave way to the reality of only about $50 million the first year. After two years, Jem was gone.

Hassenfeld was undaunted. Realizing that Jem's rock 'n' roll persona had been too restrictive, he offered a more open-ended fantasy in 1988 with his blond, blue-eyed Maxie. "She's today's teenager with a brand new look and style all her own!" the catalog proclaimed. "Whether she's hitting the books or hitting the beach, Maxie *is* what's happening with today's teens!" Hassenfeld had finally learned his lesson: Maxie was precisely Barbie's height, 11½ inches, and was priced competitively. Backed by $7 million in ads and promotions, Maxie had an encouraging first year. Mattel struck back predictably, with a segment of teen dolls. Not even Hasbro's mighty advertising could protect Maxie from Barbie. Despite almost $5 million in new commercials, Maxie did not survive 1989.

▪

Long sold in England, Sindy was a round-faced, unsmiling, somewhat frumpish character with blond hair and blue eyes when Hassenfeld bought the rights to manufacture it from a British company, Pedigree, in 1986. Sales were flagging, and Hasbro spent the next year creating a more beguiling look. The 1988 version had suntanned skin, a more angular face, and contemporary teenage style. The names hinted of Hollywood: Superstar Sindy, Supercool Sindy, and Disney Club Sindy. The new Sindy was a hit, but Stephen was not satisfied. At his direction, Sindy's persona was made somewhat younger than Barbie's. New Sindy roller-skated, listened to a Walkman, went to dances and the beach, and reclined on a Day Dreaming Bed.

The makeover seemed to work. Sindy sales in England had stabilized since Pedigree had sold it to Hasbro (and would begin to climb in 1989), and Stephen was ready to order the doll into battle from Holland to Greece and beyond. Unlike Maxie and Jem, Sindy was an established brand. And no one understood the power of an established brand better than Mattel.

Amerman got wind after new Sindy had been shown in the fall of 1988 in private previews to European buyers. Not only had Sindy's personality changed—the doll had been resculpted, with longer arms and legs and a smile. All-pink packaging replaced a box that was pink and blue. Amerman was fit to be tied. He believed the new Sindy did not merely resemble Barbie but was a clone, the new packaging a blatant rip-off.

Amerman had a particular sensitivity to developments overseas. Deploying Barbie as a beachhead in country after country in his earlier days as head of international at Mattel, Amerman had more than quadrupled the corporation's foreign revenues and seen even more impressive growth in profits, a performance that helped convince Vogelstein to name him chairman. To a considerable extent, Mattel's future now was abroad. And now Hassenfeld with his mighty balance sheet was aiming an arrow at his heart. What gave? Was a piece of the category really so strategically important to Hasbro? After two decades of eluding him, had fashion dolls become his personal demon? Or was he only trying to draw blood, just as Mattel had announced its first profit (a modest $36 million) under its new chairman?

One day during Stephen's last Toy Fair, Amerman visited Hassenfeld to urge him not to sell Sindy as designed and packaged. Stephen heard Amerman through, defended Sindy as original, then announced he was going forward.

"No one tells me what to do," he said.

Vogelstein tried intervening with Hasbro director Rosenwald, a friend and fellow New Yorker, to no avail. In late March Mattel's lawyers sent Hasbro a letter. Mattel would not seek legal redress if Hasbro agreed to immediately stop manufacturing Sindy and destroy (or turn over to Mattel) all dolls, packaging, catalogs, and advertising. A deadline of four P.M.,

April 7, London time, was set. Hassenfeld did not relent. Since buying Sindy, he'd invested some £3 million in its development and marketing.

Backed by heavy TV advertising and promotions, Sweet Dreams Sindy and her friends were beginning to appear in England when Amerman gave the lawyers the go-ahead. Barbie was hardly a stranger to litigation. The doll's first court appearance was only two years after its birth, in 1961, when Mattel tangled with Louis Marx in a patent infringement case; more recently, Mattel had sued the German maker of look-alikes Steffi and Teeny. But nothing had rivaled Mattel's response to Sindy.

The first action was in England, where in April Mattel sought an injunction to block sales. Sindy was shipped to Belgium, and Mattel's lawyers were there with a claim the doll was counterfeit. Sindy reached Holland, and Mattel's lawyers were in court with allegations of copyright infringement and unfair competition. In France the lawyers persuaded authorities to impound Sindy shipments, and gendarmes arrested the manager of Hasbro France—a mild-mannered gentleman, by all accounts—in his office on a criminal charge of counterfeiting. So it went through 1989 and into the early 1990s in Germany, Greece, Denmark, Hungary, Spain, Turkey, New Zealand, Australia, and Hong Kong, where the Hasbro vendor that manufactured Sindy had its offices.

Amerman's darkest fears were revealed in an affidavit of Sandra M. King, his girls' marketing manager in England. "If the defendant is allowed to sell its new-style Sindy doll," King declared, "there may no longer be any need for some shops to stock both dolls and some may choose to stock only the Sindy doll. This could also have a knock-on effect on the rest of Mattel's range of products since shops which choose not to sell Barbie, Mattel's flagship product, may lose interest in stocking the rest."

Legally the crux of the matter was originality. Sindy and Barbie were undressed in court, and measurements were taken of bust, waist, hips, shoulders, fingers, and legs. Hair was detached from scalps to better compare the shape of heads. Mechanisms allowing bodily parts to swivel and bend were studied. The color and detail of eyes, eyelashes, and eyelids were examined, and the long-standing association of the color pink with little girls' fantasies were explored. Whether children too young to read could reliably differentiate between the dolls was a major point of contention.

"When a number of Sindy and Barbie dolls are lined up at random, one really needs a magnifying glass to discover any differences," a Mattel lawyer told the Dutch court. "Sindy has become Barbie's unwanted twin sister."

Sindy's sculptor resented that. "The head of Barbie is very American looking and more like Hasbro's Maxie doll," she declared. "I set out to retain a European face."

The Mattel lawyer drew the Dutch judge's attention to noses: "The new Sindy nose is slightly turned up, more so than the nose of the old Sindy dolls and therefore bearing a stronger resemblance with the Barbie nose."

Sindy's sculptor disagreed. "If one looks up the noses of Barbie and Sindy from underneath," she said, "one can immediately see that Sindy has a much more pointed nose with deeper nostrils."

Legs were also of keen interest.

"In both cases the thighs are longer than what is normal for human beings," Mattel's lawyer told the Dutch court, noting as an aside: "It is a remarkable fact that the earlier Sindy had shorter legs."

"The legs of the current Sindy are no different in length to those of Maxie," countered Bryan J. Ellis, Hasbro's managing director in England.

Furthermore there was the matter of breasts, a word neither side used.

"The plaintiffs ignore the most noticeable difference between the bodies. That is, the bust of Barbie is much larger than Sindy," Ellis said. "Barbie is known for her full, mature figure. I believe that this difference is so very noticeable that this will be the main thing that a person would spot if looking at the bodies of the two products without any clothes on."

5

A WEDDING AND A FUNERAL

I

The first time Alan Hassenfeld saw Vivien Azar, he'd just come off the tennis court. He was in Hong Kong, visiting a friend, Angela Martin, an acquaintance of Vivien's. Martin thought the two might get along. Alan came in from his match, hair disheveled, pants torn, toes sticking out of holes in his tennis shoes. He'd hurt his ankle and was limping but was making light of the situation. It was classic Alan. Vivien took one look and whispered to Angela: "Have a nice dinner. I've got to get home." And she left.

Born Vivien Meadows, she was the granddaughter of a baron and baroness who lived in Vienna and summered on a lake near Salzburg. Her father was a British citizen who'd been raised in Italy and England and gone into business in India, which, in 1946, when Vivien was born, included Pakistan. Vivien lived in Karachi until she was not quite eight, when she was sent to boarding school in England, there to become an equestrienne and captain of her lacrosse and net-ball teams. For a time she wanted to be a ballerina, then art and fashion interested her. She was beautiful—by eighteen a young woman with features reminiscent of the actress Vivien Leigh, to whom her mother also had been favorably compared. For two years she was a runway model in London and Paris, and after marrying a childhood acquaintance, she moved to Hong Kong. The marriage subsequently ended.

Hong Kong abounded with opportunity in the late 1960s and 1970s. Vivien modeled, produced fashion shows, and trained stewardesses in proper comportment. She traveled to Europe as a buyer for department stores and boutiques and, encouraged by friends who admired her taste, gradually moved toward interior design. She took a new husband: a Lebanese Arab who manufactured clothes in Hong Kong. They had two children, a boy and a girl, and during their early childhood, Vivien was not in business. She returned as they got older, establishing, with Angela Martin, Great Wisdom Enterprises, a company that designed and furnished the interiors of hotels throughout the Pacific Rim.

Vivien's second marriage was nearly over when she met Alan, in 1985.

Here's a beautiful woman, Alan thought, who's probably too sophisticated for me.

"He doesn't appeal," Vivien confided to Angela.

Their paths crossed once or twice after that. Sometime later they happened both to be in Japan—he at Tokyo Toy Fair, she on vacation—when, after a dinner Alan hosted, they had occasion to talk at length for the first time. Vivien was impressed with how Alan had deported himself with his Japanese guests—how, unlike many American businessmen, so culturally chauvinistic, he blended in. Martin had confided to her that Alan hated fish, and she'd marveled at how he'd handled what was on his plate. "It somehow sort of disappeared," Vivien would recall. "He just did it with finesse." As they talked late into the night, Vivien was pleasantly surprised. Alan did not come across as some hopeless (albeit wealthy) provincial, not as some bumpkin who couldn't recognize when his tennis shoes had seen their last, but as a well-traveled, erudite man who had a marvelous sense of humor and an uncommonly gentle spirit for such a high-placed businessman. For his part, Alan was smitten.

Alan flew from Tokyo to Sardinia to join his mother on vacation and one evening, they went out on the balcony of Sylvia's hotel room for a drink and one of their chats. Sylvia's need to be in constant touch with her children, her eldest especially, was a source of wonder at Hasbro. Among the stories insiders told was the time she'd called Stephen from Moscow to have him summon her a cab. Stephen was in New York, or so the story went.

"By the way, how did you and Vivien get along?" Sylvia said when it was evident Alan would not be forthcoming. She'd known Angela Martin many years and had met Vivien before Alan had.

"It was fine, Mom," Alan said. He began to blush. This was like being a teenager again, awaiting her verdict on a girl.

"Do you have anything more to tell me?" Sylvia asked.

Alan said he did not.

"Fine, if that's the way you want to be about it," Sylvia said. "Your only mother, you won't talk to."

Alan relented. "There is something special between us," he said. "We'll just have to see what it is."

Sylvia had always been particular about her children's companions, especially their romantic involvements. Alan's adult interests had not been nice Jewish girls. He was attracted to women such as the shapely blonde, a G.I. Joe showroom model, he'd dated before Vivien. Sylvia was not amused. She'd been scandalized when her younger son told *The Wall Street Journal,* in its front-page profile of Hasbro in 1975, another of the reasons international business was for him: "He says he enjoys not only the traveling," the paper noted, "but the unusual social life his travels afford as well, including one year dating a Swedish airline stewardess and another 18 months dating a Filipino model." In truth, the Filipino had been Tina, a professional ballet dancer; Alan had indeed dated a model, but she was a Taiwanese woman named Lillian. With the exception of the showroom model, Alan hadn't been romantically involved with a non-Asian in more than a decade.

If Alan married Vivien, Sylvia's daughter-in-law would be a Protestant and Alan's stepchildren would be teenagers, hardly ecstatic that their parents had broken up. Alan would not have any children of his own, for Vivien had hers and, having reached her forties, was not interested in more. But in every other regard, Vivien measured up. Vivien shared Sylvia's appreciation for the better things in life. Vivien always looked her finest. Vivien had real class. If they were serious, Sylvia would bless them.

"I can honestly tell you it's not going to be easy," she told her son. "I just want you to know that if this is what you really want—I think the world of Vivien, and you'll never have to worry about me questioning you."

II

WHEN ALAN ANNOUNCED his engagement early in 1989, he'd been president and chief operating officer of Hasbro, reporting to Stephen, for five years. His primary responsibility remained international, which, with the acquisition of Milton Bradley, had changed overnight from licensing and manufacturing to a business with significant sales, marketing, and research and development components. Alan had succeeded quietly, nearly doubling revenues since the acquisition to almost $500 million annually. He spent much of his time in London, at the European headquarters that Stephen had built with Robert Beckwith's assistance, a glass-and-metal building as architecturally and artistically distinctive as West Twenty-third. Most of the rest of his time was spent in Rhode Island.

"I'll live wherever makes you happy," Alan told his fiancée.

Vivien had a flat in London, which she intended to keep. Alan suggested their American base be New York, but Vivien was not keen on the city. She preferred Boston, and she and Alan rented an apartment there while the house they bought was gutted and rebuilt. America was an adjustment for Vivien. "Although I'd lived what sounded like a very exotic, wordly life, I was very naive," she said. "I had never used a dishwasher in my life." She chuckled, recalling her first try, when she loaded ordinary dish detergent and the machine filled half their apartment with suds.

Fashion was one of Alan's accommodations. "Nothing ever fits me," he said, "and I hate shopping." Vivien took matters into her own hands, buying his clothes and shoes after measuring him and tracing the outline of his feet. But he still preferred blue jeans and loafers, and wore them whenever he could.

After Merrill's death, Sylvia had left Rhode Island for an apartment on New York's Fifth Avenue, near the headquarters of many of the Jewish organizations she served. She'd kept her residence in Palm Beach, and it was there that Alan and Vivien had their wedding, on the grounds of a small museum, in April. A reception followed at Club Colette, a private dinner establishment. Only about one hundred people were invited, among them Verrecchia, Bernstein, and Beckwith, at Stephen's request. On this special day, at least, Stephen did not seem sick. He greeted guests with his customary charm and paid tribute to the new couple in an emotional toast. But by May he was failing again. With her background in fashion, Vivien was knowledgeable about AIDS. She asked Beckwith if

Stephen had the disease, but, respecting Stephen's wishes, he could not answer.

"Alan, your brother has AIDS, I'm sure of it," Vivien said to her husband. After all the denial, Alan suspected she was right.

III

AT ABOUT THE SAME TIME, a week or so before Hasbro's annual meeting, Robert Beckwith again urged Stephen to unburden himself. If he couldn't face Sylvia, he had to tell his brother.

"If you truly love Alan," Beckwith said, "you've got to bring him into this."

Stephen would not. Perhaps someday, perhaps someday soon—lately he seemed more favorably inclined to that possibility than before: had not Beckwith joined him at Alan's wedding?—but not then. Stephen still would not acknowledge he was dying. Neither would Alan, who did not know how to approach a big brother who could not approach him. Even a celebrated fraternity had its limits.

Certainly Alan had to wonder about his brother's sexuality, especially after Stephen broke off his engagement to a woman in the 1970s and no romantic female relationships followed. Alan knew the rumors. He knew Beckwith, of course, and saw him constantly with his brother. But unless Stephen broached the subject, it was not something Alan believed he had the right to get into. "We never interfered with each other's personal lives unless advice was asked. We had our own rules," he would say many years later. If Stephen explained his maladies as the aftermath of endocarditis, then that was the story to be believed and told, despite evidence to the contrary. "Blind," was the word Alan would use repeatedly, sadly, to explain his part in the telling of the tale. "I had created my own world."

It was a world somehow more comfortable for all of the Hassenfelds than the real one, now poised to intrude in such manner as could not possibly be ignored.

In his quarter century at Hasbro, virtually all his adult life, Stephen had never missed an annual meeting. He was determined to preside over this one, even though Beckwith had begged him to let Alan stand in. At ten o'clock on the morning of May 17, 1989, Stephen walked to a podium on West Twenty-third's lower-level plaza, where not two and a half years ago he'd celebrated completion of Hasbro's stunning new look with a party that had been the talk of New York's design community. Sylvia was in the audience, along with the rest of Hasbro's board, the company's senior executives, Beckwith, and a few shareholders. Stephen talked about a new line of cars, his hopes for Playskool, the Nintendo threat, and the corporation's prospects for the quarter and the year.

"I've been in this business twenty-six years," he said. "I hope, the good Lord willing, I'll be here another twenty-six years, because I love it."

Those who knew read less into Stephen's words, as carefully crafted as ever, than into the nuances of his performance. Once he had been an impassioned speaker, but now his voice had lost its power. He leaned on the podium for support, something he'd never done.

Only one person remarked on this. It was Verrecchia, whose later white-collar restructuring and factory closings would earn him a reputation as a man without a heart.

"Take him home," he whispered to Beckwith. "Take care of him."

Less than a week later Stephen was hospitalized. Hasbro made no announcement, and only family and their very closest friends were allowed into his room. Beckwith visited once, but his presence thereafter was not welcome. After a day, Stephen seemed to have stabilized. On the afternoon of May 24, Alan and Larry Bernstein flew to New York from Atlanta, where they'd been negotiating the final details of a licensing agreement for Cabbage Patch dolls, which Stephen (and John Amerman) fervently wanted. They took a limousine from the airport to the hospital, and it was there, seeing the "Precautions" sign on Stephen's door, that the fantasy of endocarditis ended.

Stephen listened to the latest on Cabbage Patch and complained good-naturedly about the hospital food. Alan and Bernstein found a restaurant nearby and brought Stephen a chicken sandwich and a piece of chocolate cake. "See you later," Bernstein said, and kissed his boss good-bye. He was heading back to Rhode Island. Alan was staying the night, with his sister, mother, and Vivien. Perhaps in the morning they would all discuss what could no longer be kept secret.

Hours later Stephen's heart arrested, and he went into a coma from which he never awakened.

6

■

BEAN COUNTING

I

*A*lan Hassenfeld got in the lovingly preserved Mercedes-Benz coupé his parents had given him on graduation from college and drove to Warwick, a suburb of Providence. It was August 1990, fourteen months after Stephen's death. Alan parked inside the gates to Lincoln Park Cemetery and walked west, past tightly packed lots, past the more spacious area along Hassenfeld Avenue where Osias, Hillel, Herman, Henry, and Marion Hassenfeld were buried. He continued toward the cemetery's prettiest and most remote corner, where, in a choice lot bordered by an evergreen hedge, Stephen lay next to Merrill.

Alan came here often, to reflect, to let his father and brother know how he was doing. He was anxious now, for he was about to change the lives of five men who'd stood by him here as Stephen had been lowered into the ground. One by one they'd thrown a spadeful of earth onto the coffin, a final farewell to someone they'd loved and respected and to whom they owed great fortune.

For a while after being named chairman and CEO, Alan had not touched his brother's management team. Most of Hasbro's top executives were in relatively new positions, the result of the restructuring Stephen had undertaken in December 1988 in an effort to rekindle the company's growth. One of the Three Musketeers, Larry Bernstein, was president of the Hasbro Toy Division, the corporation's promotional arm, direct successor to Merrill's business; another, Steve Schwartz, was president of the new Playskool division, for preschool products. (George Dunsay, the third Musketeer, had left Hasbro.) Al Verrecchia had been rewarded with the presidency of manufacturing, executive vice president Barry Alperin with greater responsibilities for acquisitions and strategic planning. George Ditomassi had remained head of games, essentially Milton Bradley. (A relative newcomer to Hasbro, John T. O'Neill, had succeeded Verrecchia as chief financial officer.)

Although Alan had been president and chief operating officer since 1985, none of Stephen's senior executives had reported to him. Alan saw them at product line reviews and budget meetings, but these were fleeting contacts; he knew them as much through Stephen's eyes as his own: "I was an outsider," he recalled later. During the summer and fall of 1989 he'd watched as the old guard maneuvered. Except for John O'Neill, who'd achieved his career objective by reaching CFO, all wanted a crack at something bigger—at the very least, they did not intend to lose an inch of what they had. None was shy in letting his desires be known to the new boss.

Alan had made his first moves in December. He promoted O'Neill to executive vice president and named London-based Norman Walker, a friend with whom he'd worked for years, president of European operations; these were easy steps, free of repercussion, the kind of benign decision he had little trouble making. His other move in December was an attempt to please Verrecchia, whose ambition was to be president and whose overall expertise Alan badly needed, and Alperin, friend of Stephen and board member. Alan gave Verrecchia and Alperin curious titles: co–chief operating officers, or co-COOs, an inherently unstable dynamic that temporarily relieved him of something he hated, a hard choice. Verrecchia's co-COO duties included manufacturing and administration. Alperin kept acquisitions and legal services, areas where he had experience, and gained responsibility for sales and marketing in South America and the Pacific Rim, areas new to him.

As Alan neared the end of his first full year as chairman and CEO, the politicking got ugly; by attempting to please two people, he'd pleased none. Verrecchia was critical of Alperin for refusing to leave New York for an office in Pawtucket, Rhode Island, the tired old industrial city that was home to corporate headquarters. A noted supporter of the fine arts, Alperin could not imagine returning, especially now that Stephen, the only person at Hasbro he'd considered his intellectual equal, was gone. Verrecchia (and others) complained that Alperin was better suited to strategic thinking than marketing or sales, hard-hearted disciplines where he had scant experience. Alperin feared Alan would put Verrecchia in charge of marketing, where Verrecchia was undistinguished. Schwartz and Bernstein each had his own agenda. So did Ditomassi. Sometimes lost in all the bickering was the greater good of Hasbro.

"Alan, you've got to do something," Verrecchia said. "Pick who you want. Go to the outside. But you've got to make some decisions."

Alan stood by the grave, the sounds of songbirds in the nearby trees. On Merrill's death, Stephen and Alan had commissioned a monument from Chaim Gross, an expressionist sculptor who'd been born in Galicia a year after Henry and Hillel had left for America. His piece, a depiction of two lovers embracing, was intended to symbolize Merrill's relationship to his wife. Alan looked at it now, sunlight picking up flecks of gold in the polished green marble, and talked to Stevie, as he had the night before his funeral. Only this time he was not seeking guidance so much as a blessing. After more than a year, his mind finally was made up.

▪

Later that week, Alan summoned Verrecchia and Ditomassi to his office and told them they were his choices to run the company. He did not specify who should do what, although a logical division was evident. "You guys go figure it out," he said. "Split it in half, figure out titles, and come back with a plan."

Ditomassi and Verrecchia both wanted to be Alan's second—whether as president or (sole) chief operating officer, title mattered less than position. Since that road was closed, at least for now, there was nothing to do but follow Alan's unconventional instructions. Given that neither man would take a backseat to the other but were both loyal to Alan, Verrecchia and Ditomassi looked at the cards and in fifteen minutes dealt their hands. Ditomassi was a natural to keep games—his entire career had been at Milton Bradley, based in East Longmeadow, Massachusetts, where he lived. Virtually all of Verrecchia's twenty-five years had been in domestic toys, based in Rhode Island, his home, so he took that: marketing, sales, manufacturing, and administration. Since Ditomassi had experience overseas, he also got international (although Alan kept a direct role and Norman Walker had primary day-to-day responsibilities for much of the world, a subpartition that would create its own confusions). In sales volume terms, the division between Verrecchia and Ditomassi was roughly fifty-fifty. The prestige was comparable as well; for the time being, both were content. But privately both doubted a corporate structure born of the desire to accommodate personalities could endure. Privately each hoped Alan someday would hand him it all.

In the new scheme, Alperin kept legal and acquisition responsibilities but lost his South American and Pacific roles. He was named vice chairman, but he was not pleased. He did not believe the new structure was intelligent, especially Verrecchia's larger role in marketing, and he told Verrecchia and Hassenfeld that—unwisely, as the remainder of his career at Hasbro would prove. "I think it's wrong," he said, but Alan had cast his lot. It remained to be seen how Bernstein and Schwartz, the remaining two major players, would greet the new order. Like Alperin, neither was Verrecchia's biggest fan. He was the consummate numbers guy.

II

VERRECCHIA'S FATHER, A COMMONER, emigrated from Italy to America in the 1920s at the age of sixteen. Alfred Sr. became an engraver in Providence, home to a jewelry industry that prospered as textiles declined, and eventually into business with two of his brothers; Verrecchia's mother, Elda, was the bookkeeper. They did not employ hundreds, as did Hassenfeld Bros. Inc. in the 1950s, but the business prospered, allowing the Verrecchias to relocate to Cranston, a suburb—at first to a modest house in a working-class neighborhood, and later, when Al was in high school, to Dean Estates, a place of manicured lawns and two-car garages.

Verrecchia had no desire to join the family business. Stress regularly came home with his parents, prompting arguments and periodic separations, some lasting weeks. "You were always trapped in between who was right, your mother or your father," Verrecchia recalled. "I saw that and I said, 'Jesus, I don't need that grief and aggravation.' " Elda wanted her son to be a doctor, like her brother, but Verrecchia wasn't interested. He enrolled in the University of Rhode Island without a clue about what he wanted to be. He did not apply himself to his studies, and after being placed on academic probation at the end of first semester sophomore year, he left for a sales job at a department store. This was not what a proud immigrant had in mind for his college boy. Verrecchia was still a disappointment in his father's eyes when he married Gerrie Macari, a girl he knew from high school. Gerrie encouraged him to return to URI, and he did, in September 1964, as a major in accounting, his mother's discipline—one that appealed to his academic strength, math, and his profound need for logic and control. Here was a man who could tell you how many suits he had and exactly the order in which they hung in his closet.

The reborn Verrecchia was an A student. When a professor who'd left URI to become controller of Hasbro offered him a part-time position there in 1965, the year after Stephen Hassenfeld became Merrill's assistant, he took it. His first assignment, at $1.75 an hour, was auditing invoices in accounts payable, a monotonous job requiring concentration, attention to detail, and boundless patience, qualities that would serve him well in the long years ahead. Verrecchia worked forty or more hours a week, frequently past midnight, even though he was still in school and he and Gerrie were starting a family. After more than a month, he was finally done. "What was the purpose of this?" he asked his boss, Robert S. Fell, the controller. "I haven't found many errors at all." Fell responded with a series of questions about materials, suppliers, prices, and measures. Verrecchia had every answer. His real business education was under way.

Verrecchia was promoted next spring to junior accountant, at $2.15 an hour. He'd developed a new standard cost sheet for every commodity used in Rhode Island manufacturing and was frequently on the factory floor. He found waste, of items as small as rubber bands, and devised means to reduce it. He became immersed in inventory control, depreciation, the general ledger. Fell encouraged scrutiny, not blind acceptance of numbers. "Ask questions," Fell would say. "Why? How come? Do you really have to do it that way?" When Verrecchia graduated from URI in 1967, he accepted full-time employment, at $165 a week.

He followed Fell as controller in the early seventies, when Hasbro's survival was in jeopardy. His duties included ones Merrill and Stephen did not want to dirty their hands with, but which were necessary to keep the company in business. Assuring a constant supply of plastic resin and cardboard, used in bulk throughout the factories, was a particular challenge. Retailers began filling their warehouses in summer with toys man-ufactured in spring—but withheld payment to Hasbro until goods began to move off the shelves in autumn. Suppliers didn't want explanations of this nutty industry's seasonal cycles; they wanted their money in ninety days, not sometime after Christmas. Verrecchia was reduced to taking to the road to beg. "Just give me more time," he would plead. Sometimes he succeeded; other times he got back in his car and drove somewhere else. He borrowed heavily at high interest from local banks, and when he'd used up his credit with them, he went to a Chicago specialist in risky loans that charged even more. He analyzed the company payroll, discov-ering that roughly 70 percent of checks handed out on Fridays didn't clear banks until Monday, 20 percent showed up on Tuesday, and so forth into the week. He managed his scarce dollars accordingly. He learned dozens of tricks. Any wiggle room there was, he took.

Occasionally Verrecchia would approach Stephen. "We don't have the cash, we're doing different things to try to stay afloat," he'd say.

"Well, what are you doing?" Stephen would ask.

Verrecchia would answer: "Do you really want to know?"

To which Stephen would say: "No, not really."

And that was that.

Verrecchia stayed because he enjoyed much of his work and many of the people. He stayed because Stephen, upon becoming president, com-mitted himself to the balance sheet and the situation began to improve. He stayed because of promotions—to treasurer in 1974—and pay—$34,000 a year in 1974 and $54,000 by 1980, when he became vice pres-ident of finance.

III

STEVE SCHWARTZ WAS on the golf course when his secretary reached him that Friday afternoon in August 1990, not long after Alan had visited the grave. Alan needs you immediately, she told him. It can't wait until Mon-day.

Schwartz stopped by Bernstein's office before seeing Alan. Bernstein was visibly shaken. "What's going on?" Schwartz said.

"They're making Verrecchia COO, and we have to report to him," Bernstein said.

Schwartz was astounded, then furious. "No way am I reporting to that guy," he said. Bernstein, too, was considering quitting.

The other news, Ditomassi's promotion, made sense to Schwartz. Milton Bradley's overseas business had brought Dito into regular contact with Alan, and until each had married, the two had double-dated; he was one of the few employees who could claim to be the new chairman's friend. Dito's marketing credentials were gold plated, and he'd continued to pull off the rare feat of profitably running a large, labor-intensive factory in New England at a time when most in the industry, including Hasbro's own toy managers, were looking south and overseas. His games business had consistently, increasingly, made money.

But Verrecchia—Verrecchia was the classic suit! The joke was that even in a hurricane, his hair would remain unruffled! To Schwartz, suits were the stepchildren of the business: useful with the chores, perhaps, but not worthy of a seat at the head table. That was for marketers, people with passion for product and talent for moving it off the shelves at high velocity, people like Schwartz.

A psychology major in college, Schwartz had been casting about for a job when he read a newspaper article about Ideal Toy Co. and decided selling toys might be fun. He worked alongside another Ideal salesman, Larry Bernstein, in the early 1970s before progressing to marketing. In 1978 Bernstein, at Hasbro now, called to see if he'd consider coming to Rhode Island. "Where's Rhode Island?" Schwartz joked. One meeting with Stephen Hassenfeld was all it took to bring him on, as vice president of marketing and product planning.

That friction existed between Verrecchia and Schwartz was no surprise; the intrinsically uneasy relationship between finance and creativity breeds rivalries in many industries. But Verrecchia and Schwartz's relationship was pointedly without warmth. When Schwartz had picked a loser, Verrecchia would quip: "Why don't you guys just stick a dollar in a box and ship it that way. It's cheaper." To which Schwartz would respond: "If you think it's that easy, why don't you come on over here and give it a whirl? Because it is one thing sitting there counting the money, but we are the guys who have our asses on the line."

What was with Alan? Schwartz knew what the party line would be: in terms of manufacturing, distribution, administration, and the balance sheet, Verrecchia was without peer at Hasbro. And it was true: Verrecchia had greater technical breadth than anyone. But did Alan really believe a bean counter was more vital than a marketer? Alan was so laudatory of Verrecchia—how he'd been there when Stephen died. But that couldn't be it; others had been there, too. Certainly it wasn't great friendship: Alan had intersected with Verrecchia over the years, but no more than anyone else. Was it a matter of trust? Ambitious though he was, Verrecchia would never be behind a palace coup. Was Verrecchia some sort of father figure to Alan, now that Merrill and Stephen were gone? Verrecchia was the only senior executive who'd been at Hasbro longer than Alan himself.

Or was Alan punishing Schwartz? Despite his gentle nature, Alan had an explosive temper—a withering, sometimes sarcastic fury that could reduce underlings to the point of tears. Several of Schwartz's people had felt its heat, and Schwartz had repeatedly chastised Alan. And while he'd supported Alan for the chairmanship, Schwartz did not believe him the genius Stephen had been, particularly when it came to product and marketing. Alan was the globe-trotting kid brother. Brilliance might lie within, but naming Verrecchia COO was hardly a promising omen.

Schwartz found Alan in his office. A black-haired man with a bushy mustache and intense eyes, Schwartz was not possessed of delicate emotions. He was not a man with a poker face.

"Why do you have to make a move?" he said. "I mean, you've got strong people. You have Norman in Europe. You have Dito at Bradley. You had me over here. You have Larry over here. You've got Al over there. Why do you have to consolidate?"

Alan said this was how he wanted it. He did not say that he was prepared to lose Schwartz, but he was, albeit reluctantly; as valuable as he might be to Hasbro, Alan believed, Verrecchia was more so. The company could prosper without him, if it came to that. Alan's own product and marketing skills, Alan believed, were greater than Schwartz gave him credit for.

Schwartz said it would have been one thing if Alan had brought in someone distinguished from outside. But Verrecchia? "We don't like each other," he said. "We haven't liked each other in thirteen years, and I'm not going to put myself through what I know is going to happen working for him. So it's just better for everybody—the company and me and Al—if I resign."

"Think about it tonight," Alan said.

"I'm not going to change my mind," Schwartz said.

"Talk to Al," Alan said.

"I don't want to talk to Al," Schwartz said. "I have nothing to say to him."

On his way out of the building, Schwartz passed Verrecchia. "I guess you won," he said, and was gone.

·

In the ensuing publicity, Alan was not available for comment. He left that job to Verrecchia, who praised Schwartz in his remarks to the press. Wall Street was less than thrilled. One analyst called Schwartz one of the "guiding lights" of Hasbro's growth in the eighties, and another said: "I don't think the company is permanently crippled without Steve, but I think it's a loss."

The uproar seemed to have subsided when, on October 17, *The Wall Street Journal* ran a scathing front-page story under the headline A HIGH-FLIER IN THE '80S, HASBRO LOSES ITS TOUCH FOR PICKING HOT TOYS. CHAIRMAN DIES, TALENT LEAVES, AND CREATIVITY SUFFERS. The lengthy piece did not state outright that Alan was not the manager his brother had been, but the implication was unmistakable. "Hasbro's earnings peaked in 1986," the article read, "and with sales essentially flat for four years and possibly dropping this year, the company may lose its No. 1 spot to a resurgent Mattel." The *Journal* noted that only a week earlier Hasbro had laid off ninety white-collar workers in Verrecchia's new division, the largest such layoff in company history (in the local coverage, it was again Verrecchia, not Hassenfeld, who'd been available to comment). In meticulous detail, the *Journal* chronicled the cooling of Hasbro's eighties hits, noting especially the recent decline of G.I. Joe.

The story angered Alan—many years later it was first in a file he kept of such broadsides. This wasn't the hometown paper. This was the solemn voice of Wall Street, its every page scrutinized by major shareholders, investors, and members of the Hasbro board, who so far showed no inclination to replace Alan or sell the company. But if Alan had learned one thing at Stephen's side, it was how quickly loyalties can change when big money is at stake.

IV

THUS IT WAS with more than ordinary interest that Hassenfeld observed the agony that autumn inside Tonka Corporation of Minnetonka, Minnesota, the third largest toy and game company in the world and one of the last independent giants left. Swamped by $612 million in debt it had assumed acquiring Kenner Parker Toys Inc., shortly before the stock market crash of October 1987, Tonka was hemorrhaging. As the fall of 1990 passed and the bleeding went unchecked, its chances of survival diminished by the day.

Even wounded, the company was a magnificent entity, a cornucopia of golden brands. Few boys would have named any but Tonka when asked their favorite toy truck, and Play-Doh, Nerf, and Easy Bake Oven were timeless moneymakers. The Parker Bros. division had Sorry!, Risk, and Trivial Pursuit, huge sellers year after year, as well as the most enduringly popular (and immensely profitable) board game in history: Monopoly. Among the Kenner division's long line of hits were Strawberry Shortcake, Care Bears, and numerous blockbuster movie tie-ins, including Robocop, the Real Ghostbusters, and Star Wars toys, which had buried G.I. Joe in the late 1970s. Kenner's latest hit was product tied to Batman, Warner Bros.' 1989 blockbuster. Kenner also had president Bruce L. Stein, a thirty-six-year-old whose marketing gifts were said to rival those of Schwartz and the only other person routinely mentioned in the same breath, Jill Barad of Mattel.

Hasbro's relationships with studios predated Mr. Potato Head, but since Flubber, the Hassenfelds had been wary of drawing too close to Hollywood. Stephen especially was cautious. In 1982 he'd masterminded a deal in which Warner invested heavily in Hasbro, but his motivation was less licensing rights than Warner's cash and its transfer to Hasbro of subsidiary Knickerbocker Toys, which sold Raggedy Ann and Andy. Stephen preferred to focus attention on TV series that featured his toy characters Joe, My Little Pony, and Transformers (all three became highly rated programs in the 1980s). For purposes of advertising, it was hard to beat a medium that went directly into living rooms every day. Nonetheless, even Stephen had expressed interest in Kenner when Tonka was looking at it in 1987 (the price turned out to be too high). Kenner certainly had experienced fiascoes, but it understood the strange tango of movie licensing better than any toy company.

For Alan, Tonka would be more than an acquisition that would nearly double the size of Hasbro, a move sure to quiet skeptics, at least for the moment. It would be an opportunity to distinguish himself in one of the few pieces of business, Hollywood, that Stephen had not mastered. And in the unscientific but all-important arena of image, to which even Wall Street was susceptible, it would be a watershed for the new chairman, as his chief operating officer for domestic toys knew well. "I really want this for the company," Verrecchia said, "but especially for you. Because once this is done, Stephen's shadow won't be constantly over you."

Hassenfeld assigned the job of overture to Alperin, who discovered that Tonka chairman and CEO Stephen G. Shank was courting someone else. He was talking to John Amerman, who had recently hired David M. Mauer, Stein's predecessor at Kenner, a move that surely would give Mattel the inside track. In late October, unbeknownst to Amerman, who was eager for a deal and increasingly confident that one was about to be arranged, Alperin managed to get Shank and his chief financial officer to dinner with him and Hassenfeld.

7

■

STAR WARS

I

"Normally I would never presume to ring a bell," Alan Hassenfeld said as he stood at a press conference and rang one, "but if we were outside, you would hear a strange phenomenon. From all corners of our state, church bells are ringing."

They were, more than a hundred total, an outpouring that would have seemed a transparent attempt to make the evening news but for the moral authority of the men and women standing with Hassenfeld: rabbis, priests, ministers, nuns, Episcopal and Catholic bishops, the president of an Ivy League university. They'd come to the State House to join Alan in calling for "a new dawn, a new day, a rebirth of the old ideals of ethics and morality," a lofty ambition they hoped to achieve through the work of a new coalition. Hassenfeld had agreed to chair RIght Now!, as the group was called. It was two weeks before Christmas 1991.

The press conference was in the Rhode Island General Assembly's House lobby, chosen because it symbolized democracy's promise and, lately in Rhode Island, democracy's opportunities for graft and corruption. One of the former House speakers whose portrait hung near where Hassenfeld stood had resigned in disgrace as chief justice of the state supreme court, his next job, when his ties to organized crime had been revealed; another had been indicted on federal extortion and racketeering charges after leaving office. The powerful current speaker's nickname was "Prince of Darkness," for the manner in which he allegedly cut deals and rewarded cronies with the choicest state jobs. RIght Now! sought more than state house reform. It sought to restore dignity to the state's reputation, ridiculed as "Rogue's Island" on national TV. The reputation was not ill deserved. Malfeasance at the highest levels of government and commerce had precipitated the near collapse of Rhode Island's credit union industry, Pawtucket's mayor was serving a federal prison sentence for extortion, and a convicted felon was mayor of Providence. A superior court judge recently had been charged with accepting bribes, and a family court judge had pleaded guilty to defrauding four banks. And this was the short list. Rhode Island, it seemed, was a sewer. Cleaning it was not a job for the fainthearted.

Facing no questions about amortizations and earnings, Hassenfeld was confident and relaxed. He indeed made it onto the evening news, where he'd last appeared in September, when he'd launched the campaign to build Rhode Island's first children's hospital with a $2.5 million gift and a commitment to raise millions more. With RIght Now!, editorialists and columnists once again lined up to pay tribute. "Astonishing," wrote the *Providence Journal*'s M. Charles Bakst, a political columnist who was notoriously tight with praise. "Hassenfeld, the 43-year-old Hasbro chief executive, came across as a gee-whiz, when-are-these-guys-going-to-wake-up crusader."

It was enough for a twinge of that Tom Hanks–in–*Big* feeling again. Until 1991, Hassenfeld's most visible philanthropic role had been as head of Hasbro's annual Giving Tree campaign—a worthy endeavor, to be sure, but hardly one to put him on the track for recognition as an outstanding humanitarian. Now he was leading the broadest political coalition in Rhode Island history, one whose only aim was to do good.

∎

The surprise was not that a Hassenfeld would be associated with a cause. The surprise was where its battles would be fought. Alan's grandfather and parents had steered clear of the political arena, and while Stephen's philanthropy had had high visibility, he, too, had had no desire to experience the searing personal scrutiny leadership of a reform movement would invite. As the legislative fight degenerated into a brawl, Alan was regularly roughed up on radio talk shows, and politicians on the Prince of Darkness's side could barely contain their scorn whenever he returned to the State House to lead a demonstration, watch a debate, or testify on a crucial bill. How hypocritical of a manufacturer with factories in Asia to claim he was concerned with making his home state a better place to live! How sanctimonious that Hassenfeld should preach open government, then ban reporters from all but a few meaningless minutes of his coalition's steering committee meetings! And wasn't his true motivation a hidden desire to someday be U.S. senator? Who was he kidding?

Hassenfeld was gracious throughout. In fact, he had the notion he might seek office someday, but RIght Now! was not the platform to get him there; when and if the time came, his wallet would be vastly more effective than past association with do-gooders. Like his grandfather, who'd been delivered from poverty and pogrom, Hassenfeld simply believed in giving back, just not the conventional way.

"I never wanted to follow the path that was there," he reflected later. "I didn't think that's what life was for."

11

UNLIKE TOY FAIR 1990, when Wall Street had yet to return a verdict on Hasbro's new chairman, Alan had arrived triumphant at Toy Fair 1991. Alperin and his negotiators had delivered Tonka on terms and for a price that would prove to be a steal.

The deal had taken longer than Alan had desired. Since the October dinner, Alperin had met again with Tonka chairman and CEO Shank and his managers, retained an investment adviser, and opened a dialogue with Tonka's bankers, whose interest was to curtail their mounting losses. But New Year's Day had passed without an agreement. Dissatisfied with the pace, and suspecting that Mattel was somewhere in the picture, Hassenfeld authorized Alperin to send a letter to members of the Tonka board, urging them to speed matters up. "We are treating all aspects of the subject matter of this letter as highly confidential and, accordingly, are making no disclosure at this time regarding our interest in acquiring Tonka," Alperin wrote. It was not quite a bear hug, but the threat of one in the event of inaction was clearly implied.

Two weeks later the deal was consummated. As it turned out, Hasbro bid marginally higher than Mattel, but price was not what swayed Tonka's board and bankers: cash was. Armed with the strongest balance sheet in the business, an inheritance from his brother, Alan had been able to put up all cash for Tonka (and its debt). Although its financial position had improved greatly of late, Mattel could offer only a combination of cash and stock for Tonka.

Alan's $486 million deal, one reporter wrote, "would secure, perhaps for years to come, the company's role as the world's largest toymaker in sales, leaving Hasbro's closest competitor, Mattel, far in the distance." Alan was in clover. When some analysts suggested that the terms might have been too generous, he was good-naturedly dismissive, even uncharacteristically arrogant. In one story he reminded a reporter how his brother had responded to similar criticism of the Milton Bradley acquisition: "Steve used to say: 'You pay a vintage price for a vintage wine.' "

■

In El Segundo, California, the city just south of Los Angeles where Mattel had its headquarters in a new high-rise, John Amerman was steaming. Well into January he'd believed he was on the brink of getting Tonka. So confident was he that he'd spread word inside Mattel to expect formal announcement any day. Now Hassenfeld, that oddball with the rubber bands, had swooped in and stolen it away.

It was a humiliating loss. Fully recovered from Intellivision and He-Man, Mattel had crept to within $50 million of Hasbro's revenues in 1990 (and had posted slightly higher earnings), but now it would end 1991 $500 million behind Hasbro, which had become a $2.1 billion company overnight. The dollar gap was less irksome to Amerman than his maddening frustration with games, a business he, like the Hassenfelds, had been unable to generate from within. At an analysts' conference, Mattel was left to brag about the hiring of "a game expert extraordinaire" who'd worked at Milton Bradley and Parker Bros., both now in Hasbro's camp.

But this was no time to mope. Amerman had not gotten to where he was by taking defeat lightly. In El Segundo, the CEO and his inner circle began to consider other options for growing Mattel's market share. The most surprising would turn out to be the most enticing.

▪

By the time church bells rang throughout Rhode Island, it was permissible, if only for the moment, to think of Alan without reflexively conjuring up his brother's ghost. Some who knew the company especially well even dared to observe that with his obsession for minutiae, Stephen might have had more difficulty managing the post-Tonka Goliath than Alan, who was comfortable delegating large chunks of the business. The cover of Hasbro's annual report for 1991 featured a Mr. Potato Head atop a Play-Doh model of the globe, symbolic of the old Hasbro and the new. Inside was a photograph of a smiling chairman surrounded by an ethnically and gender-diverse group of children. In his effusive but unpretentious way, Alan wrote of his pride in his employees, company, and philanthropy, notably the Hasbro Children's Hospital. He spoke of growth, of stability through diversification, of international expansion—a respectable, if hardly original, vision for the company.

But much of his message concerned his vintage wine.

Tonka was markedly different from any other Hasbro acquisition, and not only because of its price, over $100 million more than Stephen had paid for Milton Bradley. Tonka put Hassenfeld into the heart of Hollywood, gave Hasbro a virtual monopoly on the U.S. games market, and came with a wealth of brands in traditional toys. It came with underutilized factories in Texas and Mexico, where the costs of production were far cheaper than in New England. It also, for the first time, brought a powerful division into the fold that competed directly with an existing one. Like the Hasbro Toy Division, whose president was Larry Bernstein, Kenner, headed by Bruce Stein, was heavily into TV-promoted products—a business of high risks, heavy volume, and, by necessity, large egos. Like Hasbro Toy, Kenner had made fortunes in action figures, the industry's most punishing category with the possible exception of fashion dolls. Rather than fold Kenner into Hasbro Toy, or vice versa, Hassenfeld decided to keep both independent. "We want to retain their corporate cultures with their talented people who have a track record of successful product development," he wrote in his annual report.

What he did not anticipate was how Kenner would change Hasbro, and ultimately him, forever.

III

ON THE DAY Bruce Stein graduated from Pitzer College, a small school near Los Angeles, a city with a strong pull on him, his father asked about his progress getting into medical school. Stein could no longer hide the truth. "I haven't applied and I'm not going to," he said. So what were his plans for the future? "I'm going to spend the summer with my cousin Harvey," Stein said. Harvey lived a laid-back existence on Venice Beach, where roller-skating and pickup basketball were the impassioned pursuits. Venice Beach was where a young Jim Morrison a decade before had dropped lysergic acid and written songs for a band that became known as the Doors.

Stein's father handed him a ten-dollar bill. "Buy yourself a pair of bongo drums," he said. "This is the last penny you're getting from me."

Venice Beach was both dead end and opportunity. Stein's listlessness forced him to confront a sobering reality, one Alan Hassenfeld never had: He was on his own, and he had no money. He met young men in similar circumstances, and together, there on the beach, between pickup ball and jobs in telephone sales, they concocted profit-making schemes, custom jewelry and earthquake survival kits among them. They were not groundbreaking concepts, but they were entrepreneurial, and creating them pleased Stein, whose imagination was more fertile than most. Dad was pressuring him for a postgraduate education, so that autumn he applied to business schools. He was accepted at the University of Chicago, near where he'd grown up, and in January he enrolled.

Here, too, he was contrary. His classmates were all eager for investment banking and management consulting, the glittering career paths of the time, and Stein couldn't envision anything more dry. He took the required finance courses but gravitated toward marketing, a discipline based on understanding and manipulating human desires and needs. Stein had studied psychology in college and fancied himself, rightly so, a good student of the consumer's mind. Marketing also would bring him deep into pop culture, a realm whose high priests, movie stars and directors, excited him. And it would provide a gainful outlet for his creativity, which, as applied to market dynamics, he later explained like this: "Nobody wants a three-quarter-inch drill bit. What they want is a three-quarter-inch hole. People see the world differently. I always see the hole.

And so for me always the step is to back up and put something—create something—that fills that hole."

His first job after earning his MBA was at Armour-Dial, the soap and deodorant firm. He was involved in a packaging color change and wrote an ingenious plan to market Dial to Hispanics, who, he'd learned through research, often shampooed with soap. Stein wanted to bring his shampoo idea to a full-scale Spanish-language test market, but the company declined. "You're like a diamond in the rough," a superior said to him. "You're a strategic thinker, but we can't get you to do the basic stuff." In other words, he had ambition and vision and was bored silly with scutwork. Fed up with Armour-Dial's arthritic attitudes, he left after two and a half years for a job at Ogilvy & Mather, the Los Angeles advertising giant that counted Mattel among its clients.

Ogilvy immersed Stein in TV, by way of the Mattel account. He examined years of Barbie commercials, testing and retesting each in focus groups until he understood which were effective, which weren't, and why. He applied the knowledge to new commercials, so successfully that Mattel soon offered him a job. He resisted, for Ogilvy was speedy with his promotions: account supervisor, management supervisor, vice president by the age of thirty. He was living in Santa Monica, not so very far from Venice Beach, driving a company car, and earning excellent pay. In June 1985 Stein relented, lured by one of the few marketers who had much of anything to teach him: Judy Shackelford, the Mattel executive who was developing the segmentation strategy that would send Barbie to historic sales even as Intellivision was nearly bringing her company down. Stein accepted the position of vice president of marketing, with responsibilities for Hot Wheels and Popples. Jill Barad was his peer. Stein had been at Mattel barely a year when Shackelford left and a headhunter contacted him to see if he had any interest in becoming senior vice president of marketing at Kenner, a position that would put him first in line for president. He calculated the time it would take to reach the top at Mattel, what with the ages and ambitions of those ahead of him, and in January 1987 he was on a plane to Cincinnati, Ohio, a city that very definitely was not L. A.

▪

Kenner was one of the survivors of the golden age of toys, although survival had been at the cost of losing family ownership. Founded in 1947 by brothers Albert, Philip, and Joseph Steiner in a building on Kenner Street in Cincinnati, Kenner's first memorable product was the Bubble-Matic Gun. Give-A-Show projector was introduced in 1959 and was followed four years later by the Easy Bake Oven, the company's first classic brand. The Steiners sold Kenner in 1967 to food giant General Mills, which purchased Parker Bros. the next year; in 1970 General Mills merged Rainbow Crafts, originator of Play-Doh, into Kenner. Spun off from General Mills after Star Wars had subsided, Kenner Parker Toys Inc. was independent when Stein arrived. It was not happy, nor was it fat. More than seven hundred blue- and white-collar workers had been laid off the year before, and memories from a bitter strike earlier in the decade lingered. The corporation had been only slightly profitable in 1986, after losing almost $100 million in 1985, its first year on its own. Kenner was like a veteran boxer: a little the worse for wear, but undoubtedly wiser, and with the talent and determination for another shot at the title. Certainly the Machine was still there, consisting of licensing chief Jim Black, the most successful Hollywood liaison any toy company had ever had; Jim Kipling, a lawyer skilled in negotiating licenses; and a design and development group with a gift for translating film properties into best-selling pieces of plastic, a task vastly more difficult than most believed, until they tried it.

Although he would manage several internally developed toys to profitable performances, Stein would delight his eventual employer, Hasbro, with what he and the Machine made happen with Hollywood. The big studios were not stingy deodorant makers: they regularly rolled tens of millions of dollars on projects, and millions more were brought to the table with fast-food and merchandise tie-ins. Stein recognized the enormous potential of this new synergy (or "supermarketing," another term also coming into vogue)—how it could only lead to greater things for all parties, of which the large toy companies, with their mighty distribution channels and powerful TV advertising, were second only to the studios themselves. But Stein brought more than a sharp picture of how children's culture could be directed to the Machine. Like many of the stars and directors themselves, he was a movie junkie, with broad and eclectic tastes: Woody Allen, Steven Seagal, movies about sports and animals, fantasy flicks. He understood the relationship of movies to television, where the best children's properties lived on and on, and he knew the cultural nuances of trendsetting Southern California as no lifelong resident of

Cincinnati ever could. He had Hollywood style. Dark haired, tan, fit from daily sessions at the health club, Stein was the sort of man whose presence was noticed. He favored stonewashed denim shirts, chinos and athletic shoes, and contact lenses. He'd learned the art of stroking egos without sounding phony. He was a real player, or was about to be.

Stein worked for then president David M. Mauer, whose background, like many at Kenner, included time at Cincinnati neighbor Procter & Gamble (Zest and Downey were among his brands). Mauer heeded sales data, not feelings; when a toy had peaked, it was time to cut your losses and get out. "We were not emotionally married to our product," he explained. Stein's influence began with the 1988 line, which saw the introduction of Starting Lineup, licensed plastic likenesses of professional athletes that were Stein's idea. Robocop, Police Academy, and Ghostbusters II action figures reached the market in 1989, followed the next year by Beetlejuice and Batman figures, based on the first Warner Bros. movie, whose resonance in the popular culture seemed to rival that of *Star Wars*.

Stein almost missed Batman, the comic book character who would make him a star. Kenner had been offered the property eight months before the film's release but had passed; eight months wasn't enough time to create a distinctive toy line, and the script Stein read hadn't done justice to what he saw on a Cincinnati screen one day in the summer of 1989, after *Batman* had opened to a record-breaking box office. What he saw made him physically sick: a property with extraordinary continuing toy potential. "What crumbs can we get?" Stein pleaded in a call to Dan Romanelli, Warner Bros.' consumer products chief. "We've got to have a piece of this! I don't care how late it is!" Stein wound up getting a license to sell a limited line in 1990 and a contract for a rapidly expanding one thereafter.

Stein became president of Kenner in October 1990 when Amerman lured Mauer to Mattel, but realizing his ambition came amid growing peril. Tonka had purchased Kenner shortly after Stein's arrival, and the parent corporation's worsening financial woes were eating away at the division, sucking out profit that should have been reinvested in research and development. Tonka did not have the resources to let Stein pursue the biggest movies anymore, but that was increasingly moot: the studios were spooked. Stein had Batman in his 1991 line, but Beetlejuice and Ghostbusters were fading, and the only fresh properties he'd been able to scrounge were Robin Hood and Bill & Ted's Excellent Adventure, hardly at the top of anyone's A list. "The first toy line to combine real rock 'n' roll with the fantasy of time travel," the catalog copy proclaimed, "Bill & Ted's Excellent Adventure promises to be *the* boys action line of 1991!" It had no such promise, of course, and it would be an embarrassing dud. The year 1991 looked to be a bust for Kenner, with revenues not half the $310 million of only two years ago.

▪

In Stein's ideal world, Mattel would have bought Kenner. Mattel's urgent need for winning action figures would have made him an instant sensation in El Segundo, and Mattel paid better than Hasbro and was but half an hour from Hollywood. And Stein objected to how Hassenfeld and Verrecchia carved up Tonka Corporation; like a child who comes into a family through remarriage, he envied his new siblings. He did not like losing Play-Doh to the Playskool Division, and he wanted Tonka trucks but was beaten to them by Larry Bernstein. On the other hand, he got Parker Bros.' Nerf, a foam-sports brand with tremendous unfulfilled promise. And he had the new bosses' unqualified support for what, at best, would be a rebuilding year. Backed by the best balance sheet in the industry and carrying as open a checkbook as Verrecchia could offer and still sleep at night, Stein returned to L. A. a player again. He already had the toy rights to the *Batman* animated TV series and the movie *Batman Returns,* a certain winner, headed for a 1992 release. Now he could close a deal on the toy rights to *Terminator 2* and go after Steven Spielberg's *Jurassic Park,* which was creating a remarkable buzz, even by Hollywood standards, long before it went into production.

Meanwhile, Stein had some unsavory chores. Certain services that Hasbro could provide better or more cheaply elsewhere had to be eliminated in Cincinnati; considering its gloomy projections for 1991, Kenner would have hope of achieving Verrecchia's divisional profit goal only by also cutting sales, marketing, design, and administrative costs. And having discovered substantial unused capacity in Tonka's more economical Texas and Mexican factories, Verrecchia had quickly decided to close Kenner's Ohio plant. All of this added up to hundreds of layoffs. Except for Kenner's factory, which Verrecchia would completely wipe away, it was up to Stein to decide who stayed.

Identifying candidates was less difficult than notifying them once the decision had been made. Some had been at Kenner for years—had children, mortgages, and auto loans. Stein had to twice call one well-liked veteran into his office before summoning the fortitude, if that was the word, to let him go. Stein tried to look ahead, to Hollywood. It's right for everybody else left in the company, he told himself. We're going to be able to go back out and sell this company to the entertainment community as "We're lean, we've got the tightest group right now, and we're going to make the most of your property."

A hundred white-collar workers were gone when, late in the year, it was over. Stein summoned his remaining staff to an empty floor in the old downtown headquarters, which was being vacated for cheaper leased space, friendlier to the bottom line. "We are structured now so that we cannot just survive, but we can thrive," Stein told those who were left. "And when we hit it like we know we will, ultimately we're going to make a lot of money." It was the first time Stein had delivered such a speech, but it would not be the last.

IV

"YOU'RE FAMILY," Alan Hassenfeld said to Larry Bernstein. "You can't go."

It was August 1990, shortly after Alan's cemetery visit, and Bernstein was threatening to follow Schwartz out the door, for many of the same reasons. The difference was that Alan had a special fondness for Bernstein. Hired by Stephen Hassenfeld in the precarious seventies, Bernstein had found Schwartz and Dunsay, Musketeers Two and Three. He was often at Bristol and Museum Tower. He indeed was family, in a way Schwartz, and even Verrecchia, never had been.

"I'm going to have my mother call you!" Hassenfeld said. His sister, Ellie, too. He meant it as a bit of Jewish humor.

"Please don't," Bernstein said. "This is between me and you."

After securing a three-year contract and a $40,000 raise, Bernstein relented. Then he went to see his new direct boss.

In temperament and many other ways, Verrecchia and Bernstein were polar opposites. Bernstein favored boat shoes and jeans, was more or less a schlump regarding his posture and hair, and was paunchy, although he still had a football player's rugged build. Like a schoolboy first setting eyes on a pretty girl, he fell quickly and excitedly for new toys. He was animated to the point of being supercharged, a quality that could inspire, confuse, or annoy, depending on who you were. No one had ever written down a joke or saying uttered by Verrecchia (or Alan Hassenfeld, for that matter), but Bernstein's people frequently recorded his comments—sometimes years or months later posting them in a presentation theater before a meeting. "Collectors are a pimple on the elephant's ass," Bernstein once said, comparing middle-aged men who buy G.I. Joe to the much larger youth market. Of inventory, he observed: "When it's not moving, you're sitting on a mountain of shit. When it's moving, you put shit on the table and it looks like gold." On not having all the answers: "If I did, I'd go sit in an office and have people come and pray to me." And on what salesmen should tell their buyers about key products: "If you don't carry it, we burn your business. And if you don't promote it, we break your leg."

"Al, I just want you to know something," Bernstein said. "I told Alan I didn't think you were the man for the job."

Verrecchia said nothing.

"But I've decided to stay," Bernstein continued. "And given the fact that I've decided to stay, I want you to know you have my loyalty. I will work for you."

"That means a lot to me," Verrecchia said.

Bernstein couldn't leave it there. "I just want you to know how we are going to operate," he said. "If I think you're wrong, I'm going to come in and close the door and go right down your throat."

"No problem," Verrecchia said. He thanked Bernstein, then did something uncharacteristic: he embraced him. Two resignations of top marketing talent would have been no way to inaugurate the new era. In 1990 Verrecchia needed Bernstein.

But Bernstein figured he had to be thinking: I don't like the way he operates. I think he is a flake, an unmade bed. He even looks like an unmade bed.

Which, in so many words, is just what Verrecchia was thinking.

▪

Son of a salesman, Larry Bernstein was raised in a postwar Brooklyn neighborhood that had a fish market, a grocery, a theater, a barbershop, and two synagogues. His friends were mostly Italians and Jews. Captain of his high school football team senior year, leading scorer in New York schools, all-city, all-state, all-American, he saw his name splashed across the sports pages every week. What would endure from that experience was wisdom from his coach. "Football is a metaphor for life," Moe Finkelstein said. "You are going to get knocked down and you are going to lose. And the measure of the man is what he does with himself once he gets up and goes at it again."

Bernstein was recruited by dozens of colleges and chose Boston University, which had a football program he hoped would get him to the pros, his only ambition, besides girls, at the age of eighteen. "I'll get the Hebrew National endorsements!" he used to joke. Conference rules excluded freshmen from playing varsity, but sophomore year, Bernstein was the starting halfback. He also was flunking, and after first semester he was asked to leave. He went home, to reflect on Coach Finkelstein's words and his father's unique rephrasing of that same philosophy: "Don't be a piece of shit floating on the tide. Control your destiny." Next fall Bernstein was readmitted to BU. He'd forfeited his scholarship, so he took loans and two part-time jobs. He was a student now, on the dean's list when he graduated with a bachelor's degree in business in 1965. It was a rebirth oddly reminiscent of Verrecchia's.

Bernstein had no desire to sell toys, but when he answered an ad for a position at Ideal and was offered the job, he took it. It was in retail services—essentially stocking shelves—which might have led to sales if he hadn't been laid off after Christmas. Still, he'd found his calling, working with product he liked and the colorful characters who peddled it. Hired as a salesman by Transogram, whose revenues paralleled Hasbro's, he was stationed in 1966 in Memphis, where he encountered Wally Haas, a Hasbro representative who'd lost most of an arm in an accident. At the Atlanta toy show, Haas kept needling Bernstein, jabbing him with his stump to make his points. "Do I have to take that from him?" Bernstein asked his boss. No, his boss said. "Mr. Haas," Bernstein said, "if you hit me with your arm one more time I'm going to fucking kill you. I'm going to take that thing and stick it up your ass and bury it right to your throat." Haas stopped needling Bernstein, but continued to beat him on orders.

It was a lesson learned, one of many. Bernstein was getting an education—not through confrontation, for the most part, but by paying attention. "Learn from the old men," his father had advised. "They'll want to teach you." Bernstein came to understand the value, and limitations, of a good story—that jokes alone don't close a deal, although they help smooth the way. He learned to schmooze without seeming obsequious, egotistical, or deceitful, a rare skill. He learned the deepest secret of sales: that in his heart of hearts, even the toughest buyer wants to believe the great things a great salesman promises. He learned whom to hit, how to turn on a dime, when to call time-out.

"When I was out on the road I was playing professional football in a metaphysical sense," Bernstein recalled later. "And I got good at it."

▪

Bernstein had left Transogram for better opportunity in the Boston office of Ideal when, in 1975, Stephen Hassenfeld offered him a job as Hasbro's West Coast regional sales manager. Stephen struck Bernstein as "namby-pamby" but also likable and smart. Stephen offered better pay and a transfer to California. Bernstein accepted immediately.

Two successful years later, Stephen wanted him back in Rhode Island; Ideal had a respectable games business, and he figured Bernstein's earlier experience there might benefit Hasbro in that category. Bernstein sensed that Stephen was more intense than before—more convinced that Hasbro was bound for glory. Made a marketer, Bernstein found one winner from an outside inventor: Hungry Hungry Hippos, the only Hasbro game to survive long enough to be incorporated into the Milton Bradley line. But his most significant contribution of that period was recruiting Musketeers Two and Three. That accomplished, Stephen named Bernstein head of companywide sales, in 1979.

Larry was almost insanely loyal to Stephen—he would speak unblushingly, many years after Stephen's death, of his love for this man who had made him a millionaire by age forty. His devotion transcended monetary gain, or respect for uncommon intelligence and vision, or the fact that demanding as he was, Stephen allowed his people to fail, a necessary prerequisite of success in an industry of high risk. Outside of his family and Robert Beckwith, no one was closer to Stephen than his head of sales. It surprised no one that Bernstein was the last person except for the Hassenfelds to see Stephen before he lapsed into a coma or that after Stephen died, he, first among many others, prominently displayed a framed photograph of the dead chairman in his office.

▪

Stephen's restructuring of Hasbro shortly before his death was meant to reignite domestic toys through the crisper focus dividing the company would bring. Bernstein became president of the Hasbro Toy Division just as the salad days, as he'd called them, were beginning to fade. As *The Wall Street Journal* had not failed to notice, Transformers were disappearing, My Little Pony was going down, and G.I. Joe had peaked and was in retreat. The net result was that overall pretax profit in domestic toys dropped from 19 to 2 percent in just three years. That Hasbro Inc. could remain profitable, with the continued faith of Wall Street, was testimony to the wisdom of Stephen's balanced portfolio. Without his vintage wine, George Ditomassi's Milton Bradley, the corporation would have been in dire circumstances.

Despite the turn of the wheel, Bernstein was enthusiastic about his division's prospects as he went to work for Verrecchia in August 1990. After almost twenty-five years in promotional toys, he believed the business was more art than science; apply all the cold Procter & Gamble discipline you wanted, he believed, at the end of the day this was still a business of cycles and luck—a business, as Stephen always preached, where product, Bernstein's forte, truly was king. Sizzling yesterday, cold today, you could be red hot again tomorrow with a single hit.

Certainly there were signs that philosophy would serve Bernstein well during his first two and a half years under Verrecchia. His New Kids on the Block line, based on the popular rock group, did $47 million in sales (and, with a 70 percent gross margin, millions in profit) in 1990. Despite initial orders for only one hundred thousand units, Bernstein ordered production of half a million Go-Go My Walking Pups, a mechanized toy he loved and many others hated—and sold every one. His division had Cabbage Patch dolls, Stephen's final legacy, and Tonka trucks, a brand with tremendous long-term potential. He snared the license to World Wrestling Federation figures from a competitor that had soured on them, and he made the line a hit. Not everything he touched turned to gold: such action figures as Bucky O'Hare were disasters despite heavy television promotion and programming. ("One of my great follies," Bernstein remembered of Bucky O'Hare. "It died the death of a thousand dogs.") Still, overall Hasbro Toy Division revenues grew at a healthy rate in the early days of Bernstein's presidency and the division was profitable, although only in single digits.

Bernstein began 1993 with an old salesman's optimism.

His girls' toy group was bringing two innovative large dolls to market, and Kirk Bozigian, his vice president of marketing for boys' toys, was introducing several promising new action-figure lines. Transformers were back after a two-year hiatus. Gone since the seventies, foot-tall figures had returned to the G.I. Joe line after testing off the charts in focus groups, and Bozigian was seeking to capitalize on the latest video-game phenomenon with a Street Fighter II segment in Joe. Bernstein had confidence in Bozigian, who'd lifted Joe sales from $65 million in 1990, an eight-year low, to more than $100 million in the year just ended. Once again it seemed G.I. Joe would save the day.

If there was a caveat, it was how competitive the action-figure market had become since Star Wars and reborn Joe had redefined the genre. The wild success of those two lines had drawn scores of imitators. Action figures were an almost $1 billion business now, having quadrupled in a decade, and the pressure was unrelenting and intensifying, especially in-house. The toughest competitors Joe faced in 1993 were Batman and Jurassic Park, from sister division Kenner. Word was that *Jurassic Park* had what it took to be one of the biggest blockbuster movies of all time. Merchandise associated with it would surely experience Spielberg magic, and marketers would become superheroes.

BOOK TWO

8

X - M E N

I

One morning in August 1993, nine boys said good-bye to their moth-ers and followed a stranger into a windowless room in an office building in Natick, Massachusetts. The stranger closed the door and, for the next ninety minutes, questioned the group. For this and seven similar focus groups, Hasbro was paying $28,000, a tiny fraction of the millions it spent annually on market research. Kirk Bozigian had authorized the expendi-ture. He sought to learn the alarming but hopefully constructive details of something he already knew: suddenly, G.I. Joe was getting creamed at retail.

Ron Rentel, who worked for Consumer Eyes Inc., a New York firm, introduced himself and had the boys do the same. They were eight to ten years of age and had been identified through screening as "users" of Joe. Four of the eight focus groups would be with nonusers.

Before starting, Rentel urged the boys to speak up: everyone's opin-ion, he emphasized, was equally important. "If you like vanilla ice cream—hey, great," he said. "If you like chocolate—hey, great. Is one right or wrong? No. It's not a fact. It's something you like." Rental urged patience regarding the toys that were hidden under sheets; in due time, he said, they'd get to them. He had the boys arrange their name cards on the table so they were visible to the videocamera, hidden behind a two-way mirror that took up most of a wall. Several of Bozigian's marketers and researchers were back there in the sound-deadened darkness, notepads in hand.

"Anybody read comic books here?" Rentel said.

Most hands went up.

"Which ones are good?" Rentel asked.

"*X-Men* and *Spider-Man*," one boy, Robert, said.

"*Punisher*," said Adam.

"What's the story there?" Rentel said. "What happens in *X-Men* or *Spider-Man*?"

"They were human, but they got mutated," Robert said.

"Interesting," Rentel said. "Cool." And when was the last time Robert had read *X-Men*?

"Yesterday," Robert answered.

"And *Punisher*," Rentel continued, "what about that one? What do you like about it?"

"All the guns and fighting," Adam said.

Asked to name their favorite video games, the boys mentioned *X-Men, Street Fighter II,* and *Sonic the Hedgehog 2.* Asked what movies and TV shows topped their lists, the boys cited *Ren & Stimpy, Beavis and Butt-head, Home Alone 2,* and *Jurassic Park,* of which one boy said: "I saw it three times." Spielberg's film had lived up to its advance billing. Having opened with a record $50 million, an astonishing total for a single weekend, *Jurassic Park* was well on its way to becoming the highest-grossing film in history.

Marvel still published the *G.I. Joe* comic every month and the Joe animated TV series was still on in most major markets, but so far not one boy had named the property in any context. And these were users. In the next hour Rentel would attempt to find out what had gone wrong.

▪

Their likenesses appeared everywhere in catalogs, advertisements, and packaging, yet children were rarely seen inside Hasbro. The company operated an observational laboratory called Fun Lab at its world headquarters in Rhode Island, but the entrance was separate, and access elsewhere within the cavernous complex was denied. An annual Halloween party drew hundreds of kids, after hours and under carefully controlled circumstances. Family Day at the New York showroom, established by Stephen Hassenfeld for the end of Toy Fair every year, had been discontinued under Alan when executives complained to him of being too exhausted. Except for their own children, marketers' interaction with their consumers was limited.

Their own children, therefore, were influential. Marketers regularly brought home prototypical (and production) toys from Hasbro and competitors. Like well-provided pilgrims, they journeyed religiously with their families to malls, movie theaters, bookstores, arcades, computer outlets, and fast-food restaurants, and especially to the shrine, Toy's "R" Us, which had the largest selection of mass-produced toys of any merchant in the world. They monitored family TV preferences and listened attentively at the dinner table to the latest buzz from playground and school. Larry Bernstein told the story of how his young son was the most persuasive voice warning of Joe's staleness in the late eighties, when sales were dipping, and Bozigian attached reverential importance to the product opinions of his six-year-old son, Colt, who more than once had alerted his unsuspecting old man to new currents in children's culture.

When they wanted hard data, marketers turned to formal research. Focus groups were but one kind. Hasbro and its consultants continually conducted one-on-one interviews with children and their parents, most frequently mothers, who made toy-buying decisions in greater percentages than fathers. Substituting tokens for money, they sent children shopping through selections of toys. They polled. They questioned children before viewing ads, requestioning them after to determine if desire had strengthened. They subscribed to databases that tracked industrywide sales by category, region, and chain. Calls to Hasbro's toll-free consumer hot lines were recorded and analyzed. Coupon redemptions were scrutinized, as was correspondence to fan clubs such as G.I. Joe's. To gauge the effectiveness of promotional campaigns, Hasbro hired firms to record the date, content, and audience size of every broadcast and print story about the product; for an additional fee, Hasbro could obtain tapes and photocopies. To help interpret studies, the company retained distinguished experts such as E. Troy Earhart, Ph.D., former commissioner of Rhode Island's Department of Education, who consulted for Playskool. Few universities or academicians had the mass of information Hasbro had accumulated about the desires and needs of children. It was proprietary treasure, available only for internal use.

Despite its sophistication, which computers had raised to new levels, market research could lead to mischief. Enthusiastic young marketers (and some neither enthusiastic nor young) needed reminding that if an infallible test truly existed, every product would be a champion out of the gate. The oft cited example was the 190,000 blind taste tests that convinced Coca-Cola Co. in 1985 to introduce New Coke, which left actual consumers so unimpressed that the company was forced, amid wide ridicule and at substantial cost, to reintroduce its original formula under the name of Classic Coke. The best marketers trusted their instincts and smarts, using research less to confidently predict winners than to weed out likely losers. In cases such as G.I. Joe in the summer of 1993, research provided clues that, properly interpreted, might direct a product out of a slump.

For his Joe study, Bozigian did not want poor kids—no one ever wanted them—or nerds. He wanted boys with money or easy parents, or both, boys who were cool—the action-figure market. The firm that had recruited the boys for Rentel to question, Dorr & Sheff, had begun with telephone preinterviews that followed four pages of custom guidelines written for Hasbro. Responses indicating an unsuitable candidate were tagged TERMINATE. Household income under $20,000 warranted a TERMINATE, as did any boy who'd been involved before in toy research. Acceptable candidates were required to "like to/have" at least three of the following: read, create things, a lot of friends, draw or paint, play team sports, playact, and talk on the telephone. Likewise, the Natick boys had all been able to define, identify, or describe at least three of these: Rollerblade, Crystal Pepsi, Beavis and Butt-head, Dennis the Menace, Gameboy, Ren & Stimpy, and the saying "Don't have a cow, man." Having made the cut, they'd disclosed all the action figures they owned, how often they played with each, and when they'd last received a toy within each line. These were boys on the leading edge of mass children's culture—boys with a power, unknown to them, that surpassed any superhero's.

•

"What's good about Joe?" Rentel asked the group. "Come on, guys, help me out. I've got to find out!"

"Rocket launchers that really do shoot," Robert said.

"He has all these cool weapons," said Keith.

"War," said a third boy.

"I don't know," said another.

And these were users!

Like a masterful teacher, Rentel had talent for keeping young children on track without stifling their enthusiasm. He seemed spontaneous but worked from a script. Unobtrusively he kept a close watch on time, in order to explore every assigned topic in the allotted hour and a half, for which each boy would earn $25.

As the session neared its end and the boys were seriously fidgeting, Rentel had discovered why the G.I. Joe series was no longer popular with these boys ("repeats and stuff"). He'd learned that they wanted change in the Joe line. He'd elicited at least part of the reason they considered X-Men much more exciting than Joe ("X-Men have like superpowers and stuff" and the toys were bigger). He'd shown models of figures and vehicles planned for next year's Joe line, getting detailed responses on all. With storyboards he'd identified favorites from potential segments in the 1995 line, already in early development (among the themes boys independently suggested would be cool: "G.I. Joe with rip-off arms and legs" and "wounded G.I. Joe with bloodied legs and guts").

Just when time was almost up, Rentel left the room to check something with Jackie Fradin, whose research group had hired Rentel for Bozigian's study. One selection of toys remained hidden under a sheet.

"Let's go see what's over there!" one boy said.

"Yeah!" Robert agreed.

Their pent-up energy burst, and most of the kids bolted from the table. "They're watching," one who remained seated reminded them gravely. He was ignored, but before they could check out the mystery toys, Rentel reappeared.

"Here he comes!"

The boys scattered back to their seats.

"Okay," Rentel said. "You want to see what's back here?" He removed the last sheet, revealing a variety of store-bought figures that were on the market that summer.

"Cool!"

"Killer!"

"Can we take these home?"

They could not, nor could they touch anything. "What's got your attention here?" Rentel said.

X-Men and Aliens, the boys agreed.

"Which of these would you want but your mother won't buy for you?"

"Aliens," a boy said.

"Why?"

"Too much money."

"How much influence does your mother or father really have in this kind of decision?" Rentel asked. It was a rhetorical question.

"Not too much, right?" Rentel said. "It's what you want."

11

ABOUT THE TIME the boys in Natick were earning their $25, Bernstein, Bozigian, and a dozen of the Hasbro Toy Division's senior marketers, researchers, and designers gathered in the Greenhouse Cafe, a private dining room at corporate headquarters, for a day-long G.I. Joe summit. Admen Joe Bacal and Tom Griffin were up from New York. Many had been in the old presentation theater twelve years earlier when Stephen Hassenfeld had made the most critical product decision of the company's last twenty-five years. All had visited the current chairman's office, where Alan kept a glass case of original G.I. Joes, which he'd inherited from Merrill. They knew this was not just another toy.

Begun with the optimism of a G.I. Joe marketing plan Bozigian had called "Ascension to Greatness," the year had quickly soured. Research had revealed weaknesses in key ads and ratings for the TV series were falling; the last fresh programming had aired two years ago, an eternity in TV, and no new production had been approved. Outlicensing income, an indicator of a property's resonance in the culture, was in its fourth straight year of decline. And just when Joe needed a break, the competition was unusually formidable. Riding the success of two of the highest-rated children's programs, both from Fox Children's Network, the new powerhouse in kids' TV, X-Men and Batman toys were superheated, as were Stein's Jurassic Park toys. All of this had contributed to sluggish sales and worsening prospects for Joe. Bernstein had started 1993 intending to sell

$144 million in the line. The forecast last month had been taken down yet again and was now off a third.

"We've got to change," Bernstein told the men in Greenhouse Cafe. "Otherwise we're extinct."

They were rich with ideas. Perhaps they should launch another nationwide "Real American Hero" contest or push deeper into the collector's market. Find new twists on the usual store and coupon promotions or fire up the fan club, which had been languishing of late. Throw a coast-to-coast party for Joe's thirtieth birthday next year. Freshen the TV, if the financing could be found, or try again for a feature-length film, subject of on-and-off discussions with Warner Bros. for years; meanwhile, how about a direct-to-store video? Bozigian wanted ads instructing kids how to play with G.I. Joe, an idea inspired by his son. (After observing Colt playing with his Joes as lone soldiers, Kirk had shown him how much better two large, opposed forces were. "It was like a light bulb went off in his head!" Bozigian said.) Much discussion concerned Marvel, which published X-Men and Joe comic books. X-Men was outselling Joe more than six to one, and Hasbro's marketers believed that, in part, was because Marvel had assigned the hot title its finest talent and farmed out Joe to the second team. This infuriated Bernstein, who wanted the lawyers to find a way out of Schwartz's famously arranged contract so Hasbro could give Joe to another house. "I want to scare Marvel! I want to kick the shit out of them!" he said. "We're the biggest toy company in the world, damn it!"

But no one disagreed that the deepest root of Joe's problems was the most basic element of all, the toy.

"We're a victim of our own success," said Bozigian, who admitted to a share of the blame. Once again, Joe had strayed from the real-life military persona that had underlaid his success, regardless of era: like Joe in the mid-seventies, contemporary Joe was confused. The 1993 line had Ninja Force Joe, Streetfighter II Joe, Mega-Marines Joe, Mega-Monsters Joe, Battle Corps Joe, and Hall of Fame Joe, the relaunch of the twelve-inch figure. Stores still carried most of 1992's line, which included Super Sonic Fighters, Drug Elimination Force, Talking Battle Commanders, and Eco Warriors, billed as "poseable environmental warriors" and featuring such items as Septic Tank, an enemy vehicle. Merrill would not have recognized his poseable fighting man. He'd become a sponge, soaking up whatever came floating down the stream of culture.

Yet so many of these newfangled characters looked the same—same weapons, same colors, same sneering smiles. Designers had stagnated after a decade on the brand, to the point that they themselves characterized some of their work as "cookie-cutter," about the worst creative knock artists (as they fancied themselves) could take. Worse, at 3¾ inches, the magic number in 1982, the basic figure was perceptibly shorter than Batman and X-Men. Less bulked-up, too.

"We cannot kid ourselves," Bernstein said. "We've got to start putting out some exciting product." That meant originality, because, as Bernstein explained to laughter, "every new thing that comes along is exciting because a kid has the attention span of a gnat."

Bozigian had brought some encouraging statistics to today's summit. Research revealed that 87 percent of U.S. households with boys age five to ten recognized the name "G.I. Joe," and 40 percent owned something from the line; owners, on average, had 13.5 figures and vehicles, greater than for any other brand. Jackie Fradin's research also showed that only 6 percent of mothers had "a problem" with Joe—in other words, an overwhelming 94 percent did not object to the violence, or not so strenuously as to forbid their sons' play. Not quantified was nostalgia: Joe had endured long enough that millions of fathers, like Bozigian, had played with the toy when they were boys. While difficult, the task ahead could not compare to carving out a new brand.

Bozigian had not waited for the summit to begin the battle. Packaging and market research were working on a new look for retail, and ads were being rewritten. Those changes could have impact on late 1993 and the first half of 1994. Looking to late 1994 and early 1995, Bozigian was hoping to introduce Sgt. Savage, a World War II hero who, preserved through cryonics, suddenly appears in today's world. The Savage figure would be almost an inch taller than basic Joe, a tiny increment Bozigian believed would be humongous in a boy's mind.

Bozigian also believed the Hasbro Toy Division had largely missed recent tidings from the world of comics. In just one year, according to Hasbro research, total sales of comic books and related paraphernalia had doubled, to $600 million; upstarts such as Malibu and Dark Horse were giving Marvel and DC, the industry leaders, a run for their money. Behind the boom was fresh storytelling: superheroic fantasy was undergoing another of its periodic transformations, with heroes and villains alike becoming deadlier and more grotesque. The hottest titles did not have

Clark Kent quietly ducking into a phone booth to become the Man of Steel. They had outlandish mutations creating hideous characters capable of inflicting (and enduring) unspeakable injury and pain. "In your face," as Bacal put it. The fall of communism, some hypothesized, had opened the door to new demons.

Bozigian passed around an issue of Q Unit, one of the new titles.

"This is really great," Bacal said.

"If the comic book people are doing this stuff, we have to push the envelope, too," Bozigian said.

"How far are we willing to go?" Bacal wanted to know.

▪

When Bozigian gathered many of the same people for the first of two brainstorming sessions a few weeks later, he came loaded with toys, comic books, and a document he'd labeled "Ultra Top Secret." Even the wise guys on the Joe team, and that was almost everyone, indulged Bozigian in his military affectations. He was a well-liked man, and if that was how he motivated himself, fine. This was still the toy business, after all. Eccentricity was still allowed.

The top-secret document was a storyline Bozigian was proposing for a new segment. Under it, Joe's longtime enemy, Cobra, had escalated his quest for world domination, and in response, a new unit of superheroic Joes had been assembled. "Some have undergone radical experimental surgery to enhance their normal human abilities," Bozigian wrote. "Some are mutant forms of humankind altered by the effects of radioactivity, nuclear waste, and/or depletion of the ozone layer. One is rumored to be a god!" Bozigian proposed names for fifteen members of the new force, including Megatron, Wizzo, and T.A.N.K. But Bozigian was open-minded; these were only preliminary ideas. His sole precondition was that X-Soldiers, the segment's working title, had to be somehow connected to the military. Much of the first session was spent debating radioactivity as a mutagen and reviewing competitive product. One toy that intrigued the team was Super Soldier, a G.I. Joe Hall of Fame knock-off who wore a black eye patch and carried an implausible personal arsenal: submachine gun in one hand, rifle in the other; survival knife on one leg, machine pistol on the other; machete and sword on waist; second knife on one biceps; and pistol, bazooka, and second sword slung across his back. And all for only $15.

With Bozigian out of town, brainstorming resumed a week later under the direction of his marketing manager, Vinnie D'Alleva.

"I called up my nephew, who's eight," designer Dave Kunitz reported. "He and his friends got together and created some characters." They included Anti, a warrior who gained his superpowers when bitten by a mutated ant, and Delta, the absentminded scientist who becomes horribly grotesque when he eats one of his experiments by mistake.

"I don't have nephews," said another designer, Jeff Thompson. "I only have nieces. They say, 'Send Barney.' "

"Well, he's a mutant," quipped Greg Berndtson, chief Joe designer. On the brand since the days of the Three Musketeers, he had more history than almost anyone.

Bill Young's contribution was "Flatulon, Master of Pressure."

"He could have like a huge thumb—'Pull my thumb!' " Thompson said.

The discussion turned serious. Everyone agreed the new Cobra would have to be more evil than ever, in order to support conflict on a grander scale. Perhaps an explosion from deep within the earth or a radiation cloud from outer space could touch everything off.

"Something's missing," D'Alleva said. He didn't think they were pushing the envelope. He advised looking at X-Men, where bad guys sneak into hospitals to snuff the terminally ill.

That piqued the interest of Don DeLuca, senior design director, who said Cobra ought to kidnap children. "You want to get edgy," he said, "we'll get edgy."

Once kidnapped, Kunitz suggested, the children could be injected with substances to make them mutants.

"They need material for genetic engineering," DeLuca agreed. "They break into nurseries, day-care centers, and grab kids."

"Alan won't buy it," D'Alleva said.

"Okay," Kunitz said. "They kidnap teenagers."

"What would make it more palatable would be if they stole not just kids, but whole families," D'Alleva said.

Berndtson objected.

"What do you have against stealing children?" Kunitz said.

"It just bothers me," Berndtson said.

"I think it's a fear and a fantasy of a child, being stolen."

"You don't need to be a superhero to steal a kid," Berndtson argued. "Any sleaze from an alley can steal a kid."

"Instead of going down that path, I'm going back to the original concept of breaking into military installations," D'Alleva said.

DeLuca chided D'Alleva for chickening out but was nonetheless wry in his assessment of their profession. "Do you realize," he observed with a chuckle, "it's only us and cereal companies that have the authority to fuck with kids' minds?"

III

KIRK BOZIGIAN GREW UP on TV westerns, World War II movies, and comics of all sorts. His heroes were his grocer father, his merchant grandfather, and Ted Williams—and at the age of forty-two, he still idolized them. He attended a Catholic college preparatory school with the ambition of an appointment to West Point, thence to become an airborne ranger, but poor eyesight and mediocre grades in math and science put an end to that. He majored in humanities in college, earned a master's degree in TV and radio journalism, and, after jobs in public relations and advertising, accepted a copywriting position at Hasbro. It was 1978. A product manager by 1981, Bozigian was in the old presentation theater when Stephen decided to bring Joe back. His contribution was the top-secret "dossier" on the back of every blister pack—the bio card, intended to be clipped, that told each character's background, specialty, and favorite weapons. The dossiers were an expedient, inexpensive way to amplify the new Joe storyline.

Long before working for Bernstein, Bozigian was a fervid collector. His comic collection had thousands of issues and was worth a small fortune, but Bozigian had no desire to sell even one; his grand ambition was only cataloging what he had. He'd bought his first G.I. Joe in 1964 at F. W. Woolworth in downtown Providence and had gone on to amass untold hundreds of action figures, vehicles, and accessories, and at an age when many men in his station in life played golf, he still built model airplanes and spacecraft. "I'm a geek, what can I tell you," he said on a tour of his collections, which filled half a basement and a good portion of a spacious garage. He reached into a box and held up a jet no bigger than his palm. The landing gear was broken, the rear stabilizers missing.

With his thumb he scratched the blue paint, revealing an earlier coat of red underneath. "This is the first model I ever built," he said. "I was four years old. An F-86 Sabre jet; I don't even know what company made it. I remember it was in my dad's store. I remember building it with him and then painting it with—believe it or not—my mother's nail polish!" He talked of his plans to gradually entrust his son, Colt, with care of his precious plastic.

"I guess it's remembering a piece of history, trying to preserve a piece of history even if it's your own personal piece of history," Bozigian explained. "Who knows? Maybe a thousand years from now, some archaeologist is going to unearth this house and come up with these G.I. Joe figures and get some insight into us as a culture."

▪

"What does it do?" Colt asked his father.

"Well, it rolls fast," Kirk said.

It was the summer of 1989, and the Bozigians were on one of their trips to the mall. Kirk had offered to buy his son, then two and a half, an 89¢ Hot Wheels car.

Colt wanted a $3.99 Sonic Flasher car, which, with its battery-operated lights and sounds, did a lot more than roll. He wanted what Dad and his Hasbro buddies called sizzle.

Bozigian had just been named vice president of marketing for boys' toys in the Hasbro Toy Division (by Bernstein) when he related this anecdote to his designers and marketers, in December of that year. Joe's sales were flagging, and Bozigian believed he could correct that by giving every vehicle and every figure sizzle—in this case, weapons that fired projectiles. Stephen Hassenfeld had never allowed them ("G.I. Joe weapons do not shoot," he'd made sure his catalogs proclaimed), just as he'd never allowed the comic or TV program to depict injury or death. His prohibition was so stern, and so well-known, that no one dared ask him to reconsider. But Stephen was gone now, if remembered in the photographs that Bozigian, like Bernstein, kept of him in his office. Perhaps the new chairman would be less rigid. Certainly Alan needed every additional penny of revenue he could get, with the business as flat as it was the year he succeeded his brother. Bozigian figured their best chance was not to bounce some half-baked concept off him, but to show real excitement at the next product review, a month away.

Berndtson got right on it. There were no technical obstacles to shooting weapons—dart guns had been around for decades, and action figures such as Teenage Mutant Ninja Turtles already had launchers and guns. Over the years Berndtson had tinkered with several spring-powered mechanisms of his own design. As Turtles' sales soared past Joe's, he, like others, had been increasingly frustrated by Stephen's intransigence. "We felt like we were playing with one hand tied behind our backs," he said. With Bozigian's blessing, he went back to four new vehicles already approved for production in 1990, retrofitting them with missile and mine launchers that could be incorporated into assembly without expensive and time-consuming retooling. If Alan sanctioned them, the 1991 line would be designed ground up with new armament in mind.

Bozigian repeated his story about Colt and his Sonic Flasher to Hassenfeld at the line review. "If my two-year-old son is telling me he wants toys that do something," he said, "today's *generation* of kids wants toys that do something. It's not enough to have toys that move or pose."

Berndtson brought out his vehicles and placed them under the chairman's nose. Berndtson had attached the prototypical weapons with glue, but they worked. Bozigian demonstrated one by shooting a Joe figure.

Colt had asked what a toy did. "This is where I answer my kid's question," Bozigian said.

Bozigian had coined two terms in connection with his proposed revolution. "Every figure in the line is going to have a 'toy-ized' feature," he said, meaning a firing projectile, a flying mechanism, something more than poseability or wheels. And that feature would be "burst-able," meaning it would be called out on the package in an explosion of color.

Alan asked if the weapons had passed safety. They had. They did not fire with force to puncture skin or injure an eye.

The room was silent, all eyes on the new chairman. Alan was on the shore of the Rubicon.

"This is the shot in the arm the brand needs," he said. "Let's go for it."

Whatever the cultural implications, and some would see them as deeply unsettling, it was the correct business decision. In the first full year with shooting weapons, 1991—aided by the patriotic fervor that accompanied Desert Storm—sales of G.I. Joe rebounded sharply. The next year they surpassed the $100 million plateau for the first time in three years. Bozigian and his people had never stood taller.

I V

THE SENIOR EXECUTIVE SUITE at Hasbro headquarters was off Main Street, the name given to the long, broad, skylight-brightened corridor that divided the old brick building on Newport Avenue in Pawtucket where machine tools and (later, when Merrill Hassenfeld bought the place) G.I. Joes and other toys had once been manufactured. Many of the same architectural and design luminaries who'd created Hasbro's showroom had guided the old factory's rebirth in the 1980s, and their contemporary tastes were evident in the stylish reception area that led to the three offices in back. No matter the hour, the doors were always open. They did not even have locks.

Alan's office was the middle of the three. But for the absence of a bunk, it could have been a college dorm. Hassenfeld and his family owned or controlled almost eleven million shares of Hasbro stock, valued at roughly a third of a billion dollars (other investments added many millions more to their worth), but Alan preferred ratty old gym and duffel bags to carry his belongings on his worldwide travels, and between trips they often were in a heap on the floor, next to his beloved tennis racket. He wore jeans whenever he could and sometimes, lost in thought, would slip his bare feet out of his loafers or mindlessly finger his rubber bands, which never left his wrists, not even in bed. A pack of Parliament cigarettes, an ashtray, and matches were always on his desk. Admirers, detractors, and wishful beneficiaries were constantly sending letters and cards, and the latest batch awaited his attention in a pile prepared by his longtime secretary, Sandy Marks, a down-to-earth, middle-aged woman many employees counted as a friend—and whom Alan called sweetie when he wanted something, Sandra when he was angry, and Sandy in the ordinary course of events. Phone messages, often including one or more from his mother, made another pile, which he endeavored daily to reduce. A sentimental man, Alan did not let a friend's birthday or anniversary pass without sending a card or a gift; employees and business associates were remembered on such occasions as well. Alan was a prodigious letter writer. He did not have a computer, nor did he know how to use one; he ran his business from yellow legal pads, just as Stephen had. Usually lying around was the latest Nerf gun, with which he jokingly threatened his managers, notably during budget meetings—to which, for a laugh, he also sometimes wore a hard hat.

There was no mistaking the chairman's pride in his company's products. Merrill's G.I. Joes were on a table facing his desk; depending on what was hot, a Batmobile or other toy was next to them. His walls were decorated with twelve framed cartoons featuring Mr. Potato Head, including several from Gary Larson's *Far Side*. He had the photograph of him with Stephen from that long-ago America's Cup summer, a doll with a junior doctor kit his sister had made for their father when she was a girl, and his name spelled out in both Scrabble letters and Playskool wooden blocks. He had books on toys and books on China, and a set of the classic works of Poe, Faulkner, Cooper, Crane, Thoreau, and Twain. "I spent a lot of time with those characters!" he said. "They gave me some good days, and they gave me some very bad days."

Hassenfeld's visitors were as likely to be Henry Shelton, an ex-priest who was Rhode Island's foremost advocate for the poor, as fund managers for institutional investors. Reporters often came by, more intrigued by a different irony, the one behind Tom Hanks's *Big*. Hassenfeld and his public relations chief, Wayne Charness, played to this, emphasizing all the wild and crazy fun grown-ups had in this multibillion-dollar business. Photographs illustrating stories invariably showed Hassenfeld surrounded by toys. "Where else could I climb on all fours playing with a train and, when a banker walks in, look up at him and say that I'm only doing my job?" he told one national magazine. "Uh-oh, it's happening again," went an *Esquire* profile of Hasbro published before Stephen died. "Take the visitors from the Chamber of Commerce on a tour of the cafeteria. Get the Wall Street analysts away from Alan's office. You mean? Yes. He's at it again. The president of Hasbro Inc. is sitting back, hugging Bingo the Bear. No, it's worse. He's talking to Bingo the Bear. His Gene Wilder face has collapsed into the silliest of Gene Wilder smiles. He is cooing stuff like, 'I love to hug you, Bingo.' "

Such scenes were only part artifice, and the smaller part at that. Hassenfeld enjoyed the toys more than any other aspect of his job. He had a photographic memory for product, Hasbro's and its many competitors'— could recite color schemes, game play, inventors, and jingles for items not manufactured in thirty years as easily as those presently on the shelves. At line reviews and other meetings, Hassenfeld was genuinely emotional about toys he liked and toys he didn't: A real coup for a marketer or designer was eliciting a public compliment, typically rendered with an "awesome!" or "right on!" Hassenfeld insisted on personally shooting every new weapon, kneading every new play compound, and trying out every new special-feature doll, and he only half-kiddingly demanded a prototype of the most exciting stuff for his own. Unlike Verrecchia, who infrequently ventured an opinion on the look of a toy, package, or ad (and then usually only when asked), Hassenfeld had sound instincts—good "product sense"—and Stephen's death had freed him to be more forceful in that regard.

▪

The room to Hassenfeld's left belonged to Alperin, but he rarely used it, preferring instead his office in the New York showroom. To the right was Verrecchia, which meant (as other executives had not failed to remark) that when the chairman wanted a heart-to-heart chat, there was but one place to go. This only added to the mystique still surrounding the relationship between Hassenfeld and his chief operating officer for domestic toys three years after his promotion.

Verrecchia's office was as precisely arranged as his hair. Financial sheets and sales reports awaited his attention in carefully squared stacks. He kept his calendar on his new computer, a modernistic all-black machine that evoked an image of the *Star Wars* villain Darth Vader, and the handful of notes he needed were in neat handwriting on a small white pad. He did not smoke. He had several pictures of his wife, three college-age daughters, and son, a young marketer in Bernstein's division. He had one original G.I. Joe and figures from Kenner's Starting Lineup and Jurassic Park lines. Gold-lettered leather-bound volumes of legal documents from all of Hasbro's major acquisitions took up several feet on his bookshelves. He had an honorary doctoral degree in business administration from Johnson & Wales University, was on the Rhode Island Board of Governors for Higher Education (which oversaw his alma mater), and was president of the Rhode Island Public Expenditures Council, a government watchdog group. He was a major benefactor of the University of Rhode Island and would, in 1997, personally contribute $250,000 of the $1.5 million Hasbro would give the school to endow a business college chair. He was, in short, an upstanding citizen.

Unlike many at Hasbro, Verrecchia displayed no photograph of Stephen, but there was a gift from him on one wall: a framed enlargement of a passage from a story *The Wall Street Journal* had run in 1984. "Hasbro generally was profitable throughout the mid-1970s but it was often squeezed for cash because of overstocked inventory and overdue receivables, recalls Alfred Verrecchia, the senior vice president for finance," the article read. "He says Stephen Hassenfeld, who joined the company in 1964 and became president ten years later, aggravated the problems by heavily advertising products that, as it turned out, didn't sell." Stephen had signed the article "Thanks ever so much." Verrecchia chuckled when explaining the circumstances of the story. Stephen never would have tolerated such comments, nor Verrecchia dared to make them, if Hasbro hadn't been on its fabulous streak.

Of all the people still at the firm, only Alan had worked more closely with Stephen than Verrecchia, and Verrecchia's professional relationship had been five years longer. Verrecchia was one of the few who spoke candidly of the dead chairman's complex emotional palette—as though Stephen truly had been mortal, not the godlike "architect of the modern toy company," as proclaimed on his plaque in the Toy Industry Hall of Fame. His candor was not disloyalty; on the contrary, Verrecchia had always been a dutiful soldier, beginning with Stephen's earliest days, when he'd urged people in and out of Hasbro to give the boss's fresh-faced young son a chance, and continuing during the company's climb to the Fortune 500—a climb that was hardly smooth or direct, as Uncle Harold remembered well. Unpredictable in his moods, charming one minute and coldly intimidating the next, Stephen had given his chief numbers guy fits.

"Stephen was an individual who could create every emotion conceivable to mankind in you," Verrecchia said, "all in the space of a day. He could be warm and wonderful and generous, and you really wanted to love him, at eight o'clock in the morning. And at four o'clock in the afternoon you wanted to stick a knife in his heart and cut his fucking soul out."

V

FOR ALL THE glittering headlines, digesting the Tonka Corporation had proved daunting to Hassenfeld and Verrecchia. Tonka had five factories, eight distribution centers, and nine offices scattered across nine countries and five states. Integrating Parker Bros. had been the least problematic. Hassenfeld closed Parker's sole factory, in Salem, Massachusetts, and shifted production of Monopoly, Clue, and the rest of its titles to Milton Bradley's East Longmeadow plant. For the time being he kept Parker's design, marketing, and sales organization freestanding. It reported to Ditomassi, the master of making money.

Tonka's toy pieces, which Verrecchia supervised, had been more problematic.

It had made common sense and was relatively simple, logistically, to close Tonka's corporate headquarters in Minnesota and move production from its Cincinnati factory to underutilized plants in Texas and Mexico. Distribution was not so easy. Tonka had different information systems from Hasbro's, and shifting production to the Southwest created need for a new shipping network. And there were powerful new external forces at work. Following consumers, who increasingly bought their toys at discount chains, the bulk of Hasbro's business was gravitating to four retail giants: Toys "R" Us, Wal-Mart, Kmart, and Target, part of Dayton Hudson. All were placing new pressures on suppliers, notably with just-in-time inventory, a system of shipping on demand that shifted much of the warehousing burden back to manufacturers. To help sort this out, Verrecchia in the postacquisition period had hired a management consultant: Meritus, a joint venture of IBM and Coopers & Lybrand, the accounting firm. Meritus had worked with several corporations, although never one that made toys.

Still, the thorniest issues were not making and transporting goods; for the most part, you were not dealing with an artistic or creative enterprise, not with egos. In acquiring Tonka, Hassenfeld and Verrecchia had wrestled with Kenner—which, once the factory was closed, was essentially a design, marketing, and sales organization. They could have moved the division to Rhode Island, but the cost of losing talent was too high. Similarly, it made no sense to fold Bernstein's division into Cincinnati. Verrecchia had opted for the General Motors model. He'd kept Kenner independent and hoped, like the managers of GM, that all of his divisions would thrive.

By the summer of 1993, all were not. Kenner had returned a solid 13 percent pretax profit in 1992—the Hasbro Toy Division, only 6 percent. Powered by Batman and Jurassic Park, Kenner was headed toward a champagne-popping 20 percent profit in 1993; it was conceivable that Hasbro Toy, home of ailing Joe, would lose money that year. Such glaring inequities only highlighted other troubles. Hasbro Toy and Kenner were competing constantly for the same Hollywood properties, and the fact that Kenner was winning the best was eating into morale at Hasbro and giving some at Kenner dangerous false confidence that they would be forever on a roll. The Playskool Division, headed by Dan Owen since Schwartz's stormy departure, was still disappointingly shy of its profit targets, having averaged less than 5 percent annually since coming to Hasbro Inc. with Milton Bradley in 1984. And what of the two smaller divisions reporting to Verrecchia: Playskool Baby and Kid Dimension, the direct import arm? Did it make sense for all these salesmen to be calling on the same accounts separately? Certainly overhead costs were not to Verrecchia's liking. Meritus, in its study of distribution, had confirmed his belief that the time was ripe for scrutiny of everything in his half of Hasbro. Hassenfeld agreed.

"It's becoming painfully obvious that having five divisions is not working," Verrecchia would say. "The question, Alan, is: Is it the fact that we're organized inappropriately? Or is it the fact that the organization is fine, it's just that we don't have the right people in those slots?"

Verrecchia was inclined to believe the answer was a little of both. So was the chairman. With due respect to his brother, he believed there were elements within Hasbro that had failed to change with changing times.

"In some places up top maybe we've had a little bit of, you know, hardening of the arteries," Hassenfeld would say. "We need bypass surgery." It was a distinctive metaphor, one he would return to in the next year as the operation promised more and more to be bloody.

V I

THE MENU FOR the private dinner Bernstein was hosting in the Greenhouse Cafe for his top executives and Verrecchia on October 26, 1993, was among the Hasbro's chef's finest: wild mushroom and barley soup, mesclun salad, choice of Asian grilled swordfish or herbed seasoned chicken with cream sauce. Dessert was apple-cranberry pie with vanilla-bean ice cream.

As the men sipped wine and sampled the hors d'oeuvres, they made small talk. Verrecchia had bought a place in the Caribbean; Lee Bitzer, Bernstein's vice president of sales, and John Buntel, the Hasbro Toy Division's engineering chief, had news about their boats. Bernstein had his usual stories. Stephen had built the Greenhouse Cafe so that he and his men could combine business and dining, two of his dearest pursuits, without having to leave the grounds. His stated intention was to privately run Rhode Island's finest restaurant, and those who'd experienced it would not have disagreed. Glass roofed, with evergreens on the terrace to hide a parking lot, the café had recently been redecorated in a Japanese motif by Vivien Hassenfeld. Spindly vines grew up an old brick wall, and a tiny waterfall tinkled into a small pool in a corner garden. You could almost imagine you were in the shadow of Mount Fuji, not Pawtucket, Rhode Island, birthplace of the American Industrial Revolution.

Dinner ended and the mood darkened. Unspoken but keenly felt were two recent developments that had made news. One was Mattel's recent purchase of Fisher-Price, Playskool's longtime nemesis in the baby and preschool business. Fisher was not only a gem in its own right; its acquisition meant Mattel's sales volume would again rival Hasbro's, and possibly surpass it. "I'm not afraid of this one," Hassenfeld had told reporters. "I'm looking forward to it." But privately he knew what Wall Street would do. With two corporations each knocking on $3 billion in sales, Wall Street would recast the toy industry as a horse race like never before. In that kind of race there could only be one winner.

The other development was internal. Record corporatewide third quarter results had just been released, and Dito's games group had come in for high praise. But not the highest. That had gone to Stein's division, which, in part on the strength of Jurassic Park, had racked up a phenomenal 40 percent increase in sales. "Kenner has had a magic," chief financial officer John O'Neill told the press. "Literally almost everything they have touched has had success." Even Playskool, which was riding the crest of Talking Barney, had received a public compliment. But not a word about Bernstein's division, and with reason. Last summer Bernstein had been forecasting 1993 sales of $498 million ($131 million more than 1992 had turned out to be), the best volume since the banner year of 1986. By the time he'd returned from Toy Fair in February, Bernstein had started walking the forecast down, until now, with only two months left in the year, he was predicting revenues of less than $350 million. Profit was looking to be a few million dollars, at best. As Verrecchia was about to point out to the men in the Greenhouse Cafe, he could get a better return on a passbook savings account at the local bank.

G.I. Joe's worsening misery was but part of the reason for Bernstein's troubles. Two special-feature dolls he'd banked on for a huge fourth quarter had been killed—one after an ice cold reaction at Toy Fair, the other after a weak performance in test market. Chainsaw Steel Monster, a Tonka truck that had extraordinary presence in a commercial, was delayed when an engineering design error was discovered as it was headed toward full production (plastic had been specified for its gears when only steel would tolerate the abuse the toy was supposed to take). Soft Walkin' Wheels, another promising Tonka toy, slipped a year when an Asian vendor encountered difficulties manufacturing it in the quantities needed to support its heavy advertising campaign. And two of Bozigian's favorite new boys' lines—Conan and Wild West C.O.W.-Boys of Moo Mesa—had not caught on, despite television programming and encouraging research. Bernstein liked to believe that 1993 had turned into an unusual demonstration of how cruel fate could be. "Murphy has been putting in overtime this year," he joked.

Verrecchia saw things differently; he didn't ascribe so much to chance. He was impressed with how Kenner went about marketing: with research, strategic planning, and cold discipline, matters MBA candidates had drilled into them at business school. Verrecchia had spoken to Bernstein about this, but never as chillingly as tonight in the Greenhouse Cafe.

"The way you go about selecting product," he said, "is in a very herky-jerky emotional manner in terms of it's in it's out, it's in it's out, it's going to be red it's going to be blue, it's back to red again."

Verrecchia's words seemed to hang in the air. The only sound was Vivien's waterfall.

"I'm spending money in R and D, engineering, a whole host of dollars, and I'm not getting any results," Verrecchia said. "I could have taken all that money and just put it in the bank and earned six and eight percent with no risk at all. You're not giving a return to shareholders, and it's not been just a one-year proposition—you've been given an opportunity. Now either you turn it around or we've got to make changes."

■

For once, Bernstein only listened. The events in 1993 had mellowed him, much as being suspended from Boston University had; after a career at large corporations, he was nothing if not a realist. The simple fact of the matter was that Verrecchia had the chairman's ear, the power. And now he had these button-down consultants, snooping around everywhere and speaking a language all their own. Brought in to study distribution, Meritus had signed another contract for a full-scale analysis of Verrecchia's entire operation, and they were holding closed-door meetings, running computer programs, and asking the sorts of questions whose true purpose you could only guess. *Reengineering the Corporation: A Manifesto for Business Revolution* had recently been published, and Verrecchia had a copy of the best-seller in his office, on a bookshelf where the eye might wander sitting across his desk from him and his computer.

Bernstein desperately wanted to bring his division back—not to please Verrecchia, but for his people, who were not financially set for life, and for his pride. He remained unconvinced toys could be reduced to science—maybe detergents or soaps could be—but he nonetheless had instructed Duncan Billing, his vice president of marketing, to begin work on a strategic plan for the Hasbro Toy Division, the first such ever. Billing had come to the dinner with a preliminary document labeled "Hasbro Toy 2000." It identified product selection, development, planning, and high cost base as the critical issues.

Bernstein had invited Verrecchia to dinner with the idea that he might have some helpful suggestions. He had not expected a lecture.

▪

Verrecchia was not humorless, as many who had only fleeting contact with him believed him to be. On the contrary, he could tell a decent enough joke, and raising four children had provided him a stock of stories about the comical escapades of family life. He liked to tease the chairman, a registered Republican, for his public support of Bill Clinton and the money he gave to many liberal candidates and causes. His nearly thirty years in toys had given him a dry appreciation for the industry's inherent ironies, and he delighted in tweaking Hassenfeld for his near paranoid concern for product safety. "That's why you have two eyes," he said once, his voice perfectly deadpan, when Alan expressed worry about a proposed spiked football. "In case you lose one."

But Verrecchia had no humor tonight, nor did he offer any of the suggestions Bernstein had hoped for—only relentless criticism, as if something that had slowly built up inside of him was finally spilling out.

"You won't change anybody in R and D and marketing," he said. "I don't know that if you change those people that's going to turn it around—but Jesus, you've got to try something." Verrecchia invoked the memory of the dead chairman. "I can remember many years ago sitting with Stephen Hassenfeld," he said. "We used to look at the Red Sox. He'd say: 'Who the hell knows if they're going to win, but I've got to give them credit this year. At least they went out and made some moves. They're trying to shake the tree a little bit.' "

"Next time no food for you," Bernstein joked when the evening was at its end. "You get nasty when you eat!"

When Verrecchia had gone, Bernstein said to his people: "Go past the anger. I hear what he is saying. We've got to cut costs."

As he drove north to exclusive Wellesley, Massachusetts, where he lived in an old Victorian (his summer home was in the coastal town of Rockport), Bernstein was discouraged, but he was not defeated. His presidency was endangered, but he still had command of Sliced Bread, code name for Hasbro's latest supersecret project, a virtual-reality machine. Confident that the end result would belatedly but dramatically do what Alperin's NEMO had failed to—establish Hasbro as a first-string player in video games—Verrecchia, with the support of Hassenfeld and several other senior managers, was prepared to sink $40 million or more into the project.

And Bernstein had Elvis, a line of dolls based on the rock 'n' roll idol he was soon to launch with one of the most spectacular promotional campaigns the toy industry had ever seen. A $75,000 study by Yankelovich Partners Inc., one of America's premier market research firms, had urged caution, but Bernstein wasn't listening. His gut said Elvis would be big—big as *Jurassic Park*—big enough, he dared hope, to cover his entire profit goal for next year.

9

■

M A D E   I N   J A P A N

I

*M*argaret Loesch, the founding president of Fox Children's Network, took the call from Haim Saban in the summer of 1992, not knowing what to expect. A native of Egypt who'd been raised in Israel, Saban had produced the barely noticed *Little Shop of Horrors* for Fox and a few respectable but hardly earth-shattering properties for NBC. He was, in his words, "a cartoon peddler."

"Darling," he said, "I want to sell you a show."

"I don't need a show right now," Loesch said.

"Oh yes," Saban said. "You have a slot open next year. You have a slot Monday through Friday."

"But I don't have money for a new show for that slot, Haim."

"I make a deal with you," he teased. "You come look."

Loesch left her office on Hollywood's Sunset Boulevard and drove to Saban's Burbank headquarters, located in the shadow of the Warner Bros. lot. Saban, as was his custom, greeted her with a kiss, then brought her into a conference room and began feeding videocassettes into a player. They were clips of children's programs whose rights Saban had bought. After looking at *Samurai Pizza Cats, Bob in a Bottle,* and half a dozen others, Loesch had seen more than enough. She politely told Saban to stop.

"Listen," she said, "there's nothing wrong with these little shows. I mean, some of them are cute, most of them are soft. A few of them might be competitive, but there's nothing here I want. I want something different, something fun, something zany, something unusual, something kooky."

She was about to return to Hollywood when Saban said, "Okay, one moment," and left the room.

He reappeared a moment later with another cassette. "Please don't get mad at me," he implored. "Don't tell me it's a piece of crap. You want something different—this is different. But don't get mad at me."

"Why would I get mad at you?" Loesch said.

" 'Cause nobody likes it. I'm the only one that likes it. I can't sell it. I have it a long time."

Saban started the tape, two minutes of a show called *Dino Rangers*. Loesch watched as five ordinary American teenagers metamorphosed into karate-kicking superheroes. Assisted by high-tech fighting robots that resembled dinosaurs, the superheroes battled the intergalactic sorceress Rita Repulsa, whose cartoonish forces of evil—mutants—were out to conquer the world. It was high camp, and it reminded Loesch of *Godzilla* and other Japanese sci-fi movies she'd been enchanted with growing up in the fifties. It also uncannily resembled a pilot she'd tried to sell to the networks almost a decade ago, when she was chairman and chief executive officer of Marvel Productions Ltd., the television production arm of the comics publisher that handled, among other programs, *G.I. Joe.*

"I love it!" Loesch said.

"You do?" Saban hadn't anticipated this.

"This is what I've been looking for!" Loesch said. She asked if the fight footage had come from Toei Co, one of Japan's leading TV and film production houses. It had. She told him of her experience at Marvel when, at the urging of Stan Lee, Marvel's creative genius, she had used similar Toei material for her pilot, which every network had rejected.

"I'll do it," Loesch said, "but you have to sell it to me real cheap, Haim, because I don't have any money. I only have this morning time period—we don't get any money for it." Haim assured her they could come to terms.

Back at Fox, Loesch showed *Dino Rangers* to her creative staff.

"How could you, Margaret?" said one.

"She's lost it," said another.

▪

Loesch was newly graduated from college and living in Los Angeles when a friend suggested she seek employment in broadcasting. She laughed—what connections did she have?—but made the rounds of the networks nonetheless. When ABC offered her a job as a clerk-typist, she took it. Three years later she was a production manager. NBC hired her in 1975 to work in children's programming. She was a quick study—director of children's programs under Fred Silverman when she left four years later to become a vice president at Hanna-Barbera, legendary creators of *The Flintstones* and *The Jetsons.* As head of production for children's programs, Loesch supervised development, writing, and production and represented her properties with buyers, the major networks. Her most successful series was *The Smurfs,* a Belgian property that came to the United States on a wave of merchandising. A Saturday morning hit on NBC for many years in the eighties, *The Smurfs* drew Loesch into the potent new dynamics developing among the purveyors of children's culture as the Reagan era unfolded. "It was the first time I ever, as a creative individual, found myself sitting in meetings where I was listening to what the toys were going to be," Loesch recalled later.

Such meetings were a fact of life starting in 1984, when Loesch left Hanna-Barbera for six years as CEO of Marvel Productions. Marvel co-produced the *G.I. Joe, My Little Pony,* and *Transformers* series with Sunbow Entertainment, a subsidiary of Joe Bacal and Tom Griffin's ad agency, which did Stephen Hassenfeld's bidding. Scripts were written to include the latest toys. Loesch sought a balance between creative independence and financial reality, but it took confrontation to finally achieve it.

One day her *Transformers* team came to her with Hasbro's latest demands. "They told us to write the scripts but leave blank the characters until they figured out what toy they wanted us to promote," a story editor said.

"That's it," Loesch said. "We can't do this."

Loesch prevailed. Hasbro would not relinquish control, but it begrudgingly accepted Hollywood as a storytelling partner in a medium it had known, until the 1980s, only in fifteen- and thirty-second increments.

Such cooperation, Loesch made Stephen realize, could only be to the greater benefit of both parties.

•

Early in Loesch's career, nearly all original major network programming for children was on Saturday mornings, the only time in a busy week, broadcasters assumed, parents allowed youngsters the uninhibited viewing required to build large audiences and sustain profitable advertising rates. Sunday mornings were mostly for religious fare and a few week-in-review news shows. Weekdays were a hodgepodge. The major networks mostly targeted adults, offering news programs in the morning and soap operas, game shows, and a sprinkling of talk shows in the afternoon. Some stations locally produced a kids' show or two, but the rest of what passed for children's programming outside of educational TV on weekdays was recycled prime-time family shows and old cartoons, sold cheaply through syndicates. No major network executive in the seventies would have believed it possible to create a profitable daily schedule of original children's programming.

By the mid-eighties a sea change was reshaping children's entertainment and the mass media. Technological advances were multiplying the means of viewing, and deregulation under Reagan's laissez-faire Federal Communications Commission was relaxing limitations on children's advertising. Capitalizing on dissatisfaction with the major networks, investors found cable TV increasingly attractive, with household penetration more than doubling during the decade and the number of national cable networks almost tripling. Similarly, independent broadcast stations steadily gained market share. Barely measureable at the start of the decade, the percentage of households with VCRs by decade's end had surpassed two-thirds and was still climbing, supporting a lucrative new business in videocassette sales and rentals of old and new programming from TV and movies. Related developments in game systems, personal computers, and on-line services promised even greater fortune to those who had capital and were willing to risk it. Technology and government were not acting alone: the same demographic shifts behind the increase in spending on (and by) children that the Hassenfelds and other toy makers exploited worked to the advantage of media and entertainment executives, too. Parents of both sexes worked more, expanding TV's role as baby-sitter. Like toys and trips to the mall, TV was a salve on parental guilt, a virtually unquantifiable reality that performance-driven employees of the children's industries felt keenly themselves.

Rupert Murdoch formed Fox Broadcasting Co. in 1986 amid skepticism that even someone as powerful as he could build a fourth major network. Skepticism turned to envy as independent stations flocked to Fox and the network had prime-time programming success. Probably no one in Hollywood was better suited to realize Murdoch's ambitions in children's TV than Loesch. Having been employed by two of them, she understood networks; having sold properties in her last two jobs, she understood syndication and independent broadcasting. She knew all the major producers and most of the minor ones, such as Saban, and her experiences with *Smurfs* and Hasbro's monster hits had taught her the advantages, and pitfalls, of relationships with merchandisers. In 1990 she left Marvel, which had been acquired by Ron Perelman, for Fox Children's.

"Here's the staff I need," she told her new boss, Jamie Kellner, president and chief operating officer of Fox Broadcasting Co.

Kellner approved every position but one: vice president of marketing. He thought it unnecessary in television.

Loesch disagreed. She knew the success of Nickelodeon, a cable network for children launched in 1979 in Buffalo, New York. Due largely to the innovative ideas and exhaustive market research of former educator Geraldine Laybourne, a programmer and eventually the network's president, Nickelodeon had grown into a formidable national presence not only in cable TV, but in children's merchandising—a profitable division of Sumner Redstone's Viacom Inc. Loesch admired the unique image Laybourne had created for Nick, how children turned to it for a distinctive, irreverent form of entertainment they found nowhere else on TV. She knew how Laybourne had succeeded: with clever contests, fan clubs, advertisements, and promotions supporting superior product, the very same secrets of the Hassenfelds, who called it marketing.

"The business is changing," Loesch told Kellner. "We've now got cable, we've got videocassettes, we've got foreign, we've got co-production, we've got toys, we've got licensing—we've got everything. And you want us to create a network and be successful when those networks have been on for forty years? We've got to get our name out. We've got to establish an image."

Loesch got her marketer.

Loesch's ambition was grand. She did not intend merely to steal a piece of Saturday morning, although she would establish a beachhead there. She wanted weekdays, which, experience had led her to believe, were ripe for the picking. For Loesch had been in on the ground floor of another development whose significance had been underestimated by the major networks: first-run syndication, original children's programming produced for sale to local stations through independent syndicators. Having been spurned by the majors, the toy companies and their production partners in the 1980s had turned to these aggressive middlemen, who sold station by station, all across the country, such shows as *G.I. Joe* and Mattel's *He-Man* and *Masters of the Universe*. All were hits with kids, who didn't know or care about the business arrangements behind what was on TV before and after school every day. With her new network, Loesch could use weekdays to generate additional ad revenue and the loyalty of affiliates. She could use them to promote Fox Children's Saturday lineup, and vice versa.

Like Laybourne and Bruce Stein, her friends, Loesch had a rare talent for understanding what excited and pleased kids. Chastened by her experiences with Hasbro, she refused to be what she called "toy-driven." The programs she would buy had to appeal on the strength of their own characters and storylines. Ideally, a happy marriage of toy and TV could subsequently be arranged. For such programming, she went to the finest producers: Spielberg, Warner Bros., the late Jim Henson's firm. She knew, of course, how to bring superheroes to life on the small screen. Starting with *Batman: The Animated Series,* consistently in the top ten of all children's programs virtually from its premiere, superheroes would be her signature genre.

Fox Children's Network went on air September 8, 1990, with three hours of Saturday morning programming carried by 131 affiliates. A half hour of weekday afternoon programming began two days later, but Loesch put nothing on weekday mornings until the next year, when she started after that untapped time period with the half-hour *Peter Pan & the Pirates.* Loesch believed in nurturing, not overnight success, so she grew Fox Kids methodically, from five and a half total hours a week its first year to nineteen hours in the 1992–93 season. By the summer she agreed to buy *Dino Rangers,* Loesch had two programs in the children's top ten; the fall she launched Saban's show, six. NBC had been so badly battered by its former employee that it had abandoned children altogether on Saturday mornings.

▪

"So you really think this could be big?" Kellner said when Loesch showed him *Dino Rangers.*

"I do," she said. "There's nothing else like it, this genre has worked for twenty years or longer, kids are kids and I love it!"

Like Loesch's staff, Kellner was skeptical. He suggested she and Saban co-produce a pilot. If it tested well, he would support production of forty episodes—Loesch was so high on the property that she wanted it on six days a week. With $100,000 of Fox money and a matching amount of Saban's, a sixteen-minute pilot was shot and shown to children from the Burbank area. Just as the rangers themselves had three boys and two girls (an Asian American, an African American, and three Caucasians), the sample included boys and girls of mixed ethnic, racial, and economic backgrounds. Loesch was floored: children watching the pilot were so excited, they literally could not stay in their seats. Even more astounding was the reaction of girls. This was typical: "They got that pink ranger and that yellow ranger and they get to kick butt, just like the little boys!"

Loesch had glimpsed the Holy Grail, for it is every marketer's deepest desire to find properties with strong cross-gender appeal. She ordered forty half-hour episodes, for which Fox paid $50,000 apiece, a bargain-basement price (Bandai Co., Japan's largest toy maker and owner of the property's major toy rights, advanced Saban royalties to help underwrite production). Loesch also wanted a better name. *Dino Rangers* became *Mighty Morphin Power Rangers,* "morphin" being slang for metamorphosing.

But even encouraging research did not persuade the skeptics: since when was research infallible? "Please don't show that *Power Rangers* piece," Loesch's head of sales implored on the eve of a presentation of the 1993–94 schedule to advertisers, when some $130 million in potential ad revenue was at stake. "This isn't for McDonald's, thank you, Burt," an agent for the world's biggest restaurant chain told Burt Gould, Loesch's vice president of marketing. "We're looking for big properties."

Overwhelmed by Kenner's Jurassic Park toys, Bandai's action figures were barely noticed at Toy Fair 1993. Even Stein that February in New York good-naturedly chided Loesch. As late as August, on the eve of the inaugural broadcast, she was still fighting resistance. Pressured by affiliates who'd heard terrible rumors of this off-the-wall new show they were supposed to carry, Loesch sent station executives an episode by satellite for their private examination. The reality, the executives decided, was even worse than the rumor, and now Fox was besieged by phone calls. Loesch was on vacation when Fox Broadcasting chairman Lucie Salhany sent her a fax. "Maybe I'm too old," Salhany wrote, "but I think you have a disaster on your hands." Loesch circled the part about age and sent it back with a two-word quip: "You are." But Loesch was not cavalier. If *Power Rangers* bombed, her backup plan was to drop it, filling that daily slot with back episodes of something from the Fox Children's small but growing library.

One month after its debut, during the week of September 27, 1993, in the 7:30 A.M. Monday–Friday slot, *Power Rangers* topped all other programs among children two to eleven.

II

WHEN HE WAS LITTLE, Haim Saban used to wait with great anticipation for his father to come home. He stood on the balcony of the Sabans' third-story apartment in Alexandria, Egypt, and watched as Dad came down the street from the toy store where he worked as a clerk. Haim desperately wanted a Vespa children's motor scooter, and when Dad appeared yet another night empty-handed, Haim was certain that somehow he'd managed to fold it and hide it in his pocket, for surprise. The suspense built as his father climbed the stairs and came through the door. "No Vespa," Dad would say when he saw his son.

"I could buy the goddamn Vespa company now," Haim would remark much later.

The Sabans moved to Israel in 1956, when Gamal Abdel Nasser drove Jews from Egypt in the aftermath of the Suez War. The toy clerk became a door-to-door salesman and twelve-year-old Haim continued his education, which ended with graduation from high school. He was in the Israeli army when he joined a rock 'n' roll band, the Lions of Judea, that covered the Beatles and other sixties groups. Saban played bass but was uncomfortable onstage; he preferred managing the band, which led to concert promotion, eventually of the Israeli tours of such acts as Blood, Sweat and Tears and Jose Feliciano. He operated, at first, on others' money—offering performers advances that he paid with up-front money from ticket agencies. He was a charming young man, fluent in half a dozen languages, quick on his feet, expensively tailored, handsome in his way, frightfully smart, with an extraordinary talent for keeping names and numbers in his head and seizing opportunity where others saw none. Fate nearly ruined him at the age of twenty-nine. With $350,000 of borrowed money, Saban booked Japanese harpists for a two-week tour of Israel, to begin in early October 1973. Opening night was set when Syria and Egypt attacked Israel, precipitating the Yom Kippur War, which did not put people in the mood for string music. The tour was canceled. Deeply in debt, Saban set out for Paris, where entrepreneurs were not impeded by war or raging inflation and where the music industry was big.

He repaid his debts with profits from a growing business, begun, improbable though it was, when he signed on as manager-producer of a nine-year-old Israeli boy who sang (in French) theme songs from television cartoons. Saban sold millions of the boy's records, discovering, and quickly exploiting, a distinctive Continental appetite. "Unlike in the U.S., where there isn't much of a market for television show theme songs," he told *Forbes* magazine, "Europeans were eager to hear television-exposed music." Saban soon had deals to produce new theme songs for European broadcasts of such hits as *Dallas* and *Starsky & Hutch*. He was hard to refuse: in return for the record rights, vendors got custom tunes free. By 1982, on the strength of several hit records, Saban's annual revenues were near $10 million.

But TV, not its music, was where the real money was, and Los Angeles was TV. Saban went to California, into a booming market for syndicated cartoons. He supplied music for *He-Man* and other series and produced, in 1984, his first show: *Kidd Video,* which had a brief run on NBC Saturday mornings, enough to persuade the network to buy three more programs. Saban was prospering, but he was not satisfied. The biggest expense of TV was related to production; once shot and packaged, a show could go on to a hugely profitable afterlife in syndication, overseas sales, and videocassettes. "I realized that to be considered a significant player you need a significant library," he said. He'd been buying a cartoon here and a cartoon there for some time, but now, like some sort of mad collector, he went on a binge—purchasing eight hundred half-hour episodes in 1988 from a financially squeezed American animator and another thousand or so half hours the next year from foreign sources. His hope was resale on the world's richest market, the United States.

■

Saban enjoyed John Wayne movies growing up but did not watch TV until he was nearly thirty and regular Israeli broadcasting began. Even as a producer decades later, he rarely was a leisure viewer—*60 Minutes* and CNN news were the only adult programs of which he claimed firsthand knowledge. "I've never watched an episode of *Murphy Brown,* which I know is a very successful show, or of *The Cosby Show* or of *Roseanne,"* he said in late 1994. Business was another matter. To be successful he needed to watch children's programs, and he did, from everywhere.

He was in Japan in 1984 on business when an unusual show came on his hotel TV. Combining live action with cartoonish special effects, *Ju Renja (Ju Rangers)* seemed to be about a band of regular Japanese kids who turned into warriors in colorful helmets and skintight body suits. Thus transformed, the rangers used stylishly choreographed karate to defeat monsters that, for all Saban could tell, were grossly mutated animals, plants, and fruits. The basic idea seemed akin to Hasbro's Transformers, a line of toy cars, trucks, and jets that with a flick of the wrist turned into fighting robots. One of the hottest sellers on the American market just then, Transformers were licensed by Stephen and Alan Hassenfeld from Takara, the Japanese firm that had created them.

Though he spoke no Japanese, Saban thought *Ju Rangers* was hilarious—and as pure and wholesome as children's entertainment could be. He believed that if he preserved the monsters and fight scenes and reshot the out-of-costume rangers as American teens, it would translate to the U.S. market. Having been associated peripherally with Mattel through *He-Man,* he also saw toy possibilities. Inquiry led him to Toei, which had kept the program atop the ratings for most of the decade since its 1975 introduction by periodically changing plots and characters. Toei knew how children delighted in its goofiness and nonstop action, but the company understood the real magic was in the metamorphosing. Here were ordinary kids, boys or girls only a little older than viewers themselves, who instantly became *sentai*—superheroes capable of defeating the most hideous (if silly-looking) villains an evil alien could send to conquer planet Earth! In the real world, Mom and Dad told you what to eat, what to wear, when to go to bed—but in this fantasy place you were invincible. Somewhat different psychology was at work with the writers and producers who had sustained the show for so long. Japan's continuing fascination with its shogunal past was reflected in the rangers' mastery of the martial arts. More recent history flavored the monsters, which evidently owed their existence to some terrible radioactive event. Just as in the fifties, when Japanese movies featured Godzilla, precursor to Rita Repulsa's minions, apocalypse continued to have a hold over the only culture to endure atomic attack.

Having failed to place the property outside of Asia, a situation Loesch and Stan Lee knew all too well, Toei eventually gave the American rights to Saban for a pittance: $10,000 against future royalties, should they materialize. Saban put together a pilot he called *Bio Man,* tested it in focus groups, and, pleased with the results, shopped it around the networks and toy companies. "Stop," Hasbro's Steve Schwartz said after a couple of minutes. "This is absolutely terrible, thank you, good-bye." No one else was enthralled, either.

Having exhausted the possibilities, Saban moved on to more fruitful endeavors. He was hardly starving. By the early nineties his cartoon strategy had paid off. His privately held Saban Entertainment was supporting a Rolls-Royce (vanity plate "1 RSK TKR") and a new five-bedroom, seven-bath, ten-thousand-square-foot Mediterranean-style villa, with pool and waterfall, in Beverly Hills. His programs didn't impress Loesch, but that was beginning to change when she saw *Power Rangers.* Saban had recently sold her *X-Men,* an original series of high-quality animation. A sneak preview, on Halloween 1992, hit number one among boys.

III

IN VOLUNTARY TESTIMONY before Congress in June 1994, the height of *Power Rangers'* popularity, Margaret Loesch spoke proudly of her network's rise in only four years to the top of the children's ratings. She was an impressive witness, articulate and at ease, and the fact that she'd bothered to come to Washington (when so many of her colleagues had not) scored points with her inquisitors. Mother of a young son, she had on several occasions reflected publicly on topics, violence and materialism among them, that others of her position were not troubled by, even privately.

Massachusetts representative Edward J. Markey, chairman of the House Subcommittee on Telecommunications and Finance, a Democrat and longtime crusader for better children's TV, had called the hearing to help gauge the industry's compliance with the Children's Television Act of 1990. Among other provisions, the act was written to encourage more and better educational and informational programming to the nation's young. Markey said that with passage of the 1990 act, Congress had anticipated "new, creative, and innovative programming, the dawn of a new era," but that with few exceptions, the industry once again had been dismissive, if not contemptuous. The open television marketplace Reagan's FCC had so energetically built continued to flourish—but the bottom line, not the needs of the young, was its master.

"Last year I said that children's television was the video equivalent of a Twinkie," Markey said. "This year the Twinkie is served with an occasional vitamin, but most children's television today remains the equivalent of a trip to Toys 'R' Us. A recent ad pointed out that children will be responsible for $130 billion of their parents' purchases this year. They will buy billions of dollars of toys, and they will see approximately one hour per week of children's educational programming."

Loesch respectfully begged to differ. She cited Fox programs she deemed educational, among them her Saturday morning cartoon version of *Where in the World Is Carmen Sandiego?*, the Public Broadcasting System series. She noted the Peabody Award she'd won for Fox's *Totally for Kids* messages, commercial-length segments within programs that advised on such matters as recycling, baby-sitting, and fire safety. "But if all we can be is 'school on TV,' " she said, "we will lose our attractiveness, and lose our audience. If we can't entertain first, we will not be able to capture children's attention in order to educate them."

Loesch turned to *Power Rangers*, which appalled critics even as it continued to mesmerize kids. "We knew that children would delight in *Power Rangers* from the moment we screened it," Loesch said, "but we felt that the show's live-action format warranted some reminders." Those were in the form of public service announcements Fox prepared for each episode to teach children to differentiate between fantasy and reality "and suggest nonviolent means of conflict resolution," Loesch noted. Left unsaid was the fact that violence was the only means the rangers used in resolving their differences with Rita Repulsa's forces. And karate was the least of it. Rangers had many ancient and modern weapons at their disposal, and no fight scene was complete without a pyrotechnics display rivaling anything ever seen on children's TV.

Loesch ended by presenting three unsolicited letters received by Fox. One was from parents of a five-year-old Maryland boy. Had he not watched *Power Rangers,* they wrote, he might have lost his life when struck by a minivan. He suffered only cuts because, the parents claimed, in the instant he was midair he perfectly executed an acrobatic maneuver he and his siblings had seen on *Power Rangers.* "They are fond of practicing shoulder rolls, flips in the air, and a wide assortment of falling techniques," the parents reported. "Our children asked us to write to you to thank you and the Power Rangers for your role in this escape. They also want to recommend that you teach a lesson on your show about how to fall and minimize impact." Another letter was from the mother of an autistic boy who, it was claimed, had learned to dress himself and make his bed only after the show had been introduced as incentive. The last letter was from a preacher who despised Fox's adult fare but admired *Power Rangers* because "1), it teaches kids that you don't have to destroy an enemy unless necessary to protect others, 2), they fight monsters and not people, 3), they slowly increase their power instead of blowing their enemy away at first glance." One could only imagine the preacher's sermons.

▪

As much as they may have respected Loesch personally, critics were not moved. They did not believe that Fox, or most other providers of children's programming, were committed to educational TV. And the truth was incalculably more millions were to be made from *Power Rangers* than *Bill Nye the Science Guy.* This had always been the general rule in television; the eighties and nineties merely opened the door to greater profits and more players. By and large, Hollywood producers stuck to the proven formulas: action-oriented animation, often derived from the comics, that easily translated into (or from) toys. There was a deeply entrenched mind-set in the industry that educational TV could not be entertaining, and that even if it could, children would avoid it since it would require some degree of work, which belonged in the classroom.

"I believe programmers and advertisers are sensitive to parents' concerns, but the sad truth is educational shows don't deliver the ratings," Allen Bohbot, president of a production and media-buying firm, told *Advertising Age* in 1994. "These kids have seen it all. They don't relate to feel-good shows filled with sweetness and innocence. It's not our job to tell kids what is or what isn't good for them. And it's not our job to change the world from what it is to what it ought to be, simply because we aren't capable of doing that."

The Children's Television Act of 1990 required broadcasters to provide educational and informational programming to children but did not specify how many hours per week or when they should air. Broad latitude was thus given to the FCC in renewing station licenses, but the commission remained divided on how assertive it should be—indeed, whether government had the right to interfere with the free market at all. The result was what the Washington, D.C.–based Center for Media Education, a new watchdog group, documented for Markey's hearing. The center found that broadcasters in their renewal applications were claiming such programs as *G.I. Joe* and *The Jetsons* were "educational," and that many of the legitimately educational programs were produced on budgets a tenth or less of those of such shows as *Power Rangers,* had little or no promotional support, and were aired at six A.M. or earlier, the choice slots going to shows generating the most advertising revenue. A further hindrance was syndication, where stations routinely gave preference to programs that came with guaranteed advertising. Under this so-called barter system, a large toy maker such as Hasbro would purchase a set amount of advertising time throughout a station's schedule in return for airing a show featuring the company's toys (those toys could not be advertised during those shows, only before or after).

▪

Markey's hearing had a disturbingly familiar ring. Beginning in the late 1920s, more than a decade before TV, citizen reformers with their congressional allies had attempted to improve broadcasting. Network radio was criticized as lacking quality and depth—as decidedly noneducational—and the line between commercials and shows was faulted as dangerously blurred: a "pawnshop," was one U.S. senator's description of the airwaves in 1930. Chastened by the legislation that created the FCC in the early days of Franklin D. Roosevelt's presidency, and fearing further government regulation under the new commission, CBS chief William S. Paley in 1935 voluntarily announced new standards for his network, including time limits on commercials and a list of themes (gangsterism and disrespect for parents among them) that were off-limits for children's programs. Paley's competitors saw this as grandstanding and did not follow suit.

"Let's not go 'sissy' with the kids or they won't listen now—or when they grow up," one NBC executive commented. "We still want to raise kids with some adventure and fight and imagination. The best way to plan programs for youngsters is to let them judge." If it had been sixty years later, it could have been Allen Bohbot speaking. After CBS began to lose its children's adventure shows (and their advertising) to NBC, Paley began to ignore his own standards.

Little had changed by the 1960s when, distressed by the violence and overload of commercials to which young TV viewers were being exposed, Peggy Charren and her pioneering Action for Children's Television (ACT) began to pressure Washington. Charren and her allies believed the broadcasting industry would not reform itself, no more than steelmakers and chemical manufacturers of the time would clean up the rivers and air on their own. Unusually tenacious, and with a flare for publicity a network executive could only envy, Charren forced the FCC to hold many hearings. Broadcasters paraded to Washington—arrogant or repentant, depending on where public sentiment was at the moment (and if there was one thing that could always be counted on, it was how fickle the public was). Charren had success: in 1974 the National Association of Broadcasters (NAB) agreed that its members would reduce commercial time on children's programs, advertise only safe products, forbid "host selling," and more clearly differentiate between fantasy and reality in ads, an obstacle Hasbro overcame with clever use of a comic book when relaunching G.I. Joe in 1982.

Much of what ACT accomplished was undone under Reagan. Among other deregulatory developments, the FCC repealed a 1974 policy encouraging stations to air educational programs, and an antitrust action by the Federal Trade Commission against the NAB prompted it to disband its code in 1983. Worn down after so many years in the trenches, Charren went into semiretirement, leaving only a few liberal congressmen, academics, and the newly founded Center for Media Education to carry on. The free-market sweepstakes Reagan set in motion led to a momentary resurgence of public protest that resulted in the 1990 act. Enforcement, limited though it was, was placed in new jeopardy when Markey's party lost control of Congress in 1994 to Republicans intent on eliminating federal subsidies to public broadcasting. A sign of the times was the appearance of real-life Power Rangers on Capitol Hill in January 1995. There, at the invitation of new House Speaker Newt Gingrich, the rangers entertained the children as Republican representatives were sworn into office.

▪

As Saban's show shot to the top of the ratings in fall 1993, reports began to surface of young viewers imitating the Rangers on playgrounds and in schools. They were not demonstrating how to miraculously survive near-death experiences with minivans. They were practicing karate on their peers.

In the three decades that TV had been a fixture in American childhood, only one issue had generated more controversy than the quality of programming and advertising, and that was the effects of television violence on children. The First Amendment was more directly at stake, and the debate over what constituted quality shows paled in comparison with the heated arguments over what violence was exactly, never mind whether it caused viewers to be more aggressive. After decades of hearings, commissions, and governmental, academic, and private research, the gulf between television executives and their critics remained wide.

Loesch was a rarity: a powerful member of the industry who admitted to searching her soul. "I've actually lost a lot of sleep over it," she acknowledged, noting that she had rejected shows offered to Fox after judging them to be excessively violent. She did not put her most popular show in this category. "I really in my heart of hearts don't think what we're doing is hurting kids," she said. "I don't believe that the violence in *Power Rangers* is causing violent behavior or altering behavior." Nonetheless, after observing her son's reaction to a sneak preview, she'd considered it prudent to include public service announcements at the end of each show. "When I first brought the *Power Rangers* home and showed my son—he was four—he ran around the house, you know, imitating," she said. "I just stopped and I remember walking over and I put my hands on his shoulders and said, 'Honey, listen. You can pretend to be a karate champion, you can pretend all you want. You can jump through the air, but you can't kick the cat'—I literally said that—'you can't kick the furniture, and you can't kick other people.'"

Depending on the temperature of the debate, the purveyors of violent TV defended their shows or supported some form of restraint, usually of the other guy's programming. They cited old studies, urged new studies, and relished coming back at busybody reporters with reminders of the graphic nature of the evening news. Children's programmers pointed to adult shows as vastly more pernicious, argued that young children could reliably distinguish between real and fantastic, and questioned the responsibility of parents who did not monitor their children's viewing—a salient argument, since research both sides accepted as valid disclosed that even conscientious parents who are home with their children rarely know what they are watching all the time (children home alone, of course, had free rein). Conversely, the programmers spoke glowingly of kid empowerment and choices, as confirmed in the Nielsens. Most rejected the argument that out of an abundance of caution, programming to such an impressionable audience should err on the side of being tame or that there might be a more deeply philosophical principle involved than debating the complexities of cause and effect—that given a chance to be ennobling, they'd let money guide the way.

Defenders of the status quo trotted out the red herring of research, claiming that little or no credible evidence existed that TV violence could harm young viewers. In fact, the evidence was overwhelming— and not merely credible, but indisputable. The U.S. surgeon general, the National Institute of Mental Health, the American Medical Association, the American Psychological Association, and many distinguished university scholars all had found a link between violent television and socially detrimental behavior and attitudes. In its landmark 1992 *Big World, Small Screen,* a review of decades of TV research around the globe, the American Psychological Association concluded: "Television violence can lead to desensitization as well as to aggressive behavior. Children and adults who are exposed to television violence show reduced psychological arousal, and they are less likely than unexposed individuals to seek help for victims of violence or to act on behalf of victims." This was not the language of equivocation.

Ironically, two pieces of the industry's own research during the *Power Rangers* era wound up on similar ground. Both grew out of the same periodic national uproar, when Markey and like-minded congressmen were threatening strong measures against broadcasters—notably a ratings system and the V-chip, a device built into television sets that allowed offensive programs to be blocked. Markey and his allies sounded unusually determined this time; perhaps more research would keep them at bay.

The first study, funded by the National Cable Television Association and conducted by four major universities and a private think tank, found that virtually no violent shows portrayed violence as bad and thus something to be avoided, if not actively discouraged; it also concluded that public service announcements were ineffective in changing attitudes about violence. The second study, the University of California at Los Angeles's "Violence Monitoring Report," which was funded by Fox, CBS, NBC, and ABC, argued that the level of violence throughout TV was excessive (although diminishing), at least on the major networks. Researchers noted the vast potential of TV for good and criticized the producers of certain children's programs for failing to realize it. *Power Rangers* was singled out for especially harsh criticism. Anticipating the reaction by defenders of the show such as Loesch and Saban, UCLA confirmed that no human was hurt or killed on *Power Rangers*—but that was precisely the point: never seeing consequences, young viewers could easily come to believe that violence really wasn't so bad after all.

I V

The Wall Street Journal had checked in with its front-page examination of violence and *Power Rangers* the very day in December 1994 that Haim Saban reflected on his show. He was in his office, an expansive, expensively furnished space whose walls were covered with framed magazine articles that shamelessly glorified his success. The corporate maid brought cappuccino, and every now and then Saban glanced at a row of clocks, which told the time in several cities around the world. Through plate-glass windows, he had a panoramic view of the San Gabriel foothills, shimmering like gold in the late autumn sun.

"I'm telling you *Power Rangers* is a positive show for kids," he said. "I would challenge any of these other cartoons to have such a positive impact."

Introduced at about the same time as the program, Power Rangers toys had sold at a dizzying rate, initially outstripping master licensee Bandai's capacity to manufacture them. Parents lined up before dawn for first crack at new shipments, and a black market arose in the newspaper classifieds. "Other than the Cabbage Patch craze of '83," Toys "R" Us head Michael Goldstein told *Newsweek,* "I've never seen anything like this."

Sales exploded in 1994, and by December, toy sales were projected at nearly $300 million for the year. Merchandise from Saban's dozens of other licensees would sell at a similarly torrid pace. At royalty rates of 8 percent and more, Saban's take for 1994 alone would be tens of millions. Except for the administrative expenses of an in-house licensing division and the salaries of the flacks who helped stoke the media frenzy, it was just about all gravy.

Like his superheroes, Saban had been transformed.

Entertainment Weekly had just listed him in its annual Hollywood Power 101 Issue—he ranked ahead of Bill Cosby—and by the next fall he would have nine children's series on the air: four nationally syndicated, three on Fox, and two on the new United Paramount Network. A *Power Rangers* movie and national live tours would be in the works. Saban Entertainment's corporate headquarters would be moving to Saban Plaza, a twenty-four-story building on Westwood's Wilshire Boulevard. He would be invited with Bill Gates, Ted Turner, Michael Eisner, and others to investment banker Herbert A. Allen Jr.'s elite Sun Valley conference, and he would attend President Clinton's 1996 V-chip summit.

In December 1994, more than a year into the phenomenon, Saban had already wearied of the bad press. "There is not an episode of *Power Rangers* that doesn't teach you a lesson," he declared. And they were? "The importance of teamwork. The environment. It's a multiethnic group. It's the only show on television that has a male African American superhero." Saban's son was taking karate lessons, as Dad made a point of noting. "As the father of a six-year-old, whom I encourage to watch *Power Rangers,* any day of the year I would rather have my son run around and acting martial arts than running around shooting out of a realistic-looking wooden gun and playing cowboys and Indians," he said.

"You don't like *Power Rangers?* This is America!" he said. "What am I—in the censorship business? You don't like it—push the 'off.' "

V

POWER RANGERS TOYS were only threatening to turn the American action-figure market upside-down when Larry Bernstein and Kirk Bozigian convened a series of meetings to map out the thirtieth anniversary celebration of G.I. Joe. It was the second half of 1993, the year of trouble; Joe's thirtieth was in 1994. Bernstein had wanted to spend $2 million on events, but with his division's worsening performance, he'd cut that by over half. Still, almost $1 million could buy a respectable observance. Cone/Coughlin Communications, a Boston public relations firm, was hired to help draw up a plan.

Hassenfeld insisted on personally approving it, and he brought Verrecchia with him to the meeting at which it was unveiled. Among other events, Bozigian and Cone/Coughlin proposed an international convention in New York aboard the USS *Intrepid,* a World War II aircraft carrier made into a museum; a special coast-to-coast promotion featuring limited-edition figures; a G.I. Joe "news bureau"; and Jonathan Taylor Thomas, of ABC's *Home Improvement,* as a celebrity spokesman. The crowning touch was to be the G.I. Joe skydiving team, which would parachute into air shows coast-to-coast starting next spring. Hassenfeld wanted the skydivers to visit children's hospitals. Margaret Coughlin, a principal in the PR firm, thought that was fine. Depending on local ordinances, they might be able to drop into hospital parking lots as children looked on and TV cameras captured the excitement for the evening news. "These guys can land on a dime," Coughlin said. "It's a wonderful photo opportunity." Hassenfeld liked the skydivers and other elements of the plan but overall found it lacking.

A revised celebration was proposed at the second meeting, in early October. Hassenfeld still was not pleased. "I'm not trying to be problematic," he said, "but it doesn't knock my socks off." Not much about Joe did anymore. He believed the line was dangerously fragmented, and Verrecchia, who hardly ever ventured a product opinion, had taken to characterizing the figure as puny—Stein's bulked-up Batman was more what he had in mind.

"We don't have any real blockbuster beginning or any blockbuster event we're culminating with," Hassenfeld said. "Could you skydive into the Super Bowl?"

A deeper discussion unfolded when everyone reconvened a month later, shortly after word of Verrecchia's Greenhouse Cafe remarks had leaked out, sending fear rippling down Main Street. Desperate for some immediate sizzle in Joe, whose sales continued to fall, Bernstein's people couldn't afford to wait for X-Soldiers, which would not be ready for market until well into 1995. Nor could they rely on Bozigian's pet project, the Sgt. Savage segment, considerably closer to production but still unlikely to be available until the fall of 1994, which might be too late. Looking outside, they'd found Mortal Kombat, a wildly popular video game seemingly made for toys. Using an old trick—sculpting new heads but using existing molds for the bodies, a considerable time- and money-saver—Mortal Kombat action figures could be in stores by next summer. The latest plan called for introduction of a Mortal Kombat segment as the September finale to Joe's thirtieth celebration. Not coincidentally, the home version of Mortal Kombat II, the game, would be released then, too.

▪

Whatever else could be said about it, Mortal Kombat unquestionably had edge. The game's premise was straightforward: In a series of one-on-one fights, a demon, a four-armed monster, and seven human warriors—including Sonya Blade, a busty woman in a skintight two-piece suit—battle for supremacy in the Tournament of Death, held in some mysterious and unspecified Oriental locale. Players controlled the characters' punches, uppercuts, head butts, scissor grabs, knife throws, flame throws, harpoonings, lightning bolts, fireballs, and variety of kicks. But what most disturbed many were the so-called finishing moves: round-ending maneuvers that included decapitation, immolation, vaporization, the ripping out of hearts and spines, and Sonya Blade's specialty: the burning kiss of death. All were accompanied with realistic displays of spurting blood and mangled guts.

Tepid though they were, regulations were some control of what children saw on broadcast TV. Video games were constrained only by the inventiveness of their marketers and the laws of supply and demand. Unlike television viewers, passive by the very nature of the medium, players of Mortal Kombat and its kind were active participants in violence—rewarded with points, progression to higher levels, and championships for maiming, killing, and rendering opponents unconscious. Newly on the market, the games had not existed long enough for the sort of intensive study to which television had been subjected. Some preliminary research suggested their long-term impact—especially in light of rapidly evolving technology—would rival, and conceivably exceed, TV's. No one really knew in 1993, but concern was sufficient to put Congress into another of its lathers (hearings would lead to a voluntary rating system adopted by game manufacturers).

Hassenfeld was concerned about Mortal Kombat, too.

"I'm not sure putting it in Joe is the right thing to do, especially in the thirtieth anniversary," he said. "Your weakest link can bring you down."

Verrecchia agreed. He noted that whenever reporters examined children's entertainment and violence, "the name G.I. Joe pops up all the time."

"It's now the least violent of all," Hassenfeld said, not without a degree of truth.

■

Mortal Kombat was created inside WMS Industries, a manufacturer of arcade video games and pinball machines and an aspirant to the casino slot machine market. Inspired in part by the success of a rival company's Streetfighter II, designers Ed Boon and John Tobias had sought to utilize an emerging technology: digitized graphics, which bring the high-definition realism of videotape to a game system or computer screen. Finishing moves were an attempt to improve upon the more mundane endings of conventional martial arts contests. In those, "your character, if you've beaten him, basically just falls to the ground," Tobias said. "It started out as a joke with us talking about 'wouldn't it be cool if you could do this, you could that.' We just started going on about all these different outrageous ways of ending the match." In April 1992 a prototype was placed, without advertising or promotion, in a downtown Chicago arcade. A crowd gathered immediately, and one remained throughout the test weekend. The heart-rip finishing move drew unusually favorable reaction. "Fifteen-year-old boys are into it," Boon explained. "That's why all the *Terminator, Predator,* all the slasher movies and stuff—the shock value is a form of entertainment for these kids."

Acclaim Entertainment Inc., a $480 million (in 1994) multinational corporation that had licenses for game versions of *Rambo, The Simpsons, NBA Jam,* and many other properties, had brought Mortal Kombat into homes beginning on September 6, 1993, so-called Mortal Monday. That's when versions for Sega and Nintendo machines, the most popular platforms, went on sale. It was no ordinary game launch: Acclaim spent $10 million in an unprecedented campaign that had the unmistakable feel of Hollywood. Weeks in advance of release, the company ran teasers in movie theaters and sponsored a sweepstakes; commercials appeared on network, cable, and syndicated TV, and full-page ads in game magazines proclaimed "PREPARE YOURSELF." Retailers received thousands of counter cards, banners, and seven-foot standees of Goro, the four-armed monster, and a company that packaged ads with health tips made sure Mortal Kombat got onto high school locker-room bulletin boards nationwide. By Mortal Monday, demand was at fever pitch. Worldwide, six million home units of Mortal Kombat I eventually would be sold, and four million of its sequel, helping Acclaim to record earnings.

And the violence?

"I think these things are blown out of proportion," said marketing vice president Sam Goldberg. "As far as 'Does this game lead to other violence and other issues?' and things like that, I tend to doubt it. I really do, because I just don't think that's real. I think most people see it and have been quoted as saying: 'Hey, it's a game, what's the big deal?' "

▪

But at least one person wasn't cavalier. Producer of two Arnold Schwarzenegger blockbusters, *True Lies* and *Terminator 2,* and eager to come to terms with Hasbro for a G.I. Joe movie, Hollywood-based Larry Kasanoff had secured the screen rights to Mortal Kombat. He had much more in mind for the property than a $20 or $30 million movie. He wanted books, comics, videos, a TV special, an animated series, live-action tours, merchandise of all variety, certainly a line of Hasbro toys—all synergistically feeding one another as they built to a crescendo of profit.

"The world is intellectual properties published across all media," Kasanoff said. "The whole point is orchestrating a cross-media event, and to do that you need everyone's support. It's like getting bipartisan support in Congress." Troubled that the title's connotations might impede the cause in more conservative quarters, Kasanoff cleverly emphasized another definition of the word "mortal" in his instructions to his screenwriters and on his rounds of prospective licensees and promotional partners.

"Mortal Kombat is the oldest tournament in the history of the world, held once a generation, where a few human beings are called upon to rise to the occasion and defend the fate of the earth," he explained. "Mortal Kombat is about saving the world for mortals."

·

Hassenfeld personally approved all of Hasbro's major licenses. Mortal Kombat presented him with a dilemma. *Power Rangers* having been spoken for, Mortal Kombat was one of the hottest licenses available in fall 1993, an all-but-certain bet to add some zest to a badly flagging division. On the other hand, Hassenfeld was aware of the graphic nature of the game, even though he had not played it. After soliciting opinions from his executives and Wayne Charness (who was opposed), Hassenfeld tentatively decided to take it, on the condition that he read the script to confirm the movie would be rated PG-13. He insisted on regular briefings as the movie and toys moved toward production. And WMS Industries did not get slot machine rights to Monopoly or Yahtzee, which the company wanted as part of the deal. Reluctantly WMS agreed. They wanted the titles so badly that they were willing to wait, in the hope that Hassenfeld someday would lose his objections to the Hasbro name being associated with casino gambling.

Still, Mortal Kombat gave Hassenfeld a degree of discomfort.

"I'd like to keep it as far away from the thirtieth as we can," he said at the final G.I. Joe anniversary planning meeting. "I don't want to spend all of the time on this positive thing answering negative questions." Nor did he want Mortal Kombat introduced at February's Toy Fair, for the same reason.

Bernstein and his people stayed behind after Alan and Verrecchia left. Bernstein was worried that without Mortal Kombat, Joe at Toy Fair would be the same old story—a story that was now a threat to their very livelihoods. "There's no real meat," he said. "We've got a hole here."

"The only thing we can do is tease Sgt. Savage," said one of Bozigian's marketers.

Bernstein didn't believe that would be enough. He thought they could have private showings of Mortal Kombat, by invitation to the top buyers only, and still technically be acceding to the chairman's desires. "I honestly believe we can turn the forbidden fruit into something great," he said. "Everyone loves the inside deal."

"I still have a question if we ought to do it," a salesman said.

"You have to give the kid what he really wants," Bernstein replied. "We are marketers. We are not social engineers."

10

■

THE KING LAYS AN EGG

I

The two-tier, semicircular theater known as the Tank was filled to over-flowing the morning of December 1, 1993. Larry Bernstein had summoned his Hasbro Toy Division sales force from across the continent for three days of review and planning. Behind a partitioned turntable, marketers and designers prepared their toys and rehearsed their presentations. Outside the Tank, urns of coffee, containers of yogurt, and baskets of fresh pastries and fruit had been arranged. Nearby were banks of telephones, awaiting the salesmen, who could not last much more than an hour without ducking out to check on progress of the fourth quarter, even in good times the most critical of the entire year.

Bernstein took the floor at eight. He did not have notes or a prepared speech, only a head full of numbers he knew painfully well. An exceptionally strong Christmas might save an otherwise nightmarish year, but the prospects for a miracle were dimming by the day. After the Greenhouse Cafe dinner, Bernstein had brought the forecast down $6 million more and would take another $6 million off within the week. Rumors ignited by Verrecchia's remarks had swelled to near hallucinatory proportions, and you couldn't walk the length of Main Street without hearing the latest. Bruce Stein was replacing Bernstein. Ginger Kent, Kenner's senior vice president of marketing, was replacing Bernstein. The division was being folded into Kenner. The division was being eliminated. Layoffs were imminent.

This was fact: People were testy and increasingly afraid. The G.I. Joe designers, already endowed with a distinctive brand of gallows humor, were outdoing themselves in describing how bad things were. "We couldn't sell tourniquets at the scene of a train wreck," Don DeLuca quipped. Greg Berndtson was only somewhat less grim about the prognosis. "It's coughing," he said, "but not coughing blood yet."

"We got a mountain to climb," Bernstein began. Ditomassi's games division, Kenner, Playskool, which had the Barney license—all had Hassenfeld smiling this holiday season, Bernstein said. "The one unit that's suffering is us," he said. He threw out some numbers as proof.

The Tank was deathly silent.

Bernstein repeated Verrecchia's assertion that with the division's current performance, it would be smarter to put their money into a certificate of deposit. "At the end of the day," he said, "I have to go down to Alan with his trick-or-treat bag and put something in it. If there ain't nothin' coming out—as they say in corporate parlance, you farted."

No one laughed.

"If I'm scaring you, good, because I've been scared for a long way out," Bernstein said. He confirmed that one of Verrecchia's options was closing the division, with the loss of well over one hundred jobs. "That would be a capper for my career: 'I took the Hasbro Toy Company into the toilet.' They'd have a plaque for me at the town dump."

But grim as things were, Bernstein wasn't giving up just yet. The division had a new special-feature doll and an activity toy that had tested off the charts. They had Mortal Kombat and the rights to a Streetfighter movie and the science-fiction epic *Stargate*. The problems with Soft Walkin' Wheels and Chainsaw Steel Monster had been resolved, and both were cleared for production. A number of 1993 introductions appeared headed for a strong second year.

And Bernstein had Elvis. Wave after wave of Elvis dolls, which he envisioned sweeping across the nation on a glorious promotional tide, enticing middle-aged women with memories and money to burn—up to $50 per doll. Bernstein was euphoric that morning, rhapsodizing about Elvis. He knew intimately the merchandising possibilities of high pop culture, having reaped a windfall with his New Kids on the Block figures before the rock group had faded. Elvis was forever—sixteen years after his death, research confirmed, Elvis music and memorabilia sold as strongly as ever. "The Sun Never Sets on a Legend," was Bernstein's caption for his campaign.

The dolls may well have been the finest likenesses of the singer ever brought to mass production. Their look was crafted by Shelley Smith, one of the industry's premier designers who'd researched such minute details as the decoration on Elvis's guitars and the cut of his gold lamé suit. Each doll depicted the singer at a different stage of his career: Teen Idol Elvis, Jailhouse Rock 45 RPM Elvis, Aloha from Hawaii Elvis. Wave One, the first trio of dolls, would reach market in limited quantities in late December, with national distribution no later than January 8, the fifty-ninth anniversary of Elvis's birth; assuming success, Wave Two would follow in summer, starting with the August anniversary of his death. Five waves were in various stages of development, along with an Elvis & Pink Cadillac special that would retail near $200. The basic doll cost Hasbro an average of $6.29 to manufacture (plus a 10 percent royalty to the company that managed Presley's estate); at $50 in some stores, about $10 cheaper at the big discount chains, Hasbro and the retail trade would have unusually high margins. Played right, everyone won.

"If Elvis is the hit it could be," Bernstein told his sales force, "it will cover the entire profit goal for this division." It might also offset some of the volume Power Rangers toys were poised to take from G.I. Joe, and the rest of Kirk Bozigian's action-figure lines, in 1994.

•

The U.S. Postal Service's plans for an Elvis commemorative stamp had generated enormous free publicity when, in fall 1992, Steve D'Aguanno, Bernstein's head of research and development, suggested Elvis dolls. D'Aguanno was seeking new uses for the expensive molds that made the bodies for twelve-inch-tall G.I. Joe Hall of Fame figures. Bernstein was excited immediately. In January, with the Elvis stamp selling in untold millions and media outlets tripping over each other for stories about the craze, he dispatched his girls' marketing chief to Memphis to meet with Elvis Presley Enterprises Inc., which was immediately interested. Hasbro's marketing and design departments went to work. When they saw Smith's early models a few weeks later, the people at Presley Enterprises were ecstatic—and these were not even the final outfits or head sculpt-ings. A contract was signed, with a $1.5 million guarantee. The Memphis firm's strictest artistic constraint was that no matter how many waves were produced, Hasbro must always depict Elvis as a rock 'n' roll icon, never as the pill-popping, bloated caricature he was at his death. Bern-stein and Smith, an Elvis fanatic, would never have thought otherwise.

Bernstein went in September to the Sheraton Bal Harbour, a resort on a twelve-acre private beach outside Miami, with a marketing and pro-motional plan for Elvis that rivaled Hasbro's Jurassic Park campaign. The Bal Harbour that year was the setting for Hasbro's Pre–Toy Fair, an an-nual, invitation-only precursor to February's New York Toy Fair that gave important buyers an early look at the next year's products. Their re-actions often led Hasbro to fine-tune lines and, occasionally, kill them. When Toys "R" Us talked, Hasbro listened.

The plan included nearly $2 million on TV commercials, another $1 million in print ads, and almost $1 million more in direct mailings, radio sweepstakes, and six thousand life-size standees for stores. The earliest dis-cussions of sales volume had assumed three hundred thousand dolls in each wave (one hundred thousand of three separate dolls), but those numbers were too conservative for Bernstein—each wave, he believed, could be nearly a million pieces. "Prove to me you have a business here," Verrecchia said, and Bernstein authorized the Yankelovich study. The ini-tial results, available before Bal Harbour, were disappointing: Elvis dolls would sell briskly, potentially for years, just not at the levels to which Bernstein already was committing the factories and materials suppliers in China. But Bernstein was nothing if not a gambler. Instinct told him that once in motion, the Elvis express would roll over everything in its path, including cautionary research and the skepticism of a boss whose strong point was numbers, not popular culture.

Bal Harbour was where it all was to begin. Buyers toured six large rooms of toys and then, seemingly done, were led into a darkened the-ater. A wall of video monitors sprang to life with a custom video of Elvis footage and snippets of his best-selling songs. Narrated by Kasey Kasem, the voice of American Top 40, the video closed with Kasem's pitch for Hasbro's "fully poseable, authentically detailed, stunningly crafted twelve-inch figures," a phrase that echoed of Merrill Hassenfeld's G.I. Joe, not inappropriately, considering the original use for the Elvis-body molds. The lights went up, revealing New York actresses performing the first of several song-and-dance routines, all choreographed by a New York director. It was enough to convert the buyers into true believers. "Ship me first!" they beseeched as dolls were handed over for inspection. Of the largest retailers, only Kmart, notoriously skittish with big-ticket items, was subdued. Wal-Mart's chief toy buyer, flown in on the Hasbro jet, was so enthusiastic that he persuaded Hassenfeld to rent another jet to bring the whole show to corporate headquarters, in Arkansas, so that senior management—the good ol' boys—could not possibly misunderstand what a huge deal Elvis was.

As Bernstein had predicted, the media was drawn in, too, beginning on November 8, when he unveiled the line at a press conference in Hasbro's New York showroom. Reuters, the Associated Press, and the Bloomberg business wire service covered the announcement, and *USA Today* teased its story on the front page. CNBC, CBS, CNN, and the E! entertainment cable network had stories, and network feeds brought an abundance of local pieces in twenty-four of the top twenty-five TV markets and many smaller markets as well. It seemed something more was going on than reporters happening on yet another Elvis sighting. If the unrestrained enthusiasm of their stories even remotely reflected basic consumer desire, the doll would be unstoppable.

As a lark, Bernstein put forty-five dolls on end cap at a small store in a Providence suburb the weekend before Thanksgiving—unadvertised, at $44.99 apiece. Eighteen sold within an hour, with the rest gone soon thereafter. Christmas week, again without advertising, 6,500 dolls left Wal-Mart stores; the next week, ordinarily a dead time for toys, the chain sold 9,500. By early January Elvis sales had achieved escape velocity just about everywhere. Bernstein was so encouraged that he instructed his market researchers to begin exploring twelve-inch Beatles and Marilyn Monroe dolls.

•

Elvis sales seemed only to be pausing—one of those momentary dips even hot properties experience, easily reversible by throwing more ads on TV—when Bernstein laid off twenty-two people in mid-January. This was part of the cost-cutting strategy he'd instructed his managers to devise last fall and a gesture to his boss in the wake of the Greenhouse Cafe dinner. Verrecchia was unimpressed. Most of the dismissed were lower-level workers: a sample maker, a darkroom technician, a typographer.

None were from the highest ranks, where Verrecchia believed significant change was long overdue. But Bernstein didn't have the heart to cut deeper or go after friends. He'd lost enough sleep already.

"You know, when you start talking about trimming the company," he reflected just before the layoffs were announced, "executives—to save their sanity, I guess—sit around and say, 'Well, we will take a few heads out of the business.' They speak in euphemisms, and they think they do that convincingly, so that they don't go mad. But the real issue is that sooner or later—whether it's three A.M., when CNN is on—the ghosts come into your living room and they carry their babies with them, and their wives are pregnant, and they can't get a job, and it's really tough."

Last of the Three Musketeers, Bernstein doubted even Elvis could save them now. But he still hadn't given up. When had the future in this nutty business he so loved ever unfolded according to expectation or plan? Who'd given Stephen Hassenfeld good odds back in 1975, when he'd hired Bernstein and Al Verrecchia was begging for better terms on plastic resin just to keep the molding machines going? Who ever would have believed Hassenfeld Bros. of Pawtucket, Rhode Island, would one day be the largest toy company on earth?

II

On February 10, 1994, the day before the first buyers were to visit the Hasbro showroom at Toy Fair, Verrecchia presided over a meeting in the mezzanine-level conference room where Hassenfeld had been elected chairman nearly five years before. Stein; Playskool president Dan Owen; Senior Vice President of Employee Relations and Human Resources Sherry Len Turner; a Meritus consultant; and David Hargreaves, chief financial man on Verrecchia's staff, attended behind closed doors. This was the steering committee for the restructuring Verrecchia intended for his half of Hasbro.

They were part of a larger group of senior managers that had met first in September for two days of wide-ranging and confidential discussion at a Boston hotel. Meritus had gone to Boston with an overview of the domestic toy industry, a critique of Verrecchia's operations, and a map toward a strategic vision, whose cornerstone would be internal growth leading to higher profits and thus enhanced shareholder value. With its distribution analysis as the springboard, Meritus had delved into the very core of Verrecchia's operations. The consultants found strengths, but numerous alarming weaknesses. If Meritus was to be believed, domestic toys was perilously close to crisis. Product development was haphazard, inefficient, and slow. Retail trade relations were poor, with too many late deliveries and out-of-stock items. Information systems were archaic. Training was inadequate, and leadership left much to be desired. The problems transcended those resulting from the acquisition of Tonka. And not even Kenner was exempt.

Several meetings had followed the one in Boston, and they'd brought Verrecchia to a conviction: with Hassenfeld's consent, he'd decided to build a new house.

By the time of this meeting in New York, the rough shape of the structure had emerged. Unbeknownst to anyone but the chairman and the executives at this session, Verrecchia had decided to replace his three major (and two minor) product divisions with category management, a scheme in which all research, design, development, and marketing functions would be organized under a single executive reporting to him. Similarly, all of sales would be within a unified "account management" organization. (Manufacturing and administrative services would be largely unaffected by the restructuring, and Ditomassi's games and international divisions would be untouched.) Lower-level employees would be grouped in small teams: on the category side, for instance, G.I. Joe marketers, designers, and engineers would have no other responsibilities than that toy; on account management, as an example, salesmen dedicated to Wal-Mart would sell every toy line Verrecchia had, but only to Wal-Mart.

"We don't want to approach the marketplace with G.I. Joe, Jurassic Park, Batman, and Shadow," Verrecchia told his steering committee. "We want to approach the marketplace with: What is Hasbro doing in boys' action?" Leverage, as he called it, theoretically would give the company greater clout with retailers. Buyers would be more inclined to take lower-margin staples, for fear of losing hot sellers such as Batman.

"This is not just downsizing or rightsizing or whatever else you want to call it," the Meritus consultant said.

But it was partly that. One of the goals, listed on that day's handout, was: "Rightsize/flatten the organization."

▪

Despite an atmosphere of great deliberation created by all of the flip charts, secret sessions at four locations, and hand-numbered confidential documents, Verrecchia knew early on whom he wanted as masters of his new house. He wanted Dan Owen as head of sales and Bruce Stein in charge of category management, the creative side of the business. Stein's position was the most critical of all, for while great salesmanship requires talent, the best marketing takes brilliance.

Stein had arrived at this Toy Fair the uncontested star of the corporation. His three major boys' action lines had outperformed already high expectations, helping Kenner to nearly $100 million in pretax earnings, some 70 percent of all profit in Verrecchia's half of Hasbro, and more than twenty times the $4 million (1 percent of sales, considerably less than a certificate of deposit would have earned) that Bernstein's division wound up contributing. Stein had beaten Bernstein and all other comers for the master toy license to Saban's *VR Troopers,* a TV series he hoped would cash in on the success of *Mighty Morphin Power Rangers,* which it closely resembled. Kenner was the heavy favorite to get *Gargoyles,* a Disney series Mattel coveted, and while *The Shadow,* a summer-of-1994 movie, was shaping up as a dud, Batman—which had no movie this year, but a Fox program with continued high ratings—looked good for $75 million or more. Kenner had Shaq Attack, a line of toys licensed by NBA superstar Shaquille O'Neal. Stein expected another $30 million from the second year of Jurassic Park. And Littlest Pet Shop, a line of minidolls that went head-to-head with Mattel's popular Polly Pocket, was sizzling. In appreciation for all this, Verrecchia had given Stein a $1 million bonus. Verrecchia had never rewarded anyone that handsomely. His own bonus for 1993 was only a third of that.

Far from being pleased, Stein was ticked off.

The bonus would not be his all at once, but paid over three years, an arrangement that aggravated a continuing complaint. Stein's importance to Hasbro was arguably as great as Jill Barad's to Mattel—yet his salary was $325,000, less than half of Barad's, and his total compensation paled in comparison with hers: $5.4 million. Hassenfeld didn't believe in paying that kind of money to a divisional president, a philosophy that further irked Stein in light of the nearly eleven million shares of stock the chairman and his family owned or controlled and the $872,000 salary,

$600,000 bonus, and 210,000 stock options he gave himself in 1993. Stein had been over all this before with Verrecchia—had mentioned the feelers from Mattel and especially the studios, which, with their Hollywood rates, made Barad's compensation look like chump change. He'd been over all this and gotten nowhere.

"I hate being unappreciated," Stein said. "I have told him so many times that compensation is an issue for me. And not just for me." Key designers, he noted, were approached constantly with better-paying offers to leave Kenner. "I'm talking people out of it all the time," he said.

Stein's displeasure went deeper than money, to Verrecchia's proposed restructuring. He believed (as Verrecchia did) that reconfiguring one-half of Hasbro without simultaneously tackling the other was foolish, although he understood that Verrecchia's hands were tied by the chairman, who was unwilling to tackle such a momentous task, with its difficult personnel choices, in one fell swoop. He did not think integrating preschool into the markedly different business of promotional toys was smart, nor did he believe sales should be separated from marketing and development to the extent Verrecchia proposed. Were he in charge, Hasbro would have a handful of executives at the very top, with three presidents just below: of toys, games, and international. He saw himself in charge of toys, if not more.

"Nobody knows right now if it will work," Stein told Verrecchia at the Toy Fair meeting, "but we've got a lot of smart people who'll make it work as best they can."

In early 1994, before a representative of Ron Perelman's Marvel Entertainment Group quietly got in touch with him, he still counted himself in their camp.

III

TO THE WORLD AT LARGE, it was the same old Larry Bernstein who rolled into New York that February in a limousine from Pawtucket. He'd swapped his jeans and sweater for a suit, as he traditionally did for Toy Fair, and he was brimming with fresh stories and jokes. He worked the showroom masterfully, all smiles and radiant enthusiasm for a terrific new Hasbro Toy Division line. Even Toys "R" Us chairman Charles Lazarus, notorious for demanding low prices, could not rattle him.

"How much?" Lazarus asked, picking up a Cabbage Patch Baby Surprise doll.

"Twenty-one," Bernstein said.

"You're kidding. That's a joke."

"It's not," Bernstein said.

"There's a fifteen-dollar rebate in the box," Lazarus quipped. Of course there was no such thing. "It's not going to sell," Lazarus declared.

That was Charles. Starting in 1948 with the National Baby Shop, a children's furniture store in Washington, D.C. (where his father had a bicycle repair business), he'd built Toys "R" Us into an $8 billion chain with more than nine hundred stores in the United States and twenty foreign countries. He could be forgiven if he spoke with assurance about a toy's prospects at retail. And Bernstein, who'd known Lazarus for decades, could be forgiven if he respectfully disagreed with the chairman's obsession with rock-bottom pricing.

One afternoon after the buyers had cleared out, bound for the restaurants and bars, Bernstein gathered his top people to review the overall reaction. This would be a blue-collar year, he said—a lot of hard work with the prospect of a decent wage and maybe more. "You've got an opportunity," he said. "Talk up your successes."

He was worried about Elvis, more than he let on. By late January that momentary dip had become a two-week slide at Wal-Mart; Bernstein had upped the advertising, to no effect. No one was panicked, but the seeds of doubt were sown, on characteristically fertile soil.

For this, after all, was the toy business, where expectations created by manufacturers regularly came back to haunt them. Even Stephen Hassenfeld, with his Jem and his Maxie, had learned this the hard way . . . and still never really learned it at all. What if Elvis sales kept dropping? the retailers were beginning to worry. What if a few weeks of Wave One hadn't whet this ferocious appetite Bernstein had made them believe in—but taken the edge off it altogether? Who would buy the hundreds of thousands of dolls collecting dust in their warehouses? One solution would be to drop the retail price, thereby forcing Hasbro to make amends with markdown money or free goods. That would be fine by the likes of Charles Lazarus, who'd mastered the art of turning adversity to his advantage—but for Bernstein, it would mean undercutting his margins, thereby compromising, if not ruining, the multimillion-dollar advertising on which future waves depended. It was indeed a vicious circle, one

Bernstein had seen before. "We're promoting a phenomenon and we're not creating a phenomenon yet," he said. As Toy Fair dragged to an end, he was pleading with buyers to hold their prices. But already there was word from the West Coast that a small chain had broken ranks.

Bernstein's hopes for Elvis now were less that success would save his presidency than buy time for his people—provide breathing room to re-demonstrate their worth. By Toy Fair, Bernstein was privately resigned to a reduced role, or no role, in Verrecchia's new toys organization.

▪

Verrecchia had invited Bernstein to the first strategic sessions, and as winter neared and the future took shape, Bernstein had made good on his August 1990 vow to speak his mind. He was skeptical of the concept of leveraging and, like Stein, did not believe promotional and preschool toys made for a good marriage. "You cannot explain to me, none of these consultants can explain to me, nor will I accept their explanation," he'd said as a whole room listened and his boss simmered, "how you can make Playskool more competitive to Fisher-Price by putting it in this part of an organization. There is a guy at Fisher-Price who gets up every morning. He is called a CEO, and he dies for Fisher-Price. They have a sales organization that does nothing but sell Fisher-Price. Their leaders do not have this combined so-called mix of responsibility for the rest of the product line. You don't get down into the lower ranks and have a sales-person who's calling on a small account who is carrying the entire line."

After that, Verrecchia stopped inviting him to meetings. Which was all right by Bernstein, for it was one less demand on his time, already stretched thin by his new passion, Hasbro's virtual-reality game project.

Whatever pleasure Bernstein derived from his job these days came from Sliced Bread. This, not Elvis, was the real pot of gold at the end of the rainbow—an affordable system enabling players wearing head-mounted displays to experience the illusion of being inside three-dimensional worlds. Neither Sega nor Nintendo had brought such a machine to market, although both wanted to. Bernstein's hopes were pinned on a unique multimedia microprocessor—a microchip—and Hasbro's technology partner, David Sarnoff Research Center, the Princeton, New Jersey, firm that invented color TV, among many other marvels of the age.

"I'm absolutely thrilled," Bernstein said. "I want to do this one project, and God, I really want it to work."

If it did, it would be more than a laurel for him and for Hasbro. It would fulfill an old friend's dream. Unable to find a distinctive entry into the booming video-game market of the early eighties, Stephen Hassenfeld had seen frustration become smiling fate when Milton Bradley was put into play. But acquiring the games company did not dissuade him from his belief that video games, despite their erratic performance, were a serious, long-term threat to traditional toy makers. Even after abandoning NEMO, at a loss of $20 million, Stephen had not given up. "We will continue to look at technology," he'd said when announcing NEMO's demise shortly before his death. Sliced Bread was Hasbro's first try since.

Even Verrecchia was bewitched by virtual reality, so much so that he'd helped persuade Alan Hassenfeld of Sliced Bread's merit, despite strenuous objections by O'Neill and Alperin, who as head of NEMO had learned some bitter lessons about hardware. Verrecchia had already spent some $25 million on Sliced Bread and was prepared to spend tens of millions more, an astounding gamble, by toy company standards, on an unproven concept. Maligned as a bean counter, Verrecchia had a reputation as someone who avoided risk. Undertaking Sliced Bread had already proved the reputation wrong. Shepherding it to success would do far more. It would establish Verrecchia as a daring pioneer—in product, of all things.

I V

NEARLY A MONTH AFTER Toy Fair, Verrecchia summoned his senior and middle-level managers to the Tank for a firsthand presentation of what had been accomplished at all those closed-door meetings, by now the subject of rampant speculation on Main Street. Bernstein greeted Stein, who was fresh off a plane. Bernstein's worst fears about Elvis had materialized, with the retail price having dropped as low as $19.99 in some outlets, a desperate situation that created the perverse phenomenon of negative sales one week at some Wal-Mart stores when angry shoppers demanded $20 refunds for dolls they'd purchased at $39.99. The whole corporation knew Elvis was dead, but Bernstein, never a whiner, put a good face on things. He shook Stein's hand, and the two traded small talk as they found their seats.

Never loose before a crowd, Verrecchia, tanned from his annual Caribbean vacation, was unusually intense that morning. Wayne Charness had been conscripted to supervise the audiovisuals and provide a postpresentation critique for tomorrow, when Verrecchia would bring the rank and file up-to-date in a cafeteria session that would be videotaped for those unable to attend. Internal communication, albeit on Verrecchia's terms, was one of the principles the steering committee had agreed to at its Toy Fair meeting.

"We are still the number one toy company in the industry," Verrecchia began. He acknowledged, however, how close the leaders were. Hasbro had closed 1993 with record sales of $2.747 billion; Mattel, now the parent of Fisher-Price, with a record $2.704 billion, a mere whisker behind. And Mattel had the license to the movie expected to be the children's blockbuster of the year, Disney's *Lion King.* It was not inconceivable that for the first time since Stephen's fabulous run, Mattel this year could be bigger than its rival. Still smarting from losing Tonka, Amerman was making good on his promise to Wall Street that Mattel would find other ways to aggressively grow.

Verrecchia outlined the trends in U.S. toy manufacturing and retailing. One of his slides showed market share in traditional toys: in the last eight years Hasbro's had increased from 12 to 17 percent, Mattel's from 8 to 15 percent. Just as in the cola wars, Verrecchia noted, "the trend of industry consolidation is likely to continue, with one company emerging as the dominant player." Similarly, Target, Kmart, Wal-Mart, and Toys "R" Us, the top four toy retailers, were amassing market share and now accounted for two-thirds of all business from Verrecchia's factories; the top ten totaled 79 percent. The days of the mom-and-pop toy store were strictly numbered.

"Our strategic goal is straightforward: to be the dominant player in the traditional toy industry in 1997," Verrecchia said. That meant increasing his operation's revenues from $1.2 billion to $1.9 billion. Such growth was a critical component of Alan Hassenfeld's larger corporate objective: to increase earnings per share by 15 percent a year, the expectation Hasbro had given Wall Street. Fifteen percent was a benchmark for growth companies in many industries.

Verrecchia recapped the highlights of Meritus's study and outlined the next step in the restructuring: so-called activities analysis, a computer-assisted study of what everyone in his half of Hasbro did, a prelude to the blueprint for what everyone would do. He was now open for questions.

What will the new structure look like? someone wanted to know.

Verrecchia said he didn't have a detailed plan yet—that if he did, he wouldn't be spending so much for Meritus. "I'm not afraid to rip it up by its roots and turn it upside-down, nor am I afraid to keep it as it is," he said.

Lee Bitzer, Bernstein's sales chief, wanted advice on stopping all the rumors his people were hearing in the field.

"You could start by telling people to shut up," Verrecchia said.

Another executive said many employees assumed the twenty-two lay-offs within Bernstein's division were but the first cuts in a process bound to get bloodier. Another executive called attention to a story on the front page of the statewide newspaper that morning. Providence-based Fleet Financial Group—like Hasbro, a company that recently had reported record profits for 1993—was eliminating 5,500 jobs, some 3,000 by lay-off.

Verrecchia responded that his initiative was not a head-count exercise, although layoffs could not be ruled out. "We're not targeting six months from now a Black Friday or anything like that. There isn't a day when everyone is going to wake up and their desks have all been moved around."

Stein had little sympathy for worrywarts. He reminded the room of the many ownership and personnel changes Kenner had been through over the years and of how Rhode Island essentially had been static. "In some sense," he said, "the Hasbro organization has been seduced by its own success."

•

The old presentation theater where Stephen Hassenfeld had brought G.I. Joe back to life was the setting for the activities analysis session involving some fifteen of Bernstein's top R&D people, most of whom had been with the company since Hassenfeld was alive. While one of the Meritus consultants, a pudgy-faced man barely out of college, was setting up the overhead projector, Don DeLuca entertained his friends.

Few in DeLuca's circle believed analysis was anything but a ruse, possibly to protect Hasbro against the inevitable lawsuits, in any event an insult to their intelligence. They assumed almost everyone at Kenner was safe and the consultants already had a long list of the heads that would be taken out of the Hasbro Toy Division. For some time now the guys had been joking about their future after Hasbro. "Time to get the ladder hooks back on the truck," DeLuca would say, a reference to work he'd taken restoring a house a decade ago, when he'd been laid off from his previous job. He was in rare form today: "Should the shutters be the same color as the trim? May I acquaint you with the dessert menu? May I check the oil? Looks like about a nine iron from here!"

The consultant started his slides, which explained the questionnaire they were about to fill out, subsequent steps in the three-month analysis, and the rationale behind it all. "It's a pretty open process," the consultant said. "We're not trying to hide anything here."

"This is the kiss of death," DeLuca said when he received his questionnaire, on which he was to describe what he did in a typical week.

Almost fifty, DeLuca had been at Hasbro a decade, rising from senior designer to senior design director, in charge of two dozen people. He was an expert model maker and designer of mechanisms, and his creativity had helped shape G.I. Joe, Tonka, Transformers, and many other brands in Bernstein's division and Playskool. DeLuca was something of a Renaissance man. He'd majored in sociology and engineering at Brown University and earned a master's degree at the Rhode Island School of Design, one of the nation's foremost art schools. He designed and built boats, restored cars, and, as a twenty-year-old, had crossed the Atlantic in a thirty-seven-foot yawl. He was not shy with his opinions. If a person was an idiot, he was an idiot; it was no more complicated than that.

DeLuca loathed Meritus and the people on Sherry Len Turner's employee relations staff who worked closely with the consultants. He was not alone. The sight of the restructurers on Main Street would provoke a torrent of whispered vulgarities even from ordinarily soft-spoken secretaries. Employees coined unflattering nicknames for them, ridiculed their jargon, and made special note of the fact that Turner's previous employer had been Frito-Lay, maker of corn chips, which did not exactly rank with Barbie or G.I. Joe on their list of notable achievements. DeLuca would see them clustered together at lunch and imagine they were sharing a fantasy: that soon they would don their executioner hoods, sharpen their poleaxes, and get down to what restructuring was really about.

Black humor aside, DeLuca framed the issue in moral terms. He was no stranger to such judgments, having described his own industry's role in children's lives in such stark terms at the X-Soldier brainstorming session. "Why do they have the right to fuck with people's lives like this?" he said of the restructurers. "They'll answer to a higher power someday."

∎

"We've got people deciding our fate who, I think, don't really understand our business," Kirk Bozigian said a short while later. What Bozigian didn't know was that the people who did, the influential marketers at Kenner, already believed that G.I. Joe's troubles could be laid at his feet. Their belief would only strengthen as the restructuring progressed to the point where they would question whether Bozigian even deserved a job.

Bozigian had rented a conference room at a nearby Comfort Inn and invited key people involved with G.I. Joe and other boys' toys to discuss their future—and what, if anything at this late stage, they might do to determine it. The twelve marketers, designers, and engineers here with Bozigian were angry. They were angry at Bernstein. They were angry at delays and indecision, which Bernstein's worsening prospects had exacerbated. They were angry that senior management apparently had forgotten their considerable successes in boys' toys, while Kenner's failures, such duds as Savage Mondo Blitzers (a line of characters named Bad Fart, Loaded Diaper, Eye Pus, and the like), seemed to have been conveniently overlooked. They were angry at themselves for G.I. Joe, which, in its thirtieth anniversary year, was bound for epic disaster. Bozigian related the story of how his son, Colt, six now, had chosen an X-Men figure over a Joe on his last visit to Toys "R" Us because X-Men were more exciting. "That's pretty ego deflating," Bozigian said. "But I stood there and said: 'You know, he's right.' "

They were angry that Bernstein's division, direct heir to Stephen Hassenfeld's legacy, had become the laughingstock of the corporation. "We're the patient," DeLuca said. "We're in intensive care. Everyone in the fucking hospital is going to come in and look at our guts."

Doing anything about such a mess was another matter. True, they could unite behind Sgt. Savage in an effort to convince the sales force and retail trade that the new segment was the shining future of G.I. Joe. But that alone would not satisfy the man who had Hassenfeld's ear. No one knew exactly where Verrecchia and his steering committee were heading, but the talk on Main Street was of Michael Hammer's *Reengineering the Corporation*.

Bozigian went to the blackboard and wrote: "We need balls."

"We've got to get ahead of the curve," Joe Morrone, an engineer, agreed.

Whatever happened in the coming weeks, DeLuca noted, they were in a different boat than Bernstein and his kind. The high-muck-a-mucks were financially secure. "You know what bothers me?" DeLuca said. "They walk away from this smoking heap of shit."

"And I can't send my kids to college," said sculptor Ken Ellis.

V

ALTHOUGH HE HAD personally fired people and employees had been laid off during his tenure, Stephen Hassenfeld had never subjected Hasbro to a full-blown restructuring, with its consultants, activities analyses, and widespread fears of termination. As Verrecchia proceeded, Alan had no desire to learn the gory details. Like Bernstein, many of those whose survival was in jeopardy were old members of the family.

"I have a tendency to like everybody as long as they're devoted and they're working and all of that," Alan said. "The most difficult thing for me basically has been the willingness to let the process happen without interceding. Because I'd find an excuse to intercede for everybody."

But he was sold on Verrecchia's intentions, even while visibly distancing himself from them. Verrecchia would host three cafeteria meetings before the restructuring finally went down, and there were countless other smaller sessions, but Hassenfeld attended none. His most tangible involvement was an open-door policy: making himself available, as he described it, to hold hands.

•

Outside Hasbro, Hassenfeld was still thought of as the gutsy hero of Rhode Island's ethics reform movement. It was an accurate perception. RIght Now!, the coalition he'd forcefully chaired, had succeeded in cleaning up government to a degree even the optimists had not dared hope the day a hundred church bells rang throughout Rhode Island. Thanks to the coalition's efforts, legislation had been passed and signed into law making it all but impossible for political insiders to staff state government with their cronies. Campaign finance reform had been instituted, the statewide ethics commission fortified, and four-year terms established for governor and other general officers, a change that freed officeholders from the constant fund-raising and politicking that came with biennial elections. The secretive process by which state judges were appointed had been replaced with an open, less easily corruptible system. "Rogues' Island" no longer worked as a knock on Hassenfeld's home state.

Mission accomplished, RIght Now! had faded, liberating Hassenfeld for other agendas. As Meritus and Verrecchia's steering committee moved toward denouement, Alan went to Washington to receive an award from the Consumer Product Safety Commission for the Playskool 1-2-3 High Chair and was called "one of the truly good guys" among manufacturers of children's goods by the commission's chairman. He spoke with Sarah and James Brady at an antigun rally at the State House and greeted President Clinton when he journeyed to Rhode Island to promote a national health care plan. The Urban League recognized his philanthropy, and Johnson & Wales University awarded him an honorary doctorate.

But more than anything, it was the hospital he and his company had played such a major role in getting built that delighted him during that time. He could not talk about the Hasbro Children's Hospital without becoming highly animated—both feet tapping madly, his words rushed, his face refreshed by a boyish grin. Hassenfeld had not only committed $2.5 million to the building and, quietly with his family, another $1.5 million to establish a chair in pediatrics at the Brown University School of Medicine—he had promised his involvement would not end with a ribbon cutting. He'd vowed to be a supporter through the years. The early returns showed he was a man of his word.

"This happens once in a lifetime," he'd said shortly before the hospital was dedicated, early in the year. "This is something no one can take away from us. This is pure. Sometimes dreams do become reality."

11

■

BLACK TUESDAY

I

Alan Hassenfeld seemed equanimous, even gregarious, when he arrived at the Tank for the Hasbro Toy Division's management line review at the end of the first quarter of 1994. He'd just returned from Cincinnati, where he'd had bountiful praise for Bruce Stein's new product line. It was still chilly enough for a scarf, and Vivien must have been out of town, for he was wearing blue jeans. All of Hasbro Inc.'s top executives were on hand.

"Good morning!" the chairman said after settling himself at the center seat at the horseshoe-shaped main table.

"Good morning, Alan!" said some three dozen executives, designers, salesmen, and lawyers. A first-grade teacher could not have hoped for better from her class.

Cabbage Patch was the first line presented. It was quickly apparent how long the day was going to be. Hassenfeld liked some of the dolls for 1995 but hated one called Baby Go Bye Bye and was visibly angered by Pretty Sew 'N Style, which reminded him of Hassenfeld Bros.' 1950s sewing kits.

"It just looks old and tired," Alan said. "Darn it, make it contemporary!"

Things improved momentarily after Cabbage Patch. Hassenfeld liked a doll called Twist 'N Style Tiffany, although he considered the packaging "amateurish," which it was. He applauded the concept and price of No More Boo Boos Betsy but thought the color-change effect lacked the drama for a good commercial. "There is something missing," he said. "You in marketing have got to think: How do you capture [excitement] on the camera?"

Bernstein had pretty much held his tongue. He was counting on the next item on the agenda, Dr. Hallie's Hospital, a girls' line, to score with the chairman.

Bernstein had flipped when he'd first seen the concept, brought to Hasbro from an outside inventor, two months ago. He was convinced it was that most precious of commodities, a truly revolutionary toy—the first, to his knowledge, to combine the girls' play pattern of nurturing with superheroism, the domain of boys. The idea was deceptively simple: Women are the surgeons, radiologists, pediatricians, nurses, and everyone else in position of authority at a big-city medical center. Bernstein was so excited, he intended to call Margaret Loesch, who surely would want Dr. Hallie's Hospital as a Fox series. "The network will go absolutely bananas over an issue like this," he'd said. He spoke of breaking paradigms, of complex levels of meaning for girls and their mothers, of romance, conflict, and resolution. "This is not 'Hi, what did you have for lunch?' This is 'There was an earthquake! Get the OR ready! I've been operating twenty-four hours already!' All this heroic stuff," Bernstein had said in a meeting preceding today's that Hassenfeld had not attended. "You just wrap yourself in mom and apple pie with every mother, every feminist."

One of Bernstein's marketers set the stage for Hassenfeld. "Women are the ultimate heroes," she said, "because women are the ultimate caregivers." After screening a video, the marketer and a designer brought out models of the toys: small play sets and figures about the size of 3¾-inch G.I. Joe. The initial offerings would include an operating room, nursery, and pediatrician's office; assuming success, the concept would be broadened in later years. Bernstein asked Hassenfeld for his reaction.

"Dito?" the chairman said.

Ditomassi said he really liked it but wanted to know why Bernstein was not targeting boys, too.

Hassenfeld agreed. "It's a great, great concept. Why are you cutting your market in half?"

Bernstein explained this was superheroes for girls, not boys.

"Where the hell is the dollhouse?" Hassenfeld said. "I don't think you're going to show the trade your conviction unless you're willing to step up to the bar." He wanted something, like a deluxe G.I. Joe or Barbie play set, that had gigantic presence on a shelf. Parents looked for big boxes for Santa to leave under the Christmas tree.

Bernstein explained that the smaller play sets could be placed together on a table or the floor—creating a dollhouse without walls, as it were.

"You're underwhelming me," the chairman said.

"Let me go through this without you reacting."

"I have reacted." Hassenfeld made a crack about this being a monarchy, but it did not relieve the tension. People were frozen in their chairs. Within minutes word would travel down Main Street to the far ends of headquarters that things were getting nasty in the Tank.

Close friends had urged Bernstein not to tangle with the chairman when he was on one of his tears, but Bernstein this time did not heed. He didn't believe Hassenfeld understood Dr. Hallie's Hospital. He rearranged the figures and began again: "This is very much like room settings—"

Hassenfeld cut him off. "I'm not going to argue this out in public," he said, furious, "but I'll tell you I think you missed some huge window of opportunity."

"We're arguing semantics," Bernstein said.

"Give me a center."

"Fine, we'll give you a center."

"I really do feel passionate that you do need something to bring it together," Hassenfeld said, calming. "And you need it in the first year."

The chairman always met privately with his divisional executives after management line reviews for a second, often more candid, critique. Bernstein came to his office the next day. Hassenfeld praised a number of lines, including Mortal Kombat, to which he'd given final approval. "The script is pretty special," he said. "It has mystical undertones. It's not maiming, killing, anything like that . . . there's not a gun in it." He gave G.I. Joe fair marks, having been unimpressed yet again by the basic 3¾-inch segments but pleased by where Kirk Bozigian was taking Sgt. Savage and X-Soldiers. But Hassenfeld was no happier today than yesterday with several other lines. "I gave you the lowest rating I've ever given a product: a zip," he said of In My Pocket. Along with reinsisting on a dollhouse, he rejected the medical play set's name, Dr. Hallie's Hospital. And he, and Verrecchia, were still ticked off at the packaging for Twist 'N Style Tiffany.

"That package stunk," Verrecchia said. "That package never should have got to a management review."

"It was a judgment call," Bernstein said. He promised to change it.

Hassenfeld wouldn't let go. He was troubled that the package had proceeded so far through development without someone seeing what was so evident to him. "We've got to be demanding of our marketing people," he said. "They should have an answer for every question we could ask. No different from when I prep for an analysts' meeting, when they do their darnedest to trip me up."

Hassenfeld went through the rest of his notes, and the meeting was over. "Some really exciting fun things," he said, "and some lemons."

"Hey," Bernstein said. "You have to kiss some frogs."

■

As his faith in the Hasbro Toy Division had dwindled in 1993, Verrecchia had prepared Hassenfeld for the possibility that Bernstein might have to be replaced. It was a slow process, for this was not just anyone. Bernstein's roots at Hasbro were almost as deep as Alan's. He'd been there when Stephen died. He liked Alan, and Alan liked him. They shared a love of good times, a passion for toys, and an aversion to hurtful personnel decisions. It was not lost on Verrecchia that Alan had taken fourteen months after Stephen died to name his own team—and that when he had, he'd fired no one. Verrecchia built his case on the division's numbers, increasingly disappointing as 1993 had progressed and likely to be worse in 1994.

One afternoon in April, sensing Hassenfeld was finally resigned to the inevitable, Verrecchia went next door to his boss.

"Alan," he said, "I'm going to talk to Larry tomorrow."

Hassenfeld did not object. Hasbro's arteries were clogged, nowhere worse than in the Hasbro Toy Division. Bypass surgery was clearly indicated.

The next morning Verrecchia called Bernstein into his office. "Larry," he said, "I think the time has come."

He did not need to say more. Bernstein had been expecting this call for some time now, and he immediately offered to step down. Verrecchia said he was not naming a replacement; until the restructuring was in place, the division would be run by senior vice presidents reporting as a group to him. Bernstein's sole responsibility from now on would be Sliced Bread. He would keep his office, his pay, and his benefits. He would keep a measure of dignity.

Contrary to what many would believe, Verrecchia did not delight in moving Bernstein aside; they did, after all, go back a long way and Bernstein was a good guy who told one hell of a story. But Verrecchia did not have remorse; if anything, he regretted not having moved sooner. "I tried to give Larry and that team an opportunity," he reflected later. "I think we gave them too much time relative to the company. Why? I don't know—friendship, loyalty, been around for a while, give him a shot. Who the hell knows why? Why do you keep the quarterback in that one more game—then you say, 'Hey, I should have hung it up.' "

Bernstein's ego took a blow, but there was also relief, even a sort of welcome (if fragile) tranquillity, as when the guns have been silenced after a terrible battle. The fate of his division was completely out of his hands now, he'd done all he could, and Sliced Bread was getting more and more exciting. Scheduled for release in late 1995, the game had the potential for billions of dollars in sales and millions in pretax profit. For a new-product company, the rewards would be more than monetary: the big risk takers attracted the best inventors, the ones most likely to come up with the next G.I. Joe or Barbie. For Bernstein, who'd had charge of the project from the start, it was one more shot at glory.

"I'm on my last quest, so to speak," he said. "The lights are showing green all the way down the line."

What he did not know was that Verrecchia already was quietly looking for someone else to handle his $25 million-and-quickly-growing bet, now the largest such in Hasbro history.

II

AS SUMMER NEARED, Kirk Bozigian was beginning to believe no job was safe, but he remained optimistic he would have a position when the dust had settled. No question G.I. Joe had suffered of late, but Bozigian had sixteen years of exemplary service to Hasbro, and he was sure that still counted. He'd conceded mistakes in Joe and written a strategy guide, more than an inch thick, on how to rebuild his beloved brand.

Substantial progress had been made since last August's Greenhouse Cafe summit. Hasbro's lawyers had drafted a contract with *Mortal Kombat* producer Larry Kasanoff to produce a G.I. Joe film for Warner Bros., at no cost to Hasbro, and a writer was deep into a script. Kasanoff had plans for a video game and live tour, among other attractions. Griffin Bacal Inc.'s Sunbow Productions was arranging financing for a new G.I. Joe television series—for Fox or the new Warner or Paramount networks, they hoped. Dark Horse, a hot West Coast firm, was eager to replace Marvel as publisher of the Joe comic. And Sgt. Savage, the freshest new look in Joe in years, was cleared for production. It was scheduled to reach the market in January 1995, giving the sales force the remainder of 1994 to clean retail shelves of old Joe. Bozigian's biggest setback had been X-Soldiers. Shown prototypes, boys in focus groups had been disinterested. The concept needed work, and the line was unlikely to reach market before the summer of 1996, if then.

One morning in May, Bozigian walked from his office to a presentation theater in a newly renovated section of corporate headquarters. He was wearing a thirtieth anniversary denim shirt and carrying a stack of documents. Bozigian greeted the senior members of the Hasbro Toy Division's sales force and passed out condensed versions of his strategy guide. He acknowledged the sorry state of Joe at retail, then informed the salesmen that of 257 action-figures lines introduced from 1982 through 1993, only 28 had been successful. "You know what the batting average is?" he said. "One oh nine. That's how treacherous this is." The salesmen and -women hardly needed reminding.

Bozigian's chief marketer on Joe, Vinnie D'Alleva, who was wearing a thirtieth anniversary watch and ring, walked around the room, handing everyone a manila envelope that was marked "Top Secret" and sealed with a gold stamp.

"Don't open this," he said. No one did.

Bozigian was an armchair military historian. He had an extensive home military library, and one of his favorite activities was reading about Napoleon, MacArthur, and other great generals. He often quoted from their writings or speeches during G.I. Joe presentations, and he liked to think his marketing campaigns owed a small debt to their thinking. He reminded the sales force of all the headlines D-Day had been getting lately as the fiftieth anniversary of that heroic landing drew near. "We've taken a look at all that and said: How do we bring G.I. Joe back to his military roots?" Deafening sound filled the room as the monitor flickered on. The Griffin-Bacal ad agency had prepared a sizzle video, designed to kindle interest in a new product. It featured World War II combat footage intercut with scenes from the movie *Patton,* in which George C. Scott plays the title role. "From out of the past to save the future!" the narrator announced as the camera zoomed in on Sgt. Savage figures.

"The documents we handed out to you can now be opened," D'Alleva said when the video ended. "It has secret information on how Sgt. Savage was developed."

The sales force found a five-page marketing plan inside their envelopes. The cover was a color rendering of Savage by Joe Kubert, the legendary artist whose *Sgt. Rock,* a DC Comics title, had been one of the most popular World War II comics during Bozigian's youth. Bozigian had hired Kubert to draw the new line's package art. His participation was prompted by more than nostalgia. Bozigian's resolve to create Savage had strengthened considerably last year with the rumor (still unsubstantiated) that Warner was making a *Sgt. Rock* movie starring Arnold Schwarzenegger. Mattel supposedly was willing to pay a staggering $5 million up-front guarantee for the rights to the toys, which would be targeted at the heart of the action-figure market, one of the last categories (with games) where Mattel remained a weakling.

D'Alleva held a Savage figure next to a basic Joe. Savage was taller by about three-quarters of an inch and substantially beefier. "This is not a puny G.I. Joe anymore," he said. "He's muscular. He's heavy-duty." Finally, a line with edge. "This is hard-core—down-and-dirty, gritty military," D'Alleva said. "We've even got bullet holes in the packaging."

Bozigian told the Savage story, which he, D'Alleva, designer Greg Berndtson, and others had concocted over the last year: In June 1994 a Joe squad discovers a mysterious frozen tomb in a secret medical laboratory in Berlin. Its occupant, an American G.I. captured by a mad German fifty years ago, is flown to Langley Air Force Base, where scientists revive him. "Robert Stephen Savage, a man out of time, is reborn," Bozigian said. "He does not understand what women are doing in the military. He doesn't understand why soldiers don't salute snappily when an officer walks in the room. He has totally different values." Savage favored World

War II vehicles and aircraft, outfitted with the weapons of today, an incongruity no more outrageous than teenagers metamorphosing into Power Rangers. Savage fought with his Screaming Eagles, a band of contemporary military renegades, against the forces of General Blitz and his I.R.O.N. Army—who suspiciously resembled, but were not identified as, Nazis. Bozigian had his sensitivities.

"It's time for something bold, guys," Bozigian said. "This is bold."

"And it's only the beginning," D'Alleva added.

In closing, Bozigian talked of the corporate microscope everyone in the room was under, especially now that Bernstein was no longer divisional president. Famous on Main Street for his unconventional attire—he favored psychedelically bright colors and hardly ever wore a jacket or tie—Bozigian had outdone himself today. He removed his denim shirt, revealing a white T-shirt underneath. He turned so the salesmen could read what was printed on back:

> Bottom of the Ninth.
> Down by three.
> Bases loaded.
> Full Count.
> Two outs.
> . . . NO FEAR!

Bozigian reminded the room of the emotionally charged speech he'd delivered before Toy Fair. In it he'd quoted General Creighton Abrams ("They've got us surrounded again . . . the poor bastards") and urged the sales force to be aggressive with the buyers in New York. " 'Attack' is the theme," he'd said at that earlier meeting, "not just for boys' toys, but for the Hasbro Toy Division. When you walk into Puppy Surprise, think attack. When you go into Treasure Rocks, attack. Elvis, attack. Makeup Beauty, Fantastic Flowers, Real Power Toolshop, Fashion Plates, attack!" Bozigian had had the entire sales force shouting with him: "Attack! Attack! Attack!"

Sgt. Savage was worthy of a new cry, Bozigian said today. "No fear!" he shouted.

"No fear!" the salesmen shouted back.

"No fear!" Bozigian shouted louder.

"No fear!"

"I just don't see it," an executive for Target, a Big Four account, said when the room had quieted. He could not but think of Elvis.

■

Bruce Stein was all business a week later when he arrived at a Holiday Inn near Rhode Island's principal airport for the third meeting of the category (or product) management design team, which he chaired. A second team, headed by Playskool president Dan Owen, was working separately on a new sales department. Verrecchia had given them broad authority not only to come up with the final blueprint for his new domestic toys organization, but to decide who would have positions and who would not.

"If you're into pain avoidance," Stein said, "this isn't the place to be."

Verrecchia had created the teams in April. Fresh fear had gripped Main Street with their announcement. "Not being on a team doesn't mean you've been shot and should get your résumé out on the street," Verrecchia told his senior and middle-level managers from whose ranks members were chosen. But it was difficult to be blasé if you'd been passed over. And it was impossible not to believe team members had the inside track to the best positions in the new organization. Stein's top two marketing people were on his team, as was Playskool's marketing head, Sharon Hartley, a friend of Owen's—but no marketer from the Hasbro Toy Division. In all, six of the category team's eleven members were from Kenner, and only two from Hasbro Toy.

Stein's team and two Meritus consultants were at that day's meeting, in a hotel conference room. Stein paced as he spoke. In their two earlier meetings, he noted, they'd danced around a central issue.

"Every time Al has presented this he's said this is not about head count reductions," Stein said. "I think it should be." He reminded everyone of how he'd made Kenner lean in the immediate postacquisition period. "Nothing drives me crazier than walking around the building and seeing people who are busy but not passionately busy," he said. "The people who are watching the clock are not going to help us." He took special note of longtime Rhode Island employees, some of whom, he maintained, had been protected by heritage, not kept because they performed. Kirk Bozigian, he'd been told, belonged in this group.

"The weaker family members in the end don't survive," Stein said. "Sorry."

"Sharpen your pencils," said Hartley.

III

A FEW DAYS LATER, early in the afternoon of Friday, June 10, Stein left Kenner and drove to a small airport on the outskirts of Cincinnati. Only the man he was meeting knew what he was up to. Stein parked his car and went into the offices of Million Air, which provides aviation services to corporate clients. William C. Bevins Jr., chief executive officer of Marvel Entertainment Group Inc., had just flown in from New York. Stein and Bevins went into a room to discuss some last minute details of a contract they and their lawyers had been negotiating for weeks. Less than forty-five minutes later, the two shook hands. Bevins got back on his jet. Stein returned to Kenner.

He was in New York on Tuesday, June 14. He spent most of the day with Hasbro executives in a windowless room at Coopers & Lybrand, IBM's partner in Meritus. Verrecchia's restructuring steering committee was meeting next week, possibly to set the date for the new organization to be implemented, and Stein's category management design team was supposed to be wrapping up. Since the last meeting, the head count had risen from twenty-three to eighty-one, and names were being freely discussed, not only of candidates for termination, but of employees who would be promoted and outside executives Stein wanted to hire. The team was still dickering, and Stein was impatient. Despite all the activities analysis and examination of personnel records, he believed that it was all but impossible to make scientific decisions past a certain point.

"We may have as much luck throwing a dart," he said of junior-level Hasbro Toy Division marketers, whom no one on the design team knew, except perhaps in passing. "We can talk about this forever, trying to justify and find out what these people do." That night Stein went to the East Coast premiere of *Wolf,* the Jack Nicholson film. Nicholson, Candice Bergen, Diane Sawyer, and Home Shopping magnate Barry Diller were among those in the audience with him.

Two days later, on the morning of Thursday, June 16, Stein called Verrecchia from Cincinnati.

"I've got good news and bad news," he said.

The good news was that Stein had persuaded a vital part of the Machine, Ron Hayes, to stay at Kenner. Highly influential in the distinctive, moneymaking look of Batman toys, Hayes had been offered a job at Warner Bros.

"The bad news," Stein said, "is I've got to leave the company."

Verrecchia was nonplussed. Stein had threatened to seek greener pastures before, and knowing Bruce, Verrecchia believed he probably would again. But this was no idle threat. Marvel CEO Bevins was offering him a salary of $1 million a year, over three times what Hasbro paid, and incentives and stock options potentially worth millions more, to be the entertainment group's president and chief operating officer.

"That's quite an offer," Verrecchia said. "It kind of catches me by surprise. Give me a couple of seconds. I'll call you back." He went next door to Hassenfeld.

The power behind Marvel was Ron Perelman, its chairman and a major investor through his MacAndrews & Forbes holding firm. Perelman had come a long way since being outmaneuvered by Stephen Hassenfeld for ownership of Milton Bradley. He'd bought a cigar company and a stake in Pantry Pride, a food firm. He owned Coleman Company, a leading manufacturer of outdoor products, and Revlon Group Inc., the multibillion-dollar cosmetics firm whose spokeswoman was supermodel Cindy Crawford. He was chairman and controlling shareholder of New World Communications Group, a television producer and station owner that just the day before had announced the hiring of Brandon Tartikoff, the famously successful former NBC programmer. Marvel had an interest in Toy Biz, a medium-size toy company, and owned Fleer Corporation, which sold trading cards. Along with Warner boss Terry Semel, Perelman now counted Diller and superagent Michael Ovitz as friends. In ten years he'd made great strides toward becoming a media and merchandise mogul. He was a player now, not a pretender.

Perelman had sent out his first feelers to Stein in February. He wanted him to run Toy Biz, but Stein wasn't interested in a medium-size toy company. Marvel was another matter. Stein recognized the value of its extensive library of characters—Spider-Man, X-Men, and the Incredible Hulk were but three—and he knew exactly how to use Perelman's expanding influence to drive those characters deeper into children's culture. "Between being able to do a TV show through the New World group, to be able to do the publishing and the trading cards and the toys—I think you've got every major form of product that a child knows an intellectual property from," Stein explained. He was persuaded that Perelman, like Larry Kasanoff and like himself, understood how rapidly the old order was crumbling and what the shape of the new one would be. He did not get a strong sense that Hassenfeld did. Stein worried that Hasbro's fabulous past had hobbled it for tomorrow. He foresaw the day when traditional licensing, which had made Kenner millions and which so excited Hassenfeld, would be extinct. "You will be like the dinosaurs of the past," he said, "unless you have people who are visionary, who are willing to take a shot at investing in a vision." By itself, he did not consider Verrecchia's restructuring a vision.

■

Ordinarily unflappable, Verrecchia was stunned as the news sank in. Stein's departure would leave a huge hole at Hasbro, one not easily filled, for marketing talent of his caliber was rare. And this was a double whammy. Stein would be a competitor now, at a company that was rich with underdeveloped brands. Verrecchia and Hassenfeld considered counteroffering, but before they came up with anything concrete, Stein sent a fax confirming his resignation; already word had leaked out to Wall Street.

Given that the road to the very top had a couple of firmly anchored people in Stein's way, Verrecchia had doubted he would end his career at Hasbro, and he was certainly aware of Stein's discontent with compensation and his objections to the new structure. But he'd never expected Stein would leave at this most critical juncture, just as the domestic toy division was about to be reorganized.

"It's a significant downer," Verrecchia said a short while later. "The timing was terrible. I can tell you I've been staring at my ceiling for the last several nights thinking about it."

Stein's departure made headlines in *The Wall Street Journal* and *The New York Times* and was picked up by the Bloomberg business wire and the Associated Press. Hassenfeld was quoted in Hasbro's release. "We are sorry to see Bruce go," he said, but he implied no harm had been done: "With Kenner's 1995 product line already put together, we don't believe we will miss a beat." Hassenfeld did not mention that he'd immediately called the major studio heads with reassurances and flown out the very next week for personal visits, stopping in Cincinnati to address Kenner employees, who were as stunned as Verrecchia.

Privately the chairman was incensed. Hasbro would not have matched Marvel's offer, but Hassenfeld wished Stein had given greater notice of his leaving, which would have provided him a head start on damage control in the financial and entertainment communities. Alan empathized with Verrecchia.

"They had built up a very good rapport," he said. "At the end of the day, it was like sticking a knife in Al's back."

▪

The sting had lessened a week later when Hassenfeld convened one of his presidents' meetings, held periodically to review corporatewide strategy.

"Couple of empty seats," Hassenfeld joked.

"I'm doing my job cutting costs," Verrecchia said with a laugh. "What about you guys?"

"Let's call it Black Thursday," Hassenfeld said, "and be thankful the cloud has passed."

He was referring to more than Stein's resignation. In what would turn out to be an unfortunate coincidence, forecasts also were updated at this time, and Hassenfeld and CFO John O'Neill had chosen June 16 to announce that Hasbro expected its second quarter to be lackluster. In a morning press release, Hassenfeld predicted revenues and earnings would be down compared with the year earlier quarter, in part because Jurassic Park and Barney toys had not carried strongly into 1993. Hasbro ordinarily did not make such announcements. This was calculated to head off complete surprise, with potentially enormous damage to the stock, when the actual results were released in the middle of July. Nonetheless, shares fell $3, to a fifty-two-week low, in heavy trading on June 16.

But for O'Neill, the situation likely would have been worse.

Hassenfeld presided over financial conferences, issued press releases, and met from time to time with big investors, but it was the chief financial officer who prepared for those conferences, helped draft those releases, and was always at the chairman's side in investor meetings. O'Neill managed Hasbro's day-to-day contact with Wall Street, fielding calls from analysts and fund managers, putting the spin on Hassenfeld's announcements, and interpreting the numbers. He was well cast for his role.

Rugged and tall, with graying hair, O'Neill laughed heartily, had a good selection of jokes, and was honest, which gave him credibility. Lowering expectations was not his customary job. Since becoming CFO, he'd more often been the bearer of good news.

In the flurry of calls that began June 16, O'Neill elaborated on what Hassenfeld had said in the release. He talked about Jurassic Park and Barney and retailers' growing fondness for just-in-time inventory, which pushed shipments (and payments) into the second half. He looked ahead, toward what Hassenfeld had predicted would be modest full-year growth and a product line for 1995 that had the chairman "enthusiastic." He succeeded so well that within a few days the word on Wall Street was that Hasbro was experiencing nothing more than "a one-quarter hiccup," in the words of one analyst. O'Neill had not, of course, dwelled on the possibility that Bernstein's Hasbro Toy Division might lose money in 1994, nor had he mentioned Playskool's historically thin profit margins, which had long irritated him and were so thin this year that Dan Owen's division, too, might end the year in the red. He had not discussed his doubts about Sliced Bread or the concern he had with Verrecchia's restructuring now that Stein was gone.

Hassenfeld praised O'Neill for managing Wall Street, and the presidents' meeting moved along. There was much to discuss. Another battle was brewing in Congress over children's TV, and media specialists with Grey Advertising, which had a major account with Hasbro, joined the meeting to bring Hassenfeld up to speed. A woman from Grey said her child had come home from nursery school with a note urging parents to ban viewing of *Power Rangers,* which teachers blamed for an increase in schoolyard aggression. "Now you have mothers talking about a motherhood issue," a Grey employee lamented. "It's real bad."

The meeting ended on restructuring.

"We're going forward," Verrecchia said, "even though Bruce Stein has left the company."

"Is there a great deal of fear out there?" Hassenfeld asked.

"I would rather use the word 'anxiety,'" Verrecchia said. "Not a whole lot I can do about it." He recounted his efforts to keep employees informed, notably through his cafeteria talks, but asserted there was only so much that could be done to allay concerns. "If you sit in the men's room long enough, you hear all kinds of rumors going around," he said.

Hassenfeld asked Bob Stebenne for his observations. President of Verrecchia's Kid Dimension Division, the direct import arm of Hasbro, Stebenne had been at Hasbro many years and knew the culture as well as anyone. He was one of the few senior executives in whom rank-and-file workers regularly confided. Hassenfeld had learned to value his commentary.

"We're dealing with people's lives, and it can be difficult," Stebenne said, choosing his words carefully. So what was he hearing? " 'Cold and cruel,' " he said. " 'What happened to the old Hasbro?' " And: " 'We're all on this train and no one knows where the train is going to stop.' "

Based on what they'd been able to learn, O'Neill informed the group, Wall Street had a markedly different view. " 'We see this as a very positive event,' " O'Neill said he'd been hearing. There was a reason *Reengineering the Corporation* was a best-seller.

IV

SUMMER DRAGGED ON. New rumors sprouted, spread, and withered away, like weeds in the hot July sun. Head counts changed. Verrecchia wrestled with the vacuum left by Stein. He also found the person he wanted for Sliced Bread. Before her appointment was disclosed, on a morning in early August, Bernstein went into Verrecchia's office. Bernstein took one look at his boss's face and knew.

"This is not working, Al," Bernstein said.

"You're right," Verrecchia said.

Both agreed neither was happy. The two had been arguing a lot over Sliced Bread lately, but it was not the technical nature of the issues in dispute so much as that Verrecchia had lost faith in Bernstein.

"This is going to be very difficult for me," Verrecchia said.

"It's not going to be difficult at all," Bernstein said.

"I'm going to ask for your resignation."

"I want to give it to you." Bernstein did not know Verrecchia had found his replacement; he knew only that he was tired. "You obviously don't trust me," Bernstein said. "If you don't trust me, you're out of your mind to keep me around, and I don't want to stay. Who needs this shit? The project is too goddamn important for you and me to screw it up. Go get somebody you like and that's it. Just be fair to me. I've been here nineteen years."

Verrecchia gave Bernstein a generous severance package. But money wasn't an issue; Stephen long ago had taken care of his friend. Bernstein went from Verrecchia's office to Alan's, to thank the chairman for all the good years. The two promised to stay in touch, and Hassenfeld was adamant that, business aside, Bernstein could always count on him in time of personal need. They hugged and said good-bye.

After two decades at Hasbro, more than half his adult life, Larry was gone.

Not long after leaving, when he had more consulting opportunities than he could handle and he'd been asked to become a partner in another toy company, Bernstein looked back. He was not bitter, nor did he have regrets. He recalled the days when the Three Musketeers made the exciting calls and Verrecchia sat with his mechanical pencils and calculator off to the side. "Now it's Al's turn," he said. "He gets to set the rules. If I wasn't smart enough to play by his rules, then I should suffer the consequences. I mean, I can be angry about it. I could be pissed. I could hold a grudge. I could do everything else like that, but I cannot deny the man his right to play, to set the rules the way he wants."

V

ON ABOUT THE DAY that Hassenfeld and Verrecchia parted company with Bernstein, personnel chief Sherry Len Turner took control of a small room near her office. The room had a telephone, a table, half a dozen chairs, and a wastebasket whose paper contents were emptied into a shredder. It had no windows. Turner made the janitorial staff give up their keys. To get in, you had to see her or one of her trusted lieutenants. Turner knew about such things from her days at Frito-Lay. She called this space the war room.

Verrecchia regularly visited the war room. So did Dan Owen. He'd gone to Verrecchia after Stein resigned and asked to run marketing as well as sales. After considering his options, Verrecchia had decided to accommodate him. Owen would be president of the entire new organization—the very title Stein might have taken, had it been offered. Owen did not have Stein's flair, but he had marketing experience and his sales credentials were beyond reproach. He'd run Playskool profitably since succeeding Steve Schwartz, albeit not at levels that approached Kenner's profits or thrilled Hassenfeld or O'Neill (or Verrecchia or Owen, for that matter). Verrecchia considered Owen an excellent overall manager and feared that if turned down, he'd leave. Verrecchia could ill afford that. He had no one else like him inside his half of Hasbro, nor did he have the time to search outside. The restructuring was too far along. The Hasbro board had given its approval at its summer meeting. Along Main Street, the anxiety intensified by the day.

If the rank and file had seen the war room, anxiety undoubtedly would have become paranoia. Lists of employees with their salaries, years of experience, and titles were on one wall, the latest computer-generated charts of Owen's new organization on another. The charts showed the new structure and chains of command. Names filled many boxes, but others were empty. With mere days until the restructuring was to go down, the fate of dozens of employees remained unresolved. Some were deemed meritorious, and the only question was where they best belonged. Others had little support from Verrecchia or Owen, or their managers, and their prospects essentially depended on a convoluted process of elimination based, in part, on politics and uninformed opinion. The phone was often in use to Cincinnati. How strong is so-and-so in girls' sculpting? Is she a team player? What did his skills assessment show? Would he be willing to move? Some boxes defied filling. They would be filled later, with hiring from outside. "Fresh blood" was another goal of the restructuring.

The yellow list, so called because it was written on legal paper, had the names of employees for whom there would be no box. Executives Verrecchia had personally decided must go were at the top of the list. Bernstein was there, of course. So was Bernstein's head of sales and the senior vice president of marketing services, who'd just appeared in the *Hasbro Herald,* enthusiastically discussing how a new retail merchandising program he'd devised would improve sales. Executives not personally designated by Verrecchia were on the list: among them the head of engineering for Playskool, who was marking twenty years at Hasbro and would be honored, five days before being terminated, at a service anniversary dinner (his smiling face was in the anniversary book, which was titled "Thank You," two pages after Hassenfeld, who was celebrating his twenty-fifth).

By the beginning of the first full week of August, Verrecchia had decided he could not wait past the middle of next week to pull the trigger, as the war roomers called it. Productive activity had virtually ground to a halt in Rhode Island, and many employees were losing sleep and subsisting on Pepto-Bismol. The 1995 line was largely finished, but 1996's was increasingly in jeopardy. Headhunters for Mattel were clandestinely exploiting the situation with promises of security, promotions, raises, and an exciting new life in sunny Southern California, and Verrecchia was afraid of losing valuable employees. Bruce Stein was among those taking advantage of the situation. He'd barely arrived at Marvel when he'd tried to lure Ron Hayes, the same designer he'd persuaded not to leave for Warner Bros. in his final days as president of Kenner.

Starting Thursday, August 11, the war room was manned around the clock. Wary of age discrimination lawsuits, Verrecchia submitted the yellow list to legal analysis. Fearful of rocks being thrown through the windos—or worse—Turner pulled her office blinds and was careful to check her tires before driving home. Security, counseling, and outplacement firms were briefed, and internal and external communications plans were developed. With much of the nation's attention on Woodstock's twenty-fifth anniversary concert, Verrecchia and the war roomers worked through the weekend. Bozigian was one whose fate remained unresolved. The people in Cincinnati didn't think much of him, but he had enough support in Pawtucket to ensure his employment, if not his status. Without his knowledge, he'd been penciled in for team leader of Transformers, subsequently considered for the G.I. Joe leader spot, then put down for a middle-level retail merchandising position. Owen initially thought he needed four such spots but before the weekend was over had decided he needed only two. Bozigian was not one of them. He remained in limbo, along with many others.

But time was marching on. By Sunday evening, Verrecchia had decided to pull the trigger on Tuesday.

▪

Verrecchia himself terminated several high-level executives on Monday. Meanwhile, with less than twenty-four hours to go for everyone else, Owen and his managers continued to seek the final composition of several teams, including G.I. Joe. Turner's staff produced severance packages, but they were about the only ones being productive in Rhode Island. The rumor mill had confirmed that tomorrow was the day, and employees gathered in small groups to speculate on the meaning of the increased traffic in and out of the war room. Bozigian had company in his office all day. He'd started a list of those Verrecchia had let go, and it was growing by the hour.

After most people had gone home, Verrecchia, Owen, and the war room crew went to the Greenhouse Cafe. It was crowded with representatives of the perversely named Right Associates, a national management consultant firm that specialized in the logistics of downsizing, and Hasbro department heads, supervisors, and others responsible for terminating the nearly one hundred people Verrecchia had not personally handled. Many of the terminators were friends of the terminated. Most had learned only in the last few hours that they would have jobs, that their names were in boxes.

Turner began with general comments about tomorrow, which employees would memorialize as Black Tuesday but that she called transition day. Her speech was rich with such euphemisms. Tonight was notification training, which was preparation for tomorrow's separation meetings, which brought soon-to-be-ex-employees to outplacement services Hasbro provided to help them transition into new opportunities. When Turner finished, Verrecchia went through slides he would present tomorrow afternoon to a cafeteria gathering of those who were left. "Wednesday is not the end," he said. "It's the beginning."

The Right Associates representatives had the floor. A video film and a pamphlet everyone was asked to take home for their bedtime reading were the centerpieces of the presentation. After introducing himself, the head consultant attempted to show the video, but the connection between player and monitor was faulty, and broadcast TV came on the screen. It was *Wheel of Fortune*. A few people giggled nervously as the wheel spun, then watched in disbelief as it stopped on "LOSE A TURN." The head consultant was not amused; judging by the look in his steel blue eyes, it was doubtful he ever was. The connection was fixed and the film, *Managing Separation Meetings: Restructuring,* began. The film was chock full of practical tips, clearly the result of long, firsthand experience with misery. Notifiers were advised to conduct their sessions in private—spending, at most, seven minutes on each. "More time," the announcer said, "is usually not productive." Shock, denial, anger, or depression could be expected, but no emotion, certainly not sympathy or pity, should be shown in return. "Notifiers should not try to control these reactions, and certainly never discuss them with the individual," the voice said. In extreme cases, security should be swiftly alerted, but it was inadvisable to have guards in the room or posted by the door. Notifiers should not argue, rationalize, or be receptive to counterarguments, and, like goods sold at auction, all decisions were final. To illustrate possible complications, several vignettes had been shot. The acting was cartoonish, the scripts unconvincing, leaving some to wonder if the filmmakers intended to lampoon the process or were simply so bad at their craft that they themselves were in need of transition.

The last vignette was of Wallace, a hardworking, middle-aged man who'd joined the company straight from the military and risen steadily through the ranks, only to lose his job in a corporate merger.

"My God, Michael, what do they expect me to do?" Wallace pleaded with his notifier. "I'm not a kid anymore! I've been here a long time!" Wallace was crying. "I don't know what my poor wife will do. She is so nervous. It'll kill her, Mike. It'll kill her."

Now Wallace was sobbing, an appropriate opportunity for Mike to display compassion, if such was to be forthcoming.

"Wallace, why don't you take a moment to regain your composure?" Mike said, and left the room. Here was a soul mate for the man with the steel blue eyes.

"This is *Reefer Madness* for the nineties," whispered John Gilda, head of licensing and promotions in Rhode Island.

V I

TUESDAY, AUGUST 16, was one of those splendid New England days—breezy and warm, not a cloud in the sky or any humidity. Cars began pulling into the parking lot behind the old brick building at 1027 Newport Avenue in Pawtucket at seven A.M., same as usual. Employees greeted the daytime guard, always a friendly sort, and headed down Main Street past a series of small conference rooms to their offices.

"That's scary," said Carl, a marketer for Bozigian. Coming in, he'd spotted a man in a gray suit in one of those rooms. The man had a stack of manila envelopes and seemed to be waiting for someone. If Carl had looked closer, he would have noticed his steel blue eyes.

Bozigian was in his office, across Main Street from the chairman's suite. People drifted in and out. No one could sit for long. "A moving target is hard to hit!" someone joked. At a quarter to eight no one had heard anything, but it was far too early to relax. Over in R&D, designer Don DeLuca waited by the phone. With his ever-more-vocal criticism of the restructuring, he was convinced he would be the first fired, so several weeks ago he'd instituted his ten-minute rule. The rule stated that everything that could not be boxed on ten minutes' notice had to be cleared out of his office, and he'd methodically stripped it of the many personal maps, navigation charts, postcards, photographs, and mementos that had made it one of the most distinctive spaces at Hasbro. Monday afternoon, he, Greg Berndtson, and many of the longtime G.I. Joe and boys' toy designers had reminisced. They didn't know the new shape of things, but they knew an era was ending.

"We were analogous to a platoon in World War Two that had somehow survived thirty battles and no one had gotten killed," DeLuca said. "Now, this bunch of know-nothing fuckheads were going to take this most talented boys' group in the business and scatter them to the winds." After reminiscing, DeLuca had scrounged four large boxes for the last of his things. He suspected there would be a rush for empty boxes Tuesday morning.

At eight o'clock Carl answered his phone. It was Duncan Billing, the Hasbro Toy Division's senior vice president of marketing, a good-natured native of Britain who'd come to Hasbro through Kenner, where he still had friends. Carl disappeared into his office. Exactly five minutes later Carl emerged. His face was blank. "It's been nice working with you," he said as he shook hands. After stopping at his desk to get his pictures of his wife and baby, he went to see the man with the steel blue eyes.

"I can't believe it," said one of Bozigian's marketers. "No one's safe." He'd written Carl's performance review. It was complimentary.

Vinnie D'Alleva's phone rang. D'Alleva literally jumped out of his chair. A voice with a British accent said: "Please come into my office." D'Alleva was ashen. But it was only one of DeLuca's wise-guy friends, with a little black humor.

In rest rooms, women were weeping. People were hugging friends and clearing out desks. Their phones and voice mail were dead, their card keys deactivated.

But the motorized, self-guided cart that delivered the mail was making its regular rounds. It stopped outside Bozigian's office. "That's the future of this company," Bozigian said. "Robots." His list was growing rapidly. Larry Bernstein's son, a boys' toys marketer, was on it. The head of packaging, Playskool's R&D chief, and many lower-level employees were on it. Most were from Rhode Island. In all, 105 people would be let go, for a savings of some $7.5 million (some of which later would be given back to new hirings). The ranks of middle- and lower-level managers had been especially thinned.

"It's over," a manager in design announced at ten forty-five.

▪

Hassenfeld was not seen until afternoon, when he went to the front of the jam-packed cafeteria and proclaimed: "Welcome to the screening of a new blockbuster movie!" Like survivors of a fiery plane crash, almost everyone looked dazed. They had jobs, but it was difficult to rejoice imagining the scenes that were unfolding as former colleagues went home to their families.

"I know that the past few months and especially today have been difficult, and for this I apologize," Hassenfeld said. "The Chinese talk of change with two characters: trouble and opportunity. The trouble is past, and now, together, we must seize the opportunity and build for the future."

Privately, Hassenfeld was less chipper.

"Look, these are not happy days for me because there's a lot of soul-searching that goes into this," he said. But he supported Verrecchia without qualification and had not touched a name on the yellow list. "This company is no longer one person or five hundred people. It's a family of twelve thousand, and I must worry about the entire group," he said. "That's a simplistic way of putting it, but that's the reality. What you have to do is the most good for the larger group."

Hassenfeld spoke to the cafeteria assembly for about three minutes, twice using the word "passion" to describe his support for the restructuring, then turned over the microphone to the man he pointedly called his partner.

When the speeches were finished, employees were notified of their new assignments. Two girls' teams were based in Rhode Island, and four were in Cincinnati, more or less the status quo. Two boys' teams were in Rhode Island, seven in Cincinnati. All nine preschool teams were in

Rhode Island, along with the four activities teams. Packaging and market research, previously split between the sites, went to Cincinnati. Engineering, also previously divided, was in Rhode Island.

The shocking news was G.I. Joe.

As late as Saturday the Joe team had been penciled in for Pawtucket. On Sunday Ginger Kent, the Kenner executive who'd been put in charge of all boys' and girls' toys, had asked Verrecchia if he objected to transferring Joe to Cincinnati. He did not; for some time he'd wanted what he described as a fresh set of eyes on the line. Verrecchia informed Alan, who also blessed the move. Both knew how high emotions would run on Main Street, for Joe had never had another home, but that did not stop them. "I wish it could be different, but that's not my job," Verrecchia said. "My job is to turn the brand around and get Joe back on its feet and make sure the company grows and is profitable."

Only one Rhode Islander, a designer who agreed to relocate to Ohio, continued on G.I. Joe. Rejected for a retail merchandising job, Bozigian at the last minute had been penciled in as team leader of Play-Doh.

VII

No one outside Hasbro knew what had befallen G.I. Joe's makers when, four days later, Bozigian bounded to a podium and barked: "Attention!" The crowd inside the USS *Intrepid,* a World War II aircraft carrier made into a museum in New York, snapped alert. "Thank you for slogging through this heat and joining us aboard this historic ship to salute thirty years of America's greatest hero, G.I. Joe," Bozigian said. "There's a lot of history aboard this ship, and today we're going to make some more."

His audience was eclectic. A few children and women were present, but most were grown men, several of whom wore dog tags, were dressed in camouflage combat gear, or had G.I. Joe tattoos. A middle-aged collector who'd written one of the many books on the action figure wore a general's uniform. Writers for toy and hobby magazines took notes alongside reporters and cameramen from the mainstream media. Sales of the action figure continued to plummet toward modern lows, but *The New York Times* and the many others covering the first G.I. Joe International Collectors' Convention, highlight of the thirtieth anniversary celebration, didn't know that. They were attracted by other numbers: almost ten thousand people in New York this sweltering weekend for what feminist writer Susan Faludi, in a piece for *Esquire,* would call "the largest doll party ever held in the U.S." Dealers had set up long rows of booths, and the wait was two hours at the satellite store Toys "R" Us had opened on the *Intrepid* for first sale of the thirtieth commemorative line. By Sunday afternoon the store would move some $200,000 of the figures, a two-day retail record. Another record was set at Christie's East, when an original Action Pilot Joe went for $5,750 at a charity auction. "The top lot of the sale even topped Barbie," a Christie's spokesman said.

Quoting General Douglas MacArthur, Bozigian observed that old soldiers never die, only fade away. Thus it was that after a dozen years of valiant service, the standard 3¾-inch G.I. Joe figure was being phased out—to be replaced by something quite literally bigger. Bozigian recounted the Sgt. Savage story, rolled a sizzle video, and said: "Let me introduce you to the new leader of the G.I. Joe team!"

A six-foot-nine, 315-pound young man rippling with muscles and dressed in fatigues burst into the conference. "Sergeant Robert Steven Savage reporting for duty, *sir!*" the actor shouted with a salute.

"At ease, Sergeant," Bozigian said.

Bozigian unveiled the new line as the audience crowded in. "As a young boy," Bozigian said, "I played with G.I. Joe and dreamed of going to West Point. As an adult, I get to command the world's largest standing army: G.I. Joe and his forces of over three hundred and thirty million action figures sold since 1964." Bozigian was too absorbed to pay attention to two strangers standing to one side, out of the glare of the lights. They were Kenner marketers: Chris Connolly and his immediate supervisor, Elizabeth Gross, two of Joe's new keepers.

▪

Bozigian's voice betrayed none of his true feelings in announcing Sgt. Savage; like his final action figure, he was heroic to the end. He was similarly composed that evening at West Twenty-third, where for $300 a ticket collectors dined on cold chicken, listened to speeches, and left with a limited-edition figure that sold for $700 the next morning back on the *Intrepid.* Saturday's dinner was on the same bottom-level courtyard where Stephen Hassenfeld had made his last public appearance five years earlier at Hasbro's annual meeting. That irony was not lost on Hasbro employees. Indeed, the dead chairman had been on the minds of many all week. Lightning had struck corporate headquarters on Thursday, and the charge had traveled through the roof, visibly through the building, and out an underground cable to the parking lot, where it blew out the windshields of cars. "Stephen," a number of longtimers had whispered.

"You guys really are nuts!" Bozigian said as he began his speech. The collectors laughed, even though some were peeved at paying $300 for cold chicken. Bozigian recounted how without Merrill's Movable Fighting Man there would have been no Batman figures, no Teenage Mutant Ninja Turtles, and no Power Rangers, the mention of which drew jeers. Bozigian led a round of applause for the nearly three dozen Hasbro workers who'd given up a summer weekend to come to New York for the convention, then singled out the people who'd worked with him on Joe over the years. He took off his shirt, revealing a T-shirt D'Alleva had designed a while back. "The Few, the Proud, the G.I. Joe Team," it read.

"This is a special secret message from me to you," Bozigian said to the old guard. "Remember that. Be proud. You guys all deserve it."

Some of Bozigian's employees were misty-eyed, and his wife was crying. She'd seen her husband after Black Tuesday, when he'd come home with a monstrous headache, taken aspirin, and lain down on a couch and cried. Colt couldn't understand why Daddy wasn't working on G.I. Joe anymore, and he already was losing his long-held desire to work for a toy company when he grew up. Kirk's reflections were in a similar vein. He'd lost many friends in the restructuring, employees he believed were worthwhile. "When is it all going to end?" he said. "When are companies going to realize they have an obligation to more than their shareholders?"

12

SHARKS

I

Jill Barad was charming and persuasive when she outlined to the creator of Cabbage Patch Kids the many wonderful things she would do for his dolls. She was fashionably dressed, and her lipstick, makeup, jewelry, and hair unquestionably were those of a woman *People* magazine had selected as one of the world's "50 Most Beautiful People." It was the summer of 1994, and Barad had journeyed from Mattel's headquarters in a California high-rise to Cleveland, Georgia, the rural town that was home to Original Appalachian Artworks, Xavier Roberts's company. Roberts had created Cabbage Patch in the 1970s and seen it become the most sought-after girls' toy of the mid-1980s. Hasbro had manufactured the dolls since 1990. Its license expired at the end of the year.

Barad spoke to Roberts of Mattel's strength: five consecutive years of record revenues, with 1994 certain to be the sixth, and the best year ever for profits. She reminded him of the remarkable success of Barbie, which had grown from $430 million to more than $1 billion in sales in the eight years that her boss, John Amerman, had been chairman and CEO and she'd been associated with the doll. She touched on Mattel's other core brands: Disney licensed products, Hot Wheels, and Fisher-Price. "We know how to do brands better than anybody," Barad said, then impressed on Roberts how Mattel also was unequaled in retail merchandising, the in-store display of goods. Roberts had long been envious of Barbie's pink aisle, forty feet long in some of the bigger chains—of how arrangement, signage, and packaging, all carefully orchestrated and controlled by Mattel, combined to create an almost irresistible impulse to buy, especially when young girls were in tow.

Barad asked Roberts and his staff to leave the room. When they returned they found a mock-up of a retail display. Like a scene from Babyland General Hospital, the folksy shop in Cleveland where visitors could buy Cabbage Patch Kids at their mythical place of birth, the dolls were surrounded by cabbage plants and sunflowers—fake, of course, but nonetheless pleasing to the eye. Some dolls held sunflowers in their doughy little hands. Barad passed out sunflower pens and sunflower notepads and continued with her pitch. Mattel's Cabbage Patch Kids, she said, would be larger than Hasbro's and would wear more colorfully contemporary clothing. "Back to the future," she called it—a funky flavor of today with a reminder of the look of a decade ago, when more than nineteen million Kids had been sold in one year in a category, large dolls, where a million seller was the benchmark of unqualified success. Barad promised Mattel would outdo Hasbro on promotion, advertising, and public relations, although dollar figures were not discussed. She was confident Mattel could make a success of Cabbage Patch overseas, where Hasbro by its own admission was foundering. As president and chief operating officer, she had authority to offer generous royalties and a large guarantee.

A millionaire before he was thirty, Roberts liked what he was hearing. He could not but be flattered by Barad's smile and the way she made eye contact with him when she spoke.

▪

Sixth and final child of a woman who sewed quilts and a grade-school dropout whose nickname was "Happy," Roberts had grown up dirt poor. With Mom's help he made his first dolls in 1976, when he was studying macramé and weaving at a local college. He was twenty. "I called them Little People," he told a biographer. "We used to say we found them in a cabbage patch. You know, that's what mothers tell their children when they ask, 'Where did I come from?' " His first sales were to customers of the gift shop where he worked to support his studies. The look was unique, as was Roberts's down-home marketing: these were not dolls, he insisted, these were babies, and they were "adopted," not purchased.

Word spread. Demand grew. Roberts founded Original Appalachian Artworks and opened a factory. Swamped with orders, in 1982 he signed a license with Coleco to produce the dolls after Mattel, Kenner, and Hasbro had all passed. Once again the big corporations had been blind.

But for Cabbage Patch, Coleco, a manufacturer of swimming pools and electronic games, almost certainly would have disappeared into bankruptcy. Like Mattel's Intellivision and Milton Bradley's Vectrex, its ColecoVision gaming platform and related home computer, ADAM, were victims of the collapse of the video-game market in the early eighties. Cabbage Patch returned Coleco to profitability. The company sold 2.8 million of the dolls in 1983, all it could make, netting $62 million. Frenzy that year became coast-to-coast hysteria the next, giving Coleco $504 million in revenues from the dolls and accessories. In 1985 Cabbage Patch sales totaled $613 million, a volume Barbie had never approached. Flush with sudden riches, Coleco ignored a lesson of the toy business Merrill Hassenfeld had learned painfully with G.I. Joe, and which had driven his oldest son to a balanced portfolio. Coleco planned on $450 million in Cabbage Patch sales in 1986 but realized only $247 million; nothing else in its line took up the slack. In 1987, when a comparatively meager $139 million of dolls were sold, Coleco lost $105 million. The next year, in May, Coleco laid off 475 workers and its stock hit a fifty-two-week low. In July it filed for Chapter 11 reorganization in U.S. Bankruptcy Court.

Stephen Hassenfeld watched Coleco's demise with excited anticipation. He had no desire to play white knight, but he wanted Roberts's babies. So did Amerman, for the same reason: despite its recent misfortunes, Cabbage Patch was the only major large-doll brand of the era with proven durability. Stephen instructed Barry Alperin to strike a deal. Among the challenges was persuading Roberts that Hasbro, the action-figure leader, could do better than the maker of the best-selling doll of all time. Alperin and Larry Bernstein, whose new division would get the Cabbage Patch Kids, played the Mattel card brilliantly. "We felt Hasbro would put the most into it," recalled Della Tolhurst, president of Original Appalachian Artworks. "They did not have the distraction of a Barbie." In final discussions when he was hospitalized, Stephen had slipped into a coma by the time Hasbro announced agreement to purchase Coleco's assets, for $85 million, on June 16, 1989. Included with Cabbage Patch Kids were two classic board games Stephen, like Amerman, had also wanted: Parcheesi and Scrabble (the North American rights only).

Hasbro had lofty ambitions for its new dolls. Bernstein intended to add new segments and revive the spirit of Roberts's early days, when no two Little People looked exactly alike, and he planned to spend millions on a new television campaign reemphasizing the adoption mystique, lost in the ruins of Coleco. "Cabbage Patch goes way beyond being a doll," he told a toy magazine. "It's part of our culture now, and we think with some tender loving care we can bring it back to some very respectable sales levels." A photograph of Alan Hassenfeld clutching an armful of the dolls appeared in *USA Today*. "Hasbro is going back to the basics," Roberts said in admiration. "The love."

From a low of $55 million in 1989, the last year Coleco had any involvement, sales doubled in two years under Bernstein's command, prompting no less an authority than *Business Week* to declare: "They're back!"

They were, but only momentarily. A decline that began in 1992 accelerated in early 1994 as the Hasbro Toy Division came unglued. The division's woes, which prompted Bernstein to make deep cuts in advertising, were not the only factor. His marketers had decided lower-priced dolls could achieve higher volumes and thus greater overall revenues, but lower cost had been achieved by sacrificing detail, which consumers noticed and did not appreciate. And a strategy of targeting mothers in advertising had drawn focus away from core doll users: girls four to seven who wanted something cool, not the old-fashioned wholesomeness that appealed to their moms. Like G.I. Joe, Cabbage Patch was in trouble.

Hassenfeld and Verrecchia began to suspect Roberts might seek other suitors at the beginning of 1994. They wanted to keep the license, but not at any cost; because of how the Coleco deal had been amortized, Hasbro had not seen any profit from Cabbage Patch in the first four years and probably wouldn't in the fifth year, given the dismal sales projections for 1994. Nonetheless Cabbage Patch had potential, and Hassenfeld was willing to pay handsomely, if not obscenely, for the rights. "I think we're the best people to handle Cabbage Patch, and we're going to fight damn hard for it," he vowed.

Verrecchia's dialogue with Tolhurst, who did Roberts's negotiating, intensified in the spring of 1994. Verrecchia assured her that his restructuring could only benefit the brand, but with the Hasbro Toy Division in such turmoil, he assigned Kenner the job of devising a new strategy. Bruce Stein participated before he left Hasbro, and Ginger Kent took personal charge. Hundreds of man-hours were invested. After a summit session in May, Kent, five marketers and designers from Cincinnati and Pawtucket, and an outside advertising executive made the pilgrimage to Georgia. It was June 21, the day Stein's resignation made the papers. Verrecchia led the delegation.

In critical respects, Hasbro's Cabbage Patch Kids Growth Strategy, outlined in a forty-five-page illustrated document, was virtually identical to what Mattel would offer. Hasbro promised new segments, a stronger retail presence, enhanced promotion, extensive advertising, and television programming. Hasbro would send the Kids to Atlanta for the 1996 Olympics as team mascot, a high-visibility title they'd carried to Barcelona in 1992, and explore using the dolls as spokespeople for national literacy, immunization, and get-out-the-vote campaigns. "Ingrain CPK into American culture," the document declared. Kent pledged to commit Hasbro's most talented large-doll people to the brand.

"I have the most talented people on the brand," Roberts said. "What I don't have is management's support." He didn't believe Verrecchia and Hassenfeld loved his babies.

So Roberts was soliciting affection elsewhere. Verrecchia already knew Hasbro was competing with Stein, who'd recently made a presentation in Georgia. Before leaving, Roberts told him Mattel was due in next month, too.

▪

Like Verrecchia, Barad had arrived in Georgia with a show of force, including her top Barbie marketer, and Jeanne Olson, a large-dolls specialist. Barad had lured Olson to Mattel only this spring from Hasbro, where her last job had been, of all things, marketing Cabbage Patch. Olson knew the folks at Original Appalachian Artworks intimately, of course, and she was especially well acquainted with a man who'd been with OAA barely a month. He was, of all people, Tom Prichard, who'd given his notice at Hasbro only two weeks before Stein. Before leaving, he'd preceded Olson as Cabbage Patch marketing chief.

When Barad wrapped up her presentation, she knew she'd scored. "They absolutely blew our socks off," Tolhurst would recall. Roberts was especially impressed with how Barad held and hugged his babies, so tenderly, as if they were her very own. The only drawback was the long shadow of Barbie, but Barad had been prepared for that. Barbie could never get in the way of the Cabbage Patch Kids, she asserted, for the brands were aimed at distinctly different regions of the developing female psyche—the one promising ravishing fantasy, the other providing a vehicle for nurturing nineties play. Roberts was inclined to agree. He bought Barad's contention that in large dolls, Cabbage Patch would be Mattel's core brand, its one true love.

Barad hadn't journeyed to this southern backwater on a lark. She had her heart set on a brand, and she was ready to close the deal immediately, with the unusual offer of five years of royalties up front, if that's what it took to best Hasbro. It was no hollow offer. Mattel was wallowing in cash that summer. With Amerman's blessing, Barad could just about write the $25 million or so check on the spot.

Roberts was sorely tempted, but for the moment he declined; for all Barad's solicitations, it would not be an easy call. Hasbro's financial position was at least as strong as Mattel's, and Roberts was sufficiently fond of Hasbro's designers and marketers to have hired one. He was impressed with Ginger Kent's growth strategy and the people in Cincinnati. As summer went by, he still hadn't made up his mind.

Hasbro and Mattel, meanwhile, had been fighting bigger battles.

I I

A GRADUATE OF DARTMOUTH COLLEGE and Dartmouth's Amos Tuck School, John Amerman was trained in the marketing of packaged goods. His first job was at Colgate-Palmolive, where he managed Ajax, helping to create its White Knight commercial and the slogan "Stronger Than Dirt." Amerman left for Warner-Lambert in 1965 and was president of its American Chicle Division, maker of Chiclets gum, before joining Mattel in 1980. Kitchen cleanser or precious playthings, Amerman saw little difference. Starting with a recognized name, a brand, a company manufactured a quality product. It innovated continually, while preserving core identity. It used research to test products and marketing plans. It created memorable advertising, which was aired broadly and repeatedly. It promoted extensively and was ever mindful that its most precious real estate was shelf space in stores. It was a complex and expensive proposition, but properly executed, it could enable a toy maker to defy the traditional laws of a fickle business.

"We've used the techniques that have worked in selling detergent or shampoos or cosmetics or whatever it may be to apply them to toys," Amerman said. "The nice part about it is it works."

The debacle of He-Man and Masters of the Universe had left Amerman less interested in building brands from the ground up than in expanding Barbie and Hot Wheels, Mattel's core products when he took over, and bringing outside brands into the fold through acquisition or partnership. His first move was in October 1987, when Disney granted Mattel a license to design, manufacture, and market infant and preschool toys based on Mickey Mouse and other Disney characters. The agreement made Mattel an immediate presence in the preschool and infant categories and gave Mattel the inside track on bidding for the toy rights to Disney's high-profile entertainment properties. The fourth of Mattel's core brands was Fisher-Price, acquired in 1993.

Naming a new chief executive officer is always a roll of the dice, but seven years after E. M. Warburg, Pincus & Co., Inc.'s John L. Vogelstein and Lionel I. Pincus had put Amerman in charge of Mattel, their gamble had paid off, and not only in record revenues and near record earnings. Like Stephen Hassenfeld in Hasbro's dark seventies, Amerman had made the balance sheet a priority, and his diligence had reaped rewards. Mattel began 1994 with over $500 million in cash reserves, almost triple what Hasbro had. It was money just burning to be spent.

Even in personnel, Amerman had excelled. One of the rare male executives who was not threatened by a woman, he early on recognized unusual ability in Barad, who, in spirit at least, bore an uncanny resemblance to Ruth Handler, Mattel's founder and one of the first female executives to break through the glass ceiling in corporate America. Aggressive and smart, Barad was the younger daughter of Emmy and Golden Globe Award–winning director Larry Elikann. An English and drama major in college, she played Miss Italian America, a nonspeaking role shot in a day, in a forgettable Dino De Laurentiis film. She did not thereafter see her future on screen, although the lessons of show business would serve her well in marketing. She took a position with Coty Cosmetics training department store demonstrators and, after marrying Paramount Pictures producer Thomas Barad, moved to Los Angeles, where she joined an ad agency, had the first of her two sons, and, in 1981, became a $38,000-a-year product manager at Mattel. She rose fast, with Barbie. Amerman named her president of the girls' and activity toys division in 1989, president of Mattel USA the next year, and corporate president and chief operating officer in 1992, in line to succeed Amerman himself, twenty years her senior. In 1993 her compensation was $5.4 million, the figure that took Bruce Stein's breath away. (Mattel took care of her husband, too. Thomas Barad owned 50 percent of a company that received $500,000 in 1994 and another $1 million in 1995, for production of a Barbie infomercial.)

▪

Inside Mattel, in marketing especially, the pressure was relentless. "Churn and burn," was one common insider's description of company culture. Employees who fell short of expectations feared for their jobs, with good reason: the chairman had inaugurated the modern era by terminating five hundred employees, and they were hardly the last to be let go. "If it isn't a fit, we're pretty quick to cut the person loose," said Glenn Bozarth, senior vice president of corporate communications. "You just can't have someone who's in the way, who's not pulling his weight."

There was no mollycoddling inside Mattel's gleaming new high-rise, no resting on laurels, and no tolerance for stupid mistakes, sustained failure, or open criticism of the top. It helped to be in Barad's good graces, and many employees spoke privately of their tireless efforts to please her. Certainly they tried to emulate her fashion sense. In marked contrast with Hasbro, where the chairman himself favored jeans and people such as Kirk Bozigian received compliments on their T-shirts, Mattel tolerated only traditional corporate dress, with the exception of Friday, a regularly scheduled "dress-down" day. Among marketers, dress shirts and ties were universal on men at all other times, and the women dressed as if auditioning for *Melrose Place*. Hair was a solemn consideration at Mattel. Men wore theirs short, and beards were all but unknown; women understood the critical importance of mirrors and trendy stylists. In the birthplace of Barbie and Ken, how could it have been otherwise?

Whatever one's opinion of such Southern Californian folkways, the formula worked. The company kept attracting the kinds of people Ruth

Handler and now Amerman and Barad liked: creative, intelligent types who were highly motivated by money. If you couldn't cut it, tough luck; someone inside or out was eager for your place. "It is a culture where paranoia runs deep, where people are worried about somebody stabbing you from behind because they will," said a highly placed Mattel insider. "It's a predator or prey business, and you have to decide which you'll be."

•

Almost without exception, stories in the popular press flattered Amerman and Barad and spoke glowingly of their working relationship. This was not happenstance. Mattel cultivated its image carefully—not to cozy up to the mass media so much as to reinforce perception where it really mattered, Wall Street. Being near Hollywood and allied to a major studio helped with public relations, as did Glenn Bozarth. Bozarth was very effective at keeping nettlesome reporters away from his bosses, whose offices were on the fifteenth floor of headquarters in El Segundo. Conversely, like the finest agent, he had an excellent nose for those likely to praise Mattel.

Amerman typically was portrayed as the white-haired, expensively tailored, hardworking master strategist who nonetheless understood the value of a little fun. A *Los Angeles* magazine profile, for example, opened with him in his office playing with Gymnast Barbie. After a recitation of some impressive numbers, the piece closed with Barad saluting her boss's sportive spirit. " 'He has a wonderful confident self that is not embarrassed or afraid to make this place fun,' " Barad said. "And you should see him sing and dance." Amerman, the writer breathlessly informed readers, had announced bonuses in rap verse and performed at company gatherings in top hat and cane as one of the Toy Boys. Amerman's 1993 compensation was more than $7 million, and he lived on the Pacific Ocean, in exclusive Palos Verdes. He had not one but two ranches for his Thoroughbreds and German shepherds. But at such moments, at least, he was one of the guys.

Because she was one of the few female senior executives of a Fortune 500 company and was so photogenic, Barad had become a media darling. The occasional writer hinted of guile in her climb to the top, and one had to wonder why many executives had left during her rise to power (they'd left voluntarily or hadn't met high standards, was Mattel's response); but most celebrated her ascent and could not avoid the obvious, if glib, comparisons to the doll that had accompanied her. Barad posed for an ad for *Forbes* magazine with Barbie, and her *People* magazine photo had her sprawled coquettishly on satin bedding surrounded by thirty-five Barbies dressed in bikini, western outfit, and evening gown. "Princess of Power," *USA Today* dubbed her in 1988 in one of the pieces that began the legend. "Queen of the Aisles," *Brandweek* proclaimed.

She lived in Bel Air, home to movie stars and directors, in whose company she and her husband traveled. It was not unusual to spot the Barads at such events as the Academy Awards, AIDS benefits, or Fire and Ice, the annual Warner Bros.' charity ball. She knew Madonna and Sharon Stone, and Demi Moore had accepted her invitation to tour Mattel headquarters. She took great pride in the way she dressed, which was tastefully eye-catching and often in red, the color of the company logo, or pink, the color of Barbie. She favored heavy lipstick and sometimes wore a yellow bumblebee pin. When asked about it, as she inevitably was by admiring reporters, she explained that it was a gift from her mother. "The bee is an oddity of nature," she said. "It shouldn't be able to fly, but it does. Every time I see that bee out of the corner of my eye, I am reminded to keep pushing for the impossible." Barad was nothing if not quotable.

Nurtured by her handlers, her story had become legend. Bozarth's official biography of her noted that "since 1982, the year she became marketing director for Barbie, Barad and the world's most popular doll have been on the fast track." It was a true statement, but an incomplete one.

Bozarth did not mention that Mattel's segmentation strategy, the foundation for the doll's explosive sales of the 1980s and 1990s, was largely the brainchild of her (and Stein's) former boss, Judy Shackelford, named Mattel's first female vice president in 1978. Rather than envisioning one doll with many accessories, which was how Barbie traditionally had been sold (Ruth Handler's razor/razor blade strategy), Shackelford saw a market for many dolls, each with a distinct theme and outfit. Segmentation divided Barbie into such categories as hair play, glamour, and lifestyle, encouraging purchases of more dolls, which yielded greater profit than outfits sold alone. But there was no denying that Barad was influential. She contributed to Shackelford's groundbreaking 1984 "We Girls Can Do Anything" campaign, which put Barbie in the mainstream of contemporary social change—thus opening another big sales window. Perhaps better than anyone at Mattel, she recognized the enormous value of Barbie parties and PR events, such as those over which she presided at Toy Fair.

When Shackelford left in 1986 to become an independent inventor, Barad became the final authority on the most celebrated, and profitable, doll of all time.

"Before John and I were around, basically it was a business of you'd buy your Barbie and then you'd buy a lot of clothes," Barad said. "Today a little girl needs Barbie one, Barbie two, Barbie three, and Barbie four to the average American girl owning eight. For the simple reason that each one is positioned against a specific play pattern that is unique from the other. So therefore multiple purchase became essential and became natural and so went the increase in the business."

Amerman believed that basic play patterns are universal. "We find in the toy industry that the wants and desires of boys, girls, mothers, dads round the world are the same," he said. "Little girls like to comb hair, they like to change clothes. Boys like to race cars across the table or across the floor. They like to have fights between bad guys and good guys." Research confirmed Amerman's observations. What divided scholars was whether these play patterns, as marketers called them, were biological or cultural and whether in a rapidly changing world they were good.

III

As it turned out, neither Hasbro nor Mattel had been able to score a knockout in their battle over Sindy, Stephen Hassenfeld's European fashion doll. By the spring of 1992, three years after the first legal skirmishes, three years after Stephen was dead, courts had banned Sindy from some countries and permitted it in others. Hasbro had continued to ship the disputed head and pink packaging into some markets and was using an old Maxie head and white packaging in others. Both sides had appealed unfavorable decisions but were facing years of delays before appeals would even be heard. Sporadic settlement discussions begun late in 1989 intensified. Three full years into it, Hasbro and Mattel were like bareknuckled boxers at the end of fifteen rounds: bloodied, still standing, but no longer entirely sure why they'd climbed into the ring. With legal costs mounting into the millions of dollars, Alan was increasingly receptive to a truce. (Sindy was not the only dispute between Hasbro and Mattel. After more than a year of litigation, the companies had reached a settlement over Kenner's Miss America fashion doll line, another Barbie look-alike, introduced before Hasbro had completed its acquisition of Tonka.)

A week before Christmas 1992, Barry Alperin, Hasbro's main contact with Mattel on the matter, packed his briefcase and took a chauffeur-driven car to New York's Kennedy Airport. Amerman and Barad were waiting for him in a small conference room in an airline's Admirals' Club. They exchanged pleasantries, and Alperin opened his briefcase. Five different freshly sculpted Sindy heads were inside. Alperin gave them to Mattel's leaders, who asked to examine them privately. Alperin left the room. Hasbro had already agreed to move away from all-pink packaging. If Amerman and Barad found one of the new heads acceptable, Mattel would finally drop its lawsuits.

When Alperin returned, Amerman and Barad had chosen a head. It was shaped slightly differently from Barbie's, and the features, while similar to an outsider, were not as close as before. Amerman wanted to know how Mattel could be certain Hasbro would use it. He suggested Alperin leave it; Mattel's people could copy it and send it back. Alperin excused himself and called the London office, which, he learned, had duplicates of the heads. Alperin shook hands with Amerman, kissed Barad, and said: "Thanks. This is what we all should be doing."

And it was, for about a year.

I V

AMERMAN WOULD BE INDUCTED into the Toy Industry Hall of Fame at a black-tie dinner in New York at the end of Toy Fair 1995. It was Alan Hassenfeld's turn in 1994. The Sindy affair at last behind them, Amerman joined his rival on the dais, and their photograph was published in the *Hasbro Herald*. In his personal tribute, Amerman called Alan a "special" person who stuck to his principles and competed aggressively but fairly. "What makes Alan so unique is his heart and his soul," Barad declared in her tribute. "I can truthfully say Alan has always been there for me."

Had he been allowed into his competitor's showroom, a city block from his own, Hassenfeld would have seen Street Sharks, Mattel's latest attempt to crack the boys' action market. A man who'd worked for Kirk Bozigian before joining Mattel demonstrated the toys to buyers. "These guys are the ultimate predators," he said as he closed the jaws of a hand-puppet shark on Hasbro's signature toy. "They can take a bite out of G.I.

Joe!" In truth, except for Hot Wheels, a winner since its introduction in 1968, Mattel had been unable to establish an enduring boys' brand, and its record in action figures was as frustrating as Hasbro's in fashion dolls. Not even its long association with the entertainment industry seemed to help. While the company from Rhode Island was reaping windfalls from Batman and Jurassic Park, Mattel saw its Hook and Last Action Hero figures perish quietly at retail.

Games continued to be equally vexing to Amerman, who envied brands like Monopoly, which had prospered sixty years and promised to be a global producer indefinitely, especially now that the interactive age had dawned and enduring classics could be made digital. Unsuccessful in building a games business from inside, and beaten to Tonka, Amerman was scouring the globe for other game makers he might buy. Having had encouraging if modest success in 1992 with the acquisition of International Games, maker of Uno, a well-known card game, Amerman in early 1994 was eager for more.

▪

Even as he wore a tuxedo to pay tribute to Alan Hassenfeld, Amerman was plotting against him, and not only for games. Any major brand was worth a look. The month after Toy Fair, Mattel announced the purchase of Kransco, a San Francisco company that made the Hula-Hoop, Frisbee, and Power Wheels, a popular line of battery-powered ride-on vehicles. Hasbro had considered buying the company but did not value it as highly as Mattel, which paid about $260 million, some $100 million more than what Alan was prepared to offer. He did not consider Kransco a big loss.

But Amerman's next move, for ownership of a small British games company, J. W. Spear & Sons, rattled him—both for its boldness and for the headlines that reached Wall Street just as John O'Neill was working overtime to contain the damage from lowered second quarter expectations. Spear had the international rights to Scrabble and was run by old friends of the Hassenfelds. Hasbro owned a quarter of its stock, and Alan had long assumed that if the Spear family ever left the business, they would sell their stake to Hasbro, which would give him control. Hasbro offered £7 a share when they decided to get out, but on the advice of an investment firm Spear rejected that price as too low. Hasbro reluctantly went to £9 and thought it had a deal when, barely an hour before the midnight deadline (on June 4) for competitive offers, Mattel delivered a surprise bid for £10. Hasbro went to £11. Mattel countered with £11.50. Hasbro declined to go higher, and on July 11, Mattel claimed victory.

Hasbro executives comforted themselves in Spear's relatively small size, the knowledge that Scrabble translates poorly into many languages, and the gain of more than $20 million on sale of Hasbro's interest, but the defeat was nonetheless unsettling. "We feel very much about games like Mattel feels about Barbie and fashion dolls," George Ditomassi said. "It's our business, and there shouldn't be anybody else in the business but us." Newly wary, Hasbro approached the games division of another British firm, John Waddington, which owned Clue and the British rights to Monopoly. Negotiating in extreme secrecy, lest Mattel find out, Hasbro succeeded in an acquisition, announced in November.

Meanwhile the companies were competing on other grounds. Hasbro's big summer movie license was for *The Shadow,* which flopped as film and toy, while Mattel cleaned up with Disney's *Lion King.* Envious of Lego's dominance in construction toys, Hasbro and Mattel sought an international marketing partnership with the makers of a promising new line, K'Nex, and Hasbro won. Both companies looked at Western Publishing's games and puzzles unit, maker of Pictionary and Outburst, and Hasbro prevailed. Capitalizing on his friendship with Nickelodeon president Geraldine Laybourne, Hassenfeld struck a deal to sell a new line of Nickelodeon toys. Amerman cried foul. How could Laybourne do such a thing? Mattel had Gak, a Nickelodeon-licensed compound that was taking share from market leader Play-Doh! But even at Nick, which cultivated an image of good old-fashioned friendliness, loyalty was second to profit.

In the midst of it all, Hassenfeld took a few moments to muse. He knew that with Kransco and Spear, Mattel almost certainly would finish 1994 ahead of Hasbro in sales volume for the first time in a decade, but he believed Amerman and Barad had earned it. Losing the top spot seemed not to trouble him. "There are so many different number ones," he said. "I'd like us to be number one in volume, number one in return to our shareholders, and number one in being considered the most socially responsible or humanistic company." Achieving all three, he was discovering, was more difficult than he'd ever imagined.

V

GINGER KENT COULDN'T WAIT any longer. It was early on a Saturday morning in September, and the opening of Pre–Toy Fair was only hours away. The Cabbage Patch sets were up, the 1995 line was ready for buyers' inspection, and Hasbro still hadn't heard from Original Appalachian Artworks. Tolhurst had promised a call the night before, but midnight had passed without it. Kent found a phone and dialed her at home. The call roused Tolhurst from a sound sleep. The wrangling had gone past one A.M.

"We're going with Mattel," Tolhurst said. "I'm sorry."

Kent asked why. Tolhurst said what had tipped them was Mattel's core brands philosophy, international marketing, and retail merchandising. It could not have been financial, for Mattel's offer was virtually the same as Hasbro's: $25 million over five years.

"You're making a terrible mistake," Kent said.

"I guess only time will tell," Tolhurst replied.

When Verrecchia and Hassenfeld learned of the decision, they jointly authored an internal memo thanking the people behind Hasbro's effort and reassuring them they all still had jobs. "While our preference would have been to keep the Cabbage Patch license, the brand was clearly not what it once was," they said. "Losing this slowing brand will just not have that much of an impact."

Privately Verrecchia had a somewhat different slant. He'd watched the year unfold with greater trepidation than his boss. He believed Hasbro needed more of Mattel's killer instinct, and he'd had that conversation with Hassenfeld. "Look over your shoulder once in a while," he'd advised. "When you see this big white thing coming at you with its mouth open, he might bite! Don't sit there and stick your head in it and assume he's not going to close his jaw. You're going to get eaten." Verrecchia's words would turn out to be prophetic, although not remotely as he imagined.

13

■

EXTREMES

I

*A*lan Hassenfeld had but two dictates when he met with the new keepers of G.I. Joe not long after Black Tuesday. The first was that the line
needed sharp focus. "We tried to be all things to all people, and you
can't," he said. The second was that Joe had to remain military, albeit
broadly defined. "I'm open for any construct," he said. "It doesn't have to
be pure hard-core military."

Thirty years of documents, computer files, sculptings, drawings, and
mechanisms were still being packed and shipped to Cincinnati, or thrown
away, when Ginger Kent and her marketers got down to the nitty-gritty
of reinvention. Unlike their predecessors on Joe, they brought to the task
a strong background in consumer packaged goods. Kent, a Wellesley College graduate who held a master of business administration degree, had
come to Kenner from Procter & Gamble, where she'd worked on
Pringles, the snack food. Tom McGrath, the new boys' supercategory
manager, also had worked at P&G; his responsibilities there included Tide
laundry detergent and Dawn dish detergent. Elizabeth Gross, the third of
Joe's new managers, had cut her marketing teeth at Fruit of the Loom;
she also had an MBA. Chris Connolly, the new Joe team leader, was a cer-

tified public accountant whose first job after college had been at Price Waterhouse. He'd subsequently taken marketing jobs at Carnation and Heinz Pet Products, where, his résumé noted, he'd been instrumental in setting an all-time record for shipment of 9-Lives pet food: more than thirty-three million cases of the stuff in 1991. Connolly's most recent assignment at Kenner was senior product manager of Nerf, responsible for such toys as the Crossbow, Sharpshooter II, and Ripsaw Blaster. Thirty-three years old, he was the only one of the four who'd played with G.I. Joe as a child.

Operating on the assumption that nothing from Rhode Island was sacred, the new keepers quickly discarded X-Soldiers. Development of all other concepts was halted immediately, and there was no enthusiasm for Sgt. Savage, but that line was already in production. Kent nonetheless considered ordering the factories to stop, with whatever they'd already made written off as a multimillion-dollar loss, on the theory that no Joe in 1995 would whet buyers' appetite for new Joe in 1996. Then again, burned by the precipitous decline of the last year, retailers might never want Joe back; precious shelf space could be lost forever. The risk was too big. With Verrecchia's assent, Kent continued production of Savage, in greatly reduced volume.

With Hassenfeld's directive in mind, Kent convened a brainstorming session at the end of September. Everyone felt pressured, for in order to make a 1996 introduction, they would have to develop new figures and vehicles, from scratch, considerably faster than the year or more it ordinarily took. They had to create a successful new mythos—a dicier proposition than merely determining which existing stories had lost their currency, as Kirk Bozigian knew well. Kent had brought Tom Griffin and Joe Bacal into the process, and the two admen flew to Cincinnati with a document incorporating the considerable, if preliminary, thinking that had already gone into new Joe. The document summarized the toy's evolution since 1964 (much of which they'd had a direct hand in), noting G.I. Joe's many enemies over the years. New Joe would face a new breed of foes: "Crude strong men," "political fanatics," and "mystic cult leaders." Joe's mission would change, as well, from storming the beaches of Normandy to dealing with "scientific prototypes run amok," computer mayhem, and espionage. The millennium beckoned.

Chris Connolly, too, had grappled with Joe's identity since spending the weekend on the *Intrepid* in the shadows of Joe's thirtieth anniversary party. He knew the eyes of the chairman were on him, that he'd been handed responsibility for a crown jewel that had lost its luster. "The things that I grew up seeing on the news at night were body bag counts from Vietnam, but today kids grow up and watch the evening news and see much different things," he said. He listed the horrors of a new age: drive-by shootings, drug smuggling, blown-up buildings, hostage takings, airliners exploding in midair, a world where danger and death were just outside the door.

"What today's kid is concerned about is a lot different from what all the adults who have worked on G.I. Joe in the past were concerned with growing up," Connolly observed. "Today, kids fear crime, violence, drugs, and murder more than us going to war with another country."

By the end of the brainstorming, they had agreed on a general concept. New Joe would be, in Joe Bacal's words, the Green Berets for the nineties—a modernized version of the toy soldier that had succeeded so brilliantly in the eighties. The next task was fleshing out the fantasy. They had little more than a month.

▪

Meanwhile, focus groups were conducted in suburban Cincinnati, in part to learn what boys from the heartland knew about real war. Among the props the moderator used were models of the Jeep and P-40 Warhawk from the Sgt. Savage line. Using photographs and diagrams from World War II, Bozigian's group had styled them authentically. A military historian unquestionably would have approved.

"When you see these," the moderator asked eight- and nine-year-old boys, "what do you think of right away?"

"A war!" one boy said.

"A big, big, big army war," said a second.

"What war are we talking about?" the moderator said.

"The Civil War," a boy said.

"When do you think the Civil War took place?"

"A few years ago."

The moderator turned to Jarrett, a third-grader who'd quickly demonstrated himself to be the most thoughtful and articulate of the group. "Jarrett?" the moderator said. "When did the Civil War take place?"

"Well, I can't really give an exact date," Jarrett said, "but I know it was not a couple of years ago because my grandma was a little girl when the Civil War took place."

Another boy said his father had fought in the Civil War, but, alas, he had no details.

"What do you think World War Two was?" the moderator said. "Who fought in that?"

Japan was all anyone could name.

"One guy is saying Japan, but everybody else sort of has a blank look, right?" the moderator said. "Nobody really knows." Okay, then—was it older brothers, fathers, grandfathers, or great-grandfathers who'd fought? The boys weren't sure about that, either, although there was some suspicion for older brothers. "Maybe it was an uncle," Jarrett ventured.

"How long ago was it?" the moderator asked.

"Eighteen something, I think," Jarrett replied.

But Jarrett was well versed in *Superhuman Samurai Syber-Squad,* yet another television series in the spirit of *Mighty Morphin Power Rangers.* "This guy named Colin, he's evil," Jarrett explained. "He's a computer genius. He finds out this computer overlord of digital places—you know, like in computers and electronic things. So Colin sends out viruses—like megavirus monsters. This kid named Sam, he has this kind of accident, so they find out how to go onto the places. . . ."

I I

HASSENFELD FLEW TO CINCINNATI for a management line review less than two months later, in November. Kent had saved G.I. Joe for last. As the time drew near, the demonstration theater filled. Employees stood along the back and sides, next to Plexiglas-encased displays of Kenner's biggest hits of the pre-Hasbro era: Care Bears, Star Wars, and Strawberry Shortcake. Hassenfeld was front and center, surrounded by his top executives.

Chief presenter for Joe, Connolly wore a starched white shirt and tie, like virtually all of the men in Cincinnati. It was the P&G look. One of Connolly's first slides was a so-called perceptual mapping chart, brainchild of Griffin and Bacal. It categorized the top nineteen action-figure lines by user age and whether their appeal was "reality" or "fantasy." G.I.

Joe stood alone. "We are definitely on the reality side of the map," Connolly said. Nonetheless, he noted, as if anyone needed reminding, Joe had become esoteric in the only realm that mattered: the minds of children.

"We're really not a part of kids' culture," Connolly said. To prove the point, he cited Q scores, a measure of two related qualities of a person, character, or property: current awareness and intrinsic appeal. In the latest boys' research, X-Men and Michael Jordan topped the list with Q scores of sixty-six. G.I. Joe was at thirty-two, one point ahead of Minnie Mouse and only two ahead of figure skater Nancy Kerrigan.

"I'm leaving," Hassenfeld said. "I don't need this! Nancy Kerrigan! Problem is, Tonya Harding's up at fifty-two!" Everyone laughed.

"What we want to do," Connolly said, "is make military cool again, not something you do when you drop out of high school."

He summarized the new story, which Griffin and Bacal's television production company, Sunbow, already was expanding into a new animated series Verrecchia had agreed to help finance. The setting was the near future, when a band of superterrorists has emerged from the ruins of a collapsed superpower.

"These twisted, evil individuals have very strong and distinct personalities," Connolly said. "Their enormous egos and the incessant media coverage of their exploits serve to fuel their quest for destruction while attracting growing hordes of twisted militant followers." They were called SKAR, which had a nice ring (Scar just so happened to be the evil lion in Disney's *Lion King*) but stood for nothing, although Connolly later would find the words to make it an acronym: Soldiers of Kaos, Anarchy & Ruin. Naturally, only one force could stop SKAR in its quest for world domination. New Joe had the latest in weaponry—but so had the old. What really set new Joe apart was personality—what Connolly called "edge, attitude, and renegade spirit."

Connolly turned the presentation over to Dan Price, one of the designers who'd brought the new story to life in figures, vehicles, and a play set. Time had not allowed the customary construction of many finished models, but they'd managed a fairly well-refined sculpting of one: Lt. Stone, the new leader of the Joes. A hush fell over the theater as people crowded forward for a better look. Stone was a hair over five inches tall, with musculature Arnold Schwarzenegger could not possibly have achieved, even with steroids, and a face that was intimidating, if not downright mean. Price handed Stone, an old Joe, and a new Sgt. Savage to Hassenfeld. The chairman studied them silently. Stone was bigger than Savage, Bozigian's cryogenic warrior, and he dwarfed the 3¾-inch figure, the staple since 1982. But America's Movable Fighting Man had been hobbled. Stone could not bend his elbows and knees, and his waist and shoulders did not swivel. He could turn but not bend his neck. Every penny saved on a joint was another penny for muscle.

Price showed drawings of Stone's fellow warriors. Ballistic was a sharpshooter who could knock the gun out of an enemy's hand at a quarter mile: Connolly drew attention to his long hair and age, mid-twenties, and said he was "someone you could emulate, aspire to be, almost a modern-day hero." Dragon was a martial arts specialist, Freight a former professional football player. Mayday was a woman. Headbanger, later renamed Metalhead, was into MTV.

"Music pumps him up," Price said. "His machine gun is almost like a guitar."

SKAR's leader was Iron Klaw, whose hero was Genghis Khan. Scorch, another enemy, was a pyromaniac. Rage was a corrupt arms dealer, Wreckage the ultimate mercenary. After introducing SKAR, Connolly and his people showed a jet, an amphibious assault vehicle, and a tank. When a target on the tank was hit with a projectile, a hatch flew open and the driver popped into view, presumably (if unspokenly) dead. The feature was a big crowd pleaser. ("It's a grown boys' jack-in-the-box!" Kent had said on first seeing it. "Unbelievable!") Price demonstrated what eventually would be called Ultra SLAM Firepower: a pump-action weapon that shot a Nerf-like projectile much farther than any spring-loaded gun could.

"The harder you hit it, the farther it goes," Price said. "What more could you want?"

The presentation was over. All eyes were on Hassenfeld.

"Great," the chairman said. "Phenomenal!"

III

SOME WHILE AFTER BLESSING new Joe, Hassenfeld invited a class of University of Rhode Island graduate business students to dinner in the Greenhouse Cafe. Hassenfeld often made time for students, particularly in his role as trustee of several colleges. The URI students had completed a case study of Hasbro, and they presented their results with a slide show. Hassenfeld was effusive tonight. After dessert he sipped red wine, his favorite, and held court for some three hours.

He left few subjects untouched. Regarding the high costs of manufacturing in the Northeast, a situation that had prompted Hasbro to steadily reduce its local blue-collar workforce, he maintained that the retail chains, under pressure from stockholders and penny-pinching consumers, cared only about the final cost of goods, not the security of jobs. He complimented Mattel for having a fabulous year, but when the students showed a slide stating that a third of Mattel's revenues came from Barbie, his voice dropped to a stage whisper and he said: "Bitch!" He then confided, much to the merriment of all, that at a recent internal meeting he'd unbuttoned his shirt to reveal a T-shirt with the slogan "BARBIE IS A SLUT."

The discussion returned to the serious. In seeking to shape a socially responsible company, Hassenfeld maintained a strict code governing conditions in factories run by its vendors (unlike Mattel, Hasbro did not own factories in Asia). Child or prison labor was forbidden. "Every factory we work with is clean, safe, and up to standards," Hassenfeld told the students. "I can take you to sweatshops here in Rhode Island and in New York City that are much worse than anything in China." Hassenfeld was opposed to boycotts and other retaliatory measures that might help nudge other corporations to his standards. "I believe in human rights," he said in a newspaper story about Clinton's review of China's most-favored-nation status, "but tying human rights to trade is the dumbest thing we could ever do. There's more to gain in a world where we are communicating."

And while Hasbro did not permit child labor, Hassenfeld did not necessarily condemn others' use of it. He'd seen firsthand the poverty in parts of Asia, and he unapologetically approved of a young teen taking a job if it meant hope for an otherwise despairing family. He put these questions to the URI students: Is it better to give a child a steady income or uphold Western principles knowing families were scrounging through garbage for food? If local custom sanctioned child labor and conditions were verifiably humane, who was an American to deny opportunity?

"Do not put your views on another society," he said, "unless you live within and work within that society."

∎

Under the banner of Trends, the URI class had slipped in a delicate one-liner. "Violent Toys," the slide said.

Without flinching, Hassenfeld plunged into a spirited discourse that began with the relationship of television to violence. He related a conversation he'd had more than once with Japanese toy makers, who couldn't understand why America was a vastly more violent society than their own—yet Japanese television was more explicit than almost anything shown in the United States. One answer, Hassenfeld contended, was the ready access Americans had to firearms, which were exceedingly difficult for a Japanese civilian to obtain. Another was what he described as the breakdown of the traditional two-parent American family, the norm when he was growing up. Hassenfeld believed a child needs a mother and father, together, in order to thrive.

Hassenfeld went to considerable lengths to sell nothing but safe products. Toys had to pass exhaustive testing, and the word of Malcolm Denniss, Hasbro's safety czar, was law. Employees grumbled about his zeal, for it sometimes led to expensive delays or favorite concepts being killed, but Hassenfeld did not compromise. On those rare occasions when something slipped through, he was quick to initiate a recall, even if it meant embarrassment—Playskool's 1-2-3 High Chair, for example, which was found dangerously defective not long after he was honored by the Consumer Product Safety Commission as one of the truly good guys (cracks in plastic joints had caused a small number of chairs to collapse, with scattered minor injuries reported). The lessons of Flubber were not forgotten. But these were physical concerns, a peculiarity of the late Industrial Age that could be codified into readily verifiable standards. The mind of a child was something else again.

Questions about the psychological implications of violent toys had dogged Hasbro almost since Merrill brought G.I. Joe to market. Among the most persistent critics were Diane E. Levin and Nancy Carlsson-Paige, education professors at two Boston-area colleges. While acknowledging some value in war play, Levin and Carlsson-Paige argued that toys such as Joe, with their ties to TV, overall are unhealthy influences. "Forces outside the home are affecting children and their war play in ways we are only beginning to understand," they wrote in *Who's Calling the Shots?: How to Respond Effectively to Children's Fascination with War Play and War*

Toys. "What is clear to us now is that children and parents are losing control of war play and toys." But without research of the depth linking TV and violence, there was room for legitimate debate about the effects of violent toys on impressionable young minds.

To Hassenfeld it seemed self-evident that real weapons, not toys, were the issue society ought to address. He'd publicly supported a number of gun control organizations and, in 1996, would join business leaders in buying a signed full-page ad in *The New York Times* urging Congress and President Clinton to trim the Pentagon's budget. Hasbro had made only one or two realistic-looking toy guns in its history, and they'd left the market decades ago.

"I find it fascinating—absolutely fascinating—how we can legislate toys and toy guns but we can't legislate real guns," Hassenfeld said. "I just think it's wonderfully hypocritical." Hasbro had just acquired Larami, maker of the Super Soaker water gun line, when Hassenfeld spoke to the URI class. He considered the much publicized efforts of politicians to ban squirt guns in several cities an absurd commentary on modern life.

Like Margaret Loesch's or Haim Saban's response to criticism of *Power Rangers,* Hassenfeld's stock defense of G.I. Joe was its storyline. "All of the action figures that we've done are basically showing good overcoming evil," he said. "We're not glorifying the rewards of being successful in a life of crime or evil." As far as he knew, boys had imitated their warrior fathers as long as there had been wars, whether with sticks, wooden swords, plastic soldiers—or, soon, Ultra SLAM Firepower.

But in a moment of remarkable candor that brought a hush to the Greenhouse Cafe, Hassenfeld acknowledged that in the information age, toys and television are inextricably and powerfully linked—and admitted he did not understand the full implications of the combination. *Batman* was violent, he noted, but was it harmful? He doubted it. What about the violence in *Exodus? Lawrence of Arabia?* Or, for that matter, Shakespeare?

"I don't know of anyone who's grown up wrong on G.I. Joe," Hassenfeld said, conceding: "There may be." He told the students he'd accepted an invitation from activists associated with Harvard University to privately discuss TV violence as a public health issue. Discussion might help in greater understanding, but the Harvard session would bring Hassenfeld to no new consciousness. It would end with but one consensus: that the discussion should resume someday.

"Don't have the answers," Alan said. "I really don't know what is right or wrong."

IV

CHRIS CONNOLLY COULD barely contain himself when he went to Rhode Island to introduce Hasbro's outlicensing and promotions department to new G.I. Joe. He was wearing a San Diego Chargers cap, and as he paced the room, pausing only to dash off a few words on a flip chart, he could have passed for a coach the morning of the championship game.

"So much of G.I. Joe in 1996 is going to be made or broken in this room," he said. He was not quite willing to say that Joe had potential to eclipse Power Rangers, but that was the mind-set he urged everyone to adopt. Connolly related what his bosses had told him and his team in Cincinnati: " 'If you guys don't think big, you're not going to win big.' "

Lacking a blockbuster movie license as yet for 1996, Kent was counting on a resurrection of Joe to help achieve Verrecchia's postrestructuring ambitions. To help prepare the way, she was unloading the last of Bozigian's old 3¾-inch Joes at fire-sale prices, and she would manufacture only a measly $17 million or so of Sgt. Savage. Including a limited collectors' line of twelve-inch figures, Kent was hoping for up to $70 million in sales in new Joe's first year. That would put Joe in Batman's league, at least for a year when there was no Batman movie.

Television was central to Kent's expectations. No G.I. Joe movie deal had been signed yet, despite Larry Kasanoff's efforts, but working closely with Connolly and his team, Sunbow was moving rapidly toward production of the animated series, which would air on weekends beginning in the fall of 1995, theoretically enabling Hasbro to build demand for toys in the weeks before they were available. Thirteen episodes would be shot at $300,000 apiece. Hasbro was selling the program through syndication, for the networks were picky about their violence—embracing the fiery aggression of *Power Rangers* but having no interest in the military equivalent.

Unquestionably the new show would be violent. The writer's bible, which set the guidelines for scripts, encouraged firefights, explosions, detonations, and crashes. Few children's shows had ever featured a greater variety of conventional weapons: missiles, bombs, grenades, rockets, howitzers, Gatling guns, flamethrowers, tear gas launchers, and the more mundane but nonetheless useful rifles and pistols. Nor was Joe to be outdone in futuristic armament. Shark, for example, had the so-called hydroelectric cannon, which could spray choking clouds of steam, blast water with sufficient force to knock a foe unconscious, or shoot a slug of ice with the power to penetrate steel.

Cincinnati and Sunbow had developed Joe's enemies into psychotic murderers who flourished in the wasteland of a postapocalyptic world. A military genius with mighty forces at his command, Iron Klaw used a form of mind control to bend law-abiding communities to his will, and his headquarters was at the site of a monstrous toxic waste accident, where only blighted vegetation now grew. Scorch's ambition was building a bomb big enough to blow up the earth; he lived in a nuclear waste dump. The result of genetic experimentation gone terribly awry, Wreckage was part machine, able to communicate by modem by plugging a phone jack into his brain.

Rage still lived at home.

"You've seen this guy a million times on the news," the bible said. "The lonely middle-aged guy who lives with his mom and finally snaps and shoots up the place where he works." Rage's weapon drove a microchip into a victim's brain, where it could induce excruciating pain, hallucination, or schizophrenia, and his only friends were the Cyber-Hacks, who worked their evil by sabotaging the Internet. Among the other scenarios writers were asked to explore were ethnic tension, nerve gas, and time bombs hidden in jetliners. It seemed Sunbow and Cincinnati had not rested until they'd plumbed every mass fear a citizen might harbor on the eve of the millennium. Only microbes were conspicuously absent.

Despite its placement on the perceptual mapping chart, Joe was oddly unrealistic, at least to an adult. The series bible asked writers to have a humorous touch whenever possible, and hard-driving rock music was suggested for the sound track. And as with the 1980s series, writers were strictly forbidden from showing the effects of violence on humans. "Nobody dies. Ever," the bible stated, but it was a prohibition applying only to humans: Zaps, Skyrenes, robots, and androids were open targets. There were other incongruities. Bullets were unacceptable. Sidearms and rifles loaded energy packs, not lead—but cutlasses, samurai swords, and battle-axes were permissible, although knives were not. Hand-to-hand combat was allowed, but only if the loser recovered by the end of the scene. "Don't ever build a bomb or booby trap some pinhead can imitate," the bible cautioned. "It's safer to go *w-a-a-a-y* over the top in improbable outrageousness than to construct something an idiot might copy."

▪

Connolly explained that the job facing outlicensing and promotion was to use TV and the new Dark Horse comic as a springboard from which to send G.I. Joe deeper and deeper into the popular culture. He maintained the new story was an ideal hook for mothers, who feared the real-world crime, violence, and related evils the new plastic hero had committed his very existence to fighting.

"At the same time," Connolly said, "we're not handing out food packets in Somalia. We still want an edge."

Connolly handed his Magic Marker to Pat Schmidt, the head of promotions. She wrote, "GI Joe 1996: Big Ideas," on the flip chart, and the discussion began. An extraordinary variety of possibilities, some more feasible than others, surfaced over the next hour. Promotional efforts could include coupons, prepaid phone cards, an on-line magazine, a CD-ROM comic, a 3-D comic, amusement park rides, mall tours, special glasses with which children could decode secret messages from the animated series, TV contests, a club, and a retail boutique: a store within a store, a sales twist Mattel had used successfully with Barbie. Joes could be donated to day care centers and hotels that drew vacationing families. There was considerable enthusiasm for another G.I. Joe grade-school curriculum—"a do-good educational program," as Connolly called it.

In an era when even the Vatican exploited its intellectual properties with official apparel, jewelry, and books, Hasbro could count on interest in its hallowed icon from a similarly broad range of licensees. John Gildea, head of licensing in Rhode Island, recently had approached Mortal Kombat maker Acclaim Entertainment about a G.I. Joe video game. Coloring books, pogs, trading cards, and puzzles and board games (from Milton Bradley) were strong possibilities. In addition to the usual children's clothing and footwear, Connolly wanted designer apparel targeted toward an older audience—Urban Gear or Special Forces, he'd call it. Gildea approved, and he advised contacting the firm that already was marketing Mr. Potato Head T-shirts. Connolly hoped Mars Inc., the candy company, would be interested in G.I. Joe Skittles. A fast-food tie-in was a priority, as was a cereal, but Schmidt doubted the major millers would be interested. It was that old violence bugaboo again.

"These people don't want Joe," Schmidt said. "Mom buys the cereal, Mom puts it on the table. These people consider one complaint a failure." Then approach smaller companies or providers of store brands, Connolly advised. He wasn't hung up over corporate prestige. He wanted exposure.

"If we're going after eyeballs," he said, "we don't care how it gets there."

V

ON HIS NEXT TRIP to Rhode Island, Connolly met with marketers of role-play, construction, and activities toys, categories into which new Joe might fruitfully be extended. He came bearing news. A distinctive orange-and-yellow packaging was well along in development, and after much deliberation, he had found the tag line he believed best captured Joe's reengineered persona. Joe was now G.I. Joe Extreme, as in the new motto "Extreme times call for extreme heroes!" Connolly had been inspired in part by the cable network ESPN, which was sponsoring street luge, bungee jumping, and other esoteric sports that had caught the fancy of generation X under the banner of "extreme games." Connolly had confirmed the word's fresh meaning with a linguistics professor at the University of California, Los Angeles, his alma mater. When it went out of vogue, he noted, they could replace it.

Bozigian was among those who attended Connolly's presentation. In the months since being assigned to Play-Doh, he had substantially broadened that line, much to Hassenfeld's delight. Bozigian was confident that his 1995 marketing plan would increase revenues by almost 25 percent and that sales in 1996 would be nearly double when he took charge. Connolly had invited him to the presentation to see what future G.I. Joe Extreme might have in compounds.

Bozigian thought Connolly's pop-up tank was a nice touch, and he liked some of the new Joes. But he considered Klaw and his villains boring, Ultra SLAM Firepower little different from foam-tipped weapons Joe had featured before. Overall he was unimpressed. He did not consider this the radical new direction Connolly was proclaiming and Hassenfeld and Verrecchia had sought. He doubted G.I. Joe Extreme had better market prospects than his beloved Sgt. Savage.

But he did not share his opinions with Connolly. "Super job, guys," he said. Courtesy was characteristic of Bozigian, calculatedly so since the restructuring. These days he did his job quietly and seemed supportive of the new order—indeed, his superiors praised his positive attitude. Almost no one at Hasbro knew how unhappy he was, how diligently he was scheming to leave, and only once had there been a hint of his true feelings.

It came during the first postrestructuring management line reviews, on a day when what was left of the old Joe crew, all on different teams now, had presented their new lines. Bozigian followed Greg Berndtson, the longtime Joe designer whose new group (the "pink/macho" team) had charge of dollhouse and Playskool Cool Tools, including the garden snippers, weed whacker, and hedge trimmers that Berndtson had designed since Black Tuesday. Like his old colleagues, Bozigian was wearing something that looked alien on him: a starched white shirt and tie. He began his Play-Doh presentation with Batman in a Can: a plastic figure of the superhero that would be sold with a container of compound. Bozigian intended it more as a gag than a real concept and was flabbergasted at the reaction. "Wow, that's awesome!" Hassenfeld said. "Must have been one of my ideas!" But Batman in a Can was the only clue Bozigian dropped publicly about his state of mind. He would remain a good soldier until he finally left Hasbro, in early 1996, to develop toy concepts on his own.

Not everyone was playing the game like Bozigian. Months after Black Tuesday, Don DeLuca remained openly contemptuous of the restructuring. He'd brought his criticisms directly to the chairman, but the chairman had much bigger things on his mind.

14

■

KID NUMBER ONE

I

*F*ive days before Christmas Alan Hassenfeld drove from Pawtucket to Providence's Hasbro Children's Hospital, open not quite a year. PR chief Wayne Charness and two of his staff were waiting in the lobby with gurneys piled high with toys, games, and baskets of fresh-baked chocolate-chip cookies, the Hasbro chef's mouthwatering specialty. Hassenfeld was spirited. Only hours before, the Mexican peso had been devalued, bringing his Central American business to the point of devastation after years of slow but steady progress in that critical market. But business had never been the only prism through which Hassenfeld viewed life.

"This puts it all in perspective," he said as he followed the gurneys into an elevator.

The first stop was the intensive care unit. "Merry Christmas, everyone!" Hassenfeld said.

"Is that Mister Hasbro?" a nurse whispered.

Hassenfeld began his rounds, a journey through the eighty-seven-bed hospital that would last three hours.

"This is my favorite teddy bear," he told a boy with cancer. "He's going to keep you company." Another boy who would not be going home for

Christmas didn't want a teddy bear, Transformer, Littlest Pet Shop, Battleship game, or anything else Hassenfeld offered. He wanted a Power Ranger. Hassenfeld promised to send one right over. "Mighty Morphin Power Ranger—this is hurting me!" He laughed.

"Aren't you nice," a mother said. "May I ask who you are?"

"We work at Hasbro," Hassenfeld said, letting it go at that.

Childless, a fact he regretted, and stepfather to a boy and a girl who were teenagers at boarding school when he married, Hassenfeld knew young children as much from TV and movies as from real life. Yet he had a touch. Room by room he went, handing out presents and drawing out children and their families with talk about sports, movies, and the latest in clothing and TV. He did not allow the presence of sickness to visibly faze him; only occasionally, out of earshot of patients, did he let on how deeply he was moved. In deciding to play Santa Claus, he'd ruled out press coverage or internal announcement except to administrators who had to be informed. He intended to come back every year, quietly, only to cheer up kids.

■

To no small extent, it was a hospital Hassenfeld had built. Asked in 1991 to spearhead a $51 million campaign to replace an antiquated pediatrics wing at Rhode Island Hospital, he'd done more than jump-start contributions with his $2.5 million pledge. Burning the midnight oil to accommodate the demands of also being chairman of RIght Now!, the reform coalition, he had persuaded friends and business associates around the world to ante up. With Vivien he reviewed color schemes. Finding them drab, he brought in Deborah Sussman of Sussman/Prejza & Company, whose prize-winning work included Hasbro's New York showroom, to fashion a more appealing atmosphere, one that steered the mind away from sickness. He encouraged his employees to pitch in with fundraisers, works of art, and design advice, and he paid for their materials and time. He insisted their company's name, not his family's, go on the building.

Hassenfeld believed corporate success without social responsibility was immoral, and he was convinced that shareholders of the twenty-first century would not merely approve of such ethics, but demand them. Since its founding in 1984, the Hasbro Children's Foundation had donated nearly $25 million to organizations nationwide. Every year the Hasbro

Charitable Trusts awarded $1.5 million more in grants, plus a quarter of a million toys; a family trust gave another $3 million. Many companies and millionaires, of course, are generous. What distinguished Hassenfeld was his personal involvement in so many causes—his gifts of time, such as the untold hours for RIght Now! He'd traveled a distance since volunteering a few hours a week with disadvantaged minorities in Providence when he was in college.

"If you're not willing to get your hands dirty," he said, "why should anyone else?"

I I

THE OVERRIDING CORPORATE CONCERN facing Hassenfeld that Christmas was vision. What was Hasbro Inc. as the century drew to a close? What should it be five years hence? What were the long-term implications of Mattel's sudden new surge?

Certainly the industry was changing, and with it—in part because of it—children's culture. What hadn't changed was the merciless mandate of growth and profitability, the continuing price to be paid for the greatness to which Stephen had brought the family firm. Acquiring Tonka had won Alan accolades from shareholders and Wall Street, but with Fisher-Price gone to Mattel, there were no independent toy makers of that size or worldwide strategic importance left to buy anymore. And having risen only slightly in 1993, revenues and earnings were going to drop in 1994. Hasbro Inc. seemed to have reached another plateau.

Nearly six years into his chairmanship, Hassenfeld had the feeling he was almost starting anew.

He'd at least reached some conclusions about the direction he wanted to take. Where Stephen had shied away from Hollywood, he wanted Hasbro to be the only toy company the studios thought of. Where Hasbro once had boasted that no more than 5 percent of its revenues came from a single line, Alan, like Amerman, was increasingly inclined toward building brands. The untapped potential in such classics as Monopoly excited him, as did new opportunities in software and the Internet. He didn't believe Hasbro should be constrained by its identity as a manufacturer of toys, puzzles, and games. More and more he viewed Hasbro as a consumer products firm, albeit one geared toward leisure and entertainment.

"There are stations of the cross we haven't visited yet," he said. "There's a circle that's forming that we have got to be part of."

However the corporation changed, Hassenfeld knew the top structure would have to as well. Therein lay the rub.

In trying to please his favored executives four years ago in the management shake-up that drove Steve Schwartz away, Hassenfeld had unwittingly strengthened Hasbro's fiefdoms. The Tonka acquisition had only exacerbated the situation. Four groups were developing software, and three licensing departments were dealing with the film and television industries. Toys rarely conversed with games, even when both divisions had rights to the same property. Hasbro manufactured around the globe with two separate chains of command and a mix of vendors and company-owned plants. And the international sales and marketing situation was as confusing as one of Milton Bradley's one-thousand-piece puzzles: South America was run by the manager of Canada, who reported to George Ditomassi, whose office was in Massachusetts and whose primary responsibility was games; London-based Norman Walker reported to Ditomassi for Europe, but directly to Alan for Japan, Australia, and New Zealand. Efforts had been made toward common purpose, including Verrecchia and Walker recently agreeing to jointly develop a few toy lines, but these were piecemeal measures.

One decisive solution would be a corporate president with across-the-board responsibilities for day-to-day management—a corporate strongman, as it were, empowered by the chairman to straighten out the mess—but naming either of the two likeliest candidates would mean offending the other and almost certainly losing him as well. For while Ditomassi and Verrecchia were unfailingly cordial to each other, had a mutual interest in sports, and even shared a showroom office during Toy Fair, privately both had let Hassenfeld know that neither could work for the other. And Alan had never gone outside for top talent. Until he found the stomach to confront such political issues and the grief that inevitably would result, a huge roadblock would remain.

For some time now Verrecchia and Ditomassi independently had been urging their chairman to resolve the structural problems. Verrecchia, of course, had restated his case to be president (or whatever title the position required), but if that were not in the cards, he believed it was incumbent on Hassenfeld to find another solution.

"Would I like an opportunity to do something?" Verrecchia said.

"Sure. But I want the company to be successful. I own a couple of hundred thousand shares of this company's stock. If the stock goes up twenty bucks, I'll kiss somebody's ass on Newport Avenue for that to happen."

At the highest levels of Hasbro, there were rumblings.

Meanwhile there was Kid Number One, the fun-loving face Alan liked to present to the world. It was time for Toy Fair.

BOOK THREE

15

GOTHAM CITY

I

On the day before Toy Fair 1995 officially opened, Alan Hassenfeld left his office on the mezzanine of his New York showroom, sprinted down to the lobby, and breezed past uniformed security guards into the heart of West Twenty-third. A giant Hasbro Toy Group banner hung from the ceiling, and beneath it were flags emblazoned with the names of Verrecchia's brands—Tonka, Playskool, and Kenner—which would remain on action-figure packaging and in commercials even though divisions had disappeared in the August restructuring. A fixture in Hasbro's showroom since Stephen had opened it, George Ditomassi's Milton Bradley had been relocated to the Toy Building annex, where Kenner had shown its new lines in the days of Bruce Stein. Gone but eight months, Stein seemed as ancient as the Jurassic era.

Hassenfeld descended a second flight of stairs to the cafeteria, where he'd instructed staff to build a diorama of A Day in the Park with Barney, a new attraction soon to open in Universal Studios Florida. He greeted Sheryl Leach, the Texas teacher who created Barney, and she complimented the Baby Bop plush toy he was carrying and his shirt, a custom denim garment with a Barney patch sewn onto the breast. The chairman headed for the podium through the crowd of over a hundred, most of them salesmen who'd been quietly informed that skipping the chairman's Barney pep rally would not be the wisest career-building move.

Hassenfeld was in a great mood. He was hosting a dinner for analysts that evening and would give a financial presentation at the more demanding William Blair & Company conference in three days—forums at which the paramount question would be how he intended to reignite Hasbro's growth at a time when Mattel was going gangbusters. But with John O'Neill and Wayne Charness hard at work perfecting his response—and with *Batman Forever,* the presumed summer blockbuster, safely in hand—Alan could afford a little fun.

He took the microphone and said: "Good afternoon, everyone!"

"Good afternoon, Alan," the crowd responded.

Hassenfeld began by proclaiming his affection for Toy Fair. How could it be otherwise? he said—he was "a February thought," conceived by his parents here in New York at Toy Fair and an attendant every year since! There was a moment of awkward silence, and then people tittered; humor, not true confession, must have been his intent. Hassenfeld told the story of Barney's origins and then professed his true feelings for the character.

"I love Barney," he said. "Barney represents to me everything that's good."

The crowd knew he was sincere. Once stratospheric, sales of Barney products had plummeted in 1994, in large part because Leach's The Lyons Group had sold too many licenses, the penalty for which was an oversaturated market. Playskool especially had suffered. This had not diminished Hassenfeld's affection for the purple dinosaur. He expected to rebuild sales, of course, but was willing to weather the drought also because he was charmed by Barney's wholesome message.

This was not the first time emotion had influenced the chairman's product decisions. More than once, Hassenfeld had become infatuated with a property and insisted on buying it regardless of others' reservations. Babe the Gallant Pig, a plush toy based on the lovable lead character of the yet-to-be-released movie, was an example this year: few of his own people wanted the license, and buyers seeing the toy on their tours through West Twenty-third this Toy Fair were scornful. *Babe* would turn out to be the surprise movie hit of 1995 and a huge winner on the home video market. Vindicated, Hassenfeld would return in 1996 with Talking Babe.

In her remarks, Leach cited studies by Yale University child psychologists Jerome L. and Dorothy G. Singer that suggested the *Barney & Friends* PBS series was that welcome rarity in children's programming: an enjoyable show with a positive influence on its young viewers' cognitive abilities, social skills, and self-image. Leach was taking Barney global with TV, books, recordings, merchandise, and a movie. "The nonviolent programming we've built is something we feel the world is sorely in need of," she said. "Barney is trying to leave the world better than when he found it."

Verrecchia was standing in back, a devilish look on his face. He bent and whispered in a writer's ear: "Fuck Barney!" He was only partly jesting. He had 250,000 Playskool Talking Barneys gathering dust in his Seattle warehouse.

▪

Hassenfeld was the consummate host during Toy Fair. He provided breakfast and lunch daily to hundreds, and his cocktail parties, with their ice sculptures and oysters on the half shell, were reminiscent of his brother's. From his arrival before seven every morning until he'd bade his last guests good night, he was a ubiquitous if flitting presence—dashing down from his office to greet Haim Saban and his cell phone–equipped entourage; escorting Charles Lazarus through the Batcave; escaping back to his office for a quick smoke and a few minutes with his mother, sister, or wife; ensuring that George Lucas's licensing chief, Howard Roffman, was pleased with every detail of the *Star Wars* display. (After a lapse of several years, Hasbro was again marketing a line of toys based on the first *Star Wars* trilogy while campaigning mightily for rights to the all-new second trilogy, whose first title, all but guaranteed to be a box office and merchandising phenomenon, was not due for release until 1999 or later.) Despite eighteen-hour days, Hassenfeld was irrepressibly upbeat for his two weeks in New York. Many memorable moments in family and company history had unfolded at Toy Fair, a fact his Barney audience could appreciate with new poignancy.

As he watched the hordes return for second and third helpings of beef bourguignon or fresh-carved turkey, Verrecchia sometimes grumbled quietly. You could almost see him calculating the cost/benefit ratio of each piece of meat. He had nothing against lavish entertainment, provided it served some useful business purpose; but Toy Fair, he increasingly believed, did not—not enough to justify a tab (for Hasbro alone) of more than $10 million, exclusive of salaries, which were millions more. And not at a time when his Hasbro Toy Group was struggling to get on its feet. In Merrill's era Toy Fair was indispensable: wrapped in secrecy during development, the new lines were unveiled to buyers for the very first time, and orders were written on the spot. But the laws of the marketplace had changed with the emergence of modern chains and their vastly more complicated operations. Top Four accounts could not afford to wait until February to begin planning four seasons of end caps, boutiques, specials, advertising, and promotions in hundreds of stores in the United States and, lately, abroad—and with two-thirds or more of their sales at stake with just the Top Four, Hasbro, Mattel, and other large toy makers could ill afford to jeopardize relations. Senior buyers from Top Four accounts first saw new lines in private viewing the summer of the year before they went to market, in time for manufacturers to modify or kill products that were poorly received, and Pre–Toy Fair provided a second, more thorough, look. Except for movie properties that studios demanded be kept confidential, few items went unseen until February.

Verrecchia's response was predictable. He wanted to abandon New York Toy Fair (as did Mattel) and close West Twenty-third when Hasbro's lease expired at the end of the century. Hassenfeld had not committed to this course, but in light of the plateau Hasbro was on, he was increasingly inclined. The contribution to the bottom line was simply too enticing.

▪

But like Hassenfeld, Verrecchia was looking forward to 1995 Toy Fair's biggest bash, despite indirectly footing part of the $650,000 bill through royalty payments to Warner Bros., its host. Glamorous Nicole Kidman would be there, and the Hasbro brass had been invited to meet her and the other stars and director of *Batman Forever*, the Warner Bros. production widely expected to be the merchandising bonanza of the year.

Spotlights swept the wintry sky as the chairman and his people walked the several blocks to the Lexington Avenue Armory, a towering brick edifice that evoked the sinister spirit of Gotham City. Police barricades kept onlookers at a distance as guests bearing invitations that unfolded into a Batmobile were admitted. The Hasbro party was escorted to a private room, where for the next half hour they and a handful of other key licensees mingled with the celebrities. Less privileged attendees, some 1,600 in all, were directed to the armory's main floor, a mammoth space divided by a curtain. Speculation about what was behind it swirled as guests partook of hors d'oeuvres and wine in the shadow of a wall mural that featured a bit of grown-up spice: a topless Catwoman. At 6:45 P.M., the curtain parted, revealing seating and a stage. The VIPs took their reserved places. The stars remained hidden. George Jones, president of Warner worldwide licensing, crossed the stage to the microphone.

Jones spoke of record orders for Batman merchandise and of the more than $100 million Warner and its partners had committed to advertising and promoting the property in its countless iterations. The *Batman Forever* campaign had everything Chris Connolly dreamed of for G.I. Joe Extreme: a fast-food partner (McDonald's), video games (Sega and Acclaim), books (Warner and Little, Brown & Company), a cereal (Kellogg Co.), a theme park attraction (Six Flags), a hit song, an MTV video, a state-of-the-art Web site, and much, much, more, all supported by a perennially popular comic book and an ongoing top ten TV series on the number one children's network, Fox. By *Batman Forever's* June release, retail shelves would be overflowing with Batman halter tops, panties, napkin rings, edible cake decals, removable tattoos, and hundreds of other products—an approximately $1 billion global barrage led by toys from Hasbro, by far the largest licensee. Here indeed was a model for the new age.

Jones reminded the audience of the dark tone of the last Batman film, second in the contemporary series. This installment, he said, was intentionally lighter.

"I think you all know that is a real positive in terms of what's merchandisable," he said.

The licensees certainly did. Warner's previous Batman movie, director Tim Burton's 1992 *Batman Returns,* was quirky film noir replete with killer clowns, a whip-cracking Catwoman, overt sexual suggestion, and scenes in sewers. Believing that McDonald's Batman Happy Meals were heightening young children's interest in depravity, family groups had been outraged. Their protests made for unflattering headlines and editorials, including one in *The New York Times* that chastised the fast-food chain for promoting a movie in which children were kidnapped and threatened with death. With a box office $90 million less than the first Batman film, released in 1989, Warner did not need the added alarm of a spooked promotional partner to understand the urgency of revamping its franchise, arguably the brightest jewel in Time Warner Inc.'s $16 billion worldwide empire. The studio did not invite Burton to direct *Batman Forever*. Terry Semel and his co–chief executive officer Robert A. Daly, two of Hollywood's most consistently successful executives, hired Joel Schumacher—a flamboyant, puckish director whose notion of Batman was adventure and fun.

After a few words by Semel and a wave from Time Warner chairman Gerald M. Levin, who was seated near Hassenfeld, Schumacher took the stage. No petulant artiste ("a pop culture sponge," was how he described himself), he'd gone beyond lightening the tone of *Batman*. He'd been amenable to, and highly successful at, licensee relations. With his charm, and the mystique that came with a big budget, he'd been the star of the dog-and-pony shows and set visits with which Warner regaled its outside partners. Schumacher related the story of being flown to Burbank from the set of his last film, John Grisham's *The Client,* and being asked to accept the honor of directing *B3*. He complimented McDonald's for signing on again and praised Hasbro, notably the company's "geniuses" in Cincinnati.

"They're such amazing people," Schumacher said. "They've done such an amazing job." Hassenfeld's executives were elated, for licensing mogul Howard Roffman was here tonight; in the furious bidding for rights to the second *Star Wars* trilogy, such praise was priceless. Schumacher showed a rough-cut trailer of his movie, still in production. When the lights went up, five of *Batman Forever*'s stars had materialized. Only Jim Carrey, the Riddler, spoke.

"A friend of mine backstage said: 'Why don't we give the money to charity?' " Carrey flashed his goofy grin. "Yeah, you're right," he said. "There's just too much money to be made!" The licensees roared.

The screen behind Carrey rose. There, bathed in laser light and dry-ice fog, was the Batmobile, shipped cross-continent from the Warner lot. Not coincidentally, the Batmobile was the signature item in Hasbro's toy line. Music thundered through the old armory, and the speaking program ended. Like pilgrims in the presence of a sacred relic, the crowd converged reverentially around the Batmobile, some bold souls even daring to touch it. Those willing to endure a long line could have a Polaroid picture taken of themselves with it.

II

FOR THE FIRST TIME in memory, Mattel preceded Hasbro at the Tenth Annual William Blair & Company Toy and Video Game Conference. With the release of 1994 results the previous week, it was official: Amerman had dethroned Alan and now wore the crown of largest toy maker on earth. Mattel's sales were $3.2 billion, up 19 percent from 1993, with net income a record (for any toy company ever) $256 million. Hasbro's revenues had dipped almost $80 million, to $2.67 billion, and net earnings had declined, although only slightly, to $175 million. Those were Hasbro's lowest numbers since acquiring Tonka. After almost two decades, the best fairy tale in toys was no longer being written by a Hassenfeld.

Amerman started his presentation by noting that 1995 was the fiftieth anniversary of his company. Avoiding any comparison to his prime competitor—as if he needed to—he once again attributed Mattel's continuing success to the cornerstone of his chairmanship: global brands. He spoke ardently of the virtues of Mattel's latest restructuring, announced just before Christmas, in which some one thousand blue- and white-collar workers had been terminated at an annual savings of $25 million (next to it, Black Tuesday had been peanuts).

Jill Barad followed Amerman to talk about product. She began, as always, with Barbie, which had grown over 10 percent again, to $1.1 billion in worldwide sales (and was started toward another record, $1.4 billion, in 1995). "I know the question you're asking yourselves," Barad said. "Can Barbie continue this level of growth? The answer is yes!"

Hassenfeld began his address with contrition.

"It's not often I get up in front of an audience of astute financial managers and apologize for producing only one hundred and seventy-five million in earnings," he said. "Then again, it's not often that Hasbro has failed to deliver growth on the top and bottom lines." Hassenfeld blamed the vicissitudes of Jurassic Park and Barney for much of the drop-off and said Verrecchia's restructuring was an integral part of his plan to fly high again. Other elements he listed were acquisitions, international expansion, diversification into software, and better global exploitation of Hasbro's brands. But for the details, he could have been reading off Amerman's script. Amerman, however, had not mentioned philanthropy, although Mattel did give to charity.

"The success of a corporation is not just measured by its financial performance," Hassenfeld said in noting the tenth anniversary of the Hasbro Children's Foundation. "It must also recognize and be involved in the vital issues of the time."

Major presentations were followed by question-and-answer sessions to which analysts, but not competitors, were invited. Removed from the Hotel Pierre's Grand Ballroom to the intimacy of a smaller chamber, Hassenfeld was more feisty than he'd been before the larger audience. If attitude was a guide, he seemed to be adopting the mind-set of Verrecchia, who'd taken to calling Mattel the "common enemy" internally. Hassenfeld proclaimed his enthusiasm for Sindy, currently engaged in new retail battles with Barbie across Europe now that the lawsuits were settled. He railed at Tyco, America's third largest toy maker (a distant third), for returning fire against Hasbro's XRC, a promising new line of radio-controlled cars he wanted to be a major brand.

"If you think I'm angry, I am," Hassenfeld said. "I am not going to let Mattel or Tyco or anyone take business away from us. I'm going to be a bloody-minded competitor like I have not been."

Asked by an analyst to elaborate, Hassenfeld smiled and said only: "I've got some tricks up my sleeve."

•

One morning before Toy Fair ended, Hassenfeld joined a small group of marketers and senior executives in a conference room near his West Twenty-third office. The meeting had not appeared on any published schedule, and copies of the document that was discussed were collected when people left. At one point a building services employee barged in. He was after a television monitor. The discussion went dead as he took it and departed. "We'll have to kill him now," Dan Owen joked.

Sindy was the reason for the secrecy. Since before Stein left Hasbro, Cincinnati had been itching to bring the doll to the United States. Still smarting from Mattel's 1991 suit against Kenner's Miss America doll (an expensive, time-consuming distraction not unlike the Sindy morass—precisely Mattel's intent), Kent's people weren't motivated only by revenge. They wanted what Stephen Hassenfeld had nearly gone mad for: a few pieces of eight from a glittering treasure. No one entertained the fantasy of dethroning Barbie, not with Amerman and Barad at the palace gate, but a long-term U.S. business eventually generating something like

$100 million a year in revenues with a respectable profit margin did not seem delusional. There were strategic ramifications as well.

"It is critical for Hasbro to break Mattel's dominance in the fashion doll category," Kent's document stated. "Barbie's $1 billion–plus in worldwide annual sales generate the profits and cash flow Mattel uses to fund multiple initiatives against Hasbro. Furthermore, Mattel leverages the Barbie brand with the trade against us." A twelve-inch piece of plastic was indeed a formidable weapon.

Hassenfeld was encouraged by Sindy's overseas performance. Freed from litigation, Norman Walker had put the doll into all major Western European markets but Italy by 1994, and his core British business had grown bigger than ever. "We've shaken them up for once," Hassenfeld said.

But exporting that promise to America was not simply a matter of having the factories load containers for Seattle. Working with Walker's group, Cincinnati had chosen existing features, outfits, and themes they believed would work in America, blending them with original design to come up with a distinctive new look. One of Kent's marketers showed the chairman the prototypical dolls. They were stunningly executed and very cool—much more in the spirit of *Teen* magazine than, say, *Modern Bride*. "This is not your mother's Oldsmobile," Kent said.

The discussion turned to name. Walker argued that preserving the name "Sindy" had important global ramifications, but Kent was concerned with the first three letters of the word: S-i-n. Would consumers in the nation's Bible Belt seize on them as evidence of lascivious intent? The idea wasn't so crazy. Fanatics claimed to be able to see the word "sex" in a cloud in Disney's *Lion King* and to hear a character in *Aladdin* whisper: "All good teenagers, take off your clothes." And Kent well remembered Cincinnati neighbor Procter & Gamble's experience with its venerable moon-and-stars logo, which certain religious fundamentalists maintained was a Satanic symbol. After years of refuting such allegations, which reporters delighted in repeating in embarrassing stories, the company gave up and dropped the logo from its products. Perhaps Sindy could be Syndy or, more probably, Cindy. Hassenfeld suggested Sandy. "No," Owen said, "I had an old girlfriend named Sandy." Someone else came up with Bobbie. Clearly name was an issue for market research.

Exciting product without brilliant marketing, they all knew, would get them nowhere. Walker favored something less than a full frontal assault on Barbie. He thought it wiser initially to go for a sliver of the U.S. market, not a larger piece on which Sindy, like Maxie and Jem, might choke.

"Talk for yourself," Alan snapped. "I'm willing to have a scorched earth policy for a while. They're coming after games right and left." He was frighteningly angry now; Walker had touched a nerve. People shrank back in their chairs. The Cincinnati contingent bristled silently, for here the chairman went again, meddling in their business, a place they didn't believe he belonged.

"Goddamn it, I'm tired of throwing away innovation!" Hassenfeld railed. "Everything we develop in the U.K. gets thrown in the dustbin!" He was not thrilled that the international group's creativity was not getting a penny of return in the world's largest market, the United States.

When Hassenfeld had calmed, he agreed that more work was needed before launching Sindy, in whatever form, in America. He acknowledged that the process could take time—conceivably many months. Still, he knew through back channels that Mattel already had wind that something was up with Sindy. He wished to maintain that high interest in El Segundo.

"No matter what, I want Mattel to think we're doing something," he said. "I would like Mattel to have an hour of a sleepless night."

III

JOHN L. VOGELSTEIN, vice chairman and president of E. M. Warburg, Pincus & Co., Inc., and E. John Rosenwald Jr., vice chairman of the Bear Stearns Companies, had known each other for decades. Their firms had been involved in many of the same mergers and acquisitions, and Rosenwald's personal finances were managed by Warburg, Pincus. Vogelstein had attended Harvard; Rosenwald was a Dartmouth graduate. Vogelstein was a trustee of the New York City Ballet; Rosenwald, a trustee of the Metropolitan Museum of Art and the Central Park Conservancy. Both had residences in Westchester County as well as in New York City. Both were long-standing directors of the world's two largest toy companies: Vogelstein of Mattel, Rosenwald of Hasbro. And within their respective toy companies, each was an influential member of the executive and compensation committees of the board—committees where the power was. So it was not unusual that the two old friends should happen to be talking one day some two months after Toy Fair.

"You know," Vogelstein said, "I think the time has come to put our two toy companies together."

For ten minutes or so the two financiers kicked the idea around. Except for preschool and infants, where Fisher-Price and Playskool were largely redundant, the fit was hand in glove. Hasbro was the master of action figures, Mattel the best in dolls. Hasbro had the world's finest games and puzzles business, Mattel an alliance with Disney, which defined family entertainment in the nineties. Hasbro had strong ties to Hollywood; Mattel was practically in Hollywood. Hasbro had the market on foam sports with Nerf, Mattel the market on ride-ons with Power Wheels. Both companies were pursuing different but complementary paths in software. But the appeal transcended product synergy—was more than Barbie taking G.I. Joe's hand. Vogelstein and Rosenwald estimated rough savings of $200 million a year from consolidating operations, virtually all of it to be applied directly to the bottom line. The prospect of a $6 billion or bigger global children's consumer goods corporation that dwarfed all others in revenues, earnings, and shareholder value, almost certainly for decades to come, excited the two men, both of whom were stockholders in their respective firms. And it solved a daunting problem Hasbro already was facing and Mattel sooner or later would. Rosy pronouncements at financial seminars aside, sustaining double-digit growth was extraordinarily difficult, no matter how powerful the brands.

"I want to talk to you about a conversation that I've had with John Vogelstein," Rosenwald said when he called Alan. Rosenwald related the highlights of their chat and his own keen interest in evaluating a merger. "I want you to go to sleep and think about it and call me tomorrow," Rosenwald said. "I don't want you to give me an answer now."

Hassenfeld's response surprised Rosenwald, as it would others who later learned of it. "I don't have to sleep on it," he said. "We should meet. It makes all kinds of sense."

Hassenfeld called his mother, whose advice was "Do what you think is right." Then Alan told Harold P. "Sonny" Gordon, an old friend, attorney, and board member he'd recently named as vice chairman to replace Barry Alperin, who, weary of being second fiddle to Verrecchia, had finally retired.

For the moment, Alan told no one else.

IV

IT WAS A SEASON of earthshaking upheaval in the children's culture industries. Jeffrey Katzenberg, the executive behind *Lion King* and *Aladdin,* had left Disney and joined with Steven Spielberg and David Geffen to form a new studio, DreamWorks SKG, which intended to be a major player in children's television, movies, and merchandise. Having failed to purchase GE's NBC television network, Disney was pursuing a $19 billion takeover of Capital Cities/ABC, which could only fortify its many children's properties. Time Warner was after a deal to buy Turner Broadcasting System. Divisions of Viacom Inc. and Warner Bros. had launched national television networks, and each aimed for a piece of the lucrative Saturday morning market. And the emergence of the Internet was rapidly redefining entertainment for kids.

If Hassenfeld needed further proof that the ground beneath him was shifting, it came mere days after his conversation with Rosenwald. Hassenfeld was in New York for Toys "R" Us's annual fund-raising dinner when Dan Romanelli, president of Warner Bros. Worldwide Consumer Products, quietly informed him that he was creating a new enterprise called Warner Bros. Toys. The division would develop toys for existing and new television and theatrical properties, and its creative chief would be Kenner designer Ron Hayes, whose crowning achievement was Batman toys. Romanelli had won last summer's Hayes sweepstakes, finally prying him from Hasbro after Stein had been unable to get him to Marvel. Hayes's new office was still in Cincinnati, a stone's throw from his former employer.

Next morning's announcement of Warner Bros. Toys made the front page of the influential *Daily Variety.* "We will of course continue to license many of our properties to major toy companies," Romanelli said, "and at the same time create programs specifically for Warner Bros. Toys." Publicly Hassenfeld was nonplussed: Hasbro's on-the-record reaction was a confidently worded statement that nothing would change. And with no managers but Ron Hayes—whose strength was superheroes, not business plans—no factories, no sales force, and no distribution network, it was hard to imagine that Warner Toys could be a threat anytime soon. Still, Hasbro and Warner had not reached agreement on the rights to the fourth Batman movie, due in 1997. And in such image-conscious places as Hollywood and Wall Street, headlines suggesting Hasbro was somehow lacking were a headache Alan didn't need.

This was Friday, April 28. Before leaving work, Hassenfeld made arrangements to meet with Warner boss Robert Daly and Romanelli the first of next week. Meanwhile he was headed to Bermuda, where the Toy Manufacturers of America was having its annual convention.

■

"I understand John has talked to you," Amerman said. He'd found Hassenfeld poolside at the Princess Hotel in Bermuda. It was Sunday evening, and the Toy Manufacturers of America was having a cocktail party.

Hassenfeld indicated his desire to explore the possibilities. "We should get together," he said, but the two agreed now was not the time or place, for they were in the presence of many ears. Meanwhile Rosenwald and Vogelstein had arranged a May 8 meeting in New York to continue the dialogue. Vogelstein wanted to personally sound out Hassenfeld.

Although Vogelstein had quickly embraced it, merger was Amerman's idea, brought to conviction during the previous year's bruising acquisition and licensing battles with Hasbro. Why fight the enemy when the enemy could be yours? Why grow incrementally when overnight you could double in size to $6 billion, becoming a consumer products giant that ranked with Colgate-Palmolive or Gillette? What an army of global power brands he would command! Think of the marketing clout, the economies of manufacturing and distribution, the stock price, the value of stock options! Who had ever pulled off such a deal? Who had dared try? Certainly there would be issues to resolve—titles, for example. But Hassenfeld was a reasonable guy. Surely he wouldn't let ego get in the way. He probably could be convinced to take the second spot, at least until the retirement of Amerman, who was sixty-four years old. And Barad, Amerman's heir apparent, would have to be accommodated. But these were details. Given the monetary rewards to all involved, Amerman had faith they could be resolved.

For his part, Hassenfeld was obligated by his fiduciary responsibility to shareholders to at least evaluate a deal. But he was not proceeding on duty alone. Like Amerman, Vogelstein, and Rosenwald, he was awed by the scale of Hasbro/Mattel, the likes of which not even Stephen could have imagined. "Here you would have a six- or seven-billion-dollar company not shooting each other in the foot, but shooting others down," Alan said later. "If you really wanted to be an entertainment conglomerate or whatever you want to call it—the sheer size was lovely."

Personal considerations also entered into his thinking: although he and his family lacked for nothing, like most people, he would be hard-pressed to refuse another few hundred million dollars, the potential windfall from a merger. With their stock holdings, his top executives stood to benefit handsomely, too. Hassenfeld would want to preserve Rhode Island jobs. He would want the top position in the new company—if not immediately, then with Amerman's retirement, for despite some annoyances, he'd come to enjoy wearing the crown of King of Toys. And he would want to preserve his philanthropy. But like Amerman, he believed these issues could be settled.

In the days since Rosenwald's call, Hassenfeld's thoughts had wandered to his brother. But he did not feel compelled to visit Lincoln Park Cemetery this time, did not need guidance; he was only remembering. Few but Alan knew that Stephen, having accomplished his goal of building the largest toy company in history, had foreseen the day when he might want to sell Hasbro and move on to something else, perhaps full-time philanthropy—the timing and terms of such a sale, of course, to be determined by him, not outsiders. Few but Alan knew that he'd seriously considered a run at Mattel, in 1986, when the acquisition of Milton Bradley had given Hasbro tremendous financial firepower and Mattel, having lost on He-Man and Masters of the Universe, was in trouble again. Stephen had engaged First Boston Corp. to prepare a tender offer when, on a trip to California, he'd decided to drop the matter. He was concerned that the corporate environments would not marry well. "We'll never get the cultures to work together," Stephen had told Barry Alperin, who'd been overseeing the details.

Hassenfeld left Bermuda on Monday, May 1, with Verrecchia. They flew to Los Angeles, where they were joined by Sonny Gordon, the new vice chairman. They were bound for Warner Bros. and also (unbeknownst to any but them, Dan Owen, and George Ditomassi) a second, hopefully fruitful meeting with the principals of Hollywood's newest studio, DreamWorks SKG.

V

BRUCE STEIN HAD STAYED less than four months at Marvel Entertainment Group, just long enough to cross swords with executives at Perelman's Toy Biz over development of properties. Stein wanted more control than Toy Biz would give, and it was mutually agreed that Stein would leave. He'd been longing for California anyway.

Stein took up residence in a Santa Monica hotel, and the outgoing chairman of Sony Pictures Entertainment, Peter Guber, who'd once wanted to hire him, arranged for an office and use of a secretary at the studio while he contemplated his future. Stein had a number of immediate possibilities, but they were traditional jobs, which had no appeal. I just can't be a licensing guy, which is just selling, Stein thought. He considered starting a toy company with another West Coast friend, Brad Globe, longtime head of marketing for Amblin' Entertainment, Spielberg's old production company, but the hassles of inventory and distribution weren't for them. Stein was thinking on a grander scale, anyway. What had attracted him to Marvel (besides the compensation) was the opportunity to develop and market properties across many media; like *Mortal Kombat* producer Larry Kasanoff, like Semel, Daly, and Disney's Michael Eisner, Stein understood that the real value was in the idea. One of his frustrations at Kenner had been his inability to develop concepts from scratch, holistically—so that movie, TV, toy, apparel, and all else were scored from the same sheet.

DreamWorks seemed the logical place to realize his vision. Announced the very week Stein left Marvel, the new studio was in the earliest stages of construction. No walls had gone up to impede bold thinking, nor was financing a problem, for the very mention of Spielberg, Katzenberg, and Geffen in league had brought a flood of investors and elicited interest in alliances from such heavyweights as Microsoft and Sega. And Globe, Stein's buddy, would be following Spielberg from Amblin'. With Globe's input, but without pay or the promise of a position, Stein began to write a plan for a consumer products division of DreamWorks. Katzenberg asked for refinements, and when he was satisfied, he told Stein to try to make it work.

Stein began making calls. One was to Jill Barad, who was deeply impressed and more than a little envious of all Stein had accomplished at Kenner. Another was to San Francisco's Lewis Galoob Toys Inc. A third was to Verrecchia. Despite the circumstances of their parting, both men shared a fundamental interest—money—and the two had kept in touch. Early on, Stein had hinted of opportunities for Hasbro at DreamWorks. Now they had something conrete to talk about. On April 20, nearly two weeks before Bermuda, Hassenfeld, Verrecchia, and Gordon had gone to California to meet with Spielberg, Katzenberg, Stein, and Globe. Spielberg and Hassenfeld had talked a bit about their respective philanthropies and then gotten down to business. Stein outlined his consumer products plan, built on what he called the five pillars of merchandising: books, apparel, interactive, comics, and toys. Toys was foremost, for a major toy company had vast advertising and promotional resources and potential for the biggest profits.

What DreamWorks wanted, Stein said, were long-term partners who would share risk and reward for all of the studio's properties—a marked contrast to the traditional licensing agreement, in which the licensee, ordinarily contracted for a single property, pays the licensor an up-front guarantee against future royalties. DreamWorks sought another unconventional arrangement. The new studio wanted to jointly create and develop toys—not only for screen properties, but for generic toys as well. Spielberg's interest in designing toys was well-known. He'd wanted his own toy line within Kenner when Stein was president, but the idea had never come to fruition.

"We have to do business with DreamWorks," Verrecchia had said after that first meeting. Hassenfeld agreed. They left California with a pledge to return soon with their proposal. They had it when they arrived in Los Angeles the day after Hassenfeld's poolside encounter with Amerman in Bermuda.

VI

HASSENFELD'S MEETING WITH Daly and Romanelli produced no guarantees that Hasbro would remain on Batman indefinitely, nor did evidence surface that Warner Toys would impede negotiations on extending Hasbro's license at least through 1997, when *Batman and Robin* would be released. But having lost Ron Hayes, Hassenfeld had another concern: that Warner Toys would raid Cincinnati. "Keep your hands off," Hassenfeld said. "We're partners. And this is not the way partners work together."

Daly and Romanelli had a parallel concern. Hollywood was a small town; they knew what Stein was up to at DreamWorks. Was it crazy to think he might try to grab some of Warner's people?

"You stay out and they'll stay out," Hassenfeld said, for what good it was worth.

VII

AFTER CONFIDING IN GORDON, Hassenfeld had eventually informed John O'Neill and, later, Verrecchia about Amerman's grand ambition. The chairman's enthusiasm was diminishing, the deeper into it they got. Early indications that Hassenfeld could be co-chairman and next in line for CEO had become clouded by the question of where Barad fit. Hasbro's information was that her contract guaranteed succession to Amerman, providing for a multimillion-dollar payout if she were denied the post. Could she work for a man who wore rubber bands as bracelets and publicly professed his undying affection for Barney, anyway? The future of Hasbro's Rhode Island divisions remained up in the air, and the companies remained apart on pricing. Stephen's words echoed in Alan's mind: "We'll never get the cultures to work together."

Still, none of this was necessarily a deal breaker. What had potentially emerged as one was antitrust. Hasbro's lawyers were concerned that an as-yet-unpublicized Federal Trade Commission investigation of Toys "R" Us (which allegedly had pressured manufacturers to refuse to sell certain popular toys to warehouse clubs) had heightened federal interest in the toy industry. Hasbro's lawyers believed a merger of the world's two largest toy companies would receive unusually intense, and quite possibly unfavorable, antitrust scrutiny. The time wasn't right for Coke to walk Pepsi to the altar—perhaps when the Toys "R" Us investigation had blown over, as these things sooner or later always did. Mattel disagreed: unity of purpose, Amerman and Vogelstein insisted, would carry the day. Include sporting goods, video games, even personal computers (none of which either company manufactured at the moment) in a new definition of "toys," and $6 billion in revenues would be a drop in the bucket, certainly no monopolistic market share. Persuading the government might take time and money, some zealous bureaucrat with a name to make was sure to whine, but ultimately what kind of antitrust case could the FTC have?

In Florida together for an international toy conference, Hassenfeld and Amerman had dinner alone on June 17 in Sylvia Hassenfeld's Palm Beach apartment. The two had never really gotten to know each other, and what better time than now? Their conversation was pleasant enough, but by dessert it was clearer than ever what different people they were—heck, Hassenfeld didn't even golf, never mind have an interest in Thoroughbred horses or the American Kennel Club. There was something else at that dinner, and again on June 26, when the sides met all day in New York—something Hassenfeld couldn't quite put his finger on. He would later call it "tonality," a feeling that what he'd thought was a friendly merger was turning into a takeover, in which he might get skunked.

I got into this as equals, he thought after the June 26 meeting. This doesn't sound like equals to me.

Wednesday, June 28, had been set as the day to sign an agreement to exchange confidentials, the highly sensitive numbers that are the innermost guts of a business. They were needed for an in-depth analysis of the merger, and their exchange would bring Mattel and Hasbro to the point of no return. The parties were to meet at Boston's Ritz-Carlton Hotel. O'Neill and Gordon would represent Hasbro. Representing Mattel would be James A. Eskridge, its number three executive, and a man who worked for Vogelstein.

On Tuesday night Hassenfeld had Gordon, O'Neill, and Verrecchia to his Boston house. Over dinner they talked about what tomorrow would really mean.

"My God, this is crazy," Hassenfeld finally said. "Why are we doing this?"

No one had a good answer.

When O'Neill and Gordon arrived at the Ritz the next morning, they were empty-handed. They did not exchange confidentials.

Hassenfeld called Amerman to explain his qualms about the FTC. "John," he said, "this is not the most foolish idea by any stretch. At the right time, we should continue this type of a discussion."

No problem, Amerman said. He did not sound upset.

Lawyers kept contact over the summer, but neither side shifted position. In September, at the urging of Vogelstein and Rosenwald, Hassenfeld joined Barad in New York for tea. It was a pleasant get-together, without agenda. Barad told Hassenfeld that she was aware of all that had transpired and wanted him to know she would have no problem working for him. She sounded most sincere. Hassenfeld thanked her. If the merger discussion ever resumed, he'd surely keep her words in mind.

And then, nothing for weeks and weeks—only the vaguely lingering notion that someday, like star-crossed lovers whose moment was yet to arrive, Mattel and Hasbro might meet again.

"What if they were to decide to come after us at some point in time, fellas?" Verrecchia said that fall. But no one really believed they would. The thought passed from Verrecchia's mind. Too much was happening internally that required everyone's undivided attention.

◼

L I L L Y M E R E

I

*O*n the very morning that Hasbro executives were disappointing Mattel's representatives at Boston's Ritz-Carlton Hotel, Al Verrecchia was meeting with his top fifteen managers at the University of Rhode Island's Alton Jones campus, a rural compound often used as a corporate getaway. No one but Verrecchia knew what was transpiring with Mattel. They had gathered for two days to critique the restructuring, now nearly a year old, and to finalize the Hasbro Toy Group's strategic plan, which Verrecchia last fall had charged Dan Owen with writing.

After a sumptuous breakfast, Verrecchia and his group walked through the pines to Sycamore Cabin. Dress was casual, and the boss, in his Bermuda shorts, crew-neck sweater, athletic shoes, and perfectly combed hair, looked as though he'd stepped from the pages of *Gentleman's Quarterly*. Slide shows and blackboard presentations got the ball rolling. A consensus soon emerged that the team concept had been embraced by most employees. Fewer managers were overseeing larger numbers of workers, producing savings. And a confidential effectiveness survey by human resources revealed a majority of employees believed the restructuring ultimately would result in better overall performance.

The survey also showed how long the road would be. Many respondents complained about the burdens of training in areas they considered peripheral to the business of toys ("The Team Advantage," for example, a mandatory day-long session put on by consultants in which, among other useful tasks, participants had to devise survival strategies in the event of being trapped inside a building after an earthquake). Respondents bemoaned the loss of what one called "the family feeling" and resented the environment that had replaced it. "It used to be a good place to work," said respondent number ninety-two. "We didn't need things like 'crazy tie day' or 'employee craft day' or such nonsense to feel good about what we do." Asked what he'd do were he in Owen's shoes, number ninety-two wrote: "Fire all the accountants & bean counters and other hangers-on . . . eliminate the card key system . . . put an end to further surveys."

Verrecchia believed in addressing legitimate concerns, but feelings did not fit his description. "Being a fun place and being worried you could lose your job if you don't perform—I think they can go together," he said. "I also don't think we can promise a warm fuzzy place anymore. It's not a family-owned fifty-million-dollar business. It's a three-billion-dollar publicly traded company. The Hassenfelds don't control it anymore." Stockholders ultimately did.

Much of what the surveys disclosed had surfaced last fall, in roundtable discussions hosted by Hassenfeld and Owen. But confidentiality afforded employees an opportunity those sessions hadn't, and many had delivered blunt assessments of management. Human Resources had devised a rating system for the responses, and among the very lowest grades were communication, trust, and inspiration from the top.

"Do people here think management doesn't have the skills—or they're in new roles and have to learn?" Verrecchia said.

"All they see is their needs not being met," said Janice Dufresne, who worked in human resources. "They see the business not doing well."

The tension inside Sycamore Cabin was palpable. Owen urged everyone not to be defensive. Because of confidentiality, how could they know the true agenda of those surveyed? Or who, specifically, was being criticized?

"I'm going to be defensive for a moment," Verrecchia said. "Are you saying, based on the analysis you've done, there are many areas where the skills simply aren't there?"

"They don't see them," Dufresne said.

"Al, remember," said Dufresne's boss, Sherry Len Turner. "These aren't statements of fact. These are perceptions."

"Frankly, we can be the greatest managers and some people out there will think we're assholes," said Sharon Hartley.

"I rely on it," quipped Malcolm Denniss, whose product safety pronouncements always seemed to irk someone or other.

The tension had dissipated the next day, when attention turned to the Toy Group's strategic plan, whose revised but still ambitious goal was $2 billion in revenues by the year 2000 (exclusive of acquisitions), nearly double what was expected this year, with pretax profits in the range of 15 percent a year. Most of the growth in revenues would come from within existing brands: Tonka, Playskool, Batman, G.I. Joe, and others, with only about a fourth in "all others," a category including outside concepts and internal lines generating annual revenues significantly below the $100 million or more eventually expected of the major brands. Even candidates for all others would be evaluated for potential as core brands. One-trick wonders and unknowns would not be automatically excluded, but they would face a tougher audition. Hasbro was hardly alone in this. The big retailers were taking fewer and fewer lines every year, and buyers were sent to manufacturers with explicit instructions to steer clear of risky new introductions, a policy that especially squeezed independent inventors. Led by Mattel, the industry was coming to believe that if freshness and novelty belonged anywhere, it was only within the context of brands.

The new strategy was a radical shift in philosophy for Hasbro. By itself, love of great product no longer would be sufficient rationale to begin, or keep on, marketing a toy. Nor would great sales alone be justification, as had sometimes been the case in the past. Verrecchia remembered well the mid-1980s, when, rolling in money, Stephen Hassenfeld had relaxed his iron dictate about individual products carrying their own weight. "There's still a 'Steve Schwartz attitude' in some respects," Verrecchia said. "We'd rather drive sales and worry about profits later." As much as he wanted $2 billion in sales—and didn't it have a wonderful ring, $2 billion by 2000—Verrecchia did not want volume at the expense of profit. Two billion dollars in sales without healthy returns could only spell trouble with stockholders and the board.

11

IF ANYONE COULD HAVE realized Verrecchia's hopes for Sliced Bread, surely it was Sandra M. Schneider, the woman he'd chosen to replace Larry Bernstein as head of the project. She'd founded Marvel Entertainment Group's software division, been vice president of consumer software for Mindscape Inc., and been a consultant for Warner Bros. and Virgin Communications. She knew hardware and finance, and she was on top of cultural trends. She was, in short, an up-and-comer. She found progress and promise in the virtual-reality machine Bernstein had bequeathed her in August 1994, and much not to her liking. More than two full years into the project, Sliced Bread was still not close to market.

Sliced Bread was the brainchild of an outside inventor who'd brought the idea to Bernstein in 1991. The heart of his concept was a powerful microprocessor that generated the illusion of a three-dimensional world through a head-mounted display (consisting of headphones, microphone, and a liquid crystal display device that projected images directly onto the eyeball). Players would not simply be immersed in a virtual world. Using a handheld controller, they'd be able to move through it—chasing or running from monsters, for example, or brandishing a sword.

Texas Instruments had done some early development work on the microprocessor but was unable to hit a price that would make for an affordable machine. At this point, Bernstein had talked to Verrecchia and Hassenfeld about Hasbro taking on the project. They were intrigued but cautious. Yankelovich was hired to conduct a marketing study, which showed that Sliced Bread, as envisioned, could make real inroads against Nintendo and Sega. It was the siren song of NEMO again. Finished with Texas Instruments, Bernstein's inventor friend had found an eager, and distinguished, technological development partner in the David Sarnoff Research Center. With Hassenfeld's support, Verrecchia gave the project, and Sarnoff, the green light.

By Schneider's arrival, Hasbro had poured some $25 million into Sliced Bread for design and development of the head-mounted display, hand control, power supply, microchip, and several games, most under subcontract to outsiders. Schneider killed some of the games, demanded modifications of others, and hired other companies to develop three more titles. The peripherals were proceeding satisfactorily, but a final design for an affordable microchip remained elusive. And while the origi-

nal system was cartridge based, Schneider insisted on the greater capabilities of CD-ROM, just then coming into its own. All of this meant more
delays and more money. Hassenfeld was concerned. So were Verrecchia
and Schneider, although both believed the project could be saved.
Thought was given to bringing in a third partner, but Sony, Nintendo,
and others were not interested. Hassenfeld agreed to continue with
Sarnoff, but not forever. At a March 1995 meeting he'd set July as the
deadline to prove Sliced Bread's feasibility.

▪

The Toy Group strategic session had just ended when the chairman summoned Verrecchia, Schneider, Sonny Gordon, John O'Neill, and David
Hargreaves, Verrecchia's main financial man, to his office. All had read the
latest business plan for Sliced Bread, which included a $22 million na-
tional advertising campaign in the renegade spirit of Nike. It was down
to a show of hands.

"Okay," Hassenfeld said, "let's go around the room."

Characteristically, Alan saw two sides. On the one hand, the promise
of Sliced Bread remained as enchanting as ever. The technical problems
were resolved, or close to being so. He'd played the newest prototype and
seen the latest versions of software titles, and he had no doubt it would
be a one-of-a-kind game that would instantly establish Hasbro as an exciting innovator—certainly no has-been in its belated entry into the
field. Who knew how that would pay off in attracting new talent and
ideas? Who could predict what inspired new union of toy to microchip
Sliced Bread might beget? And there were political considerations. The
business plan called for selling two million units over the life of the product, with a 12 percent profit by the fourth year. Killing it now, with little but a wafer of silicon and a funny-looking helmet to show for a nearly
$45 million investment, would hardly thrill the board. Verrecchia's stand-
ing would suffer, for he had been the project's biggest champion. Losing
Sliced Bread might not end his ambition to be president, but it could
hardly advance it.

On the other hand, the retail price had risen $100, to $499. The introduction had been pushed back to the last quarter of 1996 at the earliest, when the rapidly increasing multimedia capabilities of personal
computers and the next generation of Sony, Nintendo, and Sega machines would rival, if not surpass, Sliced Bread's capabilities: what was

magic today could well be mundane tomorrow. In light of that, a fore-cast of two million in sales was iffy. It was not inconceivable that tens of millions more in development and inventory, on top of $22 million in advertising budgeted for the first year alone, would be money down the drain. Explaining that to the board, Hassenfeld knew, would make get-ting out now seem like a cakewalk.

O'Neill voted not to continue. He'd been against the project from the start.

Ditomassi was not at the meeting, but his position was known. An ini-tial supporter, he'd soured as costs had climbed.

Gordon voted with O'Neill.

A straightforward and loyal man, David Hargreaves had believed in the project until very recently. But he was a numbers guy at heart, and the numbers he needed to keep the faith weren't coming up. "I feel like a real turncoat," he said, and cast his lot with Gordon, Ditomassi, and O'Neill.

Schneider voted to go on.

So did Verrecchia. The project might fail, but no one now could ever accuse him of shying away from risk.

Despite the democratic flavor to the meeting, Hassenfeld had made up his mind before it began: the financial risks were too great, he'd decided. He thanked everyone for their input and said: "I'm killing it." He would leave it to O'Neill to explain to Wall Street, which surely would be cu-rious to learn how so many millions of dollars had been spent on virtu-ally nothing.

III

THE FIRST STRATEGIC SUMMIT of Hasbro Inc. began two days later at Lil-lymere, a corporate retreat in Saunderstown, Rhode Island, bayside sum-mer home of Edith Wharton and birthplace of Gilbert Stuart, renowned portrait artist of the early republic. From near and far they came—from Hong Kong and England, from Canada and Massachusetts, from world headquarters on Newport Avenue in Pawtucket. Never had Hassenfeld gathered his inner circle for such high purpose, which was no less than setting a course to take Hasbro into the twenty-first century.

After an informal dinner Sunday at which Hassenfeld urged candor, Verrecchia formally opened the summit on Monday morning with an overview of Hasbro 2000, the corporatewide strategy that was supposed to emerge from this and subsequent meetings. The goal was revenues of $5 billion by 2000 with high profits, an objective Hassenfeld already had floated out to analysts. "The question is: Can we do it? And how do we go about doing it?" Verrecchia said. He then spoke to his Hasbro Toy Group's proposed $2 billion contribution to the corporate total. Owen and Hargreaves, following Verrecchia, laid out a scenario under which, they maintained, their $2 billion goal was feasible.

Hassenfeld asked for comments. Gordon approved of Verrecchia's plan. Ditomassi, whose games division had increased revenues and earnings every year since he'd been in charge, was politely skeptical.

"I think it's a great road map," Ditomassi said. "It's not a slam dunk. You certainly have your work cut out for you."

O'Neill was more blunt. "I don't see a road map," he said. "I don't see the meat on the bones."

"We have them," Verrecchia said with a hint of anger. "We have a lot more we could put down. But if we put them on the table today, this meeting will deteriorate into a 1996 budget session, and a lot of us didn't come here for that." Verrecchia wanted a more freewheeling discussion. He did not want to get into the current year, projected to be below budget for his Toy Group (never mind the loftier numbers he'd had in mind on the eve of Black Tuesday). It was not inconceivable that, like Bernstein's division in its final year, the Toy Group would return a pretax profit in the low single digits. The local bank might deliver a better return.

Having made his point, O'Neill had nothing further to say.

In from London, Norman Walker presented his European plan. Like Verrecchia's, it was built around exploiting old brands and developing new. He talked of changes within his organization—nothing as drastic as Verrecchia's restructuring—and then he turned to broader issues. One was the organizational hodgepodge of Hasbro, which he compared to a basket of frogs. "There's a tremendous energy and talent," he said, "but it's not all going in the same direction." Another issue was Mattel, a company that had proved beyond all dispute to be the killer shark it fancied itself. Unless Hasbro fired up, Walker feared being left behind forever. "My personal conviction," he said, "is that 1996 is a critical, critical watershed." Little did he realize just how critical it would be.

Walker's third concern was the $5 billion goal. Without an intelligent but clear plan—a strategic vision you could essentially reduce to a mantra—five billion would be little more than numbers on a page. Walker said: "We're going to come back and say five billion dollars and people are going to say, 'What the hell have you been smoking?' Anybody can say five billion. You can say ten billion, what the hell does it matter?" It was an oblique criticism of Hassenfeld. Like Verrecchia, Walker was deeply frustrated by his boss.

The day was near its end. Before adjourning, Hassenfeld spoke. His participation to this point had largely been with questions, but now he opened up, to an extent that surprised most. Alan conceded he'd stalled on a companywide plan to accelerate development of interactive software, which all agreed was an urgent priority. He acknowledged he'd been slow in articulating a global vision, and he asked for help. Couching his instructions in a favorite metaphor, he told everyone to return tomorrow morning with a list of impediments toward achieving $5 billion by the year 2000.

"If there are true blockages," he said, "you basically have to do bypass surgery."

I V

TO REACH ALAN HASSENFELD'S home, you leave the main thoroughfare and travel a side street through a middle-class neighborhood in the old seafaring town of Bristol. You descend a hill, cross a railroad right-of-way, and turn onto a shady gravel lane. The place he once shared with Stephen is a short distance down, overlooking Narragansett Bay.

Alan has added on since his brother died, and three principal structures now occupy the finger of land between the lane and the water: a poolhouse; the original residence, now the guesthouse, Sylvia's quarters when she's in town; and the smaller house that Alan built for himself and Vivien. All are in the traditional New England summer cottage style, with weathered shingles and white trim. A deck outfitted with umbrellas and wooden chaise longues borders a small pool and waterfall, and the landscaping is rich with evergreens. Interiors are airy and elegantly appointed by Vivien with an accent on the Far East. There are no stables, no kennels, no guardhouse or chain-link fence, no private beach, no yachts anchored offshore, not even a dock or a stairway to the sea. Hassenfeld has the wealth of Croesus, but his desires and needs are simple. His idea of a fabulous day is a game of tennis with Vivien and perhaps a round of Scrabble, or dinner guests, at night.

A month after Lillymere, on the morning of Monday, August 14, Hassenfeld took time to reflect. Dressed in shorts and T-shirt, he sat on his deck and drank coffee, occasionally remarking on the sailboats on the bay or pausing to light a cigarette. He was in fine spirits, in part because he'd found truth in what his managers had said at Lillymere and was now satisfied with the need to change. They'd criticized their boss for being too involved in the minutiae of product development and marketing, for favoring Rhode Island in many counterproductive ways, for not communicating effectively with the rank and file, for "trying to be the good guy to everybody," as Hassenfeld put it.

Hassenfeld had been briefed on plans to further reduce Hasbro's Rhode Island industrial workforce, considerably costlier than anywhere else the company manufactured. Within a few months only about 250 blue-collar jobs would remain in Rhode Island, down from a peak of more than 2,000 in the 1970s. Nearly all would involve Play-Doh, for the molding machines for the last locally produced G.I. Joe toy (the Monster Blaster, an armored personnel carrier) had been cold now going on two years. Where once he'd vetoed or postponed layoffs, Hassenfeld was becoming resigned to obeying the laws of economics, not his heart.

"I have a myopia about Rhode Island, and I'll be the first one to admit it," Hassenfeld said. "Even though I want to be this great global thinker, so much of what pervades my thinking has been, how do I protect Rhode Island? Rhode Island's my home, Rhode Island's the home office. I can't look at the factory in Rhode Island—I have no right—any differently than I look at the factory in Waterford [Ireland] or the factory in El Paso or Tijuana. But I do. And I'm trying to wean myself off that." He still would not allow his name on press releases announcing blue-collar reductions (the job of spokesman would remain Verrecchia's exclusively), but inside Hasbro, at least, no one doubted a milestone had been reached.

Lillymere's atmosphere of candor had allowed Hassenfeld's inner circle to pressure him on the future. They knew elements of his vision for Hasbro but wanted him to spell out the whole, then lead the way. "As a couple of people said," Hassenfeld remarked, " 'Hey, Alan, you have a tendency to worry about some of the smaller things. If you would put the energy into the larger picture, that's where we'd really like you to focus. Instead of worrying about this one person losing a job and spending six hours anguishing over it, spend six hours on something that's more major. We're talking vision."

Hassenfeld had closed Lillymere with a pledge to define, with crystal clarity, his role at Hasbro. It was a self-examination that somehow would have to settle not only the unresolved corporate issues, but Hassenfeld's larger interests in life. Did he really need a president—and if so, who should it be? Verrecchia? Ditomassi? An outsider? Could he balance business and philanthropy with his company at such a crossroads? Where did he see himself in the year 2000? Somewhere inside of him was still a yearning to write. Politics continued to cast a spell, and Rhode Island's Republican senator probably would be retiring at century's end. Did he want to run? Did diplomacy—in the Asian arena, for example, where his would be a credible voice—have appeal? Or was he content as a captain of industry? What was he as he neared the age of fifty?

As he watched the sailboats that fine August morning, Hassenfeld seemed ready to take on the future. He hadn't a clue, of course, of the extraordinary test that would begin the very morning he returned from his Christmas vacation. He was looking ahead only as far as Wednesday, when he would share a well-kept secret with his employees and the world.

17

■

BRAND NAMES

I

The ruse Alan Hassenfeld used to get employees inside a giant tent that had materialized in the Newport Avenue parking lot was an overview of Hasbro 2000. It was widely interpreted by the rank and file as a sign the chairman was ready to communicate something about Lillymere, the subject of companywide speculation in the month since the summit. Still, as the tent began to fill on that sultry Wednesday, August 16, some employees wondered if more were afoot. The old "Sega is buying us" rumor had resurfaced, along with a new one: Microsoft's Bill Gates was picking up Hasbro. Some thought a licensing deal for *Star Wars'* second trilogy had finally been struck. Almost no one suspected anything involving DreamWorks SKG.

The tent had been transformed into an air-conditioned theater, with lighting, sound system, TelePrompTer, cameras, production booth, and wall of TVs on which crowd shots and noteworthy Hasbro commercials were intercut as employees awaited the show. A satellite link enabled live transmission to Hasbro facilities in Cincinnati, England, and Massachusetts, and tapes of the proceedings would be shipped express to the remaining outposts.

The program had been meticulously choreographed. Accompanied by wives and family members, Hassenfeld, Gordon, Verrecchia, and Ditomassi filed in and took front-row seats. The applause subsided, and Hassenfeld's chief operating officers vaulted onto the stage.

"We had originally planned on Big Bird and Barney," Dito said, "so you'll have to accept Al and me. But you know what they say."

"Yeah," Verrecchia said. "Shit happens!"

The crowd loved it. Humor was not a side of him they often glimpsed. After some words about core global brands, Verrecchia introduced his boss, "the heart and soul of Hasbro."

Hassenfeld was animated and, at first, nostalgic. "I really do sometimes wonder," he told his company of 12,500 employees, "if my grandfather, when he traveled from Poland, would have dared to dream of Hasbro as it is today. Or if my father would have dared to dream of a three-billion-dollar company. Or my brother, Stephen, would recognize our fast-moving, ever-changing company."

After restriking the global brands chord, the chairman said: "Don't you believe in dreams? In the power, the magic, the pure joy of dreams? Don't you think dreams work?" The strains of "A Whole New World," the Academy Award–winning song from Disney's *Aladdin,* filled the tent. "Dreams *do* work," Hassenfeld said. "DreamWorks—a whole new world. I love it! I mean, I dare to dream that someday I'll be able to look to my right and look to my left and there, standing on either side of me, will be the DreamWorks dream team: Steven Spielberg and Jeffrey Katzenberg. And if it hadn't been for fog on Long Island, they'd be standing here right now!"

Grounded by the weather, the DreamWorks principals were at Spielberg's summer place in East Hampton, but a phone connection had been patched through so they could address the crowd. Katzenberg spoke of Hasbro as the foundation of DreamWorks's consumer products division, Spielberg of the broad assault the studio and its new partner planned on children's entertainment. "We are going to be involved in Saturday morning television, as well as Monday through Friday script series in animation and live action," Spielberg said. "We're going to be able to ensure that the products we come up together with will have a very long shelf life."

When all was said and done, DreamWorks really had had no choice but to take Hasbro's hand. Bruce Stein had dutifully courted Jill Barad, but the stormy departure of Katzenberg from Disney, the very impetus for DreamWorks, had doomed Mattel's prospects: Michael Eisner was hardly about to bless intimacy between his primary toy licensee and an ex-employee with whom he continued to bitterly feud. Galoob had lobbied fiercely, but despite a promising new product in Sky Dancers, and success in Star Wars miniatures, the San Francisco company's size (only $180 million in annual revenues) and history of losses had gone against it. Playmates, the fourth company Stein had talked to, was too narrowly focused (on boys' action; Teenage Mutant Ninja Turtles was its signature line) to realize the new studio's merchandising ambitions.

While superficially the partnership resembled Mattel's with Disney, unique elements enabled Hassenfeld legitimately to claim a degree of innovation, of vision. Replacing the traditional system of royalties was a joint investment agreement, the fine details of which the lawyers were still negotiating. Toy and screen talent theoretically would come together at the earliest stages of a project, with ongoing creative decisions made in the mutual interests of both parties. Hasbro's right to DreamWorks's properties would be exclusive, on a worldwide basis (although, in an ironic twist in light of Warner Toys, Hassenfeld had refused to give up Hasbro's ties to other studios). DreamWorks personnel would be able to propose toys, just as Hasbro people would be encouraged to come up with ideas for the screen. Products would be sold and advertised under two banners: a Hasbro brand and a new brand, DreamWorks Toys. And the alliance was to last for what amounted to an eternity in Hollywood. It was to continue through the year 2002 and quite conceivably far beyond.

"This is a model for the rest of the industry to look at," one analyst said. Wall Street agreed. When the market closed for the week, Hasbro stock had jumped $2.

▪

By Friday morning the weather had cleared. Spielberg had been to Florida overnight on business, and Verrecchia met him at the Providence airport in his shiny new Jaguar. They drove to Hasbro, where security guards kept TV reporters across the street from the main entrance, which sported a Hasbro 2000 banner PR head Wayne Charness had positioned in hopes that it would appear on broadcasts. Pop star Michael Jackson's 1993 visit had not stirred as much excitement. Inside the lobby, a growing throng of employees was keeping vigil. Many wore "Dare to Dream" T-shirts.

The director crossed to the Minicams and spoke a few words about his love of toys and the longevity of products from certain classic movies. DreamWorks chose Hasbro, he said, because it was "the best toy company in the world." Ordinarily disdainful of the press, Verrecchia was beaming. "I hope they use that!" he said.

No one did. Nor did a Boston cable station even get his name right: in its report he was identified as Alan Hassenfeld. And a CNBC reporter interviewing Verrecchia had to remind him of last year's earnings drop and this summer's huge virtual-reality write-off. But on balance, the coverage all week was highly complimentary of Hasbro, for the first time in more than a year.

Spielberg toured headquarters, signing autographs everywhere and lingering in design centers, Fun Lab, and the model shop; he was eager to see how things were made, not marketed. After meeting up with his young son Theo and Stein, who'd helicoptered in together from Long Island, Spielberg accompanied Hassenfeld to the cafeteria for a rally. Stein was eyeing the presidency of Sony Interactive Entertainment and was being pursued by Barad, who now saw him as her chief lieutenant when Amerman retired. But almost no one at Hasbro knew any of this. Old associates greeted Stein as a conquering hero. They thought he'd rejoined the fold.

Although Hasbro sought the fruits of Spielberg's cinematic brilliance—movie properties that could be made into brands—the director told the rally his own passions were elsewhere. "My real interest is the generic toy line, the products that are what they are because they're created from your imaginations and our imaginations. They start from the ethers and they become standard operating childhood equipment in every home in the world," he said. "The original screenplay as a filmmaker interests me even more than the adapted novel—and the original toy, as a father of five, interests me more than the movie spin-offs. So I hope we'll be doing a lot of original toy making together."

For his part, Hassenfeld was unusually effusive, which was saying a lot. He named the DreamWorks announcement and the Hasbro Children's Hospital dedication as the two proudest moments of his life and said he now considered Spielberg, Katzenberg, and their DreamWorks partner David Geffen three more of Santa's elves—Alan, of course, being Santa.

He led the crowd in singing "Happy Birthday" to Theo and presented Spielberg with a twelve-inch doll in the director's image.

In a private moment, Hassenfeld noted the timing of the DreamWorks announcement, the precise one-year anniversary of Black Tuesday. "Everything that was in Pandora's box has come out and the lid is shut," he said. "We've opened up onto a rainbow about where our future is."

I I

FOR DON DELUCA the future had suddenly darkened first thing that Tuesday morning, the day before the DreamWorks announcement. The man with the steel blue eyes had reappeared on Main Street. DeLuca was among those sent to see him.

When he emerged, DeLuca made an attempt at humor and tried to force a smile, but he was close to tears. Old G.I. Joe marketer Vinnie D'Alleva, now DeLuca's team leader, was waiting in his cubicle. DeLuca had lost his office in the wake of the restructuring and, like others, had been assigned a space no bigger than a junior secretary's. About the only decoration he'd put up was *Bottom Dwellers,* a book on marine life. The book was on the outside of his cubicle, in plain view of passersby.

"That's it," DeLuca said. "Ten years amounting to absolutely nothing."

"Can I help?" D'Alleva said.

"Yeah," DeLuca said, "pay my mortgage."

"We're going to miss you."

"I don't think so."

"You're a class act."

"What am I going to do, cry? I'll do that later, on my own time."

Ostensibly DeLuca had fallen victim to Ginger Kent's desire to consolidate virtually all girls' and boys' development and marketing activities with her in Cincinnati. A majority of the fifty-six affected employees had been reassigned. Twelve, including DeLuca, had been declared surplus.

Since the restructuring, evaluations of DeLuca's performance had consistently found his skills to be lacking. Naturally DeLuca disagreed, and he'd signed his February review under protest. He did not know that as early as January Cincinnati had been set to terminate him—but Hassenfeld had personally intervened to save his job, in part because no one had sought the chairman's approval, in part because he still saw merit in

DeLuca's observations, blunt as they were. By summer Hassenfeld had been persuaded that Dan Owen and his group, not the chairman, should make such personnel decisions. DeLuca's last visit to Hassenfeld found him less than sympathetic. "I'm not doing the day-to-day stuff," Hassenfeld said. "Why don't you sit down with Dan and see if you can work things out." DeLuca had, but it proved futile. Owen accepted Kent's recommendation.

Nothing would ever dissuade DeLuca from the belief that his outspokenness, not his performance, was the reason he was terminated. Unlike Kirk Bozigian, who seemed the model employee, DeLuca was almost pathologically incapable of holding his tongue. Word of his private conversations with Hassenfeld, Verrecchia, and Owen had spread quickly down Main Street, and his public comments in various meetings were the stuff of curmudgeonly legend. He'd photocopied and passed along columns from *The Wall Street Journal* ridiculing reengineering as a wasteful, if not cancerous, fad. Visitors to his cubicle could always count on an earful. As Black Tuesday had receded and he'd remained mired on D'Alleva's team in a role he believed was beneath him, basic designer, his point of entry into Hasbro a decade ago, this man whose career not so long ago had been on the fast track wore his disapproval with pride. To say he'd become a thorn in Cincinnati's side would be gross understatement.

It alternately angered and amazed DeLuca that not everyone shared his views. How could they buy the party line that bad as 1995 was turning out to be for the Toy Group, it would have been worse without the restructuring? Didn't they see that having a suit running a product-driven enterprise was folly? That hiring marketers from Hallmark, Reebok, and General Mills, as Owen had set out to do, wasn't what Hasbro needed? That the company would be better off with people who knew toys, not corn chips? DeLuca had particular disdain for Cincinnati, which, he believed, had penalized him for his candor. He felt betrayed by Hassenfeld. "I'm sad," he said. "Here's a guy for whom everyone had high hopes."

Only a few weeks ago electric locks had been installed on almost every door along (and off) Main Street. DeLuca handed in his card key, an unnecessary gesture since he'd already been deactivated in the computer, and walked one last time to the parking lot, where, almost exactly a year ago to the day, a lightning strike had blown out the windshields of cars.

III

HASSENFELD UNDERSTOOD THE growing importance of interactive software. How best to capitalize on it was something else. Hasbro had bought a 15 percent share of Virgin Interactive Entertainment in 1993 and the next year began protracted discussions to buy, invest in, or ally with Knowledge Adventure, a California software developer in which Spielberg had an investment. Similar talks were being held with other companies, including Blockbuster Entertainment and the Learning Company. The internal situation was similarly scattershot. With Sliced Bread killed, three internal teams remained at work on software, with Verrecchia, Ditomassi, and Walker each in control of an initiative. Once again structure, not strategy, ruled.

The most ambitious undertaking was Playskool's Funware, supervised for Verrecchia by Sharon Hartley, who in turn had given day-to-day responsibility to her new-business development chief, Rod Dorman, who'd come to Hasbro from an ice skate company. Dorman had spared little effort. He ran a center in Palo Alto, heart of California's Silicon Valley, and he'd hired or retained on outside contract some of the industry's top talent—developers whose credentials included Disney, Sega, and MTV. Six maiden titles were planned for Funware, all but one an extension of an already popular Hasbro brand: Mr. Potato Head, Play-Doh, Tonka, Candyland, Alphie, and Puzzles. Dorman's presentations were flawless, and reaction to early versions of the games had been universally enthusiastic. After seeing the latest demonstrations at the November 1994 management line review, Hassenfeld had exclaimed: "Just spectacular! I can't wait! I want Potato Head first!"

But delays and cost overruns were threatening Funware by spring 1995, when Verrecchia—calculator and mechanical pencil in hand—had met with his managers to review the latest financial plan.

Only that morning Hartley had shown Owen the numbers. "I was a little shell-shocked," Owen said.

"I'm sitting here with a fairly low level of credibility," Dorman said.

"We'll get you guys a job working on Sliced Bread," said Verrecchia. He laughed, but it was the only time during the meeting that he did.

Not only had costs escalated—Dorman said he needed to hire additional staff to meet an end-of-year launch. "It's a lot more work than you can possibly imagine," Dorman's director of software development explained. "It takes a lot of people. It's like putting together a movie."

Verrecchia put his reading glasses on and turned on his calculator. "I hate to do this to you," he said as he began reading Play-Doh's numbers aloud. "Negative six fourteen, thirty-two, one fifty-two . . . this says I will have a net loss of two hundred and thirty-nine thousand on that product. Now I would ask you: Why the hell would I do that?"

Dorman said Play-Doh was one of the costliest titles to produce.

"It's not just Play-Doh," Verrecchia said. "If I look at the whole business, at the end of five years I'm going to make a million dollars."

And that wasn't profit, David Hargreaves said, since sales and shipping costs hadn't been factored in.

"So we're in the tank," Verrecchia said.

It was hard, in light of Sliced Bread, for him not to feel snakebitten about anything digital.

▪

At Lillymere Hassenfeld had promised swift action on software. Unlike the structural issues, which would linger into next year, he delivered. Lillymere was not over a week when Alan announced Hasbro Interactive, the first new freestanding division created since his brother had divided the company almost a decade earlier. Longtime games executive Tom Dusenberry, a man with proven creative and entrepreneurial talents, was named head.

There was urgency to Dusenberry's charge. As the digital universe expanded, the stampede was on for a stake in the entertainment tomorrow. Phone companies, computer companies, software developers, media conglomerates, studios, publishers, entrepreneurial Webmasters, hackers—all desperately wanted a piece of the action. Mattel certainly was in the thick of things. Amerman in 1994 had hired Douglas Glen, a vice president of Sega of America whose résumé included time at Lucasfilm Games, the *Star Wars* director's entertainment software arm. Glen was president of Mattel Media, a new division. But Mattel was not content with simply developing interactive products. The very week of Lillymere, Barad's picture had made it into *USA Today* again, this time for a story about a joint venture Mattel had formed to distribute software. Mr. Potato Head and G.I. Joe had symbolized the plastic era at Hasbro. To a large extent it was up to Dusenberry to secure his company's place in the new age.

Hassenfeld handed him everything: Funware, the games the European group had been developing (notably Battleship and Risk), and Ditomassi's Games Group's titles. He was encouraged to dip into Hasbro's extensive library of properties, and the welcome mat was out to inventors. He was free to talk to the many corporations that sought Hasbro's brands for on-line uses (Microsoft, America Online, and Disney were among those who'd expressed interest) and to create a Hasbro Web site. His market was the world, not some sliver of a fiefdom. Except for major hardware like Sliced Bread, which was expressly and indefinitely forbidden, Dusenberry essentially had no limitations.

His first crack at a budget, submitted to Alan that fall, was predicated on eleven titles in 1996 and seventeen all-new ones in 1997 (on-line applications were proceeding separately), with a five-year goal of being the largest seller of entertainment software in the business. Hassenfeld nearly fell off his chair. The memory of Sliced Bread was still raw.

"One of the things you're dealing with is a person who has been blinded and burned and had to deal with the board," Hassenfeld said. "What I'm trying to do is build a little house and, if we're successful, put on the additions. I don't want to do the mansion first."

Dusenberry was somewhat more restrained with his revised presentation, but only somewhat—just released, CD-ROM Monopoly was on its way to being a top ten title, and the industry was abuzz. His new budget showed rapid growth and a healthy pretax profit within two years. Hassenfeld was supportive but still cautious.

"This is a passion for me. I really believe totally in it," he said. "Be a lovely little flower—and then we'll pollinate the world."

I V

DRAPED BETWEEN FLAGS for the Hasbro Games and Toy Groups, the banner outside the PGA National Resort & Spa in Palm Beach Gardens, Florida, site of 1995 Pre–Toy Fair, proclaimed "Timeless Brands, Endless Fun." The brands theme was reinforced at every turn inside the exhibits, with Mr. Potato Head, Star Wars, Superman, G.I. Joe Extreme, and many more.

Only three years earlier Hassenfeld had boasted to analysts that no one line accounted for more than 5 percent of Hasbro's revenues. It was a boast intended to highlight the corporation's product diversity, a lingering echo of Stephen's fear that overreliance on a single line sooner or later spelled disaster. But big brands did not have to fail, as Mattel had proved beyond a shadow of a doubt with Barbie and Hasbro was demonstrating with Batman. Big brands were visionary. Big brands were global. Big brands were more than the sum of their parts. Wall Street was enamored of them, for, when properly managed, they provided worldwide economies in manufacturing, distribution, packaging, and advertising that translated more or less directly to the bottom line. Intent on trimming their product selection to achieve their own savings, the major retail chains lusted after big brands, since they sold in large volume at high margins—and with far less risk than untried new products. For the creative people, the inventors and the designers, this meant pressure to invest less time and energy in original concepts and more in innovation and extension of existing properties. With baby boomers having children (and now grandchildren), it meant nostalgia would be a potent force. A new word had crept into discussions of brands. It was "publishing," a recognition that what you were selling wasn't a physical object, but a sentiment or an idea—an intellectual property.

As he got religion, Hassenfeld was turning into a scourge. He hounded Cincinnati to develop a broader twelve-inch collectors' line for G.I. Joe and got on the phone to Kent whenever he had an idea for a new figure, which was regularly. He chastised marketers for neglecting such classic brands as Tinker Toys and Lincoln Logs, which had become barely an afterthought in the Playskool line. Like the demanding director of an archaeological dig, he sent staff sifting through the archives all the way back to when Milton Bradley himself was alive for old brands that might have contemporary applications. Despite it being the profit center of the corporation, he constantly berated his Games Group for not further exploiting its titles.

"I've got to drive home every day past the Barbie shop at FAO Schwarz," he said after one line review.

"You ought to find a new way home," Ditomassi cracked.

"No, I think it's the most wonderful thing," Hassenfeld said. "It gets my competitive juices going. Barbie is a billion-dollar brand. Our billion-dollar brand is games. There is no better library in the world. You just have to look at different ways of stretching the damn envelope!"

He had in mind, for example, Monopoly restaurants or a Clue TV series, which the Games Group was in fact pursuing, just not at the chairman's pace. With so much attention to brands, it was interesting to ponder whether Hasbro today would have bet the farm on a concept as farfetched as a doll for boys, as Merrill had in 1963.

Hassenfeld's favorite brand was Mr. Potato Head. His office walls had an ever-expanding collection of Mr. Potato Head cartoons, and when he posed for a full-page ad for the American Stock Exchange that appeared in major national business publications, including *The Wall Street Journal,* it was with a smiling Mr. Potato Head on his shoulder. All but the first of Hassenfeld's annual reports since becoming chairman and CEO had featured the toy prominently, three times on the cover and once with Alan in his formal portrait inside. Mr. Potato Head was one of the few toys the chairman had distinct memories of playing with when he was a young boy.

"I love Potato Head," Alan said. "He's been in the family almost as long as I have."

▪

The hype accompanying Mr. Potato Head's starring role in Disney's *Toy Story,* one of the year's most popular movies (destined to be one of history's best-selling home videos), fed a resurgence of interest in the forty-three-year-old icon, the product that launched TV advertising of toys. DreamWorks had ideas for Mr. Potato Head, as did *Mortal Kombat* producer Larry Kasanoff, Hallmark, a company that manufactured battery-powered handheld massagers, and the League of Women Voters, which sought and received permission to use Mr. and Mrs. Potato Head as "spokespuds" for their 1996 get-out-the-vote campaign. Potato Head was no stranger to public relations, having thrown away his pipe in the American Cancer Society's 1987 Great American Smokeout and appearing at the White House in 1992 to receive an award from Arnold Schwarzenegger, chairman of George Bush's Council on Physical Fitness and Sports.

Kasanoff sought monetary gain from Potato Head. Well on his way to riches from his Mortal Kombat franchise, he visited Hasbro one day in 1995 for a meeting with the Potato Head team, licensing executive John

Gildea, and Gary Serby, who worked for Wayne Charness. Gildea lately had been beating the bushes for brands. One of his recent coups was a license for *Goosebumps,* a series of scary children's books whose monthly titles were best-sellers. Among the Hasbro products that would result were Mr. Mortman and Terror Tower Executioner action figures, and Brain Bites candy, advertised as "a disgusting delight. Kids remove the brain from the skull and eat the tasty 'brain matter' inside!"

Kasanoff began by showing a clip of some frightfully realistic state-of-the-art Mortal Kombat animation and outlining the property's live tour, Web site, CD-ROM, movie sequel, books, TV special, and, he hoped, TV series. This and more was achievable for Potato Head, Kasanoff said.

But first, he cautioned, they had to better define the character and his world. He cited the research he and his Threshold Entertainment had put into developing Mortal Kombat's characters and back story. "I know everything in that universe," he said. "I know what they have for lunch, what they do, where they're going to be in five years."

In fact, Hasbro already had commissioned market research to plumb Potato Head's soul. Focus groups in Boston and Atlanta that spring had confirmed that mothers of young children had a clear impression of the character. In their minds he was married, lived in the suburbs, and was middle-aged or close to it. He was not sexy or mean, and he was wise and good, if sometimes goofy—a kind and generous sort whose moods were highly changeable. Perhaps that explained Hassenfeld's affection for the toy. Perhaps when he looked at it, he saw a plastic reflection of himself.

With the research findings as a base, Kasanoff wanted to flesh out a Mr. Potato Head who led more than one life. "He's sort of a Walter Mitty guy next door," Kasanoff said. "But he goes out the back door, and he's a secret agent. Inspector Clouseau."

Gildea said he couldn't shake the image of the Schwarzenegger character in *True Lies,* which also starred Jamie Lee Curtis. Curtis doesn't know until near the end that her mild-mannered husband is a spy.

"Mr. Potato Head has been seeing Jamie Lee Curtis, you know," Serby said.

"At Planet Hollywood," Kasanoff agreed. "You just have to be able to define how a guy can be in a movie, be with the League of Women Voters, be with Jamie Lee Curtis, and be in a game." The multiple-lives scenario was perfect, Kasanoff said. "He lives like Arnold in *True Lies . . .* when he comes home from these adventures, there's the wife and spuds."

"He's probably more Forrest Gump than Arnold," a team member said.

"His job is to go on adventures," Kasanoff said. "Or maybe it is like Forrest Gump: it just kind of happens."

V

EARLY ONE SUMMER EVENING shortly before Pre–Toy Fair 1995, a Hasbro driver went to the Cincinnati airport to meet a man in his early forties. A native of Long Island, Dave Brewi was a fifteen-year employee of Toys "R" Us who'd taken his first job, as a store manager trainee, after answering an ad in the paper. Responsible now for every action figure, die-cast car, toy truck, and radio-controlled vehicle the nearly one thousand–store chain sold, Brewi, sports fan and lover of science fiction, was the most powerful boys' toys buyer in the world.

He was chauffeured to the Precinct, a restaurant that prominently displayed photographs of previous guests Rodney Dangerfield, Tom Selleck, and ex-Reds player Pete Rose. It was a hot spot, as these things go in Cincinnati, rated one of America's top twenty-five restaurants according to a framed article from *Playboy* magazine that was mounted above the urinals in the men's room. Thick steaks were the specialty of the house, but Brewi had the $49 lobster tail and drank whiskey and post-dinner tequila sent around by Hasbro's head of sales.

Early the next morning he was in the presentation theater at Hasbro's Cincinnati offices. After a cigarette and coffee, he sat in the center seat reserved for Hassenfeld when he was in town. He was about to see the 1996 boys' line, in its entirety, for the first time.

The presentation began with Nerf. Brewi sat largely without comment until they got to a new tabletop street hockey game, which would retail for $100 or more.

"Those electronics are a total waste of money," Brewi said. "The fun of the game is not listening to street noises." The presenters were crestfallen.

"In any case," Brewi went on, "it's set up for lefties."

He was, characteristically, perceptive. The rods controlling the three main players were on the left side of the game, with the goalie rod on the right. Right-handed boys would either have to control all three players with their less dexterous left hand and the goalie with their right, or control the three with their right hand and cross over with their left to stop shots. Either way was clumsy. The salesmen moved quickly to the next item.

Brewi had no problem praising products he liked, and he relished tweaking toy people—marketers especially—for those he didn't. He was always blunt and often bitingly sarcastic. "Crappy-looking tires on that thing," he said once when shown a Tonka truck. "Whoever put all those square wheel wells—you should find the son of a bitch and kill him." On another occasion he ridiculed focus groups. "In my opinion," he said, "a lot of this market research is nothing but a crutch to validate every decision that is made."

Smart toy makers swallowed their pride and listened very carefully to Brewi, not simply out of respect for his power, but because his insights were right far more often than wrong. (He was one of the only buyers, for example, who foresaw Power Rangers as a phenomenon. He bought early and big, giving Toys "R" Us a tremendous edge over competitors when Bandai's manufacturing capacity was overwhelmed in the first year.) Privately some despised Brewi for his forthright opinions and his relentless campaign to drive down Hasbro's wholesale prices. But none ever gave a hint in his presence.

Late into the afternoon it went—Batman, Superman, Tonka, re-launched Transformers, a freshened line of Star Wars, Hasbro's entire army of boys' brands. Once again, G.I. Joe Extreme had been saved for last. Although Brewi had been consulted during development, he had not seen the finished line. There was no doubt Toys "R" Us would carry it, but how strongly it would be merchandised was up in the air. Hasbro wanted the works: end caps, banners, sweepstakes, promotions, "just an explosion in the store," in the words of Chris Connolly. They wanted the full Elvis treatment, albeit with different results.

Bruce Kandel, one of Hasbro's best salesmen, had the job of pitching G.I. Joe—a line of toys, he said, to "empower kids." After rolling a sizzle tape, he made the by now mandatory comparison of old figures to bulked-up new, showed the all-new packaging, and demonstrated the new Ultra SLAM Firepower weapons.

"Talk about action in action figures, baby!" Kandel said.

"Man, all of that for six forty-nine?" Brewi said.

"It's amazing how we do it!"

"I'm not being facetious," Brewi said. "You thought I was." It was his first comment since Kandel had started. It boded well. For Brewi it was almost a compliment.

Kandel rolled a commercial with Joe's new slogan: "Extreme Times Call For Extreme Heroes." He demonstrated the pop-up tank and the Sky Stalker jet, which fired a missile. "Oooh, baby, dispersal bomb killed everyone within one hundred miles!" After mentioning the separate collectors' line and the licensing program, and promising another figure or two by Toy Fair, Kandel was done.

Brewi wouldn't have been Brewi without a gripe. "We have all kinds of dregs of merchandise in stores now," he said. Still, old Joe was selling respectably enough. He saw no reason Joe Extreme couldn't move at double or triple the pace. In fact, he thought Hasbro's projection of more than $50 million in nationwide sales in 1996 might be conservative.

"There's potentially millions of dollars in business here," he said. "That's what we're looking for, millions."

Cincinnati was thrilled. Brewi's reaction suggested they would get their program at Toys "R" Us and similar ones at the rest of the Top Four. The new TV series was set to premiere. The new comic was due out soon. Hasbro's signature brand seemed poised for another storybook comeback.

18

MORTAL COMBAT

I

Alan spent his winter holiday with Vivien at a Thai resort, interrupting his reading and tennis only to meet with officials of a refugee resettlement agency and to visit India, where Hasbro had a small but growing investment. He spent his first day home in Bristol, catching up on correspondence. The following morning, Tuesday, January 16, he was at his desk by seven-thirty. Some two hours later the phone rang. Sandy Marks, his secretary, answered.

"Alan," she said, "it's John Amerman."

Nice! Hassenfeld thought. John's going to wish me a Happy New Year.

"Hi, John," Hassenfeld said. "Just got in from India. How are you doing?"

Amerman said he was fine, then talked a bit about his own vacation. Sitting fireside at the ranch one day, he'd gotten to thinking again about combining Hasbro and Mattel. No time was better than the present, he'd concluded, and with his board's backing, he was prepared to make an offer, the details of which he was about to send to Hassenfeld. Did Hasbro have a private fax? Hassenfeld gave him the number. There was something else Amerman let Hassenfeld know: he wanted a deal and he wanted it now, not when the spirit moved Hassenfeld. Should Hasbro fail to reply formally by the end of tomorrow, the letter would be made public. Hassenfeld said a cold good-bye and went to the machine. This was hardball. Mattel was putting a bear hug on Hasbro.

I've read about these things, Hassenfeld was thinking. I've seen them in movies. This isn't real, is it? What the hell did I do to deserve this?

The three-page unsigned letter outlined an offer to combine Hasbro and Mattel with a stock swap under which Hasbro shareholders would receive 1.5 shares of the new company's stock for each of their shares, an unquestionably attractive premium (Mattel shareholders would get their new stock on a one-to-one basis). Amerman proposed to immediately begin negotiations on other aspects of a merger, including titles and resolution of antitrust concerns, topics that had been broached last spring.

Hassenfeld showed the fax first to Sonny Gordon, ordinarily an urbane, even-tempered man not prone to vulgarity.

"Oh, shit," Gordon said.

Like his boss, he was stunned that Amerman had resorted to a threat, since last year's discussions seemed to have ended amicably—certainly without the impression that Mattel would ever make an unwanted advance. If Amerman went public, things would get very ugly very soon. Hasbro could be put into play, with the chilling possibility that Alan would have little or no say in the future of the company his family had run for most of a century.

Hassenfeld informed Verrecchia and John O'Neill and, by phone with director John Rosenwald, began to sketch out a broad strategy. Hasbro would respond to the offer through a formal vote of its board. The vote would be preceded by two analyses. One, the business, would examine the benefits to shareholders and the shape of a new company. The second analysis would be legal: Would the federal government let Hasbro and Mattel combine, and if so, at what cost? Although these issues had been visited last year, they had not been given the scrutiny a formal offer demanded. George Ditomassi, Wayne Charness, and a handful of trusted others were put to work. Hasbro engaged two outside law firms and another investment banker, to supplement Rosenwald's Bear Stearns & Co., and a New York public relations firm was retained, in the event Amerman took his case directly to stockholders. At Hasbro's request Mattel relented on its deadline, agreeing to keep the matter confidential until after next Tuesday, the earliest Hassenfeld's board could convene. Meanwhile the two sides would meet on Sunday, in New York.

As he left Rhode Island that weekend, Hassenfeld was still perplexed by Amerman's motivations. Why now, when the FTC's investigation of Toys "R" Us had heated up, not gone away? "Why are they prematurely ejaculating on us like this?" Alan joked in a rare moment of levity. Why no warning? Did Amerman really want a merger, or was he only interested in being a shark? Tremendous damage with shareholders, retailers, inventors, and Hollywood was inevitable if Mattel went public. It was hard not to wonder if Amerman would have dared to take this tack were Stephen alive. It was hard not to imagine Amerman's true feelings for Alan, this CEO with the rubber bands. With one carefully timed phone call, he seemed to have cast Hassenfeld into a real-life version of one of Hasbro's own games: Sharp Shooters, say ("Okay, all you high rollers, step right up for the ultimate game of luck and strategy!"), or old Milton Bradley's still popular Game of Life ("Your goal is to dodge bad luck and make a buck. End up with the biggest fortune and you'll retire in style as a winner!").

Certainly the offer couldn't have come at a worse time for Hasbro. O'Neill was in the middle of closing out last year's books, and Verrecchia was laboring mightily to get his critical first quarter off to a good start. Coming off the disappointment of 1995, Hassenfeld was under tremendous pressure to begin the new year with a bang-up Toy Fair.

And internal issues had nearly reached the breaking point. Despite his Lillymere pledge, Alan had yet to define his role at Hasbro with crystal clarity or address the matter of top structure. On the latter issue, some were beginning to wonder if he were paralyzed in some strange way— and what, if anything, might move him. Still hopeful of becoming president, Verrecchia especially was discontented. "It's a horse's ass. It's stupid. And it's frustrating," he said of the structure. "It'll get resolved, that I'll guarantee you. Because people will leave if it doesn't." Hassenfeld had agreed to hold a second strageic planning session, Camp 2000, this very weekend, ostensibly to address these concerns, and now he had to postpone it. He had to send Vivien, with his apologies and an alibi, to the January toy fairs in Paris, London, and Nuremberg that he always attended.

One thing seemed certain: whether he got Hasbro or not, Amerman won.

Hassenfeld touched down at La Guardia on Saturday morning with a sense of déjà vu, albeit with one critical difference: a bear hug was not dinner in Palm Beach or tea with Jill Barad. Hassenfeld's pride was now firmly in Amerman's crosshairs: if Alan would not take Mattel's hand, Amerman would fight to wrest the company Alan's grandfather had founded, his father had built, and his brother had brought to greatness. It was a matter that struck deep into Alan's soul—a matter that Amerman, a man whose entire career had been spent as a hired hand and not an heir, might never comprehend.

Still, Hassenfeld was endeavoring to distance himself from the swirl of his emotions as he checked into the Waldorf-Astoria and went to the offices of Skadden, Arps, Slate, Meagher & Flom, the law firm where Hasbro had opened a war room.

I have to be dispassionate, he told himself. My job is to marshal the best resources on analyzing this deal on an economic basis, and on a feasibility basis, and bringing that to my board. I can't worry about me.

▪

At ten A.M. on Sunday of what would be remembered inside Hasbro as the Lost Weekend, which in turn was the beginning of what Hassenfeld would call the Days from Hell, Sonny Gordon knocked on the door of the Waldorf's $2,000-a-night Frank Sinatra suite. Amerman welcomed the vice chairman and his contingent: O'Neill, Rosenwald, and another investment banker. Amerman had three men as well: John Vogelstein, Mattel Worldwide president James Eskridge, and Ned Mansour, Mattel's general counsel and secretary. Hasbro had sent word not to expect Hassenfeld.

Noting that Hassenfeld, in fact, was missing, Amerman asked if Gordon and his group were empowered to negotiate. Gordon said they were not, a point Hassenfeld's absence was intended to underscore. Their role, Gordon said, was only to gather information for their chairman and their board. Amerman was not pleased, but he did not believe Gordon was being forthright. Perhaps this was how they conducted themselves back there in that funny little state of Rhode Island. In any event, here they were. There was plenty to discuss, with or without Alan.

Amerman related his holiday ruminations and continued excitement over what an incredible entity Mattel-Hasbro would be. He spoke of his plan to retire in 1997 but said he would stay another year to smooth the transition, for he envisioned a three-year process: with the mechanics of the merger occupying the first, restructuring and integration of the various components the second, and peak performance from the new corporation achieved in the third. Amerman agreed antitrust was an issue, but it was not insurmountable in his view; as he'd said last spring, with Hassenfeld enthusiastically at his side, they would prevail.

"Together," Amerman declared, "we can do it."

Gordon and O'Neill did most of the talking for Hasbro. They went line by line through Amerman's fax, seeking clarification and reinforcing Hasbro's concerns about philanthropy, titles, and a continuing presence in Hassenfeld's home state. Predictably, Gordon homed in on antitrust. On one point there was agreement: the only way to prove whose odds were right would be to announce a merger and await the FTC's reaction. But supposing Hasbro agreed to that course, Gordon said, and regulatory approval dragged on and on, a plausible scenario? Would inventors still bring their best ideas to Hasbro, with its future dangling? Would George Lucas award Hasbro the rights to the next *Star Wars* trilogy? Would Time Warner still let it have *Batman and Robin*? Would valuable employees not jump ship—conceivably to Mattel? If the deal fell through, Hasbro would be gravely wounded, while Mattel would be all the more powerful. Or so Gordon and O'Neill maintained.

The meeting ended after some three hours. The Hasbro contingent was briefing Alan when Mattel called to request another session, and discussions resumed that afternoon in the Sinatra suite. To demonstrate the depth of their desire, Amerman and Vogelstein were prepared to sweeten their offer, from 1.5 to 1.67 shares of new company stock for each share of Hasbro's. They would guarantee a significant but as-yet-undefined presence in Rhode Island. Mattel-Hasbro would contribute $8 million annually to charity, with Hassenfeld selecting the recipients. Hasbro would name seven directors to the new board, Mattel eight. All of Hassenfeld's senior executives would be guaranteed positions, not to mention riches, for all were stockholders. In addition to becoming co-chairman, Hassenfeld would head the board's executive committee. And in the event the FTC denied the merger on antitrust grounds, Mattel would pay Hasbro a $100 million indemnity. With the exception of the indemnity, which Gordon insisted was too low, Amerman believed the Hasbro side was satisfied. Never mind Hassenfeld's coy absence: if this wasn't negotiating, what was? Amerman went to bed Sunday night certain he was on the verge of closing the most magnificent deal in the history of the toy industry. On this course, they would have to redo his plaque in the Hall of Fame.

Gordon stayed up past midnight talking it over with Alan, whose room had been checked for electronic bugs. The new price, a roughly 75 percent premium for Hasbro shareholders (making it a $5.2 billion deal), was sweet indeed. But with corporate headquarters to be in El Segundo, Rhode Island's status still seemed vague, as did Hassenfeld's real position and long-term prospects: "Co-chairman of picking dandelions," he would later quip. Alan agreed the indemnity was perilously low, and he was troubled that Mattel refused to provide it up front, through an escrow account. And nothing Gordon had heard today suggested Mattel was relying on more than faith, and Hassenfeld's hand, that a merger would clear the FTC.

Fifteen lawyers from two toy companies and five law firms met for nearly four hours Monday to thrash out antitrust. The meeting was at the offices of Wachtell, Lipton, Rosen & Katz, which had represented Hasbro in its 1984 acquisition of Milton Bradley but was now in Mattel's employ. Hasbro wanted to learn the specifics of Mattel's strategy for getting government approval. Mattel offered slogans.

"Together, we think we can get there," Marty Lipton declared. "If we don't, the money will take care of your problems." Mattel was beginning to sound like a jilted lover, reduced to the same old line in pleading for one more chance.

Hasbro was more and more inclined to break up. "We didn't see the magic formula," Gordon said after the meeting.

Indemnity also continued to divide the sides. Gordon wanted at least $250 million, placed in an escrow account, but Mattel wouldn't budge. It was a contentious issue inside the Hasbro camp as well, with O'Neill and Ditomassi more inclined than their colleagues toward taking their chances with the FTC. Verrecchia didn't know what value exactly to assign the potential damage to Hasbro, but he was sure not even $250 million was enough. "I'll give you two hundred and fifty million," he said at one meeting. "I want you to cut your right arm off. Will you do it?" The analogy angered Ditomassi and O'Neill, who thought he was being a wiseass. But Verrecchia wasn't. He was only making a point.

▪

Early Tuesday morning Amerman, Vogelstein, and Ned Mansour reconvened, in Gordon's suite, for another try at an indemnity. They got nowhere. The meeting had barely ended when Mansour called Gordon to plead for yet one more try, but the subsequent session, at Skadden Arps, yielded nothing. Minutes before the Hasbro board met, Vogelstein phoned Rosenwald in a last-ditch effort at compromise. Rosenwald said it was in the directors' hands now.

A presentation by the investment bankers followed by one from the lawyers took up most of the Hasbro board's nearly six-hour meeting. No lawyer gave the merger greater than a 25 percent chance of succeeding, and that was with substantial divestiture; one rated the odds at close to zero. Sylvia and Alan Hassenfeld had little to say, and nothing whatsoever about family or tradition.

The vote to reject was unanimous. A one-page written response was prepared, explaining the vote and cautioning Mattel that going public now almost certainly would doom the chances of a merger later, even after the FTC had turned its attention elsewhere. Gordon called Mansour at about nine o'clock to read the statement.

"Thank you for letting me know," Mansour said politely. He did not indicate when, or if, Mattel would make good on its threat to go public, and Gordon did not ask.

Hassenfeld had no doubt they would, in what he believed would be a "blitzkrieg" campaign, probably already carefully plotted. "For the first seventy-two hours, understand that until we know what type of missiles they're lobbing and where they're coming in from, we're going to be on the defensive—and it's not going to be pretty," he told his people. "After seventy-two hours, we'll begin to put up our own airplanes." His speech would be rich with such war imagery in the days ahead.

II

HASSENFELD WAS ON the phone to Vivien shortly after four P.M. the day after his board's vote when the other line rang in his room at the Waldorf. It was Gordon, with word Mattel had just issued a press release, along with a copy of a letter Amerman was sending Hassenfeld and every member of his board. In it, Amerman spoke of disappointment at Hasbro's rejection and hinted of having been deceived during the Lost Weekend.

"I hope that by making our proposal public," Amerman declared, "Hasbro shareholders will communicate to your board their strong desire for this transaction."

Many would, but those immediately demanding answers were the reporters and analysts who were on Mattel's fax list or had access to PRNewswire, publisher of company news. They would be stymied to a large extent, for all anyone at Hasbro had to say on the record was in a short press release late Wednesday and a conference call Thursday, in which Hassenfeld and Gordon read technically precise, colorless statements but took no questions.

Alan had been right. Fought largely in the media, an arena in which Mattel considered itself master, not without reason, the first engagements went decisively to Amerman. Mattel's spin was all over the coverage Thursday, when the story broke. Analysts marveled at the fabulous rewards awaiting stockholders and the nearly divine fit of the product lines. Antitrust was acknowledged as an issue, but in more than one account Hasbro's concerns came across as exaggerated, if not spurious. Some reports portrayed Amerman as the business mastermind, Hassenfeld as the brattish scion clinging to a quaint but outdated family heritage that was contrary to the spirit of 1990s capitalism. "Barbie proposed to G.I. Joe, and she won't take no for an answer," was the lead on an Associated Press piece. To sustain momentum, Amerman followed his first letter to Hassenfeld with a second, released on Friday, in which he intimated again that petulance, not substance, was all that stood in the way of a deal.

"Alan," Amerman wrote, "I have to think that if you truly believed that the transaction could not be consummated you would not have directed your advisers to negotiate all the other aspects of the transaction with us. I remain absolutely confident that if Mattel and Hasbro join together in a spirit of cooperation, any and all impediments to this transaction will be eliminated."

Spread by headlines, the smell of easy money perfumed Wall Street, driving the arbitrageurs, who feed on corporate misfortune, to a frenzy. Speculators helped accomplish something Hassenfeld had been unable to through restructuring and talk of building brands: they drove the stock to record highs, on record volumes, at one point reaching $46.75 a share, up 53 percent from where they'd traded before Amerman's announcement. Venom being the close companion of avarice, Hassenfeld was besieged with letters, faxes, and calls, none praising his humanitarianism or moral compass. It wasn't only the big boys who were irate. "Why in the world didn't you accept the offer from Mattel? You will receive a golden parachute," wrote a grandmother who owned a hundred shares of Hasbro stock. "Do not shareholders 'own' the companies in which they invest—or is that just an old cliché?" Hasbro directors received their share of vitriol as well, and on Thursday, less than twenty-four hours after Amerman went public, the first of several lawsuits was filed. Hassenfeld's mother was among those named as defendants. Even more restrained shareholders, such as Fidelity, which had hundreds of millions invested in Hasbro, wanted the deal.

As the week ended, Amerman's strategy was unfolding brilliantly. Shareholder outrage was nearing a crescendo that seemed likely to force the Hasbro board to reconsider its rejection. What few aircraft Hassenfeld had attempted to get up had all gone down in flames.

■

It was nearly midnight on Friday before Hassenfeld returned to Rhode Island from the war room. He was alone. Bone tired, still without appetite, he went to Bristol, where the housekeeper had left a three-foot plush Barney, a present from Sheryl Leach. "Barney loves you," Leach had written on the card. "You make rainbows happen, they don't." Hassenfeld was cheered, if only momentarily, as he had been by an outpouring of support from his employees.

Muzzled by the lawyers, Hassenfeld had been denied his real voice at a time he urgently needed to speak. He slept poorly Friday night. When he awoke the next morning, he began to write. He sat at his desk with its view of the lonely winter bay, listened to Irish melodies through headphones, smoked cigarettes, and let his feelings run free until late into the night. It was the first time in many years he had been compelled to turn so ferociously to the written word. Months later he no longer had a copy of his reflections, and he would not have allowed them to be published if he had; but he was willing to share their theme. The dispassion he'd sought had given way to anger and a feeling of betrayal, he recalled, at how Amerman and Vogelstein had come at him.

"I basically saw it as a very Machiavellian move where no matter what, they were going to damage us," Hassenfeld said. "And if they got us or they didn't get us, they would still be that much stronger because of what they had put us through."

Hassenfeld's writing was cathartic. When he returned to New York and the war room Sunday afternoon, he was in better spirits, if not refreshed. Mattel could throw anything at him now. He was in this to the end.

▪

Quoting unnamed "knowledgeable people" who sounded suspiciously like Mattel insiders, *The Wall Street Journal* Monday published a story rich with details of the Lost Weekend. Hasbro did not look good. Writers Andy Pasztor and longtime toy specialist Joseph Pereira had carefully examined Hasbro's fifteen-page antitrust analysis, made public during the previous week's flurry of releases, and found a curious reference to "a pending FTC investigation" of the toy industry. Hasbro had cited the mysterious case only as further evidence of the particularly intense examination it believed a merger would invite at this time, but, digging deeper, Pereira and Pasztor had discovered that the prime subject of the investigation was Toys "R" Us, accused of pressuring manufacturers not to sell certain highly popular products to some of its rivals. Toys "R" Us executives were furious that the case was suddenly in the news, and they blamed Hassenfeld personally. The second week was not shaping up any easier than the first.

"Is this worth it?" his mother asked in one of her many calls.

"Mom," he answered, "it's not even a matter of being worth it or not. This thing isn't real. It can't happen."

On Tuesday Hasbro finally got some lethal firepower to the front. Hassenfeld had called Rhode Island's congressional delegation, which included a Kennedy in the House and a senior Republican in the Senate, and their strong concerns—which they'd asked the FTC and the Justice Department's Antitrust Division to scrutinize posthaste—dominated coverage. On Wednesday a glowing letter of support from Steven Spielberg to Hassenfeld was published, along with word that the attorneys general of Rhode Island and Connecticut, where Lego had its U.S. headquarters, had joined the call for antitrust probes. On Thursday, with the arbitrageurs losing some of their ardor and the price of Hasbro stock nosing back down, *The Wall Street Journal* noted that Hasbro had raised legitimate antitrust concerns regarding the European market, which no one outside Pawtucket had paid any attention to until now. Also on Thursday, media outlets reported that Rhode Island governor Lincoln Almond had signed a measure deleting an arcane provision of state law that would have let dissident stockholders easily call a special, and potentially damaging, shareholders' meeting. Besides protecting Hasbro, the legislation was noteworthy in how it had been rushed through the Rhode Island General Assembly: in a near record two days and without the customary committee hearings or even any floor debate. Hassenfeld, it was clear, had learned a thing or two about the workings of democracy as head of RIght Now!

Amerman, meanwhile, continued to play the unwelcome suitor.

"Alan," he wrote in a third letter, "it is incumbent on both of us to finalize this transaction so that your shareholders can receive a premium of over $2.2 billion. As we have noted over the past three trading sessions, the market has warmly embraced the transaction. I genuinely believe that by working together our advisors will be able to use their expertise to address any antitrust issues." Copies of that letter, as with the previous ones, were sent to Hasbro's board. Hoping an old friend of Stephen Hassenfeld might have special influence on the dead chairman's kid brother, Amerman sent Rosenwald a personal fax. Amerman wrote that Alan's motivations "perplexed" him. "We cannot allow personal self-interests to stand in the way of shareholders of our two companies," he stated.

▪

Hassenfeld had taken to calling Mattel's faxes Scuds, after Saddam Hussein's missile attacks during the 1991 Gulf War. Back in Pawtucket on Friday, February 2, less than a week before the first buyers would descend on West Twenty-third for Toy Fair, Alan arrived early for work. He stopped in Verrecchia's office, decorated, like many at Hasbro, with a poster of Barbie. "Sure, Barbie is a bitch," the caption read, "but she can't have everything!"

"Any incomings?" Hassenfeld said.

"Nothing yet," Verrecchia said.

At 9:05 A.M.—6:05 Pacific Coast time—Hassenfeld's private fax machine whirred to life. Two single-spaced, typewritten pages were produced. Sandy Marks rushed them to her boss, who read with stunned disbelief. Rather than making a hostile tender offer and initiating a proxy battle, which many had expected would be Mattel's next move, possibly a devastating one, Amerman was dropping his bid.

The tone of Amerman's letter was that of a stern father chastising a wayward child. Amerman blamed Hassenfeld personally for denying his shareholders billions, now and in the future, and again implied that he'd been badly misled. The chairman of Mattel was livid: once again a Hassenfeld had thwarted him. "You elected to take drastic steps, both politically and through the media, to greatly increase the difficulty of achieving a merger in timely manner," Amerman wrote. "Your 'scorched-earth' campaign has created an intolerable climate. By acting in this manner, you have also placed Hasbro in a position from which you cannot easily retreat, even if you now wish to do so."

All manner of theories surfaced to explain Mattel's sudden withdrawal. Some speculated that Mattel was shaken by the political and legal muscle Hasbro had been able to summon—that what had been expected to be capitulation had turned into a donnybrook from which no one could escape unbloodied. Some thought Amerman feared that an overtly hostile battle against an opponent armed with two senators, two representatives, and two attorneys general would precipitate a deep look by regulators or courts at the innermost workings of his company—a disruptive and unpredictable experience, as the government's investigation of Mattel under Ruth Handler had demonstrated. But Amerman wrote nothing in his letter, nor did he say anything later, to lend credence to such suppositions; he insisted that all he'd ever wanted was a friendly merger, not a takeover fight. The truth was, the whole affair had become an unwelcome and potentially damaging distraction for him, too. "In making this decision," he wrote, "I am taking into consideration the strong relationships with our valued customers, partners and loyal employees, all of whom could be adversely affected by a lengthy battle."

"See?" Marks said to Alan. "The good do survive!"

Amerman's letter had gone out on PRNewswire, and word was spreading quickly through Hasbro and Wall Street. Hassenfeld stood at his desk, too charged to sit or even smoke, as he worked the phone and entertained well-wishers who dropped by in person. In the next hour he talked to his mother, every one of his senior executives, the mail clerk, analysts, and Toys "R" Us CEO Michael Goldstein. He reached Vivien in London, where she was holding down the overseas fort. "Darling," he said, "first round or second round, whatever you want to call it, went to us. . . . Now I have to get a flak jacket as the stock drops. . . . I love you, precious. . . . Yes, I did hang tough. . . ."

Hassenfeld hung up and quipped: "She's poor again!"

Then he allowed as how he might sleep that night, for the first time in more than two weeks.

▪

Wayne Charness had decreed Friday, February 2, Hasbro Pride Day before Amerman's retreat. It was part of a campaign, begun the week before, to sustain morale. Employees today were to wear an article of Hasbro clothing and their "To Hell with Mattel" and "Hands Off Hasbro" buttons. Lunch was billed as a Barbie-Q. Early that morning a Model Shop employee wheeled a Playskool Magic Smoking Grille into the cafeteria, positioning it next to the daily menu. He lashed a blindfolded Barbie doll to a motorized skewer and affixed one of Kirk Bozigian's 3¾-inch G.I. Joes to the controls. "I still think we should have singed her hair," he lamented.

Another employee had written lyrics to be sung to the tune of the Beatles' "Get Back." Photocopies were available:

> Barbie was a doll who thought she was a goddess,
> Wanted everything in sight.
> But she was just a plastic bimbo in a townhouse,
> And Joe, he was ready to fight.

No one, of course, had been expecting the tumultuous scene that unfolded shortly before noon. Loudspeakers blared "The Star-Spangled Banner," and a man in Mr. Potato Head costume circulated through the crowd, which spilled out of the cafeteria onto Main Street. Workers who had not yet signed a wall-size "Hands Off Hasbro" card lined up to do so. Hassenfeld burst in, blowing kisses, then he raised his arms in victory. Verrecchia, O'Neill, and Charness had ear-to-ear smiles. Gordon was still in New York, in the war room, but sent his best wishes through the chairman.

In a rally the week before, Hassenfeld had lifted the mood by relating his mother's purported reaction to his decision to spurn Mattel's offer, which would have enriched the Hassenfeld family by approximately $500 million. " 'Five hundred million?' she'd supposedly said. 'Did I take the wrong baby home from the hospital?' " The crowd had roared; no one in it, of course, knew anything of last spring's discussions, of how the chairman had been receptive to Amerman's initial overture. Hassenfeld told another anecdote this time. It was about a letter sent him last week by Leslie Gutterman, the rabbi who'd eulogized his brother and one of many private citizens who'd been pulling for Hasbro. Gutterman had sent a letter of encouragement and a $6 billion check with which he wanted to buy Hasbro, to then return the company to Alan. "He called and told me not to deposit the check until Tuesday," Hassenfeld said to laughter.

The chairman turned serious. "I could not have fought if you did not believe in me as I believed in you," he said. He called his employees family and spoke of the absolutely critical need now to enhance shareholder value. He thanked his managers, and each got thunderous applause. Then he asked Verrecchia to speak.

His voice choked, Verrecchia made an extraordinary admission. He said his restructuring must take some responsibility for dampening employees' passion for their work, a vital component of success. They needed it back, Verrecchia said, to make Mattel pay the price for all this in the place that mattered: the marketplace. He would help lead the way.

"You've got to come in every day thinking: How am I going to beat those bastards?" Verrecchia said.

I I I

FOUR DAYS LATER Hassenfeld was back in New York for Toy Fair. Casual observers noted no difference in the man. He flew through West Twenty-third same as always, enthusiastically greeting guests and escorting the VIPs. Ever the merchant, he remained attentive to the smallest details, insisting, for example, that the Mr. Potato Head display be more than doubled in size to play off the huge popularity of *Toy Story*. He allowed himself moments of mirth, joining many of his employees in fantasizing about the movie that surely would be made about the Mattel affair: *Barbies at the Gate*. Casting suggestions were being solicited, and Hassenfeld approved of the consensus to play him: Robin Williams. (Tommy Lee Jones was the unanimous choice for Verrecchia. Verrecchia himself had named the actor, before hearing anyone else's suggestions.)

But subtle clues confirmed this was no ordinary Toy Fair. Hassenfeld regularly wore a tie and always his purple "ESV" button—yet his signature scarf was absent. He had lost weight ("You can see your chin now," Sandy Marks had commented), and his pallor was sufficient for his mother to make a fuss about his eating.

On Sunday, February 11, the day before Toy Fair officially began, Alan sat in his showroom office, which was next to his brother's old space. Pictures of Stephen and Vivien were on his credenza, along with a Mr. Potato Head. His gym bag was on the floor, and the three-foot Barney that Leach had sent him was on his couch. Across West Twenty-third, a Buddy L flag fluttered in the morning breeze. Once Tonka's nemesis, the toy-truck maker had gone bankrupt, the flag left behind when its showroom was abandoned.

Tonight Hassenfeld was hosting Hasbro's annual analysts' dinner, an invitation-only affair held downstairs in his showroom. It was a smaller group than would attend Wednesday's William Blair & Company conference, and no one from Mattel would be present, but the chairman was nonetheless worried that the question-and-answer session would turn confrontational. Throughout the takeover attempt, his only public comments had been carefully scripted, legally previewed, and not open to discussion.

"There's a great deal of apprehension inside of me about how we're going to get the real story out," Hassenfeld told a writer, "about whether I'm going to be heckled." He spoke of the tremendous stress of the last month, of his frustration at not being able to address inaccuracies and innuendo. He was asked if this was what he'd had in mind when he accepted Stephen's offer to work in Japan that summer of 1969. "Are you crazy?" He allowed himself a laugh. "That was a mystical period. Who would have ever imagined this?"

The immediate future, it seemed, held further perils, some lingering from before, others newly emerged from the dust of the Mattel affair. Hasbro's revenues had reached $2.86 billion in 1995, but earnings had declined for the second consecutive year—this, after Hassenfeld at May's annual meeting had publicly predicted they would climb 10 percent or more. The company had lost money in Germany, Europe's largest market, and Japan, a critical piece of the future, was faltering. Still stinging from the takeover defense, Hasbro board members had excoriated their chairman for letting the company drift. Not since the earliest days of his chairmanship had their faith in him been as soft. Alan's response was that

Mattel had been a "wake-up call," but people were still awaiting proof. Purple buttons did not constitute it. Nor did putting the distinctive GO and upward arrow from Hasbro's most universally recognized brand, Monopoly, on the cover of the soon-to-be-released annual report.

But whatever else happened in the remainder of 1996, nothing would be scrutinized more than what Hassenfeld did, or did not do, regarding Verrecchia. Much is forgiven in business when the numbers are good. Bad numbers have a way of magnifying flaws, and Verrecchia's Toy Group in 1995 had barely made money while its sales volume had grown at less than 10 percent, not the sort of arithmetic to reach $2 billion by the year 2000. What analysts were trying to determine was if this was attributable to late aftershock of the restructuring, some particularly unfortunate dip in the ordinary cycles of fashion, or some intrinsic organizational weakness requiring a shake-up at the highest levels. Late that fall Wall Street had started to whisper that Hasbro needed a "marketing guru," a new second in command, probably someone from outside. The chairman, like his chief operating officer for toys, could not escape the whisperings.

Listening that Sunday to Hassenfeld outlining the issues that still faced him, one sensed a man looking at himself unblinkingly. Perhaps it was inevitable; unlike the atmosphere at Lillymere, the light under which he now was illuminated was unforgiving. "I'm not the penultimate, ruthless CEO. I never want to be," Hassenfeld said. "I still have to have heart."

Still unanswered was the degree to which it would harden.

▪

That afternoon Hassenfeld met with Gordon, O'Neill, Charness, and a media consultant to rehearse for that night's dinner and Wednesday's Blair conference. Hassenfeld stepped to a makeshift podium. A videocamera began recording.

"Let's go," Charness said.

"Oh, Christ," Hassenfeld said. He made a face.

"You're on," Charness said. "Be serious."

"I am."

The consultant began with rumors that Mattel's attempt had whet others' appetites for Hasbro. "Are you in play?" the consultant said.

"I do not speculate," Hassenfeld replied.

"Where is Toys 'R' Us in this?"

"We had an excellent meeting with Toys 'R' Us. We had a wonderful walk-through." In truth, Toys "R" Us remained furious with Hasbro because of the FTC investigation. CEO Mike Goldstein had lambasted Hasbro on his Friday visit to West Twenty-third, then pointedly departed before the lavish cocktail party Hassenfeld put on for his biggest customer.

"Alan," Charness said, "if you can't enhance shareholder value, will you step down?"

"I intend to enhance shareholder value," the chairman said. "That is my goal, that is my ambition, that is what I'm going to do."

With all his millions, what could possibly motivate him? the consultant asked.

"Bitchy question!" Hassenfeld rolled his eyes. "Wayne-O, I've got to work on stepping down."

"You're a rich man," the consultant persisted. "Why don't you just get out of this? Why bother to come in in the morning?"

"Oh, that's easy. This is the most wonderful business to be in," Hassenfeld said with no hint of irony.

The real questions that night turned out to be surprisingly tepid. Perhaps it was ungracious even for Wall Street to pummel a man who'd just wined and dined you. At nine o'clock, after the last analyst had departed, Hassenfeld took a leftover bottle of cabernet sauvignon to his office. "This is Alan's liquid dinner," he said. Charness ordered a takeout pizza with pepperoni and extra cheese, which the chairman nibbled between sips of wine. His only sustenance all day had been coffee and half a slice of chocolate cake at about four o'clock. His mother would not have approved.

After congratulating his boss, Verrecchia left for his hotel. Hassenfeld was alone with his chief financial officer and Charness.

"Okay, one down," Hassenfeld said.

"You did a good job tonight," O'Neill said.

"Now we've got to deliver," Hassenfeld said. "If we don't deliver this year, I wonder really if I am right for this job."

In the hall, a janitor was shampooing the carpet. Hassenfeld took off his loafers and shook seven pennies onto the floor. "Pretty soon they're going to start hurting," he said as he got on the phone to Vivien.

EPILOGUE

One day nearly a year after the Mattel affair, Alan flew home from New York, where he'd been overnight on business. A company driver met him at the Rhode Island state airport and brought him to Lincoln Park Cemetery. It was seven-thirty on a bright but cold November morning. The van went deep into the cemetery and stopped by two graves that lie at the foot of an expressionist sculpture. Alan got out. Sylvia had been here yesterday, before heading to Palm Beach for the winter.

Alan knelt by Stephen's headstone to clear dried leaves that had blown against the base, obscuring the inscription: "A strength in need, a comfort in sorrow, a companion in joy." He placed two pebbles on Stephen's headstone and two on Merrill's, a custom signifying the deceased are not forgotten. Alan told a writer accompanying him that he still visited four or five times a year, to keep his father and brother informed—aloud, provided no one was around to eavesdrop. Among other matters, Alan updated Merrill on the Red Sox and Stephen on the stock price, which that day happened to be 43⅞, a record, if the artificial highs of the Mattel takeover attempt were excluded.

Alan had recently returned from California, where he'd presented George Lucas with a one-of-a-kind action figure that had the body of

Obi-Wan Kenobi and a likeness of Lucas's head. Alan laughed, recalling how he'd dressed as Obi-Wan Kenobi for the presentation, during the biannual Star Wars Summit Meeting, a particularly important occasion this time in light of the feverish campaigning that still continued for the toy rights to the second *Star Wars* trilogy, likely to be the most valuable toy license of all time. Alan talked a bit about the quarterly pressures of Wall Street, a topic often on his mind. He talked of 1996, expected to be Hasbro's first $3 billion year, the kind of performance he'd promised analysts at Toy Fair he would deliver. He talked of 1997, which, with the rerelease of the first *Star Wars* trilogy and the release of *The Lost World: Jurassic Park* and *Batman and Robin,* he expected to be even better. But here it was, not yet January, and already the analysts were pestering him on 1998! "You can't win!" Alan said. He mentioned two recent articles on Hasbro that had conjured the ghost of Stephen. Hard on the heels of *Forbes,* which recently had published a piece, "Rip Van Hasbro," in which Alan's chairmanship had been called into question, *CFO* magazine was discreetly critical of his social causes and their perceived drag on profits. And to think neither writer knew about his latest causes: leadership positions with an ad hoc group of public and private officials who were studying better ways to feed hungry families, and Brown University Medical School's board of overseers.

Alan laughed. "They still don't get it," he said, not sounding as if he much cared if they ever did. Indeed, he was downright feisty today. He was dressed in jeans and sweater, and he wore his signature scarf. Tomorrow he turned forty-eight. The kid brother had now lived longer than the wunderkind.

▪

For Alan, the months since Mattel had withdrawn its offer had been among the most momentous of his chairmanship, now in its seventh year. Closeted with Gordon, O'Neill, and Adam Klein, a consultant whose advice he respected, Hassenfeld had spent much of the spring and early summer finally recasting the top structure of Hasbro.

When they'd arrived for work on July 30, employees had found a letter from their chairman on their desks. "I am excited!" it began. "Last week, our board of directors approved a plan that will take this company far into the next century. One that finally nails the vision that so many of you have waited patiently for." Hassenfeld was promising revenues of more than $5 billion by the year 2000, with at least a 15 percent increase in earnings every year. His engine would be global brands, driven by a new office of the chairman. The office would have eight members.

Therein lay startling news.

After a transition period, Verrecchia and Ditomassi would be relieved of their duties as chief operating officers of Hasbro Inc. Ditomassi would become president of global innovation, a position as yet only vaguely defined. Verrecchia would be president of global operations, with charge of worldwide manufacturing and distribution, and head of Asia-Pacific sales and marketing. In his letter Hassenfeld was highly complimentary of the two men, calling Verrecchia "my partner, friend and teacher for the better part of thirty years" and Dito his mentor in the games business. "This is not about reorganization or downsizing," Hassenfeld wrote. "This is about revitalizing and aligning ourselves so we can take on and conquer the global village." Besides Verrecchia and Ditomassi, the office of the chairman included Gordon and O'Neill; their duties were essentially unchanged. There would be two new faces: Klein, whom Hassenfeld had named executive vice president of corporate strategy; and a president for global marketing, the so-called marketing guru, a position as yet unfilled. The letter was not explicit on this point, but senior people understood the guru would be second only to Hassenfeld in the corporate hierarchy. He would, in essence, be president.

Of all his executives, Hassenfeld had been most anxious about informing Verrecchia of his new role. He chose the intimacy of lunch in the executive suite's small conference room to tell him. Hassenfeld was fidgety. His foot tapped furiously, and his words ran together. Verrecchia listened coldly.

"Are you a player?" Hassenfeld said.

"I don't know yet," Verrecchia said.

Ordinarily a closed vessel, Verrecchia made no effort to mask his emotions. He resented Hassenfeld's procrastination and was angry that he'd been excluded from the decision making at its most critical juncture. He supported Hassenfeld's vision but did not want it forgotten that he had been one of the earliest proponents of opening up the brands and making Hasbro truly global. An irony was in the bottom line, the place dearest to Verrecchia's heart. Thanks in no small measure to his Toy Group's improving performance, Hasbro's second quarter results had beaten expectations, causing the stock to jump more than $1. The Toy Group was on track for a vastly better year than 1995, and 1997 looked to be huge. In fact, $2 billion by 2000 was not out of reach.

In the end, Verrecchia took what Hassenfeld offered. He left his chief operating role without apology, for he remained convinced that without the restructuring, his half of the business would have slid into total disaster. "I don't regret doing it," he said. "I don't regret doing virtual reality. If you go to the plate and you just put the bat on your shoulder and hope for a walk—well, that's one thing you can do, and sometimes you get a walk. But a lot of times you're going to just strike out. And if I'm going to strike out, I'm going to strike out swinging."

▪

Caught in the soft morning sun, the graveside sculpture sparkled pleasantly. The sun flattered the final brother. He still had a trace of summer tan, his face was barely wrinkled, and a boyish twinkle was back in his eyes. But looking closely, you could see the first gray in his hair. Alan had grown a beard to play Obi-Wan Kenobi, and it had come in significantly white. "I couldn't wait to shave it off!" he said.

Unbeknownst to Alan, great excitement was building this week on the top floor of Mattel headquarters. Soon to retire as CEO, John Amerman and his successor, Jill Barad, were wrapping up a plan to acquire Tyco Toys Inc., the third largest American toy company. They were joined by Bruce Stein, who, since visiting Hasbro with Steven Spielberg last year, had gone from DreamWorks to Sony to Mattel, where he was now Barad's second in command. The Tyco acquisition, which would be announced first thing next week, would give Mattel revenues of some $5 billion the first year and several proven global brands, including Matchbox cars.

Alan had a trick or two of his own up his sleeve. He was negotiating to buy two smaller firms that would establish Hasbro in the candy business and bring him two worthy toy brands: Stretch Armstrong and Koosh. He was close to a partnership that would allow Microsoft to offer Monopoly, Battleship, and other Hasbro games over its Internet Gaming Zone.

It was a quarter to eight, time for work. Alan got back into his minivan. He was absorbed in a lapful of documents as it cleared the cemetery gates and disappeared into traffic.

▪

On their tours of the Hasbro showroom at the 1997 American International Toy Fair the following February, buyers were escorted through cavernous Superman and Batman displays to the one tiny room set aside for G.I. Joe. There they saw such figures as the Congressional Medal of Honor soldier and the General Dwight D. Eisenhower. All were twelve-inch dolls: new heads on bodies molded from machines once used to make Larry Bernstein's Elvis. All were aimed at adult collectors, at middle-aged men who'd played with Joe as boys. There wasn't a single G.I. Joe for children.

Despite the early promise of G.I. Joe Extreme, the line had died at retail, and the series had been a disaster on TV. Urgently convened focus groups made a sobering discovery: The flag had lost its power over kids. For while his latest enemies may have been the mutated villains of a postapocalyptic world, G.I. Joe Extreme was still fighting for the good ol' U.S.A.; he was, after all, still sold in a package with red, white, and blue. "The hero element is important," the researchers concluded, "but the patriotic American idea is less interesting." When new advertising failed to pump life into G.I. Joe Extreme, further development of the line was immediately canceled, the assembly lines were shut down, and the sales force was instructed to prepare for closeouts.

Cincinnati had failed, just as the culture had changed. No one knew if Joe could ever recapture the imaginations of boys—and if so, by what means, short of another world war.

▪

Alan barely made passing reference to Joe at the William Blair & Company's Twelfth Annual Toy and Video Game Conference, held again at the Pierre. He was too enthusiastic about Hasbro's blockbuster lines and prospects for a record 1997. "What a difference a year makes!" he said.

Alan went on at some length about his new office of the chairman, but he did not mention the marketing guru. Several accomplished candidates from the shoe, snack, and soft-drink industries had been interviewed, but Alan had hired none. Each had wanted not only the number two job, but also a shot someday at becoming CEO.

Alan was unwilling to make any such promises. He was where he wanted to be, casting a shadow of his own.

NOTES

Alan Hassenfeld and Al Verrecchia invited me inside Hasbro in May 1992, after I approached them with the desire to write about the design, development, and marketing of G.I. Joe, their company's signature toy. The biggest, most profitable toy maker in history, Hasbro had never been more successful. Much happened in the ensuing years, of course, and my story evolved into something very different from what I envisioned that May. Despite the twists and turns fortune took, Hassenfeld and Verrecchia never reneged on their agreement, which gave me virtually unlimited access at all levels of Hasbro. And they were hardly alone: countless others were as open throughout the good, the bad, and the always interesting. I can think of no higher tribute to Hasbro's people than the honesty and candor I found everywhere.

I was an observer of numerous events in this book, including most that took place after May 1992. Verrecchia did not refuse a single request to attend a meeting or session. Hassenfeld declined twice, when he thought my presence would inhibit sensitive discussion (the third day of Lillymere 1995 and a Sliced Bread meeting in March 1995). Both times he and others subsequently provided recollections of what had transpired. On the advice of Hasbro's lawyers, I was denied attendance at deliberations during the Mattel affair.

I had access to many confidential internal documents, on the condition I not disclose details that would affect Hasbro competitively. Since most pertained to products and strategies that would have only historic value on publication, this was not an impediment to a comprehensive narrative.

For events I did not observe, I relied on press accounts, documents, video-tapes, and recollections. I conducted ninety-eight extensive taped interviews over the course of five years and dozens of shorter duration for which I took notes but did not tape-record. Whenever possible I reinterviewed participants after a suitable period of time, as a check on accuracy. I used quotes for certain conversations that I did not witness when, in my judgment, memories were precise and accounts by the conversants were substantially the same.

The "writer" in certain scenes was me. With the exception of a person I have called Robert Beckwith, I have changed no names, and there are no composite characters or scenes.

Hasbro opened doors ordinarily closed to journalists: Warner Bros., Toys "R" Us, and Saban Entertainment, as three examples. Mattel was less forthcoming. Despite repeated written and spoken requests for more time, John Amerman and Jill Barad acceded to only one interview, at Mattel headquarters in El Segundo, California, on December 6, 1994. I was, however, in the audience when they spoke at several William Blair and Company Toy and Video Game Conferences, and I toured their New York showroom during several Toy Fairs. Of necessity I was forced to rely extensively on Mattel publications, press accounts, and interviews with current and ex-employees, some of whom left happily and others who did not; in both cases I weighed what was said with the terms of departure in mind. Senior Vice President of Corporate Communications Glenn Bozarth was courteous and helpful, given the restraints on him. We corresponded regularly, and he met with me at the 1994, 1995, 1996, and 1997 Toy Fairs in New York, and in El Segundo on December 6, 1994, and October 21, 1996.

A highly placed Mattel insider agreed to comment on draft sections of this book that chronicle the company's attempt to buy Hasbro. This person did so strictly on background.

Eventually I became a fixture at Hasbro, in possession of a card key and free to move at will. Many meetings continued through meals that were catered by Hasbro's dining services. At such times, so as to miss nothing, I accepted the company's hospitality. I also took several trips on the corporate jet, which provided additional opportunities to observe Hassenfeld and his inner circle. (Two trips to California, one to Florida, and several to New York, New Jersey, and Cincinnati were at my own expense.) I reciprocated by buying lunch or dinner for several Hasbro employees (more than once, for many), and I made a sizable donation to the Hasbro Children's Hospital. In the end, I believe, the ledger was balanced.

I agreed to let Hassenfeld and Verrecchia read the manuscript before publication, but only with the right to correct errors of fact. Neither tried in any way to pressure me into any changes of style or characterization, nor did they ask me to strike a single passage. They are truly gentlemen.

More specific notes are as follows:

Lucky Pennies

On January 24, 1996, when Mattel's offer to acquire Hasbro was disclosed publicly, a share of Hasbro stock would have been worth $53.44 if the deal had gone through, as calculated by Bloomberg Business News.

In early 1996 some 4 million shares of Hasbro stock were owned by Sylvia Hassenfeld, 3 million by Alan, and about 1.5 million by his sister. A million shares were owned by the Hasbro Children's Foundation, and the Hassenfelds had options to purchase another million.

Earnings per share in 1995 would have been $1.98 but for a $.22 write-down for the failure of Sliced Bread, the expensive virtual-reality project.

Some exteriors of *Big* were shot outside Hasbro's New York showroom.

Chapter 1

Mitch Sugarman agreed to two interviews and let me tour his funeral chapel. Details of Alan's election to chairman and chief executive officer were gleaned from the corporate minutes and interviews with Vivien Hassenfeld, Sylvia Hassenfeld, and three nonfamily board members: E. John Rosenwald Jr., Norma T. Pace, and Barry J. Alperin.

Verrecchia and George R. Ditomassi Jr. were elected to the board in 1992.

Chapter 2

Here, as elsewhere throughout the book, I made use of the *Providence Journal* and *Evening Bulletin,* which began writing about the Hassenfelds and Hasbro in the 1920s.

The history of Ulanow and Galicia: Simon Dubnov's *History of the Jews;* Celia S. Heller's *On the Edge of Destruction;* Rachel Salamander's *The Jewish World of Yesterday;* and Abraham Wein's *Pinkas Hakehillot (Encyclopedia of Jewish Communities).* Also, several historical maps from the New York Public Library.

Hassenfeld family history: The recollections and papers of Dorothy Frank Fox (half-sister of Marion Frank Hassenfeld, Alan's paternal grandmother), Sylvia Hassenfeld, and Ellie Block; records at the New York office of the National Archives; Jacob R. Marcus's *The Concise Dictionary of American Jewish Biography;* Harry Schneiderman's *Who's Who in World Jewry.*

Jewish life in Rhode Island: Geraldine S. Foster's *The Jews in Rhode Island;* Hadassah David's "Jewish Federation of Rhode Island: Fifty Years of Giving,"

Rhode Island Jewish Historical Notes, vol. 12, no. 1, November 1995; Rhode Island Jewish Historical Association archives.

Hasbro history: A 1993 official company history; preliminary research by Bill Beck, hired in 1994 to write another history of Hasbro; and Beck's interview of Harold Hassenfeld in Nashville, Tennessee, in 1994, shortly before Harold suffered a stroke. Controller Richard B. Holt and Jeanette L. Martin of his office unearthed early financial records. I also consulted Providence City Directories and Rhode Island Secretary of State records.

I never met Stephen Hassenfeld. His portrait in this and subsequent chapters was drawn from videotapes, Hasbro's annual reports and catalogs, and press accounts. I interviewed his family and many close friends and business associates, including Verrecchia, Ditomassi, Alperin, Larry Bernstein, Steve Schwartz, Joe Bacal, Tom Griffin, Nancy Rosen, Deborah Sussman, Arie Kopelman, Fred Levinger, and Margaret Thompson, his nanny. I had access to his years at Moses Brown School through archivist Frank Fuller, now deceased.

Many stories of the creation of G.I. Joe have been told, none exactly the same. As Don Levine, one of my sources, said: "Success has a million fathers, but failure is an orphan." I took great pains to write as accurate an account as possible, relying on materials in the Hasbro archives, Vincent Santelmo's *The Complete Encyclopedia to G.I. Joe,* and interviews with Levine, Stanley A. Weston, Larry Reiner, Alan Hassenfeld, and Hasbro general counsel Donald M. Robbins, now retired. I attach significant weight to Reiner's rendition of events, in part because of persuasive legal correspondence he had in his possession and a registered letter he wrote to himself on April 12, 1963, in which he describes creating the concept. Lost for many years, the still sealed letter was opened in my presence at the office of New York attorney Jesse Rothstein on November 8, 1995; Rothstein and I are satisfied the letter is authentic. Weston disputes particulars of Reiner's recollections.

A continuing 5 percent royalty on G.I. Joe sales would have yielded in excess of $75 million through 1996.

Chapter 3

Later history of G.I. Joe: Television commercials and sales films from 1964 to the present, Hasbro records, and interviews with Hassenfeld, Verrecchia, Bernstein, Schwartz, Griffin, Bacal, Kirk Bozigian, Bob Prupis, Steve D'Aguanno, Vinnie D'Alleva, and Greg Berndtson.

The trend of increased spending on toys and other children's consumer products is documented in unpublished Hasbro market research and in James U. McNeal's *Kids As Customers.* Diminishing parental time with children in the era of dual-earner couples is examined in Juliet B. Schor's *The Overworked American:*

The Unexpected Decline of Leisure, among other places. Although difficult to quantify, anecdotal evidence (cited in McNeal and elsewhere) suggests that parental guilt over spending less time than desired with children prompts greater spending. This was a recurring theme in sessions with Hasbro marketers, many of whom are themselves working parents with long hours. A further factor is the commercialization of Easter and Halloween, relatively new trends.

The history of Milton Bradley: James J. Shea's *It's All in the Game* and my examination of annual reports and catalogs dating to the 1800s. Hasbro's acquisition of Milton Bradley: press accounts, Hasbro records, and interviews with Verrecchia, Ditomassi, Pace, Alperin, and Rosenwald. Sydney L. Stern's *Toyland* and David Sheff's *Game Over* contain excellent accounts of the video-game craze of the early 1980s.

For background on the design and outfitting of Hasbro's headquarters and showroom, and the talents behind them, I read articles from *Architecture, Interiors, Building Design & Construction,* and *Print.* I also consulted Rosen's unpublished "A Guide to the Fine Arts at Hasbro."

Chapter 4

Alan's childhood: Many of the same sources as for Stephen's youth, plus Steve Fein, John Zellerback, and Eric Rothschild.

Officials from Takara Co. Ltd., Bandai Co. Ltd., and Tomy Co. Ltd. provided background information on the Japanese toy industry. Also helpful was Anthony R. Marsella's *Toys from Occupied Japan.*

The opening of southern China to the West is ably documented in Ezra F. Vogel's *One Step Ahead in China.*

Hasbro's early manufacturing in China was chronicled in photographs by Hasbro engineer Brian Prodger, who loaned me his collection and shared his recollections.

Mattel, Barbie, Amerman, and Barad: I began with an examination of annual reports, catalogs, press releases, proxy statements, Securities and Exchange Commission 10-K filings, and other company materials. Amerman's history of his company is *The Story of Mattel Inc.,* a publication based on a speech to The Newcomen Society of the United States. Among the books I consulted were *Toyland,* Ruth Handler's *Dream Doll,* and M. G. Lord's *Forever Barbie.* I found material on Barad at the alumni office of Queens College and in three newspapers that have carefully covered Mattel over the years: *The Wall Street Journal, The New York Times,* and the *Los Angeles Times,* Mattel's hometown newspaper.

Insights into the financial histories of Mattel, Hasbro, and other toy makers were gleaned from reports by analysts at William Blair & Company, Gerard Klauer Mattison & Co., and Drexel Burnham Lambert Incorporated.

Sindy: Colette Mansell's *The History of Sindy*. Comments from the lawsuits beginning in 1989 are taken from affidavits filed in the High Court of Justice, Chancery Division, London; and the District Court at Breda, The Netherlands. For further background I read documents from the District Court of Hamburg, Germany; Bobigny Commercial Court, First Division, and Paris Appeal Court, Fourth Division, Section A, both in France; Court of the First Instance of Athens, Injunctions Section, Greece; Civil Court of Brussels, Belgium; and Court of First Instance, Chamber No. 2, Valencia, Spain.

Chapter 6

My account of Alan's management moves his first months in office is based on interviews with all involved principals.

I interviewed former Tonka Inc. chairman and CEO Stephen G. Shank for details of Hasbro's acquisition of Tonka.

Chapter 7

I was at the Rhode Island State House when Alan launched RIght Now!, and I covered the ethics reform movement for the *Providence Journal-Bulletin* in the ensuing months.

Bruce Stein's background was gleaned from interviews with him, Judy Shackelford, Dave Mauer, Ginger Kent, and Tom McGrath, and stories in the *Cincinnati Enquirer* and the *Cincinnati Post*. I learned Kenner's history from these same sources, as well as from the official Kenner history.

Bernstein's background was written based on interviews with him, Schwartz, Verrecchia, and Hassenfeld.

Chapter 8

I attended the August 1993 focus groups and later viewed the videotapes.

Alan's quote about playing with a train on the floor was in the June 1992 issue of *Sky*, in-flight magazine of Delta Airlines.

Esquire's profile of Hasbro was published in December 1986.

I was at the G.I. Joe summit in the Greenhouse Cafe, but not that fall's Greenhouse Cafe dinner. Memories Bernstein and Verrecchia had of it, however, were strikingly similar, and their accounts were confirmed by another participant, Steve D'Aguanno.

Chapter 9

Like the history of G.I. Joe, the story of Mighty Morphin Power Rangers has been told in many versions. My account was drawn from an interview with Margaret Loesch at her home on December 4, 1994, and a rare interview with Haim

Saban on December 7, 1994, at his California office. I also interviewed Loesch's marketing chief, Burt Gould, and read several of the dozens of magazine, newspaper, and wire stories that have appeared.

Numerous toy companies besides Hasbro used TV programming in the 1980s to peddle their products. Among them were Mattel, with its *He-Man and Masters of the Universe* and *She-Ra, Princess of Power;* and Kenner, with *Care Bears* and *Strawberry Shortcake.* One of the best studies of this era is Stephen Kline's *Out of the Garden: Toys and Children's Culture in the Age of TV Marketing.*

For background on the Japanese popular culture (including postwar comic books, *manga*) that gave rise to *Power Rangers,* I read Douglas Rushkoff's *Playing the Future: How Kids' Culture Can Teach Us to Thrive in an Age of Chaos* and interviewed Anne Allison, cultural anthropologist at Duke University, who has studied Japanese superheroes and Toei's *Go Renja (Five Rangers)* TV series, the root of Saban's *Power Rangers.* Allison shared an unpublished paper on the subject with me.

Saban Entertainment is private. The retail sales estimate of $1 billion I cited is based on a story that ran December 7, 1994, in *The Wall Street Journal.*

I used television viewing data from the National Cable Television Association, A. C. Nielsen Company, and *Les Brown's Encyclopedia of Television.* Much of the Nielsen data was unpublished.

Two notable exceptions to the networks' early aversion to children's programming on weekdays were CBS's *Captain Kangaroo,* which aired daily since 1955, and ABC's *Mickey Mouse Club,* which aired five days a week in the 1950s.

Congressional testimony on children's TV and video games is preserved on official transcripts, many of which I read. I reviewed transcripts of Federal Communications Commission proceedings and interviewed Peggy Charren. Of the many books written on the history of children's television, I found two most helpful: Newton N. Minow's *Abandoned in the Wasteland* and Cy Schneider's *Children's Television.* Aletha C. Huston's *Big World, Small Screen* is the finest examination of the effects of television on the broader society that I have seen.

I found background on broadcasting reform in the 1930s and the "Let's not go 'sissy' with the kids" quote in Sally Bedell Smith's *In All His Glory: The Life of William S. Paley, the Legendary Tycoon and his Brilliant Circle.*

While acknowledging the Rangers' teamwork and cooperation, the University of California at Los Angeles's "Violence Monitoring Report" researchers noted that these laudable qualities were always in preparation for combat. "Producers of *The Mighty Morphin Power Rangers* might argue that the Rangers only fight monsters and the show is all fantasy," UCLA concluded. "The point defenders miss is that the shows we classify as sinister combat violence are only about violence. Alternatives to violence are rarely discussed. The shows send the message that fighting, if not fun, is at least the norm. . . . It is ironic that programming geared largely to adults, prime time, is showing promising signs in regard to violence, while that created especially for children continues to have serious problems."

Here, as elsewhere, I used industrywide sales figures for toys and games provided by the Toy Manufacturers of America and statistics from Toy Retail Sales Tracking System (more commonly TRSTS), a proprietary service of the NPD Group.

Mortal Kombat: Details of development came from an interview with Ed Boon and John Tobias, the game's creators, and from WMS Industries literature. I learned about Acclaim Entertainment Inc.'s home version from Acclaim literature and an interview with marketing vice president Sam Goldberg. I also played the game and observed players far more proficient than I. I interviewed Larry Kasanoff twice at Hasbro and once in California, in addition to attending two meetings at which he discussed business with Hasbro. I also visited the set of *Mortal Kombat,* the movie.

Denied the license to Mortal Kombat III, Acclaim suffered a huge decline in revenues for its fiscal quarter that ended on November 30, 1996. With a $19 million loss for the quarter, its survival was in jeopardy.

Chapter 10

Elvis: I did not attend Hasbro's Pre–Toy Fair 1993 but saw a videotape of the Elvis show. Press coverage was chronicled by Cohn & Wolfe, the public relations firm, which uses several services to track broadcast and print stories.

Chapter 11

Baby Go Bye Bye was the best-selling special-feature doll in 1996 in the United States, with 1.3 million units sold.

The severance packages Verrecchia and Hassenfeld gave departing employees were more generous than industry averages, according to Meritus and Sherry Len Turner's research. Verrecchia later remarked that terminating blue-collar workers affected him more deeply than downsizing executives with golden parachutes and prospects. "I'm not complaining about it and I'm not looking for sympathy," he said, "but it bothers me. It causes me to remind my children how important it is to get an education and to work hard and to have something and not to be dependent upon somebody else. It causes me to go to bed at night and pinch myself and say how lucky I am."

I relied on Hasbro's archives for background on adult G.I. Joe conventions. The first recorded by Hasbro was in 1988, when a Dallas woman put on a one-day event: For $4, conventioneers heard the president of the Daughters of the

Republic of Texas talk about her extensive collection, which she'd started in 1964. Conventions were held in Omaha in 1989, Burbank in 1992, and Pasadena in 1993. Given the vagaries of archiving, it is possible there was an adult convention before 1988.

Chapter 12

Cabbage Patch Kids: My reconstruction of Barad's presentation at Original Appalachian Artworks is based on interviews with Tom Prichard and Della Tolhurst, both of whom were there. Sources for Hasbro's side of the story were Prichard, Hassenfeld, Verrecchia, Kent, Duncan Billing, and Dena Quilici. Bernstein's quotes were to the *Toy Book* magazine, October 1989.

Barbie revenues: Bozarth, correspondence July 1996, and Barad presentation, Twelfth Annual William Blair & Company Conference, February 12, 1997.

Los Angeles magazine's profile of Amerman: August 1994. Barad's bumblebee quote: From her 1992 official Mattel biography. Amerman and Barad on Barbie: My interview of them on December 6, 1994.

The Mattel Foundation supports a number of educational and health causes. Its most ambitious undertaking in 1994, the thirty-fifth anniversary of Barbie, was $1 million in grants to health initiatives, realized from sales of the Dr. Barbie doll. "For the past thirty-five years, Barbie has supported children's dreams, and in this, her year of caring and sharing, Barbie is giving back," Barad said in announcing the grants.

Chapter 13

Focus groups: I viewed the videotape.

Chapter 15

Faced with unenthusiastic support from retailers and its own sales force, Hasbro shipped only fifty-two thousand units of Babe the Gallant Pig and Talking Babe. Every piece sold at retail.

Warner Bros.' relationship with Hasbro: Interviews with Warner chairman and co-CEO Terry S. Semel, Warner Worldwide Consumer Products president Daniel R. Romanelli, and two of Romanelli's employees: Karen McTier and Mary Yedlin. I interviewed director Joel Schumacher on November 4, 1995, and visited the Long Beach, California, set of *Batman Forever* on December 9, 1994.

Although Kenner suspended production of Star Wars toys in the late 1980s, it continued to hold certain rights to the property, which transferred to Hasbro with the Tonka acquisition. As *Star Wars'* popularity began to heat up again in the 1990s (Galoob was selling a line of miniature Star Wars figures), Hasbro brought a new line to market in 1995. Simultaneously Hasbro began lobbying for the rights to the second *Star Wars* trilogy, which was widely expected to be the most lucrative—and expensive—in toy history.

I learned of Stephen Hassenfeld's interest in buying Mattel from Alperin, his confidant in the matter.

Conducted for Connecticut Public Television, co-producer of *Barney & Friends,* the research by Jerome L. and Dorothy G. Singer, co-directors of the Yale University Family Television Research & Consultation Center, lasted from June 1993 to August 1995. Among the study's conclusions: "There was impressive evidence that exposure of hundreds of three- to-five-year-old children to ten episodes of *Barney* in their day-care settings was followed by gains in vocabulary, counting and other cognitive skills, and awareness of socially constructive behavior."

Sindy: I attended sessions in Rhode Island and Cincinnati after the 1995 Toy Fair meeting. Hassenfeld was never entirely satisfied with the look. Given the sizable long-term investment it would have required to launch it in the United States and the more urgent need to enhance shareholder value, he ultimately decided not to proceed, at least for the time being.

Chapter 16

Sliced Bread: Interviews with Verrecchia, Bernstein, Brian Prodger, and Sandy Schneider. I had access to the technical specifications and the final business plan.

G.I. Joe in Rhode Island: I was there for one of the last assembly lines, in November 1995. Workers were assembling parts that had been previously molded. For further details on manufacturing, I interviewed Craig Smith, Mike Marley, Leon Marcotte, Leona Blum, Jenny Lippe, and Beatrice Silva, all employed in manufacturing.

Chapter 17

DreamWorks: Interviews with Stein and Brad Globe. I was at Hasbro for the announcement and Steven Spielberg's visit and briefly interviewed Spielberg at that time. I interviewed him again on the set of *Amistad,* in Rhode Island, on April 2, 1997.

I attended Hasbro's Pre–Toy Fair at the PGA National Resort & Spa in Palm Beach Gardens, Florida, in September 1995.

By 1996 the Goosebumps craze was beginning to rival that of Batman, with a top-rated series on Fox, a feature movie in preproduction, and partnerships with Hasbro, Pepsi-Cola, Frito-Lay, Taco Bell, and Hershey, among others. Author R. L. Stine's books, published by Scholastic Inc., were selling at the rate of more than four million copies per monthly title.

By 1997 Hassenfeld was fond of citing Monopoly as a model for opening up the brands. That year Monopoly was being sold in seventy-five countries, twenty-six languages, and many versions, including Monopoly Deluxe, Monopoly Junior, Monopoly Junior Travel, Star Wars limited collectors' edition Monopoly, Monopoly CD-ROM (playable over the Internet), and basic Monopoly. There also were versions customized for thirty cities, four colleges, NASCAR and Harley-Davidson, and the internal use of MCI and McDonald's, which also had a public Monopoly promotion. Nineteen licensees were producing Monopoly greeting cards, golf bags, boxer shorts, and other merchandise, and several states were selling Monopoly instant-winner lottery tickets. A Monopoly restaurant was soon to open.

Chapter 18

Mattel affair: I relied on Mattel and Hasbro press releases and the later recollections of Hassenfeld, Sonny Gordon, Verrecchia, John O'Neill, Rosenwald, and Glenn Bozarth. I had conversations during the affair with Hassenfeld and Verrecchia, to gauge their mood. The matter was covered intensely by many media outlets, but *The Wall Street Journal*'s effort was consistently the finest. Bloomberg Business News wire and the PRNewsire Web site were also useful here, as in other chapters.

Although the Sinatra Suite rents for $2,000 a night to individuals, frequent corporate users of the Waldorf, including Mattel, receive a discount.

On September 30, 1997, a federal administrative law judge upheld FTC charges that Toys "R" Us illegally pressured toymakers into not selling certain G.I. Joe, Barbie, and other popular toys to warehouse clubs. "This is a case about abuse of market power," Mark D. Whitener, deputy director of the FTC's antitrust division, told *The New York Times*. Toys "R" Us immediately appealed the ruling.

Epilogue

"Rip Van Hasbro," the *Forbes* magazine piece, appeared in the September 9, 1996, issue.

"Toy Story," the *CFO* magazine piece, appeared in the November 1996 issue. Primarily a profile of Chief Financial Officer O'Neill, the story discussed Alan Hassenfeld. Tim Bui, an analyst with Ariel Capital Management Inc. in Chicago, was quoted describing him in this fashion: " 'In the past, he came across as a creative person who wanted to make toys and as a philanthropist who wanted to use Hasbro to achieve social goals.' " In a summer of 1996 meeting, however, Bui noted, " 'He didn't discuss anything but the nitty-gritty of running the business, which was music to my ears.' "

On October 14, 1997, Hasbro announced a long-term agreement with Lucas

Licensing Ltd. to make toys and games based on the next three Star Wars movies, the first of which is expected to reach theaters in May 1999. At an estimated cost of $500 million to Hasbro, the deal is the richest in the history of toy licensing. "This is a major triumph for Hasbro," Hassenfeld said in announcing the contract. "We know the power of the Force." Galoob Toys signed an agreement to make certain new Star Wars toys, but Mattel, which had also bid on rights, came away empty-handed.

BIBLIOGRAPHY

Amerman, John W. *The Story of Mattel Inc.: Fifty Years of Innovation.* New York: Newcomen Society of the United States, 1995.

Anonymous. "Grandparent Market: Grand and Growing." *The Public Pulse.* September 1993.

Barber, Benjamin R. *Jihad vs. McWorld: How the Planet is Both Falling Apart and Coming Together and What This Means for Democracy.* New York: Times Books, 1995.

Barnet, Rosalind C. "Ozzie and Harriet Are Dead: A Study of Contemporary Dual-Earner Couples." Paper presented at the Brown Bag Luncheon Series, Murray Research Center, Radcliffe College, November 30, 1993.

Bettelheim, Bruno. "The Importance of Play." *The Atlantic Monthly,* March 1987.

Brockman, Hohn, ed. *Creativity.* New York: Touchstone, 1993.

Brown, Les. *Les Brown's Encyclopedia of Television.* 3rd ed. Detroit: Gale Research, 1992.

Bruck, Connie. *The Predator's Ball: The Inside Story of Drexel Burnham and the Rise of the Junk Bond Raiders.* New York: Simon & Schuster, 1988.

Bryant, Jennings, ed. *Television and the American Family.* Hillsdale, N.J.: Lawrence Erlbaum Associates, 1990.

Burrough, Bryan, and John Helyar. *Barbarians at the Gate: The Fall of RJR Nabisco.* New York: Harper & Row, 1990.

Calvert, Karin. *Children in the House: The Material Culture of Early Childhood, 1600–1900.* Boston: Northeastern University Press, 1992.

Carlsson-Paige, Nancy, and Diane E. Levin. *Who's Calling the Shots? How to Respond Effectively to Children's Fascination With War Play and War Toys.* Philadelphia: New Society Publishers, 1990.

Cole, Jeffrey. *The UCLA Television Violence Monitoring Report.* Los Angeles: UCLA Center for Communication Policy, 1995.

Damon, William. *Greater Expectations: Overcoming the Culture of Indulgence in America's Homes and Schools.* New York: The Free Press, 1995.

Daniels, Les. *DC Comics: Sixty Years of the World's Favorite Comic Book Heroes.* Boston: Little, Brown and Company. 1995.

———. *Marvel: Five Fabulous Decades of the World's Greatest Comics.* New York: Harry N. Abrams, 1991.

Dennis, Everette E., ed. "Children and the Media." *Media Studies Journal,* fall 1994.

Dubnov, Simon. *History of the Jews: Volume V, From the Congress of Vienna to the Emergence of Hitler.* Cranbury, N.J.: Thomas Yoseloff, 1973.

Engelhardt, Tom. *The End of Victory Culture: Cold War America and the Disillusioning of a Generation.* New York: Basic Books, 1995.

Eron, Leonard D., Monroe M. Lefkowitz, Leopold O. Walder, and L. Rowell Huesmann. "Relation of Learning in Childhood to Psychopathology and Aggression in Young Adulthood." In A. Davis, ed. *Child Personality and Psychopathology.* New York: John Wiley & Sons, 1974.

Families and Work Institute. *Women: The New Providers: A Study of Women's Views on Family, Work, Society and the Future.* New York, 1995.

Foley, Daniel J. *Toys Through the Ages: Dan Foley's Story of Playthings, Filled with History, Folklore, Romance & Nostalgia.* Philadelphia: Chilton Books, 1962.

Foster, Geraldine S. *The Jews in Rhode Island.* Providence, R.I.: Rhode Island Heritage Commission and the Rhode Island Publications Society, 1985.

Freysinger, Valeria J. "Leisure with Children and Parental Satisfaction: Further Evidence of a Sex Difference in the Experience of Adult Roles and Leisure." *Journal of Leisure Research.* vol. 26, no. 3, 1994.

Gallup, George H., with Wendy Plump. *Growing Up Scared in America and What the Experts Say Parents Can Do About It.* Princeton, N.J.: George H. Gallup International Institute, 1995.

Goldstein, Jeffrey H., ed. *Toys, Play and Child Development.* Cambridge, England: Cambridge University Press, 1994.

Goulart, Ron. *The Comic Book Reader's Companion.* New York: HarperPerennial, 1993.

Greenfield, Patricia Marks. *Mind and Media: The Effects of Television, Video Games, and Computers.* One in *The Developing Child* series. Cambridge, Mass.: Harvard University Press, 1984.

Hamburg, David A. *Today's Children: Creating a Future for a Generation in Crisis.* New York: Times Books, 1994.

Hammer, Michael, and James Champy. *Reengineering the Corporation: A Manifesto for Business Revolution.* New York: HarperBusiness, 1993.

Handler, Ruth, with Jacqueline Shannon. *Dream Doll: The Ruth Handler Story.* Stamford, Conn.: Longmeadow Press, 1994.

Heller, Celia S. *On the Edge of Destruction: Jews of Poland Between the Two World Wars.* New York: Columbia University Press, 1977.

Hertz, Louis H. *The Handbook of Old American Toys.* Wethersfield, Conn.: Mark Haber & Co., 1947.

Hewlett, Sylvia Ann. *When the Bough Breaks: The Cost of Neglecting Our Children.* New York: Basic Books, 1991.

Himmelfarb, Gertrude. *The De-moralization of Society: From Victorian Virtues to Modern Values.* New York: Alfred A. Knopf, 1995.

Hine, Thomas. *The Total Package: The Evolution and Secret Meanings of Boxes, Bottles, Cans, and Tubes.* Boston: Little, Brown and Company, 1995.

Hoffman, William. *Fantasy: The Incredible Cabbage Patch Phenomenon.* Dallas, Texas: Taylor Publishing Company, 1984.

Huston, Aletha C., et. al, eds. *Big World, Small Screen: The Role of Television in American Society.* Lincoln, Nebr.: University of Nebraska Press, 1992.

Jagusch, Sybille A., ed. *Window on Japan: Japanese Children's Books and Television Today.* Papers from a symposium at the Library of Congress, November 18–19, 1987. Washington, Library of Congress, 1990.

Juster, F. Thomas, and Frank P. Stafford. *Time, Goods and Well-Being.* Ann Arbor, Mich.: University of Michigan, 1985.

Kaye, Marvin. *A Toy Is Born.* New York: Stein and Day, 1973.

Kelly, Marcy. *National Television Violence Study, 1994–1995: Executive Summary.* Studio City, Calif.: Mediascope, 1996.

Kinder, Marsha. *Playing with Power in Movies, Television and Video Games: From Muppet Babies to Teenage Mutant Ninja Turtles.* Berkeley, Calif.: University of California Press, 1991.

Kline, Stephen. *Out of the Garden: Toys and Children's Culture in the Age of TV Marketing.* New York: Verso, 1993.

Konner, Melvin. *Childhood.* Boston: Little, Brown and Company, 1991.

Lasseter, John, and Steve Daly. *Toy Story: The Art and Making of the Animated Film.* New York: Hyperion, 1995.

Leach, William. *Land of Desire: Merchants, Power, and the Rise of a New American Culture.* New York: Pantheon Books, 1993.

Levy, Richard C., and Ronald O. Weingartner. *Inside Santa's Workshop.* New York: Henry Holt & Company, 1990.

Lichter, S. Robert, Linda S. Lichter, and Stanley Rothman. *Prime Time: How TV Portrays American Culture.* Washington, D.C.: Regnery Publishing, 1994.

Lord, M. G. *Forever Barbie: The Unauthorized Biography of a Real Doll.* New York: William Morrow, 1994.

Love, John F. *McDonald's: Behind the Arches.* New York: Bantam Books, 1986.

Maccoby, Eleanor Emmons, and Carol Nagy Jacklin. *The Psychology of Sex Differences.* Stanford, Calif.: Stanford University Press. 1974.

Mansell, Colette. *The History of Sindy: Britain's Top Teenage Doll, 1962–1994.* London: New Cavendish Books, 1995.

Marcus, Jacob R., ed. *The Concise Dictionary of American Jewish Biography.* New York: Carlson Publishing, 1994.

Markowski, Carol, and Bill Sikora. *Tomart's Price Guide to Action Figure Collectibles.* Dayton, Ohio: Tomart Publications, 1991.

Marsella, Anthony R. *Toys from Occupied Japan.* Atglen, Penna.: Schiffer Publishing, 1995.

Matthews, Jack. *Toys Go to War: World War II Military Toys, Games, Puzzles & Books.* Missoula, Mont.: Pictorial Histories Publishing Company, 1994.

May, Elaine Tyler. *Homeward Bound: American Families in the Cold War Era.* New York: Basic Books, 1988.

McNeal, James U. *Kids as Customers: A Handbook of Marketing to Children.* New York: Lexington Books, 1992.

Minow, Newton N., and Craig L. LaMay. *Abandoned on the Wasteland: Children, Television and the First Amendment.* New York: Hill and Wang, 1995.

Montgomery, Kathryn C. *Target: Prime Time: Advocacy Groups and the Struggle over Entertainment Television.* New York: Oxford University Press, 1989.

Nissenbaum, Stephen. *The Battle for Christmas.* New York: Knopf, 1996.

O'Brien, Richard. *The Story of American Toys from the Puritans to the Present.* New York: Abbeville Press, 1990.

Oppenheim, Joanne, and Stephanie Oppenheim. *The Best Toys, Books & Videos for Kids (1995).* New York: HarperPerennial, 1994.

Perry, George, and Alan Aldridge. *The Penguin Book of Comics.* Harmondsworth, England: Penguin, 1967.

Postman, Neil. *The Disappearance of Childhood.* New York: Vintage Books, 1994.

Provenzo, Eugene F. Jr. *Video Kids: Making Sense of Nintendo.* Cambridge, Mass.: Harvard University Press, 1991.

Reitberger, Reinhold, and Wolfgang Fuchs. *Comics: Anatomy of a Mass Medium.* Boston: Little, Brown and Company, 1971.

Rohwer, Jim. *Asia Rising: Why America Will Prosper as Asia's Economies Boom.* New York: Simon & Schuster, 1995.

Rushkoff, Douglas. *Playing the Future: How Kids' Culture Can Teach Us to Thrive in an Age of Chaos.* New York: HarperCollins, 1996.

Salamander, Rachel. *The Jewish World of Yesterday: 1860–1938.* New York: Rizzoli, 1991.

Santelmo, Vincent. *The Complete Encyclopedia to G.I. Joe.* Iola, Wis.: Krause Publications, 1993.

Schneider, Cy. *Children's Television: The Art, the Business and How It Works.* Chicago: NTC Business Books, 1987.

Schneiderman, Harry, and Itzhak J. Carmin, eds. *Who's Who in World Jewry: A Biographical Dictionary of Outstanding Jews.* New York: Monde Publishers, 1955.

Schor, Juliet B. *The Overworked American: The Unexpected Decline of Leisure.* New York: Basic Books, 1992.

Schwartz, Barry. *The Costs of Living: How Market Freedom Erodes the Best Things in Life.* New York: W. W. Norton & Company, 1994.

Seabrook, John, "Why Is the Force Still with Us?" in *The New Yorker,* January 6, 1997.

Shea, James J., as told to Charles Mercer. *It's All in the Game: A Biography of Milton Bradley, The Man Who Taught America To Play.* New York: G. P. Putnam's Sons, 1960.

Sheff, David. *Game Over: How Nintendo Conquered the World.* New York: Vintage, 1994.

———. *Video Games: A Guide for Savvy Parents.* New York: Random House, 1994.

Singer, Dorothy G., and Jerome L. Singer. "*Barney and Friends* as Education and Entertainment: Summary of Research Studies, June 1993–August 1995." New Haven, Yale University Family Television Research & Consultation Center, unpublished results, 1995.

———. *The House of Make-Believe: Children's Play and the Developing Imagination.* Cambridge, Mass.: Harvard University Press, 1990.

Smith, Sally Bedell. *In All His Glory: The Life of William S. Paley, the Legendary Tycoon and His Brilliant Circle.* New York: Simon & Schuster. 1990.

Stern, Sydney L., and Ted Schoenhaus. *Toyland: The High-Stakes Game of the Toy Industry.* Chicago: Contemporary Books, 1990.

Sutton-Smith, Brian, ed. *Children's Play: Past, Present, & Future.* Philadelphia: Please Touch Museum, 1985.

Sutton-Smith, Brian, and B. G. Rosenberg. "Sixty Years of Historical Change in the Game Preferences of American Children." *Journal of American Folklore,* vol. 74, no. 291.

Swartz, Edward M. *Toys That Don't Care.* Boston: Gambit, 1971.

———. *Toys That Kill.* New York: Vintage, 1986.

Twitchell, James B. *Adcult USA: The Triumph of Advertising in American Culture.* New York: Columbia University Press, 1996.

U.S. Bureau of the Census. Current Population Reports, P23–181, *Households, Families and Children: A 30-Year Perspective.* Washington, D.C.: U.S. Government Printing Office, 1992.

Vogel, Ezra F. *One Step Ahead in China: Guangdong Under Reform.* Cambridge, Mass.: Harvard University Press, 1989.

Waldrop, Judith. "More Toys for Girls and Boys." *American Demographics.* December 1991.

Wein, Abraham, and Aharon Weiss, eds. *Pinkas Hakehillot (Encyclopedia of Jewish Communities): Poland, Vol III, Western Galicia & Silesia.* Jerusalem: Martyrs' and Heroes' Remembrance Authority, 1984.

Wiencek, Henry. *The World of LEGO Toys.* New York: Harry N. Abrams, 1987.

Williams, Meredith. *Tomart's Price Guide to McDonald's Happy Meal Collectibles.* Dayton, Ohio: Tomart Publications, 1995.

Zelizer, Viviana A. *Pricing the Priceless Child: The Changing Social Value of Children.* New York: Basic Books, 1985.

ACKNOWLEDGMENTS

Permitting a writer inside your world for five-plus years is not for the faint-hearted. I owe a huge debt of gratitude to Alan Hassenfeld, who despite his many public roles is an intensely private person. It would be easy to conclude that his goodwill toward me endured because of our mutual interest in writing, but that is only part of the answer. Another part is that Alan is a man of his word: having given me permission to write about Hasbro, he did not back down when events began to unfold in ways neither of us imagined in the early days of this project. Yet another reason I lasted more than five years, I believe, is that Alan truly believes a corporation can have a conscience and be socially responsible. A story of the struggle to achieve that goal might inspire others, Alan believed, while returning healthy profits.

I am similarly indebted to Al Verrecchia, who was as accessible and candid as his boss. We were the odd couple of this project—he the buttoned-down executive, me the writer in jeans and penny loafers. It worked, I think, because Al considered most business journalism to be superficial and I was willing to commit the time and energy that might make for a truer account. I never imagined I would get such extraordinary cooperation. My gratitude, Al.

Thanks to Sylvia Hassenfeld and Ellie and Michael Block, the latter a charming young man with a promising future at Hasbro. Dorothy Frank Fox, half-sister of Alan's paternal grandmother, and Joan Engle, Merrill Hassenfeld's sister, were helpful in compiling a family history.

This book would not have been possible without the gracious cooperation of many Hasbro executives. I owe a particular debt to Sonny Gordon, George Ditomassi, John O'Neill, and Adam Klein. And I would have been lost without the assistance of Tom Dusenberry, Dave Wilson, Ginger Kent, Dan Owen, Pete Kelly, Bob Stebenne, Jerry Ligon, David Hargreaves, and John Gildea. Thanks also to Bob Wann, Amy Wann, Jack Harris, Shelly Klein, Sharon Hartley, Tom McGrath, John Buntel, Malcolm Denniss, and Steve D'Aguanno. Board member John Rosenwald went out of his way to be helpful. Thanks also to director Norma Pace.

Always a pleasure to deal with, and always knowledgeable, were Wayne Charness and his staff: Paula Sacchi, Gary Serby, Audrey Basso, Gail Farrow, and Edna Collette (no longer with Hasbro). Similarly gracious were executive assistants Donna Pelletier, Sue Frisolone, Hope Fitton, Pam Wilsey, Barbara Gemme, Barbara McDonough, Nancy Gilberg, Gail Walsh, Lori Staba, and Pat Hamel. Sandy Marks and Linda Bickel could not have been more helpful or more tolerant of my endless requests. I owe a special debt to both.

Without access to Hasbro's market research, this book would have been lacking; many thanks to Kate Stanuch, Jackie Fradin, Stephanie Shimkin, Sue McPoland, Dennis Redpath, Rob Hanson, and Debbie Petashnick. Among the financial people who helped were Al Bulson, Dick Holt, and Jeanette Martin. In legal: Cindy Reed, Paul Vanasse, and the retired Don Robbins. Thanks to corporate secretary Phil Waldoks. In the New York office: Carole Pecore. At Hasbro manufacturing: Craig Smith, Mike Marley, Leon Marcotte, Leona Blum, Jenny Lippe, and Beatrice Silva. Elsewhere at Hasbro: Joe Morrone, Simon Gardner, Valerie Jurries, Rod Dorman, Anne Kirby, Debbie Boyd, A. Franklin La Barbara, Kenny Adams, Phil Jacobs, Lloyd Mintz, Ellen Holbrook, Wayne Luther, Brian Prodger, Miriam Mawle, Garry Price, Dena Quilici, Robert Slye, Bill Milner, Shelly Smith, Vinnie D'Alleva, Dave Fergenbaum, Burt Ensmann, Maria Silveira, Dave Mowrer, Sherry Turner, Bob Carniaux, Steve Hardardt, Janice Dufresne, Bridie Blessington, Mark Staub, Steve Rodyn, Cheryl McCarthy, Chuck Milington, Paul Demty, John Claster, Carol Knight, Joe Gammal, and Pat Schmidt.

I spent many days in Cincinnati and owe much to Chris Connolly, Elizabeth Gross, Kevin Mowrer, Karen Lehman, Dan Price, Ben Torres, Nick Langdon, Kurt Groen, Perry Drosos, Viv Joklik, Jim Black, Jim Kipling, Bill Hartglass, Krickett Neumann, Nancy Wynn, Bruce Kandel, and the late Mick Yeager.

▪

Many no longer at Hasbro gave willingly of their time, before and after leaving. I can think of no higher compliment to Larry Bernstein than to say that he is one of the most entertaining people I know and one of the most intelligent; he also has a very big heart. Barry Alperin directed me in many areas, and I am deeply indebted.

Kirk Bozigian, now in business on his own, was one of the first people at Hasbro to take me under his wing, and he unflinchingly was open with me through strange times; his humor, insights, and good grace throughout gave this book a dimension it would otherwise have lacked, and I owe him tremendously. Don DeLuca also was instrumental in helping me divine truths of the modern corporation; his sharp commentary, comic sense, and broad knowledge of the toy business gave me a perspective I found nowhere else. Many other ex-Hasbro employees were helpful, including Norman Walker, Duncan Billing, Tom Bowman, Tom Prichard, Lee Bitzer, Sandy Schneider, Ken Ellis, Don Levine, Neil Levine, George Miller, Bob Prupis, Greg Berndtson, Bill Young, Steve Schwartz, Carl Fritz, Fred Vuono, and Matt Lizak.

I met Bruce Stein when he was still at Kenner and spent countless hours with him (and on the phone to him) in the years that followed as he traveled the long road from Hasbro to Mattel. His observations were invariably perceptive. With humor and insight, he helped me get to the very heart of the toy industry, and for that I am greatly appreciative. Thanks, Bruce.

▪

Many outside of Hasbro contributed, notably Tom Griffin and Joe Bacal. Also at GBI and/or Sunbow: Nina Kanter, Carole Weitzman, C. J. Kettler, and Paul Kurnit. Special thanks to Nancy Rosen, Deborah Sussman, Peter Hirsch, Eric Rothschild, Sean McGowan, Diane Cardinale, Susan Faludi, Margaret Thomas, Dave Duffy, Phil West, Arie Kopelman, Fred Levinger, Steve Fein, John Zellerback, Stan Weston, Larry Reiner, Julius Ellman, Mitch Sugarman, Rabbi Leslie Gutterman, and Tom Kully, who let me attend several of his William Blair & Company Toy and Video Game Conferences, ordinarily closed to the press.

Thanks to Glenn Bozarth of Mattel and Judy Shackelford, formerly of Mattel. At Warner Bros., my thanks to Terry Semel, Joel Schumacher, Dan Romanelli, John Dartigue, Mary Yedlin, Karen McTier, Jackie Harrold, Bettina Rose and Eli Richbourg. At Warner Toy: Ron Hayes. Thanks to Brad Globe, at DreamWorks; Brett Dicker and Dave Smith, at Disney; Margaret Loesch and Burt Gould at Fox Children's Network; Haim Saban, Nicole Cerwin-Williams, and Dani Dave at Saban Entertainment; Larry Kasanoff and Suzy Block at Threshold Entertainment; Geraldine B. Laybourne, former head of Nickelodeon. Thanks to Della Tolhurst at Original Appalachian Artworks; Dave Brewi and Bob Weinberg at Toys "R" Us; Mike Bratcher of Wal-Mart; Dave Lafrennie and Peter Eio of Lego.

Several scholars helped, including Lewis P. Lipsitt, professor of psychology and medical science and founding director of the Child Study Center, Brown University, who kindly gave several hours of his time to help my understanding of the importance of toys to children; Gene Provenzo of the University of Miami; and Ezra Vogel of Harvard. Thanks to Dina Abramowicz and Fruma Mohrer of YIVO Institute for Jewish Research, New York; Peggy Charren; Susan Waddington; and Esther Elkin, my translator for certain Yiddish documents. Also, Joe Pereira of *The Wall Street Journal*, Jim Madore of the *Buffalo News*, George White of the *Los Angeles Times*, and Ira Chinoy of *The Washington Post*. Two experts on toy collecting shared their expertise: Tom Hammel, editor of *Collecting Toys* magazine, and Jack Matthews.

▪

My sincere appreciation to several people who have supported not only this, but previous books: Joel Rawson, my mentor for many years; Brian Jones, whose guidance I often seek and whose input after reading a draft was invaluable; Linda Henderson, the *Providence Journal-Bulletin* librarian who unfailingly found the endless data I needed; business writer Neil Downing, who covered the toy industry for many years; Jon Karp, my Random House editor, who patiently pushed this book to the next level; and Kay McCauley, my longtime agent, fan, and dear friend. Thanks to my daughters, Katy and Rachel, who tracked songs and music videos from *Batman Forever*, an important piece of research. And thanks to Mary and Duke Wright, gracious (if absentee) hosts during an editing.

Last, a heartfelt toast to my wife, Alexis, who listened to toy talk for years, expertly critiqued a draft, and shared the many sacrifices needed to see this project to fruition. Here's to Eggemoggin, kid!

INDEX

ABC, 67, 140, 155, 252

Abrams, Creighton, 187

Absent Minded Professor, The, 25

Acclaim Entertainment Inc., 159–60, 231

account management organization, 168

Action for Children's Television (ACT), 152

activities analysis, 175

ADAM, 207

Advertising Age, 150–51

Aladdin, 249, 252, 271

Aliens, market research on, 120

Allen, Herbert A., Jr., 156

Allen, Woody, 103

Almond, Lincoln, 295

Alperin, Barry J., 15–18, 137, 251
  and acquisition of Mattel, 254
  Cabbage Patch Kids and, 207
  managerial positions of, 86–88
  office of, 130
  Sindy and, 216
  Sliced Bread and, 173
  in Tonka acquisition, 95, 98

Amaze-A-Matics, 56

Amblin' Entertainment, 255

American Chicle, 73, 210

American Industrial Revolution, 52–53

American Medical Association, 154

American Psychological Association, 154

Amerman, John W., 65–66, 72–73, 104,
    205, 210–12, 215–17, 236
  awards and honors of, 216
  background of, 210–11
  Barbie and, 248–49
  Cabbage Patch Kids and, 65, 84,
    207–8, 210
  game makers sought by, 217
  in Hasbro takeover attempt, 4, 7,
    253–54, 256–58, 285–93, 295–97
  interactive software and, 277
  managerial style and skills of, 73,
    210–11, 215
  Mattel's finances and, 73, 76, 174, 211,
    218, 247
  public relations for, 213
  Sindy and, 76, 216
  Tonka acquisition and, 95, 99
  in Tyco acquisition, 305
anti-Semitism, 19–21

Armour-Dial, 102

Artschwager, Richard, 49
Associated Press, 166, 191, 292
Atari, 42
Audio Magnetics, 70
Auschwitz, 53
automatic bowling alleys, 25

Babe (film), 242–43
Babe the Gallant Pig, 242
baby boomers, 26, 56, 279
Baby Go Bye Bye, 180
Babyland General Hospital, 206
Bacal, Joe, 38, 61, 140
    G.I. Joe and, 35–36, 120, 123, 221–23
Bad Fart, 177
Bakst, M. Charles, 97
Bandai Co., 56–57, 144, 155, 283
Barad, Jill, 94, 102, 211–16, 288
    awards and honors of, 8, 213–14
    background of, 211–12
    Barbie and, 214–15, 247–49
    on Cabbage Patch Kids, 205–6,
        209–10
    DreamWorks and, 255, 271–73
    in Hasbro takeover attempt, 4, 253,
        257, 259
    interactive software and, 277
    Mattel's finances and, 218
    physical appearance of, 214
    public relations for, 213–14
    salary of, 169–70
    Sindy and, 216
    in Tyco acquisition, 305
Barad, Thomas, 212, 214
Barbie, xii, xiv, 4–5, 31, 34, 176, 182, 184,
        205–7, 210–15, 218, 247–50, 279
    Barad and, 214–15, 247–49
    breasts of, 69, 78
    Cabbage Patch Kids and, 207, 210
    marketing and promotion of, 69, 75,
        102, 212, 214, 231
    market research on, 69
    and Mattel's attempted takeover of
        Hasbro, 292, 295, 297
    Mattel's finances and, 226
    origins of, 68–69
    popularity of, 39, 66, 69, 72–75
    razor/razor blade principle and, 24

Sindy vs., 76–78, 216, 248–50
    size of, 27
    success of, 4, 8, 205, 214–15, 247–49
Barbie and the Rockers, 75
Barney, 124, 247, 257, 299
    pep rally for, 241–43
    Talking, 27, 134
Barney & Friends, 243
Batman (film), 94, 104, 228
Batman (toys), 6, 104–5, 111, 120, 132,
        157, 168, 190, 217, 252, 279, 283,
        306
    G.I. Joe and, 122, 229
    licensing of, 244–46, 252–53, 256–57
Batman: The Animated Series, 105, 143
Batman and Robin, 256, 289, 303
Batman Forever, 242, 244–46
Batman in a Can, 233
Batman Returns, 105, 245–46
Batmobile, 129
Battleship, 39, 42, 305
Bear Stearns Companies, 18, 44, 250, 286
Beatles, 145
Beatles dolls, 166
Beckwith, Robert, 12, 15
    and Hasbro's new offices and
        showroom, 47–49, 61
    Hassenfeld's illnesses and, 62–64,
        82–84
    Hassenfeld's relationship with, 60–62,
        64, 83, 109
Beetlejuice action figures, 104–5
Beijing, 59
Bergen, Candice, 189
Berkshire Hathaway, 13
Berndtson, Greg, 163, 186
    in brainstorming sessions, 124–25
    G.I. Joe and, 127, 233
    and layoffs at Hasbro, 200
Bernstein, Lawrence H., 15–16, 32–36,
        38, 82, 84, 100, 105–11, 124, 130,
        157–58, 162–67, 170–74, 181–84,
        201, 266, 306
    A. Hassenfeld and, 106–7, 163, 183,
        195
    background of, 91, 107–9
    Bozigian and, 125–26
    Cabbage Patch Kids and, 207–8

demotion of, 183–84
Elvis doll and, 137, 163–67, 171–74
G.I. Joe and, 33–36, 120–22, 134–35,
    156–57, 161
Hasbro's finances and, 134–37,
    162–63, 166–67, 169, 193
in integrating Tonka into Hasbro, 132
and layoffs at Hasbro, 166–67, 175
managerial positions of, 86, 88, 90, 92
market research of, 117
Mortal Kombat and, 161
physical appearance of, 106–7
private dinner hosted by, 133–37
resignation of, 194–95
and restructuring of Hasbro, 172–73,
    175, 177–78, 196
review and planning meeting held by,
    162–64
sense of humor of, 107–9
S. Hassenfeld's relationship with, 109,
    126
Sliced Bread and, 137, 172–73, 184,
    194, 263
Toy Division line reviews and, 181–83
Bevins, William C., Jr., 189–90
Big, 6, 97, 129
Big World, Small Screen, 154
Bill & Ted's Excellent Adventure action
    figures, 105
Billing, Duncan, 136, 200
Bill Nye the Science Guy, 150
Bingo the Bear, 129
*Bio Man, see Mighty Morphin Power
    Rangers*
Bitzer, Lee, 133, 175
Black, Jim, 103
William Blair & Company, Toy and Video
    Game Conferences of, 3–8, 16,
    242, 247–48, 299–301, 306
Blastoff, 34–35
Block, Ellen Hassenfeld, 60, 106, 129, 243
    birth of, 50, 52
    brother's death and, 11–12, 14
    education of, 54
    family life of, 53
    junior cosmetic kits and, 21
    philanthropy of, 14
Blockbuster Entertainment, 276

Blood, Sweat and Tears, 145
Bloomberg business wire, 191
Bob in a Bottle, 138–39
Bohbot, Allen, 150–52
Boon, Ed, 159
Boston University, 108, 135
Bozarth, Glenn, 212–14
Bozigian, Colt, 117, 121, 126–27, 177,
    204
Bozigian, Kirk, 184–88, 200–201, 212,
    216, 232–33
    background of, 125–26
    brainstorming sessions and, 123–24
    comic book collection of, 125
    design team meetings and, 188
    Elvis doll and, 164
    G.I. Joe and, 111, 120–27, 156–58,
        184–86, 202–4, 221–22, 225, 229,
        232–33
    Hasbro's finances and, 135
    and layoffs at Hasbro, 199–200
    on market research, 115–19, 122
    model airplanes and spacecraft built
        by, 125–26
    Mortal Kombat and, 161
    resignation of, 233
    and restructuring of Hasbro, 177,
        197–98, 202, 204, 232–33
    Sgt. Savage and, 157–58, 186–87,
        203–4, 222, 225, 232
    and termination of DeLuca, 275
    Toy Division line review and, 182
Milton Bradley Company, 16, 64, 86–87,
    91–92, 109–10, 173, 190, 207, 231,
    237, 241, 279
    Hasbro's acquisition of, 39–40, 43–47,
        49, 82, 99–100, 254, 290
    history of, 39–42
    in integrating Tonka into Hasbro, 132
    video game gamble of, 39–40, 42–43,
        46
Brady, Sarah and James, 179
Brain Bites candy, 281
Brandweek, 8, 214
Brewi, Dave, 282–84
Brown University, 51, 60, 176
    Child Study Center at, xiii
    Medical School at, 179, 303

Bubble-Matic Gun, 103
Bubble-O-Bill Bubble Hat, 67
Bucky O'Hare action figures, 110
Buddy L, 299
Buntel, John, 133
Burp Gun, 67–68
Burton, Tim, 245–46
Bush, George, 280
Business Week, 46, 208

Cabbage Patch Kids, 38, 44, 110, 155,
    171, 180, 205–10
  Barad on, 205–6, 209–10
  decline of, 208
  Hasbro's licensing of, 65, 84
  history of, 206–10
  marketing and promotion of, 208–10,
    219
  Mattel and, 65, 205–7, 209–10, 219
Caesar, Sid, 15
California, University of, Los Angeles
    (UCLA), 155, 232
Camp 2000, 287
Candy Land, 16, 39
Canton Trade Fair, 58
Capital Cities/ABC, 252
Care Bears, 94
Carlsson-Paige, Nancy, 227–28
Carnation, 221
Carrey, Jim, 246
Carson/Roberts, 69
Carter, Jimmy, 34
Cassidy, Hopalong, 52
category management, 168–69
CBS, 151–52, 155, 166
CD-ROM Monopoly, 278
Center for Media Education, 151–52
Cervantes, Miguel de, 53
CFO, 303
Chainsaw Steel Monster, 135, 163
Champy, James, 136, 178, 194
Charlie's Angels, 31, 65, 74
Charness, Wayne S., 129, 161, 234, 242,
    281, 300–301
  DreamWorks and, 272
  Hasbro Pride Day and, 297
  Mattel takeover attempt and, 7, 286
  and restructuring of Hasbro, 174

Charren, Peggy, 152
Chicago, University of, 101
Children's Television Act, 149, 151–52
China:
  Hassenfeld's visits to, 17, 56–59
  human rights in, 226
  toy production in, 165
Christie's East, 203
Chutes and Ladders, 16, 39
Civil War, 41, 222–23
Classic Coke, 118
Client, The, 246
Clinton, Bill, 136, 156, 179, 226, 228
Clue, 131, 218, 280
CNBC, 166, 273
CNN, 147, 166–67
Cobra, 123–24
Coca-Cola Co., market research of, 118
cold war, 26
Coleco, 65
  Cabbage Patch Kids and, 207–8
  Hasbro's acquisition of, 208
  in video game market, 42–44
Coleman Company, 190
Colgate-Palmolive, 210, 253
Columbia Presbyterian Hospital, 63
comic books:
  Bozigian's collection of, 125
  marketing research on, 116, 119–20,
    122–23
  see also specific comic books
Commodore, 42
Conan toys, 135
Cone/Coughlin Communications, 157
Congress, U.S., 152, 160, 228
  on children's TV, 148–52, 154, 193
  Loesch's testimony before, 148–50
  on violence in video games, 158
Connolly, Chris, 203, 283
  G.I. Joe and, 220–25, 229, 231–33,
    245
Consumer Eyes Inc., 115
Consumer Product Safety Commission,
    179, 227
Cool Tools, 233
Coopers & Lybrand, 132, 189
Cosby, Bill, 156
Cosby Show, The, 147

Cosmic Chasm, 42
cotton-candy makers, 25
Coty Cosmetics, 211–12
Coughlin, Margaret, 157
Crawford, Cindy, 190
croquet sets, 41
Cultural Revolution, 58–59
Curtis, Jamie Lee, 281

D'Aguanno, Steve, 164
Daily Variety, 252
Dallas, 146
D'Alleva, Vinnie, 200
    in brainstorming sessions, 124–25
    G.I. Joe and, 185–87, 204
    and termination of DeLuca, 274–75
Daly, Robert A., 246, 253, 255–57
Dark Horse, 122, 185
Dartmouth College, 44, 210, 250
DC Comics, 122, 186
De Laurentiis, Dino, 211
DeLuca, Don, 163
    in brainstorming sessions, 124–25
    and layoffs at Hasbro, 200
    and restructuring of Hasbro, 175–78,
        233, 274–75
    termination of, 274–75
Denniss, Malcolm, 227, 262
Diller, Barry, 189–90
Dino Rangers, see *Mighty Morphin Power
    Rangers*
Walt Disney Co., 5, 17, 38, 67, 169, 174,
    224, 251–52, 255, 271–72, 276,
    278, 280
    Flubber and, 25
    Mattel and, 205, 211, 218
Ditomassi, George R., Jr. "Dito," 16, 132,
    241, 254
    and Bernstein's review and planning
        meeting, 163
    big brands and, 279
    on Bradley acquisition, 40, 45
    DreamWorks and, 271
    Hasbro's corporate structure and, 237
    Hasbro's finances and, 110, 134
    on interactive software, 276, 278
    managerial positions of, 86–88, 91–92,
        304

on Mattel's attempted takeover of
    Hasbro, 286, 290
and restructuring of Hasbro, 168
Sliced Bread and, 265
on Spear acquisition, 218
in strategic planning, 266, 269
Toy Division line reviews and, 181
doctor and nurse kits, 22–23, 30, 50, 52,
    129
dollhouse furniture, 67
Donald Duck doctor kits, 22
Doors, 101
Dorman, Rod, 276–77
Dorr & Sheff, 118
DreamWorks SKG, xiv–xv, 252, 270–74,
    305
    Hasbro's interest in, 254–57, 271–74
    Mr. Potato Head and, 280
DreamWorks Toys, 272
Drexel Burnham Lambert Inc., 45–46
Dr. Hallie's Hospital, 181–83
Dr. Kildare doctor kits, 23
Dufresne, Janice, 261–62
Dunsay, George A., 15, 32–36, 86, 106,
    124, 195
    G.I. Joe and, 33–36
Dusenberry, Tom, 277–78

E!, 166
Earhart, E. Troy, 117
Easy Bake Oven, 94, 103
educational television, 149–52
Eisenhower, Dwight D., 306
Eisner, Michael, 156, 255, 272
electric cars, 25
Elikann, Larry, 211
Ellis, Bryan J., 78
Ellis, Ken, 178
Elvis doll, 137, 163–67, 171–74, 187–88,
    283, 306
    decline of, 173–74
    marketing and promotion of, 164–66,
        171
    market research on, 165
    media on, 166
    worries about, 171–72
Empire Pencil Co., 21, 31
Entertainment Weekly, 156

Eskridge, James A., 258, 288
ESPN, 232
Esquire, 129, 202
Exclamation Point (Artschwager), 49
Experiment in International Living
    program, 54
Eye Pus, 177

Faludi, Susan, 203
Far Side (Larson), 129
fashion dolls and fashion doll market:
    Hasbro's entries in, 73–78
    see also specific fashion dolls
Faulkner, William, 4, 129
Federal Communications Commission
    (FCC), 141, 149, 151–52
Federal Trade Commission (FTC), 152,
    257–58
    on Mattel's attempted takeover of
        Hasbro, 257, 287, 289–91, 294
    Toys "R" Us investigated by, 257, 287,
        294, 301, 317
Feliciano, Jose, 145
Fell, Robert S., 89
Fidelity, xiv, 293
Finkelstein, Moe, 108
First Boston Corp., 254
Fisher-Price, 5, 39, 236, 251
    finances of, 174
    Mattel and, 134, 205, 211
    and restructuring of Hasbro, 172
Fleer Corporation, 190
Fleet Financial Group, 175
Flintstones, The, 140
Flubber, 25–26, 31, 34, 94, 227
Flying Nun dolls, 73
Food and Drug Administration, 25
Forbes, 13, 146, 214, 303
Fox Broadcasting Co., 142, 145, 155, 157,
    169, 181, 185, 245
Fox Children's Network, 120
    Loesch and, 138–39, 142–45, 148–50,
        153
Fradin, Jackie, 119, 122
Frankenstein, 23
Freud, Sigmund, 50
Frisbee, 217
Frito-Lay, 176, 195

Fruit of the Loom, 220
Funware, 276–77

Gak, 218
Galloping Gourmet housewares, 31
Lewis Galoob Toys Inc., 255, 272
Game of Life, 39–41, 287
Games of the States, 42
Gargoyles, 169
Gates, Bill, 156, 270
Geffen, David, 252, 255, 273
General Electric (GE) Co., 252
General Mills, 103
General Motors (GM), 132
Bobbie Gentry dolls, 73
Ghostbusters toys, 94, 104–5
G.I. Joe (comic book), 35–36, 116, 121,
    152, 185, 284
G.I. Joe (film), 160, 185
G.I. Joe (toy), xii–xiv, 15, 31–38, 72, 81,
    107, 110–11, 115–30, 175–77,
    181–82, 197, 200, 202–4, 207–8,
    216–17, 220–25, 227–33, 268, 274,
    277–80, 306
    decline of, 12, 93–94, 110, 115, 117,
        119–20, 127, 132, 134–35, 163,
        202, 208
    Elvis doll and, 164–65
    end of production of, 32, 34, 74
    fan club of, 37
    makeovers of, 33–35
    marketing and promotion of, 26–27,
        35–37, 117, 120–23, 126–27, 152,
        156–59, 161, 184–87, 224–25,
        228–33, 245, 283–84
    market research on, 116–19, 122,
        222–25
    and Mattel's attempted takeover of
        Hasbro, 292, 297
    new story lines of, 224, 229–31
    origins of, 23–24, 26–28
    outlicensing of, 32, 37
    overseas manufacturing of, 56–58
    popularity of, 8, 27–29, 31, 33,
        36–38
    protests against, 64
    realism of, 230–31
    research and development of, 26–27

and restructuring of Hasbro, 168,
    177–78, 202
in straying from real-life military
    persona, 121–22
summit meeting on, 120–23
tag lines of, 27, 33, 232
thirtieth anniversary celebration of,
    156–59, 161, 185, 202–3, 221–22
top-secret dossiers of, 125
violence of, 227–31
weaponry of, 37, 119, 126–27,
    224–25, 229–30, 232
see also Sgt. Savage
G.I. Joe (TV show), 37, 139–40, 143, 151,
    185, 224, 229–31, 284
G.I. Joe Adventure Teams, 33
G.I. Joe Extreme, 220–25, 229–33, 278
    demise of, 306
    marketing and promotion of, 283–84
    TV show of, 229–31, 284
G.I. Joe International Collectors'
    Convention, 202–3
Gildea, John, 199, 231, 281
Gillette, 253
Gingrich, Newt, 153
Give-A-Show projector, 103
Gleason, Jackie, 22
Glen, Douglas, 277
Glenco, 38
Globe, Brad, 255–56
Godfrey, Arthur, 67
Godzilla, 139
Go-Go My Walking Pups, 110
Goldberg, Sam, 160
Goldstein, Michael, 155, 296, 301
Goosebumps, 281
Gordon, Harold P. "Sonny," 300, 303–4
    DreamWorks and, 254–57, 271
    on Mattel's attempted takeover of
        Hasbro, 251, 257–58, 286, 288–92,
        297
    Sliced Bread and, 264–65
    in strategic planning, 266
Go to the Head of the Class, 39, 42
Gould, Burt, 144
Grass, Alex, 43–44
Great Wisdom Enterprises, 80
Grey Advertising, 193

Griffin, Tom, 61, 140
    G.I. Joe and, 35–36, 120, 221–22
Griffin Bacal Inc., 185–86
Grisham, John, 246
Gross, Chaim, 87
Gross, Elizabeth, 203, 220
Guangzhou, Hassenfeld's visits to, 58–59
Guber, Peter, 255
Gutterman, Leslie, 12, 17, 298

Haas, Wally, 108
Hammer, Michael, 136, 178, 194
Handler, Barbara, 66, 68
Handler, Elliot, 66–68, 70–72
Handler, Ken, 66, 70
Handler, Ruth (Ruth Mosko), 66–72,
    211–14, 296
    Barbie and, 68–69
    illnesses of, 71
    lifestyle of, 70
    Mattel's finances and, 71–72
Hanks, Tom, 6, 97, 129
Hanna-Barbera, 140
Hanson PLC, 40
Hardy Boys books, 52–53
Hargreaves, David, 167, 264–66, 277
    Sliced Bread and, 264–65
    in strategic planning, 266
Hartley, Sharon, 188, 262, 276
Harvard University, 228, 250
Hasbro Charitable Trusts, 235–36
Hasbro Children's Foundation, 47, 235,
    248
Hasbro Children's Hospital, 100, 179, 273
    Hassenfeld's Christmas visit to, 234–35
Hasbro France, 77
Hasbro Herald, 196, 216
Hasbro Inc.:
    brainstorming sessions at, 123–25
    company culture of, 212
    corporate headquarters of, 49, 61, 87,
        128
    corporate structure of, 237–38
    design team meetings of, 188–89
    European headquarters of, 61, 82
    finances of, xi–xii, xiv–xv, 4–8, 12–13,
        15–18, 22, 25–26, 28–32, 38–39,
        45–46, 48–49, 60, 63–65, 74, 76,

Hasbro Inc. (*cont'd*)
    82, 89–90, 93, 99, 110, 126,
        130–32, 134–37, 162–63, 166–67,
        169, 174, 183–84, 192–96, 204,
        208, 210–11, 217–19, 226, 232,
        236–38, 242, 246–50, 253, 261–62,
        266–67, 271–73, 276–79, 292–96,
        299–305
    founding of, xii, 20
    Fun Lab at, 116–17
    Games Division of, 278–79
    Giving Tree campaign of, 97
    globalism of, 6, 13–14, 39, 56–59, 61,
        76–78, 82, 88, 91–92, 98, 100, 206,
        218, 234, 237, 248–50, 266, 272,
        277–78, 285, 287, 294, 299, 304
    Kid Dimension Division of, 133, 193
    layoffs at, 93, 166–67, 175, 178,
        193–201, 203–4, 226, 268–69
    line reviews of, 180–83, 223–25,
        232–33, 276, 279
    logos of, 48
    Manufacturing Division of, 65
    new image of, 47–49, 61
    New York City offices of, 47–49, 61,
        74, 82, 84
    Playskool Division of, *see* Playskool
    politicking in, 86–87
    Preschool Division of, 38
    restructuring of, 167–70, 172–79, 184,
        189–202, 204, 209, 232–33, 241,
        247, 260–62, 274–75, 292, 298,
        300, 305
    senior executive suite at, 127–30
    showrooms of, 7–8, 12, 17, 27, 47–49,
        64, 117, 128, 130, 166, 235, 241
    slogan of, 26
    social responsibility of, xv, 226
    Toy Division of, 7, 65, 86, 100, 110,
        120, 122, 126, 132–37, 162–63,
        169–70, 176–77, 180–85, 187–89,
        191, 193, 200, 208–9, 241, 244,
        260–62, 264, 266, 275, 278–79,
        300, 304
    U.S. games market monopoly of, 100
Hasbro Interactive, 277
Hasbro Pride Day, 297
Hasbro 2000, 266–70, 272–73

Hassenfeld, Alan Geoffrey, xi–xii, 28,
    79–88, 90–101, 117, 128–32,
    136–37, 167–70, 178–83, 196–98,
    216–28, 232–37, 241–44, 261,
    263–82, 285–306
    ambitions of, xv, 14, 269
    athleticism of, 54–55
    Barney and, 241–42, 247, 257
    Batman licensing and, 246, 252–53,
        256–57
    Bernstein and, 106–7, 163, 183, 195
    on big brands, 279–80
    birth of, 52
    at Blair conferences, 3–8, 16
    Bradley acquisition and, 82
    brainstorming sessions and, 124
    brother's death and, 12–15, 85
    brother's illness and, 63–64, 83–84
    Cabbage Patch Kids and, 208–9, 219
    candor of, xi
    charm of, 58
    childhood of, xi, 12, 14, 52–54
    cigarette smoking of, 7, 54, 128, 293
    corporate and personal beliefs of, 5
    dedication of, 6
    demeanor of, 3–4, 8
    design team meetings and, 188
    in distributing Christmas gifts at
        Hasbro Children's hospital, 234–35
    DreamWorks and, 254–57, 271–74
    education of, xii, 13, 52–56
    Elvis doll and, 166
    executive office of, 128–30
    family life of, 81
    father's death and, 31
    finances of, 13–14
    G.I. Joe and, 32, 56–58, 120, 126–27,
        157, 159, 161, 220–25, 228, 233,
        279, 306
    Hasbro's corporate structure and, 237
    Hasbro's finances and, 5–8, 13, 17–18,
        126, 174, 192–93, 196, 232, 242,
        247, 253, 266–67, 271, 278–80,
        299–304
    heritage of, xii, 18
    home of, 267
    honors and awards of, 46–47, 178–79,
        216–17

illnesses of, 53, 55
in integrating Tonka into Hasbro,
    131–33
on interactive software, 276–78
and layoffs at Hasbro, 178, 193–94,
    197, 201, 226, 268–69
line reviews and, 180–83, 223–25,
    233, 276, 279
literary interests of, 4, 53–56, 59
luck of, 3, 6
management teams of, 85–88, 90–93,
    106–7, 130, 183, 237, 303–6
managerial skills of, 14, 16–17
marriage of, 79–83
Mattel takeover attempt and, 4–5, 7,
    251–54, 256–59, 285–300, 302–3
on Mortal Kombat, 159, 161
Mr. Potato Head and, 276, 280–81
on new vision for Hasbro, 236–37
oratorial style of, 5
philanthropy of, 5, 13, 97, 100, 100,
    179, 235–36, 247–48, 254, 256,
    269, 303
photographic memory of, 129
physical appearance of, 3–4, 17, 79,
    82, 128–29, 180, 299, 303, 305
on product safety, 136, 227
product sense of, 129–30
on relationship between TV and
    violence, 227
and restructuring of Hasbro, 167–68,
    170, 174, 178, 193–94, 198, 201–2,
    233, 305
RIght Now! chairmanship of, 96–98,
    178–79, 235–36, 295
rubber band bracelet of, 54
sailing cruises of, 14–15
in seeking Hasbro chairmanship,
    13–14, 16–18
sense of humor of, 4–5, 80
Sgt. Savage and, 225
simple needs of, 267–68
Sindy and, 215, 248–50
Sliced Bread and, 173, 263–65
on social responsibility, 226, 235
Stein's resignation and, 190–92
on Stein's salary, 169–70
in strategic planning, 266–70, 277, 287

temper of, 92
in terminating DeLuca, 274–75
in Tonka acquisition, 95, 98–100, 105
Toy Fairs and, 98, 243, 248
toy licensing and, 147, 246, 252–53,
    256–57
toys enjoyed by, 129–30
travels of, 16–17, 54–60, 79–80, 82,
    92, 128, 226, 285
URI class addressed by, 225–28
on video games, 43
on violent toys, 227–29
Hassenfeld, Esther, 20
Hassenfeld, Harold, 21, 43, 131
    break between Hasbro and, 31
    Hasbro's finances and, 25, 29–31
Hassenfeld, Henry, xii, 20–21, 39, 47,
    52–53, 85, 87, 97–98, 271, 288
Hassenfeld, Herman, 20, 85
Hassenfeld, Hillel, 20–21, 85, 87
Hassenfeld, Marion Frank, 20–21, 52–53,
    85, 87
Hassenfeld, Merrill, 14, 16–17, 21–31,
    43–44, 47, 50–61, 85–86, 128–29,
    244, 288, 302
    cemetery monument of, 87
    death of, 30–31, 44, 82, 87
    family life of, 50–55, 60
    Flubber and, 25–26
    G.I. Joe and, 23–24, 26–28, 33–34, 36,
        56, 120–21, 128, 165, 204, 207,
        227, 280
    Hasbro's finances and, 25–26, 29–31,
        45, 271
    illnesses of, 30
    junior cosmetic kits and, 21
    Mr. Potato Head and, 22–23, 25, 67
    philanthropy of, 24
    and Verrecchia's employment with
        Hasbro, 89, 92
Hassenfeld, Osias, 19–20, 85
Hassenfeld, Stephen David, 5–6, 8, 28–41,
    43–56, 80, 82–87, 89–95, 117,
    128–31, 171, 190, 195, 203–4, 248,
    267, 277, 287, 297, 299, 302–3,
    305
    acquisition of Mattel considered by,
        253–54, 257

Hassenfeld, Stephen David (*cont'd*)
 ambitions of, 51
 artistic sensibilities and taste of, 61–62
 Beckwith's relationship with, 60–62,
  64, 83, 109
 Bernstein's relationship with, 109, 126
 on big brands, 279
 birth of, 50, 52
 in Bradley acquisition, 39–40, 43–47,
  99–100
 brother's travels and, 55–60
 Cabbage Patch Kids and, 207–8
 cemetery monument of, 302
 childhood of, 12, 51, 53
 death of, xii, 11–18, 84–85, 87, 92–93,
  109–10, 183, 215, 298
 education of, 28, 51–54
 family life of, 53
 fashion doll market and, 73–77
 father's death and, 31
 G.I. Joe and, 28–29, 31–38, 64, 120,
  125–27, 175, 207
 Greenhouse Cafe built by, 133–34
 Hasbro's finances and, 12–13, 15,
  17–18, 29–31, 38–39, 48–49,
  64–65, 76, 110, 130–31, 174, 236,
  271
 and Hasbro's new offices and
  showroom, 47–49, 61
 heritage of, 37, 39
 honors and awards of, 46–47, 131
 illnesses of, 62–64, 82–84, 207–8
 international investors' conference
  addressed by, 63–64
 management team of, 85–87, 89–93,
  106, 109, 167
 managerial style and skills of, 6, 17,
  28–32, 34, 36, 38–39, 48
 and Mattel's attempted takeover of
  Hasbro, 295
 My Little Pony and, 38
 oratorial style of, 5, 12, 52, 84
 philanthropy of, 47, 97
 physical appearance of, 48, 61, 64
 and restructuring of Hasbro, 177–78
 self-confidence of, 47
 Sindy and, 215
 strategic planning of, 262

Tonka acquisition and, 95, 99–100
 Toy Fairs and, 65, 243
 toy licensing of, 147
 TV advertising and, 140–41
 Verrecchia's relationship with, 130–31,
  137
 video games and, 64–65, 173
 workaholism of, 60, 62
Hassenfeld, Sylvia Grace Kay, 17–18, 44,
  49–55, 60, 62, 80–84, 243, 267,
  301–2
 and A. Hassenfeld's courtship of wife,
  80–82
 A. Hassenfeld's education and, 54–55
 background of, 50
 children raised by, 51–55
 junior cosmetic kits and, 21
 on Mattel's attempted takeover of
  Hasbro, 251, 257, 291, 294, 296–98
 philanthropy of, 14, 24, 53, 82
 S. Hassenfeld's death and, 11–12, 14
 S. Hassenfeld's illness and, 83–84
Hassenfeld, Vivien Azar, 17, 134–35, 180,
  235, 243, 267–68, 285, 287, 291,
  296–97, 299, 301
 background of, 14, 79–81
 Hassenfeld's illness and, 82–84
 marriage of, 79–83
Hassenfeld Bros. Inc., 50, 52, 88, 167, 180
 manufacturing endeavors of, 20–21
 origins of, 13, 20–22
Hayes, Ron, 190, 197, 252, 256
Hefner, Hugh, 69
Heinz Pet Products, 221
He-Man, 72, 99, 211
He-Man and Masters of the Universe (TV
  show), 143, 146–47
Hemingway, Ernest, 53, 56
Henson, Jim, 143
Home Improvement, 157
Hong Kong:
 G.I. Joe and, 56–58
 Hassenfeld's visits to, 56–59, 79–80
 toy manufacturing in, 77
Hook figures, 217
Hot Wheels, 5, 71, 102, 126, 205, 211,
  217
House Subcommittee on

Telecommunications and Finance, U.S., 148–49

Hula-Hoop, 217

Human Bullet, 34

Hungry Hungry Hippos, 39, 109

IBM, 132, 189

Ideal Toy Co., 23, 91, 108–9

In My Pocket, 183

Intellivision, 43–44, 72, 99, 102, 207

interactive software, xv, 276–78

International Games, 217

Internet, xv, 236, 252

Internet Gaming Zone, 305

Intrepid, USS, G.I. Joe celebration on, 157, 202–3, 221–22

Israel:
    Hassenfeld Bros. plant in, 21
    Hassenfelds' philanthropy in, 24, 53

jack-in-the-box, 67

Jackson, Michael, 272

Japan:
    Hassenfeld's visits to, 56–57, 80
    toy manufacturing in, 24, 38, 56–57, 147, 227
    TV and film production in, 139, 144, 147–48

Jem, 74–76, 171, 250

Jetsons, The, 140, 151

Jews:
    anti-Semitism and, 19–21
    in Rhode Island, 20

Johns, Jasper, 49

Johns Hopkins University, 28, 52

Johnson & Wales University, 130, 179

Jones, George, 245

Jones, Tommy Lee, 298

Jordan, Michael, 224

junior cosmetic kits, 21

junior doctor kits, 30, 50, 52, 129

Jurassic Park (film), 105, 111, 116

Jurassic Park (toys), 120, 130, 132, 134, 137, 144, 165, 168–69, 217, 247
    Hasbro's finances and, 192–93

Ju Renja (Ju Rangers), 147

just-in-time inventory, 193

Kalinske, Thomas J., 73

Kandel, Bruce, 283–84

Kasanoff, Larry, 160, 185, 191, 229, 255
    Mr. Potato Head and, 280–82

Kasem, Kasey, 165

Katzenberg, Jeffrey, 252, 255–56, 271–73

Kellner, Jamie, 142, 144

Ken, 212

Kenner Parker Toys, Inc., 100, 102–6, 130, 144, 168–70, 188–92, 200, 215–16, 241, 248, 252, 255–56
    and Bernstein's review and planning meeting, 163
    Cabbage Patch Kids and, 207, 209
    design team meetings and, 188
    G.I. Joe and, 203, 220–21
    in Hasbro's acquisition of Tonka, 94–95, 100, 105–6
    Hasbro's finances and, 134–35, 169
    history of, 102–3
    in integrating Tonka into Hasbro, 132–33
    layoffs at, 105–6
    line reviews of, 223
    movie-toy tie-ins of, 103–4, 111
    and restructuring of Hasbro, 168–69, 175–77, 202
    Star Wars toys and, 34, 37
    Stein's resignation and, 191–92, 195–97

Kent, Ginger, 163, 202, 279
    Cabbage Patch Kids and, 209–10, 219
    G.I. Joe and, 220–21, 223, 229
    Sgt. Savage and, 221, 229
    Sindy and, 248–49
    in terminating DeLuca, 274–75

Kerrigan, Nancy, 224

Kidd Video, 146

Kidman, Nicole, 244

King, Sandra M., 77

Kipling, Jim, 103

Klein, Adam, 303–4

Kmart, 132, 174

K'Nex, 218

Knickerbocker Toy Co., 38, 94

Knowledge Adventure, 276

Koosh, 305

Korea, toy manufacturing in, 57

Kransco, Mattel's acquisition of, 217–18
S. S. Kresge, 20
Kubert, Joe, 186
Kunitz, Dave, 124

Larami, 228
Larson, Gary, 129
Lassie, 27
Last Action Hero figures, 217
Laybourne, Geraldine, 142–43, 218
Lazarus, Charles, 170–71, 243
Leach, Sheryl, 241–43, 293, 299
Learning Co., 276
Lee, Stan, 139, 148
Leggy, 73–74
Lego, 218, 294
Leigh, Vivien, 79–80
Lerner, George, 22
Levin, Diane E., 227–28
Levin, Gerald M., 246
Levine, Don, 23–24
Lichtenstein, Roy, 49
Lieutenant, The, 23
Life, 39–41, 287
Li Ka-shing, 58–59
Lilli, 68
Lillymere, Hasbro strategic summit at,
    265–70, 277, 287, 300
Lincoln, Abraham, 39, 41
Lincoln Logs, 279
Art Linkletter's Magic Moon Rocks,
    26
Lion King, 174, 218, 224, 249, 252
Lions of Judea, 145
Lipsitt, Lewis P., xiii
Lipton, Marty, 290
Lite-Brite, 30
Little Chaps, 23
Little Red Book (Mao), 58
Little Shop of Horrors, 138
Littlest Pet Shop, 169
Loaded Diaper, 177
Loesch, Margaret, 138–45, 181
    background of, 140–42
    congressional testimony of, 148–50
    cooperation between Hasbro and,
        140–41
    Mighty Morphin Power Rangers and,

139–40, 143, 44, 148–50, 153–55,
    228
  on violence in children's TV
      programs, 153–54
Los Angeles, 213
Los Angeles Olympics, 48
Los Angeles Times, 70
Lost World: Jurassic Park, The, 303
Lt. Stone, 224–25
Lucas, George, 34, 243, 289, 302–3
Lucasfilm Games, 277
Lyons Group, 242

MacAndrews & Forbes, 45, 190
MacArthur, Douglas, 203
McDonald's, 144, 245–46
McGrath, Tom, 220
Madonna, 214
Magic Smoking Grille, 297
Malibu, 122
Managing Separation Meetings: Restructuring,
    198
Mansour, Ned, 288, 291
Mao Tse-tung, 17, 58
marketing and promotion, 195–96
    of Barbie, 69, 75, 102, 212, 214, 231
    of Cabbage Patch Kids, 208–10, 219
    of Elvis doll, 164–66, 171
    of G.I. Joe, 26–27, 35–37, 117,
        120–23, 126–27, 152, 156–59, 161,
        184–87, 224–25, 228–33, 245,
        283–84
    of Sgt. Savage, 185–87, 225, 229, 233
    of Sindy, 249–50
market research, 115–20, 122–25
    on Aliens, 120
    on Barbie, 69
    Bozigian on, 115–19, 122
    on comic books, 116, 119–20, 122–23
    on Elvis doll, 165
    on G.I. Joe, 116–19, 122, 222–25
    on Mr. Potato Head, 281–82
    on Sgt. Savage, 222–23
    on Sliced Bread, 263
    on video games, 116
Markey, Edward J., hearings on children's
    TV held by, 148–49, 151–52, 154
Marks, Sandy, 128, 285, 295–96, 298

Mars Inc., 231–32
martial arts, 34, 225
Martin, Angela, 79–81
Marvel Entertainment Group Inc., 122, 170, 185, 252, 263
    G.I. Joe and, 35–36, 121
    Loesch and, 139–40, 142
    Stein hired by, 189–92, 197
    Stein's tenure at, 255
Marx, Louis, 56, 67, 77
Marx Brothers, 15
Masters of the Universe, 72, 211
    TV show of, 143, 146–47
Matchbox cars, 305
Matson, Harold "Matt," 67
Mattel, 65–78, 93–94, 104–5, 169, 186, 209–19, 236, 244, 266, 277, 279
    in attempting to take over Hasbro, xiv–xv, 4–5, 7, 17, 251–54, 256–60, 285–300, 302–3
    on big brands, 279–80
    Cabbage Patch Kids and, 65, 205–7, 209–10, 219
    company culture of, 212–13
    DreamWorks and, 272
    finances of, 5–6, 13, 32, 44, 46, 67–73, 76, 99, 134, 174, 205, 210–11, 213, 218–19, 226, 242, 247, 249–50, 253–54, 295, 305
    Fisher-Price and, 134, 205, 211
    founding of, 67
    globalism of, 6, 76–78, 206, 218, 247–48, 305
    interactive software and, 277
    Jem and, 74–75
    layoffs at, 212, 247
    and layoffs at Hasbro, 197
    marketing and promotion of, 231
    and origins of Barbie, 68–69
    public relations of, 212–14
    razor/razor blade principle and, 24, 214
    Sindy and, 76–77, 215–16, 249–50
    social responsibility of, 226
    strategic planning of, 262
    Tonka acquisition and, 95, 98–99, 105
    TV advertising of, 67–69, 102, 143, 147
    Tyco acquired by, 305
    in video game market, 42–44, 46, 72
    The World of the Young program of, 70–72
Mattel Media, 277
Mauer, Dave, 104
Maxie, 65–66, 75–76, 78, 171, 215, 250
MCA, 17
Memory, 42
Meritus, 136, 188–89
    design team meetings and, 188
    in integrating Tonka into Hasbro, 132–33
    on restructuring of Hasbro, 167–68, 175–76, 179
Metaframe, 70
MGM, 23
Mickey Mouse, 211
Mickey Mouse Club, The, Mattel's sponsorship of, 67–68
Mickey Mouse pencils, 22
Microsoft, 255, 270, 278, 305
Mighty Morphin Power Rangers, 36, 155–56, 161, 169, 187, 223
    budget of, 151
    congressional testimony on, 149–50
    Loesch and, 139–40, 143–44, 148–50, 153–55, 228
    Saban and, 139, 143–44, 147–48, 153–56, 228
    toys tied-in with, 155–56
    violence in, 153–55, 193, 228–29
    see also Power Rangers
Milken, Michael, 45–46, 72
Mindscape Inc., 263
Minnie Mouse, 224
Misfits, 74–75
Miss America fashion dolls, 215–16, 248
Model United Nations, 52
Monogram Models, 70
Monopoly, 94, 132, 161, 217–18, 236, 278, 280, 300, 305
Moore, Demi, 214
Morrison, Jim, 101
Morrone, Joe, 178
Mortal Kombat (film), 160–61, 185, 255, 280–81
Mortal Kombat (toy), 157–61, 182

Mortal Kombat I (video game), 65, 163, 231
    launching of, 159–60
    violence in, 158, 160–61
Mortal Kombat II (video game), 158
Mr. Potato Head, 6, 28, 30, 46–47, 52, 67, 94, 100, 129, 231–32, 276–78, 280–82, 297–99
    market research on, 281–82
    popularity of, 22–23, 25
Mrs. Potato Head, 23
MTV, 276
Mummy, 23
Murdoch, Rupert, 142
Murphy Brown, 147
Myers, Barton, 48–49
My Little Pony (toy), 15, 38, 94, 110
My Little Pony (TV show), 140

Nasser, Gamal Abdel, 145
National Association of Broadcasters (NAB), 36, 152
National Baby Shop, 171
National Cable Television Association, 155
National Institute of Mental Health, 154
NBA, 169
NBA Jam, 159
NBC, 27, 146, 152, 155, 190, 252
    Loesch and, 138, 140, 143
Nearly Me, 72
NEMO (Never Ever Mention Outside), 16, 65, 137, 173, 263
Nerf, 94, 105, 221, 251, 282
New Coke, 118
New Kids on the Block figures, 110, 164
Newsweek, 155
New World Communications Group, 190–91
New York Times, The, 202–3, 228, 245
    on Stein's resignation, 191
    on video games, 43
New York University Medical Center, 44
Nicholson, Jack, 189
Nickelodeon, 142, 218
Nielsen ratings, 154
Nintendo, 17, 65, 84, 159, 172, 263–64

Nixon, Richard, 58
No More Boo Boos Betsy, 181

Ogilvy & Mather, 102
Olson, Jeanne, 209
O'Neal, Shaquille, 169
O'Neill, John T., 86, 300–301, 303–4
    Hasbro's finances and, 134, 192–96, 217, 242
    and Mattel's attempted takeover of Hasbro, 257–58, 286–90, 297
    Sliced Bread and, 173, 264–65
    in strategic planning, 266
1–2–3 High Chair, 179, 227
Optigan, 71
Original Appalachian Artworks (OAA), 205, 207, 209, 219
Outburst, 218
Ovitz, Michael, 190
Owen, Dan, 133, 248–49, 254
    design team meetings and, 188
    Hasbro's finances and, 193
    and layoffs at Hasbro, 197–98
    marketing responsibilities of, 195–96
    and restructuring of Hasbro, 167, 169, 196–97, 260–61
    Sindy and, 249
    in strategic planning, 260, 266
    in terminating DeLuca, 274–75

Paley, William S., 151–52
Pantry Pride, 190
Paramount, Paramount Pictures, and United Paramount, 66, 156, 185, 212, 252
Parcheesi, 208
Parker Bros., 94, 99, 103, 105, 131–32
Pasztor, Andy, 294
Patton, 186
Pedigree, 75–76
pencil boxes, 20–23
Pennsylvania, University of, 13, 21, 54–55
People, 8, 205, 214
perceptual mapping, 223–24
Pereira, Joseph, 294
Perelman, Ronald O., 142, 170, 255
    in attempt to acquire Bradley, 44–45
    in hiring Stein, 190–91

Peter Pan & the Pirates, 143
Pickens, T. Boone, 46
Pictionary, 218
Pincus, Lionel I., 72, 211
Pitzer College, 101
Play-Doh, 94, 100, 103, 105, 202, 218,
    232–33, 268, 276–77
Playmates, 272
Playskool, 39, 49, 65, 84, 86, 105, 117,
    133–34, 163, 195–96, 241–43, 251,
    279
    Barney and, 242–43
    Cool Tools of, 233
    design team meetings and, 188
    Funware of, 276–77
    Hasbro's finances and, 193, 195–96
    Magic Smoking Grille of, 297
    1–2–3 High Chair, 179, 227
    and restructuring of Hasbro, 167, 172,
        176, 196, 200
    wooden blocks of, 129
Poland, anti-Semitism in, 19–20
Police Academy toys, 104
Polly Pocket, 169
Popples, 102
Postal Service, U.S., Elvis commemorative
    stamp of, 164
Power Rangers:
    Elvis doll and, 164
    G.I. Joe and, 229
    real-life, 153
    toys, 164, 229, 235, 283
    see also *Mighty Morphin Power Rangers*
Power Wheels, 217, 251
Predator, 159
Prejza, Paul, 47–49, 235
Elvis Presley Enterprises Inc., 164–65
Pre-Toy Fairs, 165–66, 219
Pretty Sew 'N Style, 180
Price, Dan, 224–25
Price Waterhouse, 221
Prichard, Tom, 209
PRNewswire, 292, 296
Procter & Gamble (P&G), 104, 110, 220,
    223, 249
promotion, *see* marketing and promotion
Providence, R.I., Jews in, 20
Providence Journal, 97

Public Broadcasting System, 149
Punisher, 116

Q *Unit,* 123

Radnitz/Mattel Productions Inc., 70
Raggedy Ann and Andy, 94
Rainbow Crafts, 103
Rambo, 159
razor/razor blade principle, 24, 214
Reagan, Ronald, 32, 34, 37, 44, 140–41
    deregulation under, 141, 149, 152
Redstone, Sumner, 142
*Reengineering the Coporation: A Manifesto
    for Business Revolution* (Hammer
    and Champy), 136, 178, 194
Reiner, Larry, 23–24, 27
Remco, 23
Ren & Stimpy, 116
Rentel, Ron, market research of, 115–16,
    118–20
research and development:
    of G.I. Joe, 26–27
    of Sliced Bread, 263–65
Reuters, 166
Revlon Group Inc., 190
Rhode Island:
    fight against graft and corruption in,
        96–98, 178–79
    Hasbro's headquarters in, 49, 61, 87,
        128
    Jews in, 20
    poverty in, 55
Rhode Island, University of (URI),
    88–89, 130, 260
    Hassenfeld's address to class from,
        225–28
Rhode Island Hospital, 235
Rhode Island School of Design, 176
Right Associates, 198
RIght Now!, 96–98, 178–79, 235–36,
    295
Ringling Bros.—Barnum & Bailey
    Circus, 70
Riorden, Richard, 72
Risk, 94
Rite Aid Corporation, 43–44
Roberts, Xavier "Happy," 205–10

Roberts, Xavier "Happy," (cont'd)
    background of, 206–8
    Barad's meeting with, 205–6
Robin Hood action figures, 105
Robocop toys, 94, 104
Roffman, Howard, 243, 246
Roy Rogers pistol pencil cases, 22
Romanelli, Dan, 104, 252–53, 256–57
Romper Room nursery schools and day
    care centers, 30–31, 57
Roosevelt, Franklin D., 151
Roseanne, 147
Rosen, Nancy, 48
Rosenwald, E. John, Jr., 18, 250–53
    background of, 44
    Bradley acquisition and, 43–45
    on Mattel's attempted takeover of
        Hasbro, 251–53, 258–59, 286, 288,
        291, 295
    Sindy and, 76
Rose of Tibet, 53
Rousseau, Jean-Jacques, 41
Russia, anti-Semitism in, 19–21

Saban, Haim, 138–39, 142–48, 169, 243
    background of, 138, 145–48
    Mighty Morphin Power Rangers and,
        139, 143–44, 147–48, 153, 155–56,
        228
    toy royalties collected by, 155–56
Saban Entertainment, 148, 156
Salhany, Lucie, 145
Samurai Pizza Cats, 138–39
David Sarnoff Research Center, 172,
    263–64
Savage Mondo Blitzers, 177
Sawyer, Diane, 189
Schmidt, Pat, 231
Schneider, Sandra M., Sliced Bread and,
    263–65
school supplies, 21, 23
Schumacher, Joel, 246
Schwartz, Stephen A., 15, 32–37, 109,
    124, 195–96, 262
    background of, 91
    G.I. Joe and, 33–37, 121
    managerial positions of, 86–88, 90–93
    on Mighty Morphin Power Rangers, 148

physical appearance of, 92
relationship between Verrecchia and,
    91–92
resignation of, 92–93, 106, 133, 237
Schwarzenegger, Arnold, 160, 186,
    224–25, 280–81
Scott, George C., 186
Scrabble, 129, 208, 217–18, 268
Securities and Exchange Commission
    (SEC), 71
Sega, 73, 159, 172, 255, 263–64, 270,
    276–77
Semel, Terry, 45, 190, 246, 255
Serby, Gary, 281
Sgt. Rock (comic book), 186
Sgt. Rock (film), 186
Sgt. Savage, 122, 157–58, 161, 177–78,
    182, 203–4, 221–23, 232–33
    marketing and promotion of, 185–87,
        225, 229, 233
    market research on, 222–23
    story line of, 186–87, 203
Sgt. Slaughter, 64
Shackelford, Judy, 75, 102, 214
Shadow, The (film), 169, 218
Shadow, The (toy), 168
Shanghai, Hassenfeld's visits to, 59
Shank, Stephen G., 95, 98
Shaq Attack, 169
Sharp Shooters, 287
Shea, James J., Jr., 42–46
    and Hasbro's acquisition of Bradley,
        40, 43–46
    video game gamble of, 42–43
Shelton, Henry, 129
Silverman, Fred, 140
Simpsons, The, 159
Sindy, 66, 75–78
    litigation over, 76–78, 215–16, 248–49
    marketing and promotion of, 249–50
    overseas performance of, 249–50
    in U.S., 248–50
Singer, Jerome L. and Dorothy G., 243
Six Million Dollar Man, 34
60 Minutes, 147
Sizzlers, 70–71
Skadden, Arps, Slate, Meagher & Flom,
    288

Sky Dancers, 272
Slater, Samuel, 52–53
Sliced Bread, 137, 172–73, 184, 193–94
    business plan for, 264–65
    design and development of, 263–65
    Hasbro's finances and, 193
    killing of, 265, 276–78
    market research on, 263
Smith, Shelley, 164–65
Smurfs, The, 140, 142
Sno-Kone machines, 38
Soft Walkin' Wheels, 135, 163
Sonic Flasher cars, 126–27
Sonic the Hedgehog 2, 116
Son of Flubber, 25
Sony, 255, 264, 273, 305
Sorry!, 94
Sounder, 70
Space Doctor Survival Kits, 26
Spear, Arthur S., 72
J. W. Spear & Sons, Mattel's acquisition of,
    217–18
Spiderman, 116
Spielberg, Steven, xiv, 105, 111, 116, 143,
    252, 255–56, 276, 294, 305
    Hasbro venture with, 271–74
    toy designing interest of, 256
Spielberg, Theo, 273–74
Spielvogel, Carl, 44
Stargate, 163
Starsky & Hutch, 146
Starting Lineup, 104, 130
Star Wars (films), 130, 243, 246, 270, 277,
    289, 303
    G.I. Joe and, 34–37
Star Wars (toys), 6, 34, 37, 94, 103–4, 111,
    243, 272, 278, 283
Star Wars Summit Metting, 303
stationery, 22
Stebenne, Bob, 193–94
Steffi, 77
Stein, Bruce L., 100–106, 120, 143–44,
    157, 163, 188–97, 212, 214, 252
    background of, 101–2
    Cabbage Patch Kids and, 209
    design team meetings and, 188–89
    DreamWorks and, 255–57, 271–73
    Hasbro's finances and, 134

and layoffs at Hasbro, 197
    and layoffs at Kenner, 105–6
    on movie-toy tie-ins, 103–6
    physical appearance of, 104
    resignation of, 189–95, 209, 241, 248
    and restructuring of Hasbro, 167,
        169–70, 172–73, 175, 189–92
    salary of, 169–70
    Tonka acquisition and, 94–95, 100,
        105
    on Toy Division line review, 180
    in Tyco acquisition, 305
Steiner, Albert, Philip, and Joseph, 102
stock market crash of October 1987, 94
Stone, Sharon, 214
strategic planning, 260, 262, 264–70
    at Lillymere, 265–70, 277, 287, 300
Strategy, 39
Strawberry Shortcake, 38, 94
Streetfighter (film), 163
Streetfighter II (video game), 110, 116, 159
Street Sharks, 216
Stretch Armstrong, 305
Stuart, Gilbert, 265
Suez War, 145
Sugarman, Mitch, 11–12
Sunbow Entertainment, 140, 185, 224,
    229–30
Superhuman Samurai Syber-Squad, 223
Super Joe, 31, 34
Superman toys, 278, 283, 306
Super Mario Bros., 65
Super Soaker water gun, 228
Super Soldier, 123
Sussman, Deborah, 47–49, 235
Sussman/Prejza & Company, 48–49, 235

tabletop street hockey game, 282
Taiwan, toy manufacturing in, 57
Takara, 57, 147
Talking Barney, 27, 134
Tammy doll, 23
Target, 132, 174, 188
Tartikoff, Brandon, 190
Technicolor, 45
Teen, 249
Teenage Mutant Ninja Turtles, 127, 272
Teeny, 77

television:
  advertising on, 5, 22, 25, 27, 67–69,
    74, 76–77, 94, 102, 110, 120–21,
    140–43, 147–55
  Congress on, 148–52, 154, 193
  educational, 149–52
  in Japan, 139, 144, 147–48
  violence on, 153–55, 158, 193,
    227–29
  see also specific television shows
Terminator, 159
Terminator 2, 105, 160
Terron, 31
Texas Instruments, 42, 263
Think-A-Tron, 26
Thomas, Jonathan Taylor, 157
Thompson, Jeff, 124
Three Musketeers, see Bernstein,
    Lawrence H.; Dunsay, George A.;
    Schwartz, Stephen A.
Threshold Entertainment, 281
Time Warner Inc., 246, 252, 289
Tinker Toys, 279
Tobias, John, 159
Toei Co, 139, 147–48
Tokyo Toy Fair, 80
Tolhurst, Della, 207, 209–10, 219
Tomy, 57
Tonka Corporation, 104–5, 174, 176,
    241, 299
  Hasbro's acquisition of, 94–95,
    98–100, 105–6, 131–32, 168, 215,
    217, 236–37, 247
  Hasbro's finances and, 135
  Hasbro's integration of, 131–33
  and restructuring of Hasbro, 168
  trucks of, 110, 135, 283
Totally for Kids, 149
Toy & Hobby World, 29
Toy Biz, 190, 255
Toy Fairs, 16, 32, 47, 56, 64–66, 117,
    134–35, 144, 165, 167, 170–74,
    187, 214, 216–17, 237–38, 241–46,
    248, 251, 284, 287, 295, 298–99,
    303, 306
  A. Hassenfeld at, 98, 243, 248
  Batman Forever and, 242, 244–46
  costs of, 244

G.I. Joe and, 23, 27, 37–38, 64
Jem at, 74
Mattel and, 67–69
Mortal Kombat at, 161
My Little Pony and, 38
S. Hassenfeld and, 65, 243
Sindy and, 76
Toy Industry Hall of Fame, 131, 216
Toy Manufacturers of America, 253
toys and toy industry, xiii–xiv
  changes in, xv, 236
  Congress on, 149
  as fad driven, xiv
  film tie-ins with, see specific films and
    toys
  as foundation for creativity and self-
    expression, xiii
  licensing in, 23, 32, 37, 65, 84, 147,
    244–46, 252–53, 256–57
  limitations on advertising of, 36
  morality in, 37, 41
  post–World War II transformation of,
    56–57
  safeness of, 136, 227
  S. Hassenfeld's analysis of, 64
  video game tie-ins with, 158–61
  violence of, 227–31
toy soldiers, 42, 52
Toys "R" Us, xiii, 117, 132, 149, 155,
    170–71, 174, 177, 252, 296
  Brewi and, 282–84
  on Elvis doll, 165
  federal investigation of, 7, 257, 287,
    294, 301, 317
  G.I. Joe and, 203
  Hasbro's relations with, 7, 300–301
Toy Story, 6, 280, 298
Toy Town series, 42
Transformers (toys), 15, 38, 94, 110–11,
    147, 176, 197, 283
Transformers (TV show), 140
Transogram, 108–9
Trivial Pursuit, 94
True Lies, 160, 281
Trump, Donald, 64
Turco Manufacturing, 70
Turner, Sherry Len, 167, 176, 195, 262
  and layoffs at Hasbro, 197–98

Turner, Ted, 156
Turner Broadcasting System, 252
Twain, Mark, 4, 129
Twist 'N Style Tiffany, 181, 183
Tyco Toys Inc., 248, 305

Uke-A-Doodle, 67
Universal Studios, 23, 241
Uno, 217
Urban League, 179
USA Today, 166, 208, 214, 277

V-chips, 154, 156
Vectrex, 40, 42–43, 46, 207
Verrecchia, Alfred, Sr., 88–89
Verrecchia, Alfred J., xiv, 7, 32, 49, 64, 82,
        84, 86–93, 105–6, 130–33, 241,
        243–44, 247–48, 257–69, 297–98,
        300–301
    background of, 88–90, 108, 130
    Barney and, 243
    Bernstein and, 106–8, 110, 130, 163,
        183–84, 194–95
    Bradley acquisition and, 44–46
    Cabbage Patch Kids and, 208–9, 219
    comparisons between A. Hassenfeld
        and, 130
    design team meetings and, 188
    DreamWorks and, 254–56, 271–73
    on Elvis doll, 165
    G.I. Joe and, 157, 159, 224, 229, 233
    Hasbro's corporate structure and,
        237–38
    Hasbro's finances and, 16, 29, 131,
        134–37, 162–63, 166–67, 169, 174,
        192–93, 237–38, 261–62, 266,
        276–77, 300, 304
    in integrating Tonka into Hasbro,
        131–33
    on interactive software, 276–77
    and layoffs at Hasbro, 166–67, 175,
        178, 196–98, 201, 268
    and layoffs at Kenner, 105
    managerial positions of, 86–88, 90–93,
        304–5
    and Mattel's attempted takeover of
        Hasbro, 257–60, 286–87, 290, 295,
        297–98

on Mortal Kombat, 159
    office of, 130
    physical appearance of, 16
    private dinner for, 133–37
    and restructuring of Hasbro, 167–70,
        172–75, 178–79, 184, 189, 191–93,
        195–98, 201–2, 209, 247, 260–62,
        298
    Schwartz's relationship with, 91–92
    sense of humor of, 136
    Sgt. Savage and, 221
    S. Hassenfeld's death and, 16
    S. Hassenfeld's relationship with,
        130–31, 137
    Sliced Bread and, 173, 184, 194,
        263–65
    Stein's resignation and, 189–94
    on Stein's salary, 170
    in strategic planning, 260, 262,
        265–67, 269
    and termination of DeLuca, 275
    in Tonka acquisition, 95
    Toy Division line review and, 182–83
    on Toy Fairs, 243–44
Verrecchia, Elda, 88–89
Verrecchia, Gerrie Macari, 89
Viacom Inc., 142, 252
video games and video game market, 16,
        111, 231
    Bradley's gamble on, 39–40, 42–43, 46
    collapse of, 207
    Hasbro's entrance into, 65
    market research on, 116
    Mattel in, 42–44, 46, 72
    rise and fall of, 43–44
    S. Hassenfeld and, 64–65, 173
    success of, 32
    toys tied in with, 158–61
    violence in, 158, 160–61
Vietnam War, 58, 222
    G.I. Joe and, 33, 37
"Violence Monitoring Report," 155
Virgin Communications, 263, 276
virtual reality, 137, 172–73, 263, 273
    see also Sliced Bread
Vogelstein, John L., 72–73, 76, 211,
        250–51
    in Mattel's attempted takeover of

Vogelstein, John L. (cont'd)
  Hasbro, 251, 253, 257–59, 288–89,
    291, 293
VR Troopers, 169

Wachtell, Lipton, Rosen & Katz, 290
John Waddington, 218
Walker, Norman, 237
  on interactive software, 276
  managerial positions of, 86, 88, 92
  Sindy and, 249–50
  in strategic planning, 266–67
Wall Street Journal, The, 18, 110, 130–31,
    275, 280
  A. Hassenfeld profiled in, 81
  on federal investigation of Toys "R"
    Us, 7
  on G.I. Joe, 37
  on Hasbro's acquisition of Bradley, 46
  on layoffs at Hasbro, 93
  on Mattel's attempted takeover of
    Hasbro, 294–95
  on Stein's resignation, 191
  on violence and Mighty Morphin Power
    Rangers, 155
Wal-Mart, 13, 132, 173–74
  Elvis doll and, 166, 171, 173
  and restructuring of Hasbro, 168
E. M. Warburg, Pincus & Co., Inc., 72,
    211, 250
Warhol, Andy, 49
Warner Bros., 45, 94, 138, 143, 185–86,
    190, 197, 214, 252–54, 263
  Batman licensing of, 244–46, 256–57
  G.I. Joe film and, 185
  G.I. Joe toy promotion and, 121
  in movie-toy tie-ins, 104
  Toys Division of, 252–53, 256, 272
Warner-Lambert, 73, 210
Wayne, John, 147
Wellesley College, 220

Western Publishing, 218
Weston, Stan, 23, 26–27
West Point, 125
Wharton, Edith, 265
Wharton School, 45
Wheel of Fortune, 198
Where on Earth Is Carmen Sandiego?, 149
Who's Calling the Shots?: How to Respond
    Effectively to Children's Fascination
    With War Play and War Toys (Levin
    and Carlsson-Paige), 227–28
Wild West C.O.W.-Boys of Moo Mesa,
    135
Williams, Robin, 298
Williams, Roger, 20
WMS Industries, 159, 161
Wolf, 189
wooden blocks, 129
F. W. Woolworth, 20
World of Love dolls, 65, 73
World War II, 21, 34, 186–87
  G.I. Joe and, 26
  transformation of toy industry after,
    56–57
Worldwide Consumer Products, 252
World Wrestling Federation figures, 110

X-Men (comic book), market research on,
    116, 119–20
X-Men (toy), 224
  G.I. Joe vs., 116, 119–22, 177
  Hasbro brainstorming sessions on, 124
X-Men (TV show), 148
XRC, 248
X-Soldiers, 157–58, 177, 182, 185, 221

Yahtzee, 39, 161
Yale University, 243
Yankelovich studies, 165, 263
Yom Kippur War, 146
Young, Bill, 124

This is G. WAYNE MILLER's fourth book. He and his
writer wife, Alexis, are the cofounders of the Eggemoggin
Writing Center in coastal Maine. They live in Pascoag,
Rhode Island, and have three children, ages four to sixteen.
Miller is at work on a novel and his next work of
nonfiction for Random House. Visit him on the Internet at
www.gwaynemiller.com.